PENGUIN BOOK

HYPNOTISM

Derek Forrest was born in Liverpool and educated at Birkenhead School, Cheshire. After serving in the Royal Navy he studied psychology and physiology at Keble College, Oxford. For ten years he was a lecturer at Bedford College, University of London. In 1962 he was appointed Reader at Trinity College, Dublin, and in 1968 he became the first Professor of Psychology at Trinity College. Upon his retirement in 1996 he became a Fellow Emeritus of Trinity College. He is the author of a number of technical papers in various journals, and of a biography: *Francis Galton: The Life and Work of a Victorian Genius* (1974). He is a Fellow of the British Psychological Society, of the Psychological Society of Ireland and of the Royal College of Psychiatrists. Derek Forrest is married, with one daughter.

Anthony Storr qualified as a doctor in 1944 and subsequently specialized in psychiatry. From 1974 until his retirement in 1984 he worked as a psychiatrist teaching post-graduate doctors. He is now a full-time freelance writer. His publications include *The Dynamics of Creation* (1972), *Solitude* (1989) and *Feet of Clay* (1996).

Derek Forrest

HYPNOTISM
A HISTORY

Foreword by Anthony Storr

PENGUIN BOOKS

PENGUIN BOOKS

Published by the Penguin Group
Penguin Books Ltd, 27 Wrights Lane, London W8 5TZ, England
Penguin Putnam Inc., 375 Hudson Street, New York, New York 10014, USA
Penguin Books Australia Ltd, Ringwood, Victoria, Australia
Penguin Books Canada Ltd, 10 Alcorn Avenue, Toronto, Ontario, Canada M4V 3B2
Penguin Books India (P) Ltd, 11, Community Centre, Panchsheel Park, New Delhi – 110 017, India
Penguin Books (NZ) Ltd, Private Bag 102902, NSMC, Auckland, New Zealand
Penguin Books (South Africa) (Pty) Ltd, 5 Watkins Street, Denver Ext 4, Johannesburg 2094, South Africa

Penguin Books Ltd, Registered Offices: Harmondsworth, Middlesex, England

First published 1999 by www.blackacebooks.com as an illustrated hardback,
ISBN 1-872988-37-7, under the title *The Evolution of Hypnotism*
Published in Penguin Books 2000
1

For

Pam and Tansy

Contents

	Acknowledgements	ix
	Foreword by Anthony Storr	xi
	Author's Preface	xv
1	The Discovery	1
2	Mesmer in Paris	17
3	Year of Crisis	37
4	Aftermath	57
5	Somnambulism	70
6	Minor Magnetists	84
7	Vision Without Eyes	110
8	The Spread of Magnetism to Britain and the USA	125
9	Elliotson and the Okey Sisters	136
10	The Mesmeric Campaign	169
11	Braid and Hypnotism	193
12	Charcot at the Salpêtrière	213
13	The Triumph of Suggestion	229
14	The Twentieth Century	254
	Notes and references	278
	Index	322

Acknowledgements

Several persons contributed directly to the present work. Howard Smith read the manuscript and gave me the benefit of his scientific scepticism; Catherine Guy provided help in the early stages of the library search; Tansy Forrest, Elizabeth Seigne, and Catherine Whelan unearthed obscure references; Muireann Conaty and Maeve Stokes investigated the Irish dimension; Eddie Bolger prepared the illustrations; Margaret Brennan diligently prepared several drafts of the original typescript. I am most grateful to these colleagues and especially to my wife whose help and constant encouragement were responsible for the completion of the book. I should also like to thank Hunter Steele, a careful editor and enlightened publisher. Trinity College Dublin were generous in their support of my library visits.

Foreword

The phenomena associated with hypnotism are fascinatingly interesting and still only partially understood. Although hypnotism became associated with charlatans and theatrical performances, its use in the treatment of neurotic disorders has never been completely abandoned. Indeed, the current controversy concerning 'recovered memories' of being sexually abused in childhood, together with Professor John Mack's claim that, when in the hypnotic state, many patients can recall being abducted by aliens (*Abduction: Human Encounters with Aliens*, Simon & Schuster, 1994), have once again aroused considerable interest in hypnotism.

Hypnotism appears to produce a state of mind intermediate between sleep and waking in which the subject becomes particularly suggestible. Some types of illness, including a few varieties of skin disease, can be alleviated by hypnotism. Surgeons have been able to operate upon patients without using anaesthetics, because hypnotism has rendered them temporarily insensitive to pain. Other subjects become able to perform feats of physical endurance which they could not achieve when not in the hypnotic state. Hypnotized subjects may recall memories to which they have no access when normally conscious. Whether such memories are accurate is a matter of contemporary dispute. On returning to full consciousness, most subjects cannot recall anything which occurred during the hypnotic period.

Professor Forrest's book is both judicious and enthralling. It is a study in the history of ideas which demonstrates how concepts of hypnotism have changed and developed since Mesmer flourished in the eighteenth century. In the course of his exposition, Forrest gives vivid accounts of many extraordinary characters, including Mesmer himself, the Abbé Faria, Freud's mentor Charcot, and the famously eccentric Dr Elliotson, a friend of Dickens and Thackeray, who was forced to resign from his post as Physician to University College Hospital in 1838 because of his continued advocacy of mesmerism.

Forrest thinks it likely that the practice of hypnotism originated from observation of the spontaneous occurrence of trance states induced by drumming, dancing, or even prolonged staring at the flames of a fire. Mesmer, who was well educated both musically and medically, was a friend of the Mozart family, and acquainted with Gluck and Haydn. As those who know Mozart's opera *Cosi fan tutte* will recall, Mesmer employed magnets to cure his patients. This was not quackery, but rested upon the belief that there was a universal fluid which magnets could influence. Like Newton, Mesmer was worried by 'action at a distance', and his universal fluid closely resembled, or was identical with, the interstellar ether through which, so physicists supposed, the force of gravity was transmitted. Mesmer referred to the action of the the universal fluid upon the body as *animal magnetism*, and seems to have been genuinely convinced that he had made a fundamental discovery. The idea that the effects which he produced on patients might be anything to do with his own charismatic personality does not seem to have occurred to him.

Gradually, attempts at understanding the phenomena of the hypnotic trance shifted away from the realm of the physical to that of the psychological. The notion of the universal fluid was abandoned, and the relationship between hypnotist and subject became the object of investigation. Freud, who studied with Charcot during the winter of 1885-6, employed hypnotism when he first began to treat neurotic patients, and continued to do so until 1896 when he finally abandoned it. This was partly because he found that the results of the treatment were unpredictable, and that not every patient could be hypnotized. But, more importantly, he recognized that the effects of hypnotic treatment principally depended upon the patient's compliance and the doctor's authority, a state of affairs which blocked the way to any deeper understanding of the origin and meaning of neurotic symptoms.

Freud gave up making positive suggestions, and attempted to abandon the authoritarian position of the doctor by requiring the patient to take the initiative and express whatever thoughts or fantasies spontaneously occurred to him or her. However, free association, as this technique was named, was not as successful as Freud had hoped in dispelling the patient's need for an authority. When, in the course of free association, the patient revealed fantasies about Freud himself, it became obvious that the patient was putting Freud in the place of one or other parent, the first authorities in every human life. Freud called this phenomenon *transference*, and ever since his day the study of transference has been an integral part of every variety of analytical psychotherapy.

The transference phenomenon goes some way to explaining the compliance of the hypnotized subject, who may be anxious to please the hypnotist because the latter has temporarily assumed a parental role. But the human tendency to obey anyone regarded as an authority goes much further. The American psychologist Stanley Milgram demonstrated that normal people have such a strong tendency to obey that two-thirds of volunteers will inflict what they believe to be extremely painful or even life-endangering electric shocks on other human beings simply because they have been ordered to do so by an experimenter.

However, the hypnotic state itself requires further explanation. Most techniques of inducing the hypnotic state depend upon restricting the subject's attention to a single object, a light or coin or some other monotonous stimulus. When hypnotized, the subject usually becomes unaware of anything other than the voice of the hypnotist. Research has shown that people who are deprived of most sensory input by entering a dark, sound-proofed room pay particularly intense attention to any sound which is beamed at them and become much more suggestible as a consequence. The restriction of attention which is so characteristic of the hypnotic state is also a form of sensory deprivation, so it is understandable that those who are hypnotized also become more suggestible.

Insensitivity to pain in hypnotized subjects is perhaps not so surprising when one recalls that soldiers in the heat of battle may receive dreadful wounds without being aware of being hurt, because their attention is so fully engaged elsewhere. We also know that the brain produces its own pain-killers, the endorphins; and it is possible that hypnosis encourages increased production of these chemical agents.

But, as Professor Forrest writes: 'What is clear at the moment is that the nature of hypnosis continues to elude us.' He suggests that hypnosis has numerous possible applications which are too little appreciated. His valuable book will reawaken interest in the subject and encourage further scientific research.

Anthony Storr
Oxford, 1999

Preface

It seems probable that the practice of hypnotism had its origins in the early history of mankind with the chance discovery of various methods for the induction of trance states. Perhaps sustained rhythmic drumming and dancing, such as still used by tribal peoples, perhaps prolonged staring at the flames of a fire, or the taking of drugs, or sensory deprivation in a dark cave. Whatever the method, the resulting changes in behaviour were very likely to have been given a supernatural explanation.

The postulation of a spirit world with the consequent possibility of the possession of the body by an invading spirit were among the earliest forms of religious and medical belief. In the hypnotic trance human beings seemed to be more than human: they were resistant to pain and fatigue, their bodies moved apart from their own volition, they could adopt postures and perform feats beyond their normal powers. Or so it seemed, and, if so, what better explanation than spirit possession?

The association of hypnotism with the supernatural continues to this day. For example, the charismatic cults with traditions of faith healing often operate through hypnotic induction procedures, and perhaps achieve their best results by so doing. However, an attempt at a naturalistic explanation and a strenuous rejection of the ancient viewpoint first became clearly apparent during the late eighteenth century when Anton Mesmer sought a physical cause for the phenomena he produced. As we shall see, he had good reason to call this physical agent 'animal magnetism'. In view of Mesmer's pioneering initiative it has seemed appropriate to begin the present book at that date, when scientific explanations were in their infancy.

The first four chapters are devoted to the story of Mesmer and his immediate followers. Mesmer's procedures were aimed at bringing his patients to a 'crisis', without which he thought there would be no cure. This crisis took various forms, from mild sensations to fainting and even to violent fits. This was not hypnosis as we know it today. Mesmer had little interest in the trance-like states reached by some of his patients. It fell to one of his pupils, the Marquis de Puységur, to learn to utilize the deep trance and thus to initiate the study of altered states of consciousness. Puységur's career is considered in Chapter 5.

Other pioneers soon followed, and we examine the contributions of three significant figures in Chapter 6. The botanist Deleuze codified the practice of animal magnetism and made it into the beginnings of a profession; the physician Bertrand set the magnetic trance in the context of other naturally occurring phenomena, and the Abbé Faria took a new approach in denying any mysterious influence from the operator – the trance in his view depended upon qualities possessed by the subject. Writing in the 1820s, Faria was before his time, and practitioners continued to cling to the notion of an invisible animal magnetism emanating from the operator.

Chapter 7 describes the further development of animal magnetism in France, where its association with paranormal powers came under close scrutiny, in particular the supposed ability whilst in a trance to read without the use of eyes.

In Chapter 8 we chart the early spread of magnetism to Britain, which occurred over a period of years, interest being slow to develop until the visit of the Baron Du Potet in 1837. Du Potet's demonstrations aroused the interest of a leading physician, John Elliotson, who was to defend the therapeutic uses of magnetism in the face of continual opposition from the majority of the medical profession. Elliotson's crusade cost him his academic position and his medical pre-eminence; chapters 9 and 10 describe these events and the further development of magnetism in England under his leadership.

In Chapter 11 we reach a turning point with the work of James Braid, a contemporary of Elliotson but with a more critical eye. Braid was a no-nonsense surgeon whose theoretical stance resembled that of Faria in his rejection of all notions of mesmeric influence. Braid believed that he had found the causes of the trance not in the power of the operator but in the physiology of the person operated upon. His discovery seemed to merit a new terminology, and it is to him that we owe the term 'hypnotism' and its derivatives.

Braid's views led the great French neurologist Charcot to introduce hypnotism into his Parisian hospital practice during the 1880s. Charcot's view of hypnotism as an experimentally induced hysteria led to startling demonstrations and insights, but also to egregious errors. In the ensuing controversy with Bernheim, Professor of Medicine at the University of Nancy, Charcot was to prove the loser. Bernheim was able to show that it was not only hysterics who could fall into *le grand hypnotisme*; anyone of sufficient suggestibility could do so provided they knew what was expected of them. The burden of explanation was shifted from the abnormal condition of the nervous system to a psychological factor, suggestibility, possessed by everyone to a greater or lesser degree (chapters 12 and 13).

Thus the nineteenth century drew to a close. All the phenomena produced by hypnotism had now been described; it was the explanation of these phenomena which was still being sought. In the present century, when such explanations have multiplied, it has proved more difficult to isolate individuals from their research context. As psychology and the neurosciences have developed, small advances made by many people become the rule. Thus, the individual pioneers of the past do not appear so prominently in the present, and our account, in Chapter 14, becomes the story of a more developed science, but one that has still further to progress before hypnotism can be said to be completely understood. This lack of complete understanding does not, however, mean that it cannot be usefully employed, and no account of hypnotism today would be complete without some reference to the many ways in which hypnotic practice can alleviate suffering and enhance performance.

Modern attempts to understand the nervous system are helping to provide an appreciation of the changes that can be brought about by hypnotic techniques. It is probably this factor more than any other that is leading to a readier acceptance of hypnotism on the part of the medical profession. This is in marked contrast to the treatment meted out to some of the earlier hypnotic pioneers by the more conservative members of that profession. The prejudices of the establishment have not diminished, although its targets may have changed; every period must have its orthodoxy, and alternative medicine requires ultra-strong evidence before it can achieve parity of esteem even in a limited area of practice.

The present book makes no claim to be a general history of hypnotism;

such a work would have to range more widely in time and place, and should not fail to encompass the social and intellectual environment. Our story is largely confined to individual workers in England and France, the two countries which saw the important early developments in the field. The emphasis shifts in the final chapter, as it is in the United States that most of the significant recent research has occurred.

The book is mainly directed to the general reader and I have tried to keep any specialized terminology to a minimum. Among professional groups, doctors and psychologists may find the subject matter of particular interest. The precaution has been taken of consulting the primary sources and I have quoted generously from them. This liberal scattering of quotations may help the reader to appreciate the variety of unusual people, whether hypnotists or their subjects, who have enlivened popular as well as scientific debate.

Derek Forrest
Trinity College, Dublin
Summer 1999

1

The Discovery

In the year 1760 at the relatively late age of twenty-six, Anton Mesmer entered the Faculty of Medicine at the University of Vienna. Under the enlightened policy of the Austrian Empress, Maria-Theresia, the university and in particular its medical school were in process of being modernized. One of the leaders of the world-famous Leiden clinic, Gerard van Swieten, had been persuaded to leave Holland in order to head the Viennese faculty.

The main characteristic of the teaching methods adopted by Van Swieten lay in his insistence on thorough bedside diagnosis, with the taking of meticulous case notes, which were continued during the subsequent follow-up of the patient's response to treatment. The treatments themselves were still primitive enough: bleeding, blistering, purging, and other techniques of ancient origin, coupled with the new and fashionable electrotherapy, in which electric currents were sent through the body in the vain hope of restoring normal function to the malfunctioning organs.

As a student of Van Swieten's, Mesmer received as thorough a medical education as could be obtained anywhere in Europe. He was no stranger to university life, having previously attended the University of Ingoldstadt to study astronomy and allied sciences before entering the University of Vienna to read law, which was in turn abandoned for medicine. Such a prolonged education must have been unusual for the son of a humble gamekeeper and one of a family of nine children. Mesmer's biographers ascribe it to the help given to the young man by the Jesuits, and their general opinion is that he was originally intended for the priesthood.[1]

After six years in medical school he graduated with a final dissertation entitled *On the Influence of the Planets*. The title is misleading today;

this was no work of astrology. Such an interest, besides being foreign to Mesmer's own scepticism, would never have been tolerated in the scientific ambience established by Van Swieten. Mesmer's dissertation represented an attempt to bring into medicine the study of the effects on the human body thought to be produced by gravitational influences exerted by the sun and moon, then termed planets.

Mesmer's argument ran somewhat as follows: in view of the validity of Newton's theory of gravitation and his explanation of the movement of tides, it is reasonable to suppose that there might also be atmospheric tides, produced by those same gravitational forces that move the sea. These variations in the atmosphere may be linked to variations in the progress of a disease.

This idea was by no means original: an English physician, Richard Mead, had expounded a very similar theory in 1704, and much of Mesmer's thesis has been shown to have been taken from Mead's work.[2] Mead was an ardent admirer of Newton and an initiator of the study of periodicities in physiological functions. Mesmer's main alteration to Mead's theory was to claim the possibility of a direct action of gravitational forces on the human body instead of an indirect one brought about by fluctuations in the surrounding air. There must be, he thought, a material cause of gravitation, and he accordingly proposed the existence of a 'universal fluid' which was subject to an eternal ebb and flow, affecting not only planetary bodies but everything on earth and leading to tidal effects within the human body in the flow of blood and nervous excitation.

He backed his present theory with case histories and clinical notes of fluctuating illnesses, almost all plagiarized from Mead. That a medical dissertation should be so dependent on the work of another was not as unusual in the eighteenth century as it would be today, and Mesmer successfully defended his thesis in front of Van Swieten and Anton Stoerck, the Dean of the Faculty, and was thenceforth licensed to practise medicine.

For the next eight years he appears to have run a conventional clinic with the bleedings and blisterings and electrotherapy of the orthodox practitioner. His clientèle was a rich one; he practised from a large mansion on the Landstrasse, the most fashionable district of Vienna. This house and its beautiful garden had been acquired within two years of his graduation when he had married Anna von Bosch, a rich and aristocratic widow with a teenage son. The fact that she was forty-four, and thus ten years his senior, must have led to contemporary comment as it has to subsequent speculation. Certainly, his marriage enabled him to indulge his artistic interests; he was an accomplished musician, and visitors to the house included Glück, Haydn and the Mozart family.

Leopold Mozart had cause to be grateful to Mesmer, for during a fruitless visit to Vienna in 1768 when he was unable to have his son's first opera performed – largely owing to an unscrupulous producer and to jealousies among the performers – it was Mesmer who offered the use of his garden theatre as an alternative venue. Unfortunately, it proved to be unsuitable for the performance of the full-scale opera, *La Finta Semplice*, and it was necessary for the twelve-year-old composer to turn to another theme. Characteristically rapid in creation, his first operetta, *Bastien et Bastienne*, was ready for a performance in the autumn of the same year in Mesmer's garden theatre.

The Mozarts returned to Salzburg shortly after this event and it was not until five years later that they were again in Mesmer's house. Leopold wrote from there to his wife (21 July 1773):

> The Mesmers are all well and in good form as usual. Herr von Mesmer, at whose house we lunched on Monday, played to us on Miss Davies's armonica or glass instrument and played very well. It cost him about fifty ducats, and it is very beautifully made. We dined with them on Saturday and also on Monday.[3]

The glass harmonica was an unusual instrument on which Mesmer was something of a virtuoso. In its original form it consisted of bowls containing different amounts of water, the rims of the bowls being tapped to produce a melody. Mesmer played on an improved version, invented by Benjamin Franklin (who is later to re-enter the Mesmer story in a less sympathetic role), in which notes were produced by touching the rims of glass bowls of different sizes, which were rotated on a spindle cranked by a treadle. The Miss Davies mentioned in Mozart's letter had become well known for her skill in accompanying her sister who sang. Mesmer had heard them in Vienna and had had an instrument made for himself; indeed, he had taught Wolfgang Mozart to play it, and later in life the composer produced two pieces especially for it. The glass harmonica was to accompany

Mesmer to Paris and to figure in the extraordinary scenes of the mesmeric séance.

Several further letters from Leopold Mozart dating from later in 1773 refer to the state of health of a Fräulein Franzl, who was apparently a relative of Frau Mesmer. Her full name was Francisca Oesterlin and she is important to this narrative as she was the first patient treated by Mesmer according to magnetic principles. Mesmer described her symptoms in these words:

> A young woman of twenty-eight years, who lived in my house and who had suffered from nervous debility from her youth, was attacked by terrible convulsions over a period of two years. Her hysterical fever caused continual vomiting, inflammation of the bowels, stoppage of urine, excruciating tooth-ache, ear-ache, melancholy, depression, delirium, fits of frenzy, catalepsy, fainting fits, blindness, breathless-ness, paralyses lasting some days, and other symptoms.
>
> I applied the most efficacious remedies known; not leaving her out of my sight, frequently rescuing her from death's door, and I usually restored her within three or four weeks without obtaining a lasting cure; recovery did not last long before she fell ill again.[4]

Mozart's letters enable us to follow one of these cycles in her illness:

> *July 21.* We found Fräulein Franzl in bed. She is really very much emaciated and if she has another illness of this kind, she will be done for!
>
> *August 12.* Meanwhile Fräulein Franzl has again been dangerously ill and blisters had to be applied to her arms and feet. She is so much better now that she has knitted in bed a red silk purse for Wolfgang . . .
>
> *August 21.* Fräulein Franzl has now had a second relapse from which she has again recovered. It is amazing how she can stand so much bleeding and so many medicines, blisters, convulsions, fainting fits and so forth, for she is nothing but skin and bones.
>
> *September 15.* So far I have not been out to the Rotmühle, although the Mesmers have been out there for a long time and Fräulein Franzl nearly died there again.[5]

The cyclical nature of her illness was so apparent that Mesmer became able to forecast the onset of the next attack; his patient seemed to be a perfect exemplar of the theory put forward in his medical thesis. The therapeutic solution, he thought, must lie in the discovery of an agent that would enable him to control the ebb and flow of the universal fluid.

He was led to employ magnets mainly by analogy between their properties and that of the 'general system'. That is to say, a magnet's capacity to attract and repel bears a strong resemblance to the effect of the sun and moon on the ebb and flow of the tides; also a magnet seems to exert action at a distance rather like the gravitational effect. Mesmer was also aware of the use of magnets in medicine both in England and France, where some dubious claims had been made for their efficacy in curing stomach and toothache.

Artificial magnets had first been made from stainless steel by an Englishman, John Canton, in 1750, and the technique had rapidly spread across Europe. The Professor of Astronomy at Vienna University, a Jesuit priest by the name of Maximilian Hell, was in a position to supply them from his workshop, and Mesmer asked for them to be made in certain shapes. He described their effect:

> When my patient had another attack last July [1774] I fixed two horse-shoe magnets to her feet and another in the shape of a heart on her breast. Immediately she felt a burning, tearing pain, which spread up her legs as far as her hips where it was joined by a similar pain which descended from the magnet on her breast down one side and up the other to the crown of her head. As these pains dissipated they left all her joints burning like fire. The patient and my assistants were frightened by these symptoms and asked me to stop the experiment. But I insisted upon continuing and applied more magnets to her lower limbs; whereupon she immediately felt the pains descend from her body.
>
> The pains continued throughout the night and were accompanied by a copious sweating on her paralysed side. The symptoms gradually disappeared, she became insensitive to the action of the magnets, and the seizure was over.[6]

Mesmer repeated the procedure on the following day, and over the next three weeks found himself able to direct the 'painful currents', as the patient described them, by the strategic placing of magnets on the body. Thus, the magnets seemed to be influencing the movements of the universal fluid in the patient, whose symptoms were also becoming weaker.

Mesmer kept Father Hell informed of his patient's progress, only to lose priority in publication. For Hell now wrote an article in which he claimed the credit for suggesting to Mesmer that he should use magnets. Hell himself had carried out experiments with them on the human body and had cured an (unnamed) baroness of her stomach cramps. Hell went further in this theory:

> I have discovered in these shapes . . . a perfection on which depends their specific virtue in cases of illness; it is owing to the lack of this perfection that the tests carried out in England and France have met with no success.[7]

Mesmer replied immediately and claimed priority for the use of magnetic treatment; he had been preparing the patient for the external application of magnets by giving her iron tonic for a long period. In any case, he considered Father Hell to be completely mistaken in ascribing any virtue to the shape of the magnet, in spite of the fact that his own therapy had seemed to reflect this doctrine. How, he asks, could the shape of a mineral object affect the ebb and flow: the magnet was only a conductor which enabled the universal fluid to enter the patient's body. And Mesmer now, and for the first time, refers to the universal fluid in its action on the body as *animal magnetism*. He is at great pains to point out that animal magnetism is quite distinct from mineral magnetism: the mineral magnet can channel animal magnetism but it is not unique in this respect. Experiments with Fräulein Oesterlin and others had already convinced him that paper, bread, wool, silk, leather, stone, glass, water, various metals, wood, human beings and dogs, in short everything he touched, could all have as strong an influence as steel. Human beings themselves varied considerably in their ability to store animal magnetism; one in ten persons had the power to a marked degree. Such a person might have a direct magnetic effect on a patient without the intermediary of a conductor.

Convinced that he had made a fundamental discovery, he asked Anton Stoerck to examine the evidence, but Stoerck refused. The refusal was attributed by Mesmer to Stoerck's conservatism and to his fear that the Medical Faculty might be compromised by publicity. It was in consequence of Stoerck's lack of support that Mesmer decided to publish the report from which we have quoted; it was sent in the form of a letter to Dr Johann Unzer, a German physician with whom he had been in correspondence, while copies of the letter were sent to several scientific academies.[8] The letter is dated 7 January 1775, a mere six months after Mesmer's magnetic treatment of Fräulein Oesterlin began, and obviously too short a time in which to claim a permanent cure.

Further information on this point is provided by a later work of Mesmer's, his *Mémoire sur la découverte du magnétisme animal*, which appeared in 1779. In that monograph, to which we shall later return, he tells how Fräulein Oesterlin relapsed into convulsions after contracting a chill and how he took this opportunity to demonstrate the existence of animal magnetism to a sceptical Dutch physician, Jan Ingenhousz. Ingenhousz was a leading exponent of inoculation and he was in Vienna in order to carry out inoculations during an epidemic of smallpox. He had also gained a reputation for biological research, his most noteworthy achievement being the discovery of photosynthesis, and he was now interested in electrical and magnetic phenomena. The episode is best described in Mesmer's own words:

> The patient was unconscious and convulsed. I told him (Ingenhousz) that this was the most favourable moment to convince himself of the existence of the principle I had announced and for acquainting himself with its properties. I asked him to approach the patient, while I withdrew, telling him to touch her. She made no movement. I called him back to me and communicated animal magnetism to him by taking his hands; I then told him to approach the patient again, while I kept at a distance, and to touch her a second time; this resulted in convulsive movements. I made him repeat this touching many times, which he did with the tip of his finger, changing the direction each time; and always, to his great astonishment, he caused a convulsive effect in the part touched. When this experiment was over, he told me he was convinced. I suggested a second experiment. We withdrew from the patient so that we could not be seen, even had she regained consciousness. I offered Herr Ingenhousz six china cups and asked him to tell me to which one of them he wished me to

communicate the magnetic quality. I touched the one he chose; I then applied the six cups in succession to the patient's hand; when I reached the one which I had touched, the hand made a movement and she gave signs of pain.

Ingenhousz, having touched the cups, obtained the same effect . . . I proposed a third experiment to show the action [of magnetism] at a distance and its penetrating power. At a distance of eight paces I pointed my finger towards the patient; the next instant her body was in a convulsion to the point of raising her from her bed in evident pain. I continued from the same position to point my finger at her, placing Herr Ingenhousz between us; she experienced the same sensations. Having repeated these tests to Herr Ingenhousz's satisfaction, I asked him if he were satisfied and convinced of the marvellous properties of which I had spoken, offering to repeat the proceedings if he were not. His reply was to the effect that he wished for nothing more and was quite convinced, but he begged me, on account of his regard for me, not to make any public statement about the matter, so as not to expose myself to public incredulity. We parted, and I went back to the patient to continue the treatment, which was happily most successful . . .

Two days later I was astonished to hear that Herr Ingenhousz was making statements in public that were quite contrary to those he had made in my house, and that he was denying the success of the different experiments he had witnessed. He was confounding animal magnetism with that of the magnet and he was trying to damage my reputation by asserting that with the aid of a number of magnetized pieces which he had brought with him, he had succeeded in unmasking me and had proved the experiments to be a ridiculous and pre-arranged fraud.[9]

It is unclear how Ingenhousz had used his magnets during the demonstration, but the charge of fraudulent conspiracy was clear enough. Before Mesmer could compose a rebuttal, his patient relapsed again and he spent the next fortnight in intensive therapy. Now, he claims, the cure became permanent, although it is difficult to see how he could have followed up the case personally as he had been invited to Hungary in the April of 1775 and spent the remainder of that year and the next in touring abroad. It must have been during his absence that Fräulein Oesterlin married Mesmer's stepson. Evidence is provided a few years later in a letter from Wolfgang Mozart to his father:

Where do you think I am writing this letter? – In the Mesmers' garden in the Landstrasse. The old lady [Frau Mesmer, then aged fifty-three!] is not at home, but Fräulein Franzl, now Frau von Bosch, is here . . . Well, upon my honour, I hardly recognized her, she has grown so plump and stout. She has three children . . . they are all so strong and robust.[10]

Thus we have independent testimony of the great change from the emaciated Fräulein Oesterlin to the matriarchal Frau von Bosch, but we have no means of ascertaining the role played by Mesmer's intervention in her cure. After all, Hippocrates was said to have recommended marriage as a cure for hysteria!

Mesmer now made further appeals to Stoerck to consider his new form of therapy, but he got nowhere and began to feel justified in his belief that Hell, Stoerck and Ingenhousz were in league against him and were busy influencing other physicians also. Isolated professionally, his practice expanded enormously with patients who had received little help from orthodox medicine.

His fame spread from Vienna as reports of his cures of paralyses, depressions and epilepsy multiplied. In Germany, Unzer took on a patient of his own, and thus became Mesmer's first disciple. He cured a young woman of a variety of gross hysterical symptoms which followed the births of her children. In a 20,000-word clinical report he minutely documented the effects produced by variously shaped magnets which Mesmer had sent him.[11] Unzer's account was translated into Dutch by Deimann, who reported success with the technique in three of his own cases.[12] Therapeutically the method seemed to be catching on, but a setback was to come from the Berlin Academy of Sciences, to whom Mesmer had sent a copy of his paper. The report from the Academy's mathematicians and physicists was a model of clarity and concision, but involved a misinterpretation of Mesmer's theory, which was thought to deal solely with mineral magnetism. Although not denying that magnets might have an effect on the human body, the authors wisely pointed out that the cure of an illness was not a satisfactory criterion. They were dubious too about a patient's ability to feel the magnetic force, and they were quite adamant in denying the capacity of materials other than iron to take up magnetism.[13]

It is not surprising that the Academy misunderstood Mesmer; the concept of animal magnetism was, and was to remain, unclear. Mesmer had, after all, sent various magnets to Unzer for his treatment. He was using magnets himself, although he seems to have been unsure in his own mind about their necessity in some cases. Sometimes he believed it sufficient to communicate his own animal magnetism to objects or to water, and to treat the patient with these. For example, in one of his best-known cases from late in 1775, in which he treated a Hungarian baron for spasms of the neck muscles, an eye-witness account mentions the use of water:

> I had to laugh. Mesmer sat on the right side of the bed, on a stool, wearing a dark grey gown trimmed with gold braid. On one foot he had a white silk stocking, the other, which was bare, was placed in a tub about two feet in diameter, filled with water . . . Near the tub sat Kolowratek (the baron's violin teacher), fully dressed, facing the bed and holding in his left hand a malacca cane, the tip of which rested on the bottom of the tub. With his right hand he rubbed the rod up and down; many would say that this was mere hanky-panky, but I know how effective the rubbing could be in generating electricity. Mesmer and Kolowratek kept silent; the baron, covered only with a wolfskin rug, was shivering and complaining of cold; he spoke confusedly as if in a fever.[14]

Here then were the ingredients of the later famous Parisian séances, but in an undeveloped state. The tub of magnetized water with the vertical rod was to become Mesmer's aid to group therapy, the *baquet*, although in its more sophisticated form Mesmer was to keep his feet dry; the robe he wore was to become more elegant and striking; the silence was to be charged with mysterious chords from the glass harmonica; and the baron's fevers, seemingly induced by the magnetic influence, were to become the crisis, which Mesmer was to consider essential to a cure. After the visit to Hungary, which lasted some three months and which ended not in the cure of the baron but in his breaking off treatment on account of the intensity of the induced crises, Mesmer travelled in Switzerland and Bavaria. It is noteworthy that in one account of his technique during this period there is the comment:

> Anyone who has seen Dr Mesmer at work cannot fail to be impressed
> by his skill and to marvel how he effects his cures by personal
> magnetism without magnets.[15]

It seems clear that Mesmer must have progressed quite rapidly from
the reliance on steel magnets in the early stages of the Oesterlin case
(July 1774), through the discovery that other substances could be
'magnetized', as mentioned in the letter to Unzer (January 1775) and
as put into practice in Hungary early in the same year, to the frequent
but not complete abolition of these aids by August. (Mesmer himself
stated that he made no further use of magnets after 1776.[16])

An opportunity to show his powers arose in November when he was
invited by the Elector of Bavaria to visit Munich and to demonstrate
his methods before the Academy of Sciences. The most convincing
demonstration proved possible, for the Secretary of the Academy,
who could not be suspected of fraudulent compliance, suffered from
convulsions, which Mesmer was able to induce and dispel from a
distance by merely pointing or dropping his hand. The purpose of the
invitation then became clear. The Elector, having been convinced by
the various demonstrations and having listened to Mesmer's theoretical
explanation, now asked him for his opinion on the cures being brought
about at that moment by a Jesuit priest, Father Gassner.

Gassner's practice of exorcism had begun a year or two before
Mesmer's magnetic treatments. He had written a booklet in 1774 in
which he distinguished between natural and preternatural illnesses, the
former being the province of the orthodox physician, the latter being
amenable to exorcism.[17] In spite of proceeding strictly according to
Catholic orthodoxy, his activities were not wholly supported by the
Church. His successes were undoubted, and people thronged to the
small Bavarian town of Ellwangen where he was holding his services.
His reputation had spread as far as Vienna, where opinion was divided
as to whether he was a fraud or a miracle-worker.[18]

Mesmer, having produced much the same phenomena as Gassner but
with the support of a scientific rather than a supernatural explanation,
was listened to carefully when he described Gassner as a man of good
faith but excessive zeal, who probably had greater powers of magnetism
than he himself and who used these powers to cure his patients without

being aware that that was what he was doing rather than invoking supernatural aid.

Mesmer's opinion was accepted by the Elector, who ordered Gassner to stop his practices. The Church authorities took the opportunity to persuade the Emperor Joseph II to ban Gassner throughout the Empire, and Pope Pius VI completed the process by having Gassner's writings on exorcism placed on the Index. Gassner retired to obscurity, to die four years later; Mesmer, honoured by membership of the Munich Academy of Sciences, travelled back to Vienna on the crest of a wave of recognition. It was Gassner's misfortune to utilize a framework of the miraculous when the philosophy of the Enlightenment demanded a rational explanation of observable phenomena. This latter Mesmer seemed able at the time to provide, although, as events were to prove, it was the limitations of his materialistic stance (and that of his judges) that were ultimately to prove his undoing.

After his return to Vienna Mesmer spent much of the next year quietly. He tells us that it was the insistence of his friends and his own desire to see the truth prevail that led him to search for an opportunity to perform a cure sufficiently striking to convince the incredulous. To this end he took three young women into his house. The first, Fräulein Ossine, was the daughter of an Army officer; she suffered from 'purulent phthisis and irritable melancholia, accompanied by fits, rage, vomiting, spitting of blood and fainting' – a collection of symptoms almost as varied as those of Fräulein Oesterlin. A second girl, named Zwelferine (the Twelfth), was found by Mesmer in the Viennese orphanage, whose governor attested to the fact that she had been blind since the age of two. Without supplying details, Mesmer claims that he was able to cure both these patients.[19] The case of the third girl was well documented, partly because of her artistic and social position in Viennese society, her father being private secretary to the Empress, and partly because the outcome of the treatment was uncertain. It was this case that was ultimately responsible for Mesmer's departure from Vienna.[20]

When Mesmer undertook the treatment of Maria Theresia von Paradis she was eighteen years old. According to her father, she had awakened one morning at the age of three and had found herself unable to see at all, a total blindness that had persisted all her life. Having great ability as a pianist, she was in receipt of a pension from the Empress in recognition of her talent and as compensation for her disability. She had played at the

Schönbrunn Palace and also on the concert platform. The Empress had arranged for Anton Stoerck to attend her over a number of years, but both he and Joseph Barth, the foremost eye specialist, proclaimed her incurable. During the course of their treatment she had been subjected to numerous bleedings, purgings, and cauterization, also a painful form of electrotherapy in which more than 3,000 shocks had been administered to the eyeball. Her eyes bulged and jerked spasmodically, and generally only the whites could be seen. Even her father was forced to remark that her appearance was 'disagreeable and difficult to endure'.

Mesmer began treatment on 20 January 1777 and her response was immediate: from the very first touch of his hands, her limbs began to tremble, her whole body shook, and her eye spasms increased. By the fourth day, the eye movements had ceased and her gaze became normal. However, she now experienced headaches in which the pain seemed to descend along the optic nerves and to radiate over the retinae. Her nose began to swell, the pressure becoming intolerable, until after eight days there was a copious discharge of mucous. She complained of giddiness and began to feel such pain whenever light fell on her eyes that Mesmer was obliged to keep her in a semi-darkened room. He now instructed her to pay attention to the sensations in her eyes while he placed before her black or white objects. She found that she was able to distinguish them on the grounds that the white objects caused more pain. She soon progressed to being able to distinguish among coloured objects, but found it impossible to remember the names of colours. At this stage much tuition had to be given to enable her to move her eye muscles appropriately in searching for objects in her visual field.

After three weeks of treatment, during which Mesmer had always remained outside the peripheral limits of her vision, he deliberately placed himself directly before her. She appeared somewhat alarmed at the sight of him and is reported to have exclaimed, 'That is terrible to behold! Is that the form of a human being?' Thereafter she found the experience of meeting people extremely unpleasant, repeatedly fainting when relatives or intimate friends were presented to her. She was especially frightened by human noses: 'They seem to threaten me as if they would bore my eyes out.'

It is probable that this latter fear was based on her faulty distance perception. When she was taken out into the garden, she thought she could stretch out her hand to touch a tree that was in fact 1,000 metres

away across the river. Likewise, her judgement of the size of objects was
very poor. For example, she called a reservoir 'a large soup plate'. As she
moved about, objects appeared to move with her, and as she approached
the house, it seemed to her to approach her. All objects seemed to
increase in size as they neared her: for example, having dipped a rusk
in a cup of chocolate and lifted it towards her mouth, she refused to eat
it, considering it too large. In short, the newly discovered visual world
appeared to her to be so unstable that she had to be led everywhere,
although when she had been blind she had been able to move about
confidently. Worst of all, she was now unable to play the piano with
her former skill. It is not surprising that she was not completely happy
with her cure, as evidenced by reports of crying fits and declarations that
she wished she were blind again.

However, her parents were at first delighted with her progress, and
her father wrote a most sympathetic account of her cure, which was
published and widely distributed.[21] Herr Paradis persuaded Stoerck
and other physicians to examine his daughter with a view to having
her presented to the Empress. Stoerck's initial response seems to have
been positive. According to Mesmer, Stoerck told him of 'his interest
in this extraordinary case, and said he regretted having waited so long to
acknowledge the importance of my discovery'.[22]

Mesmer's belief that general recognition of the curative power of animal magnetism would follow from Stoerck's spoken acknowledgement
was shaken almost immediately. Barth examined the patient and denied
the cure on the ground that the patient had made too many mistakes
in identifying objects for it to be certain that she had recovered her
sight. Mesmer was probably right in ascribing Barth's objections to
jealousy, for it could hardly be maintained that the patient should
have been any more perfect in this respect than other patients who
had recovered their sight after long periods of blindness.[23] However,
Mesmer was always over-ready to perceive a conspiracy and it may
have been an exaggeration to impute to Barth the desire to prevent the
presentation of the girl to the Empress by conspiring with Mesmer's old
enemy Ingenhousz to have her removed prematurely from Mesmer's
care. This they were supposed to have done by sowing such seeds of
doubt in her father's mind that he resolved to take her home. It seems
more likely that he may have become concerned over her relationship
with Mesmer, which was the subject of gossip, and over the possible loss

of her fame and pension once she were cured of her disability. However, the girl was unwilling to leave Mesmer's house. The ensuing rumpus is best described in Mesmer's words:

> Her mother, who had earlier begged me to excuse her husband's behaviour, came on 29 April to announce that she intended to remove her daughter immediately. I replied that she was free to do so, but that if some mishap occurred as a result she could not count on my help. These words were overheard by the girl, who was so upset that she went into a fit . . . Her mother, who heard her cries, left me abruptly and dragged her from the hands of the nurse who was attending her, exclaiming, 'Wretched girl, you are as bad as all the other people in this house!' and in her fury she flung her head-first against the wall . . . I hastened towards the girl to give her assistance, but her mother still in a rage flung herself upon me to prevent me doing so, while shouting insults at me. I had to get members of my family to remove her before I could give the girl any assistance. While I was so engaged, I heard angry shouts and repeated attempts to open the door of the room where I was. It was Herr Paradis, who, having been told by his wife's servant, had now invaded my house with drawn sword and was trying to enter the room while my servant guarding the door was trying to prevent him. The madman was at last disarmed and he left my house, uttering imprecations on myself and my household. Meanwhile, his wife had fallen into a swoon; I gave her the necessary attention and she left some hours afterwards. But their unhappy daughter was suffering from attacks of vomiting, fits and rages, which the slightest noise, especially the sound of bells, made much worse. She had even relapsed into her previous blind state as a result of the violent blow given to her by her mother, and I feared that her brain might be affected . . .
>
> On the next day I heard that Herr Paradis was trying to cover up his excesses by spreading about the most atrocious insinuations about me, with a view to removing his daughter and proving, by her condition, the danger of my methods. I did indeed receive through Herr Ost, Court Physician, a written order from Herr von Stoerck, in his capacity as head physician, dated Schönbrunn 22 May 1777, instructing me 'to put an end to the imposture', that was his expression, and 'to restore the girl to her parents if I thought this could be done without risk'.

Who would have believed that Herr von Stoerck, being so well informed of all that had taken place in my house and, after his first visit, having come twice to convince himself of the patient's progress and the utility of my methods, could have insulted me in this manner? I had reason to expect the contrary, because being well placed for recognizing a truth of this kind, he should have been its defender. I would have thought that as Dean of the Faculty, and still more as the repository of her Majesty's confidence, the first of his duties would be to protect a member of the Faculty whom he knew to be blameless, and to whom he had time and time again given assurances of his affection and esteem. I replied to this irresponsible order that the patient was not in a position to be moved without running the risk of death.[24]

Herr Paradis now recanted and asked Mesmer to continue the treatment. After a further month's work, by which time her blindness had once again been cured, Mesmer felt sufficiently confident to allow his patient to rejoin her family, especially since her father promised to return her whenever Mesmer wished. On 8 June she returned home and shortly afterwards lapsed into complete blindness, from which she never recovered. She was never allowed to return for treatment; indeed, her parents denounced Mesmer as a charlatan.

Maria Theresia's life as a blind pianist was not unpleasant: she toured the European capitals and was sufficiently talented for Mozart to write his Concerto in B Flat Major No. 18 especially for her. It was this piece that she played before Louis XVI and Marie Antoinette in Paris in 1784; in that audience was Anton Mesmer![25]

Although Mesmer continued for a time with the treatment of his other two female patients, the considerable scandal surrounding the Paradis affair made life difficult. Stoerck was now consistently hostile and the exclusion of Mesmer from the Medical Faculty seemed probable. His successful cures seemed to bring him notoriety and opposition rather than distinction and acceptance. There was little to keep him in Vienna and much to attract him to Paris. Leaving behind his wife,[26] whom he was never to see again, he set forth determined to obtain for animal magnetism the recognition he believed it deserved.

2

Mesmer in Paris

Accompanied by one manservant Mesmer arrived in Paris in 1778. He was now almost forty-four years of age and an impressive figure, to judge from contemporary portraits. A somewhat fat but muscular physique, with pronounced facial features, particularly heavy eyebrows and a broad bulging forehead, gave a massive solidity to his appearance. He is said to have walked with a slow heavy tread, his constant attitude being one of calm deliberation. He was not a man to be easily overlooked, even in the absence of a reputation.

Mesmer's reputation, however, had preceded him to Paris. Travellers' tales and newspaper accounts of remarkable cures led to a general expectation that Parisians were soon to benefit from this mysterious therapy. But that was not Mesmer's original intention: he tells us that he first sought scientific recognition on the ground that when once the existence of the universal fluid had been acknowledged, the physicians would subsequently be compelled to accept the reality of the cures obtained through its use.[1]

Furnished with an introduction to the Austrian ambassador, Mesmer lost no time in meeting influential scientists, such as Charles Leroy, President of the Royal Academy of Sciences. Leroy was a chemist and physiologist, seemingly ideally qualified to appreciate Mesmer's discovery. Indeed, after assisting at some experiments, which, it would seem, consisted mainly in asking subjects to report their sensations when the magnetizer's hand moved over their bodies, Leroy was prepared to introduce Mesmer as a speaker at the next meeting of the Academy. According to Mesmer's account of the proceedings, not only was Mesmer not listened to but Leroy himself was unable to keep the assembly in order until it was finally reduced in numbers to a bare dozen.

Mesmer's attempts to read a statement having failed – and it must be remembered that his French was poor and he spoke with a strong German accent — a demonstration was demanded. Mesmer was reluctant, in view of the scepticism of the audience, but at last agreed to operate on an asthmatic member of the Academy. Although the patient admitted that he could sense Mesmer's influence, namely tingling in his hands and currents running up and down his arms, his replies to questions from the audience as to what was happening to him were vague and more tentative. Even the occurrence of an asthmatic attack did little to convince the sceptics, most of whom now left the hall. The patient was more at ease with Mesmer, Leroy and his two remaining colleagues, and Mesmer was able to demonstrate hallucinations of taste and smell.

In spite of the inadequacy of this first public performance, Leroy was still sufficiently interested to accept an invitation to visit Mesmer's house, where greater things were promised. Mesmer had rented an apartment in the Place Vendôme, near the city centre, where, within a few days of his arrival, would-be patients had been congregating, begging for treatment. Despite his avowed intent to avoid therapy, he found it impossible to turn away sufferers when he had what was, he was convinced, the means of curing them. Thus, when Leroy and his party came, he was able to assemble several patients for demonstration, the most remarkable being a case of dropsy whose limbs swelled and reduced at Mesmer's touch. His scientific observers appear to have been astonished at the phenomena exhibited, but were reluctant to report their observations to the Academy for fear of ridicule. Leroy went further: he was unwise enough to say that he thought the effects might be produced by the patient's imagination, and that conviction would only be established through a large number of cured cases. To Mesmer this was equivalent to a denial of truth, and he castigated Leroy at the time in person and later in print for raising such pitiable objections. There seems little doubt that Mesmer's absolute conviction strained Leroy's impartiality to such an extent that he broke off relations, and when later in August of the same year Mesmer wrote to say that he had after all followed Leroy's advice and now had many patients to demonstrate, Leroy did not even reply.[2]

Having failed with the Academy of Sciences, Mesmer fell back on the physicians. Several members of the newly formed Royal Society of Medicine had expressed interest in Mesmer's techniques. This body was only to achieve its formal constitution in 1779, its primary function being to evaluate patent medicines and, by extension, new forms of therapy. To Mesmer it seemed likely in its embryonic state to be more receptive to his innovations than would the traditional and more orthodox Faculty of Medicine, which resembled the antipathetic Viennese organization.

Two doctors, Charles Andry and Antoine Mauduit, the latter a specialist in electrotherapy, were deputized to examine Mesmer's technique.[3] As a general rule, Mesmer would sit opposite his patient with his knees outside the patient's knees while he made long stroking movements (*grandes passes*) with his hands from the shoulders down the arms to the hands, when he would hold the thumbs momentarily before repeating the process. Sometimes the passes were continued to the feet, and they might be made in contact with the exposed skin and clothing or at a distance of a few inches. Occasionally Mesmer would place one hand on the patient's abdomen and one on the small of the back in order to saturate the trunk with the magnetic fluid.

To any orthodox medical practitioner such procedures must have appeared peculiar and unlikely to be therapeutic. However, the fact remained that they were often efficacious in bringing on an exacerbation of the patient's symptoms. On the present occasion, a young epileptic girl produced sudden and severe convulsions in response to Mesmer's passes. However, neither Andry nor Mauduit was impressed, and they raised what were soon to become the most common objections to magnetic cures: the diagnosis was uncertain and the patient may in any case have been feigning the responses to Mesmer's procedures. Mauduit's reaction was unfortunately only too understandable, for the young epileptic had been his own patient whom he had treated unsuccessfully with electrotherapy.[4]

In view of the low probability of a fair report from such prejudiced witnesses, Mesmer decided to approach the Society directly with documentary evidence from patients themselves. He accordingly wrote to Félix Vicq-d'Azyr, the secretary to the Society of Medicine, enclosing an envelope of testimonials with a covering letter in which he asked for the material to be distributed to the members. Vicq-d'Azyr replied promptly: it was impossible for the Society to venture an opinion upon unfamiliar cases. The testimonials had not even been unsealed. Mesmer immediately wrote back and re-submitted the evidence. When after three months no reply was forthcoming, he wrote yet again inviting a committee to visit his clinic. A final curt note from Vic-d'Azyr convinced even Mesmer that it would be foolish to continue the correspondence:

'This organization, which has had no knowledge of the previous state of the patients submitted to treatment by you, cannot state an opinion on the matter.'[5]

Mesmer's letters to Vicq-d'Azyr had been sent from the village of Créteil outside Paris. He had moved there with a few patients in May 1778, having found the Paris apartments too small. It was at Créteil that the baquet was first developed, to enable him to treat up to thirty patients at a time. The device was probably built in imitation of the recently invented Leyden jar and was supposed by analogy to 'store' animal magnetism. Various models were developed, but typically it was a large shallow wooden tub of up to fifteen feet in diameter and one to two feet deep. It held bottles of water, previously 'magnetized' by Mesmer, arranged concentrically like spokes of a wheel. The water bottles were themselves submerged in more magnetized water which contained iron, stone and other substances, also saturated with animal magnetism. Protruding through the cover of the baquet were sufficient bent iron rods or cords for each patient to apply one to the affected part of his body. The patients sat around the tub holding hands to ensure the circulation of the magnetic fluid.

Many patients appear to have benefited from the baquet at Créteil. Among others, whose testimonials had been sent to Vicq-d'Azyr, was the Chevalier du Haussay, a forty-year-old infantry major who had contracted a fever in Martinique, which had been followed by partial paralysis. When he arrived at Créteil he could scarcely walk; with his head fallen forward, his face purple, his eyes protruding, his breathing jerky and his limbs trembling, he described himself as having the appearance of an old drunkard. Mesmer's treatment lasted more than a month and produced crises in which the patient sweated copiously. At the end of that period he was discharged looking well and walking upright with a springy step. As he stated, 'I am entirely free from all my infirmities.'[6]

Other notable successes were achieved with the Comtesse de la Malmaison, aged thirty-eight, who had fallen from her carriage and whose legs had been paralysed until she underwent magnetic treatment, and with Madame de Berny, aged fifty-four, who suffered from a film clouding her vision so that she was unable to read or write. She had been to four consultants prior to visiting Mesmer and was now also suffering from stomach cramps and vomiting. Crises in her case were marked by evacuations of the bowel, but again Mesmer was able to announce a complete cure after one month's treatment.

These three patients were of high social standing and their cures received much publicity. Mesmer's spreading influence may have provided some compensation for the snubs received from the scientists and physicians, but he still craved official recognition. If that were to come at all, it would have to come through the assistance of well-placed supporters. Possibly he had such a plan in mind when after only four months he abandoned Créteil and returned to Paris to occupy palatial quarters at the Hôtel Bullion in the Rue Coq Heron. He was now not far from the city centre and yet had a neighbouring park and lake to provide the rural setting he preferred.

With a staff of two valets, a porter, a coachman and domestics, his Austrian manservant now had new duties: he was to give one of three different whistles to announce the social status of an arrival! Whether these whistles corresponded to the three baquets which by the end of 1780 were in simultaneous operation is unclear. One further baquet was free and for the use of the poor, but such poor patients were far too numerous, and Mesmer hit on an expedient solution. He mesmerized a large oak tree at the end of the Rue Bondy and hundreds of people attached themselves to it with cords in the hope of a cure. Seats at the paid baquets were also at a premium and had to be booked well in advance, one baquet, very select and expensive, being reserved for 'ladies of breeding' who would appreciate its floral decorations. Adjoining the baquets were small 'crisis rooms', padded with silk, to which patients were taken individually if their convulsive attacks became too violent. Musicians were hired to create the most propitious atmosphere around the baquets and to help propagate the magnetic fluid; Mesmer himself often played his glass harmonica, the music of which was described by one listener as extremely penetrating and sending shivers through the nerves.[7]

The baquets were said to bring in 300 louis a month, while Mesmer's total outgoings were of the order of 1,000 louis a year.[8] Thus the operation was a profitable one.

Among his aristocratic patients was a small number of interested doctors, notably Charles Deslon, private physician to Louis XVI's brother, the Comte d'Artois. Deslon was three years older than Mesmer; blessed with a youthful appearance and a graceful manner, he was an influential member of the Faculty of Medicine. He was also to become an ardent convert to mesmerism. He began by observing Mesmer's procedures, then joined with him in assisting at the clinic on a daily basis for more than six months. Conviction was strengthened when he underwent the therapy himself:

> From the age of ten I suffered from a pain in the stomach and could not bear any external pressure or jostling. It sometimes affected my breathing so that I had to undo the buttons of my vest. I also had continual headaches and a sensation of cold in my right temple. For a long time I said nothing to Mesmer while observing his experiments. Then when I felt over-fatigued I asked him to play his harmonica or the piano for I found the music very beneficial. At last I told him about my trouble and suggested that I should be treated if he could find an opportunity. 'Good,' he replied. 'You come here every day, you are wise. You will have the treatment and keep it up as long as you like. If you do not obtain a complete cure, at least you will get half or a quarter or an eighth, and that will be so much gained.' I followed his advice, and like the other patients, I had my crises, my evacuations, liver pains, racking head-ache, and in the end the skin of my forehead was peeling. I cannot say how long the treatment lasted for it had to be done at intervals. I felt very much better for it and could tap my stomach without feeling pain.'[9]

Himself convinced of the curative powers of animal magnetism, Deslon induced Mesmer to put his views to the Faculty of Medicine. Mesmer had been preparing for publication a short account of his discovery with a more formal presentation of his theory. He suggested to Deslon that he might read his manuscript to the Faculty, and that interested members might then follow it up by observations at his clinic. Deslon invited a dozen members to a dinner, to be preceded by Mesmer's lecture. Such little interest was aroused by Mesmer's exposition that Deslon had great difficulty in persuading as many as three of his colleagues to go to watch Mesmer at work. As Mesmer drily remarked, it was easier to induce Parisian physicians to dinner than to persuade them to visit a hospital.[10]

However, the three physicians were assiduous enough in their fort-nightly attendance over a period of seven months. They were presented with a variety of cases: a paralytic, who recovered the sensations of touch and warmth after a week's treatment; an almost-blind girl, who regained her sight; cases of ulcers, and obstructed bowels. The cures were supplemented by demonstrations of the effects of animal magnetism conveyed by Mesmer's wand or hand to the sources of the patient's illness, when the patient would shriek with pain, convulse, or give other unmistakable signs of the apparent reality of the penetrating fluid.

'*Oculos habent et non videbunt*,' was Mesmer's verdict on his three observers. They refused to be convinced: they had not previously examined these cases for themselves; such cases, they pointed out, can often spontaneously remit without any treatment. Their caution was buttressed by their professional antagonism. Mesmer's final attempt to achieve recognition from a professional society was here necessarily doomed to failure.

More general recognition was coming from the appearance in the Parisian bookshops of his treatise, with an accompanying portrait. It was published in June 1779 and sold well. Under the title *Mémoire sur la découverte du magnétisme animal*, it consists of a short account of his experiences in Vienna. Written in an assertive but not unduly biased manner, it is now of most interest for the Twenty-seven Propositions with which it concludes and which were responsible for the common complaint that it was unintelligible. It is strange that this first formal presentation of Mesmer's theory should not have been more widely distributed among the learned and scientific bodies in France and abroad. That treatment Mesmer reserved for his next book, which was to omit all theoretical considerations and concentrate on the history of the movement.

Some of Mesmer's propositions, notably the first seven, can be seen to be elaborations of the ideas contained in his doctoral thesis.

1   There exists a mutual influence among the heavenly bodies, the earth and living things.
2   A universally distributed fluid, so continuous as to admit of no vacuum, incomparably rarefied, and by its nature able to

receive, propagate and communicate all motion, is the means of this influence.

3 This reciprocal action is subject to mechanical laws which are as yet unknown.

4 This action causes alternate effects which may be regarded as an ebb and flow.

5 This ebb and flow is more or less general, more or less particular, more or less compound, according to the nature of the causes which determine it.

6 It is by this agent (the most universal found in Nature) that the heavenly bodies, the earth and its constituent parts mutually influence one another.

7 The properties of matter and of living organisms depend on this agent.

As pointed out in the previous chapter, much of this theorizing has obvious forebears in Newton and Mead. In the next proposition, Mesmer deviates from Mead, who believed the tidal waves in the atmosphere affected the nervous system, by this postulation of a direct action:

8 The animal body reacts to the alternate effects of this agent, which by entering the substance of the nerves affects them directly.

An analogy with the magnet is now drawn. Reasoning by analogy was very characteristic of the thought of the period; here it led Mesmer to postulate the existence of magnetic poles in the human body analogous to those of a magnet. It was never clear where the anatomical poles were located; according to a later statement Mesmer considered one side of the body to be the polar opposite to the other.[11]

9 The human body, especially, has properties analogous to those of the magnet; different and opposite poles can be distinguished, poles which can be changed, linked, destroyed and strengthened; even the phenomenon of dipping can be observed.

10 In view of the analogy with the magnet, the property of the human body, which makes it susceptible to the influence of the heavenly bodies and to the reciprocal action of those surrounding it, has been called by me *Animal Magnetism*.

The next few propositions are concerned with the physics of the universal fluid. They have obviously been derived from his own experiments. Numbers 11 and 12 provide descriptive bases for the magnetic relationship between people; 13 and 14 refer to successful attempts made by Mesmer to magnetize a patient through a wall and at a distance; 15 is derived from his work in Hungary and with Maria Theresia von Paradis; 16 and 17 were demonstrable in every group séance where music was played in the setting of the baquet.

11 The actions and properties of Animal Magnetism, thus defined, may be communicated to other animate and inanimate bodies, which may be more or less susceptible to it.

12 This action and these properties may be strengthened and propagated by these same bodies.

13 Experiment shows that the diffusion of the substance is so subtle that it can penetrate all bodies without losing its potency.

14 Its action is exerted at a distance without the need of any intermediate object.

15 It is similar to light in that it is reflected and intensified by mirrors.

16 It is communicated, propagated and intensified by sound.

17 This magnetic property can be accumulated, concentrated and transported.

The next two propositions are perhaps the weakest links in Mesmer's theory. They provide him with an explanation for the insusceptibility of a minority of people to the magnetic influence; indeed, the occasional presence of such people could prove detrimental to magnetic induction in others. The postulation of an anti-magnetic quality leads to a ready explanation for any experimental or therapeutic result. It is, in any case, difficult to see from Mesmer's premises how another and contrary property can exist at all if the magnetic fluid is stated to be universal and responsible for all the properties of matter.

18 I have said that not all animal bodies are equally susceptible; there are those, although few in number, who have a property so

opposed that their very presence destroys all the effects of animal magnetism in other bodies.

19   This opposite quality also penetrates all bodies, it can likewise be communicated, propagated, stored, concentrated and transported, reflected by mirrors and propagated by sound. It is not just the absence of magnetism, but a positive opposing quality.

He now proceeds to underline the difference between animal and mineral magnetism, and then makes a wild claim for the future explanatory power of his system.

20   The magnet, whether natural or artificial, is like other substances susceptible to Animal Magnetism, and even to the opposed property; in neither case is its effect on iron or on the needle affected. This proves that the principle of Animal Magnetism differs essentially from that of universal magnetism.

21   This system will furnish new explanations of the nature of fire and light, of gravitation, of ebb and flow, of the magnet and of electricity.

The remaining propositions relate to illness and its cure. The reference in number 22 to cures by the magnet and by electricity firmly relegates these aids to the commonplace: anything can cure if it is imbued with animal magnetism. Proposition 23 necessarily results from the direct action of the fluid on the nerves. However, it may also be an expression of Mesmer's confidence in the efficacy of his treatment in what we should now term psychosomatic and neurotic disorders, coupled with slight reservations about its role as a universal panacea. In practice he was much more cautious in promising cures of organic illnesses, such as in Deslon's case, than were many of his over-enthusiastic pupils. Proposition 24 contains the only reference to the crisis, in spite of its pivotal status in Mesmer's therapy.

22   In their effects on illnesses, the magnet and artificial electricity have only those properties common to many other natural substances, and any useful effects that may have resulted from their application are due to Animal Magnetism.

23   The facts will show that this principle, in accordance with the

practical rules I shall establish, can immediately cure nervous complaints and, indirectly, other illnesses.

24 With its help, the physician is guided in the use of medicines, he perfects their action, and provokes and controls the beneficial crises in such a manner that he can retain control over them.

25 By making known my method, I shall demonstrate by a new theory the universal utility of the principle I employ to defeat disease.

26 With this knowledge, the physician will be able to judge with confidence the origin, nature and progress of illnesses, even the most complicated. He will check their progress and will devise their cure, without ever exposing the patient, whatever his age, temperament or sex, to dangerous or unfortunate consequences. Women, even in pregnancy and childbirth, will enjoy the same advantage.

27 In conclusion, this doctrine will enable the physician to judge the health of each individual and will safeguard him from the illnesses to which he may be exposed. The art of healing will thus reach its ultimate perfection.

It is certainly difficult to make much of these propositions as any kind of coherent system. The strange behaviour evoked around the baquet, the overwhelming evidence that some agent appeared to be at work, an agent which seemed capable of bringing about astonishing cures, these were the 'facts' of Animal Magnetism for which the public sought an explanation; Mesmer's own attempts in that direction did nothing to aid comprehension.

Pamphlets and articles began to appear to supplement this deficiency or to criticize the theory and denigrate the treatment.[12] The medical profession were particularly vocal in their opposition. Among these publications was a short work published anonymously by Jacques de Horne, physician to the Duke of Orleans, which was noteworthy for the personal nature of its attack on Mesmer, who was described as shrewd and cunning, overflowing with confidence, a mountebank operating on credulous victims; it was to set the tone for the flood of scurrilous pamphlets of the next few years.[13] Deslon's own contribution to the controversy, his *Observations sur le magnétisme animal*, was remarkable for its modesty, fluency and elegance. The stylistic contrast with

Mesmer's own publication did not escape Mesmer, who wrote, 'In his account, he has used all his skill to polish the truths which I expressed so crudely in mine.'[14]

Deslon's book opens with a long exposition of Mesmer's ideas, expressed in a less polemical manner than that of his master. He is obviously hard put to accept the notion of a universal fluid, because, although agreeing with all of Mesmer's propositions, he prefers to write of a 'physical influence' between doctor and patient, a 'creative impulse', whose free coursing through the body is a requisite of health. When this movement is checked, illness results; the effort made by nature to overcome this obstacle constitutes the crisis. Mesmer's magnetic treatment aids and abets this natural therapy by accelerating the crisis and arriving sooner at a cure.

In his book Deslon gives us a far more detailed account of Mesmer's therapy than can be found in Mesmer's writings. It is clear that Mesmer always healed by the aid of crises, whatever the illness. Deslon warns prospective patients that the therapy is, on this account, more or less unpleasant, and that perseverance and a concentration on one's cure are essentials. His main aim was to persuade his readers of the efficacy of the practice and not to seek acceptance of the theory:

> One knows that manna and rhubarb are purgative but neither my colleagues nor myself understand the mechanisms involved. The facts and our experience are our sole guides. It is the same with animal magnetism: I disregard how it works, but I know that it does work.[15]

To this end he describes in detail a dozen representative cases of the more than 300 with which he had assisted at Mesmer's clinic. They are of the usual extraordinary variety, including sufferers from tumors of the breast, near blindness and military fever. Deslon's medical status lent an authority to his writing; such a manifest heresy could no longer be ignored by his colleagues in the Faculty of Medicine. A general assembly was called for 18 September 1780, at which a most violent indictment of Deslon's conduct was delivered by a young physician, de Vauzesmes. Deslon was accused of using his authority to shield a German quack, a verdict on Mesmer which was supported by a recapitulation of the disputes with Hell, Ingenhousz and others from his Viennese past. The Academies, said de Vauzesmes, had already discussed Mesmer's doctrines and had rejected them. Deslon was now expounding similar nonsense, mere superstition in the guise of science. Not only had animal magnetism never cured anybody, but Deslon did not even know what it was; he was no better than a quack himself. Moreover, he and Mesmer distributed their books to the public as pedlars offered leaflets in the streets.

Deslon's reply was moderate, he asked the assembly to remember that violent insults were not arguments, and he requested that de Vauzesmes' document be made available to him for a more considered reply. Meanwhile, he pointed out that he was as anxious as Mesmer to have an expert enquiry into animal magnetism, and that after the serious errors committed by the Royal Society of Medicine in their refusal, for ostensibly technical reasons, to examine Mesmer's evidence of cures, it was up to the Faculty to repair those errors and incidentally to strengthen their position vis-à-vis the rival body. To that end he suggested that the Faculty should conduct an enquiry which would redound to their credit and reflect their interest in human welfare and in the pursuit of truth: they should examine a dozen patients treated by animal magnetism and compare the results with those from a comparable dozen treated by orthodox medicine.

His plea for an investigation was rejected out of hand, the verdict of the Faculty being delivered under four headings:

1 He was required to be more circumspect in the future.
2 His voting rights in the Faculty were to be suspended for one year.
3 His name would be erased from the list of members unless he disavowed within the year his *Observations sur le magnétisme animal.*
4 Mesmer's propositions were rejected.

Thus the Faculty closed its mind to heterodoxy and put Deslon's career in jeopardy, for he had no intention of disavowing Mesmer's doctrine or his own version of it. He decided to go beyond the Faculty and to use his influence in court to try to obtain a royal commission to establish the facts. The King's physician was agreeable, and the point was reached at which members of a commission were being named but then a dispute over their terms of reference arose and the project was abandoned.

Mesmer, if not Deslon, saw this as a contrivance of his enemies and decided to abandon the fight for recognition in France. He abruptly announced that he was going to leave Paris at once to seek endorsement of his discovery elsewhere.

His announcement caused a panic among his patients and followers. Two of his aristocratic patients, the Princess de Lamballe and the Duchess de Chaulnes, decided to approach the Queen. Marie Antoinette was in mourning for her mother's death and would not take an active part in the affair. She did, however, give her Minister of State, the aged Comte de Maurepas, permission to act in her name. By March 1781 a form of contract had been drawn up by which five commissioners, two of them physicians, were to be appointed to examine the utility of Mesmer's discovery. If their report was favourable, the King would grant Mesmer a château, in which he could establish a training clinic, and an annuity of 20,000 livres: on an undertaking that he would not leave France without the King's permission.

Mesmer had reason enough to be unhappy about the competence and impartiality of any commission but there was no other way forward, and with reluctance he signed the document. Maurepas, apparently with the best of intentions, communicated Mesmer's feelings to the King, who magnanimously made what seemed to be an improved offer. The commission could be dispensed with and Mesmer could take over the château immediately and claim his annuity, so long as he agreed to take into the institution three pupils nominated by Maurepas.

Mesmer's suspicions had been aroused by the change of conditions: the three pupils proved the stumbling block. What if they were to be the three members of the Faculty who had been so blind! He was convinced that they would be investigators, government spies, rather than genuine pupils. He could agree to the new arrangements only if he could choose his own pupils, and on this point he was intransigent. This attitude seemed so unreasonable to Maurepas, who had made, what seemed to him, a generous offer with only a small safeguard, an offer which had come from the King of France to an Austrian doctor of dubious past whose current practices smacked of charlatanry, it was so unreasonable that Maurepas would negotiate no further. Thus it was that Mesmer lost his finest opportunity to establish himself on French soil.

Mesmer's reasons for rejecting the offer occupy several pages of the book he was shortly to write. They centre around the view that his discovery was of greater significance than the authorities could conceive and that any offer they might make was thus an insult. Combined with this was the suspicion of others' motives which was reaching paranoid proportions. In an attempt to justify his conduct he wrote on the day following the meeting with Maurepas a long letter to the Queen.

He begins his letter with an expression of gratitude for her interest and by a denial that he is acting from inhumanity or avarice in leaving France shortly; indeed, he is prepared to postpone his departure until September and to continue with the treatment of his patients until then. He has to leave to find a government which will provide conditions acceptable to the 'austere principles' which he holds. He continues:

> In a case which is primarily concerned with human benefit, money can be only of secondary consideration. To Your Majesty four or five hundred thousand francs more or less, when devoted to this purpose, are nothing: the happiness of the people is everything. My discovery should be welcomed and myself rewarded with a munificence worthy of the greatness of the monarch to whom I have appealed. What should completely acquit me of any false imputations in this respect is that, since my arrival in your country, I have not imposed upon any of your subjects. Every day for three years I have received monetary offers; there was scarcely time to read them and, without giving exact figures, I can say that I have let a fortune slip through my fingers.
>
> *[Two paragraphs of the letter are omitted here. They mention the disappointment he incurred with regard to the learned societies and the French Government, and how these disappointments have led to his decision to leave France.]*
>
> Twenty or twenty-five patients, whoever they may be, are of no significance in comparison with the entire human race; and, to apply that principle to a person dear to Your Majesty, I can say that to give preference to Madame the Duchess de Chaulnes above the mass of the people would, fundamentally, be as wicked of me as if I were to neglect my discovery for personal interests.
>
> I have previously, Madame, found it necessary to forsake patients who were dear to me and to whom my care was indispensable. That was when I left the birthplace of Your Majesty, which was also my country. Why did no one then accuse me of inhumanity? Why, Madame? Because such a grave accusation would have been

superfluous; because, through intrigue, I had lost the trust of Your August Mother and Your August Brother.

The man, Madame, who like myself, is always conscious of the judgment of nations and of posterity, who is prepared constantly to account for his actions, will support, as I have, a reverse as cruel as this with courage and without arrogance. For he will know that although there are many circumstances when kings should guide public opinion, there is also an even greater number of occasions when public opinion irresistibly dominates that of kings. Today, Madame, I have been told in the name of Your Majesty, that Your August Brother has nothing but scorn for me. Very well! When public opinion decides, I will obtain justice; if not during my lifetime, my tomb will be honoured.

The date of 18 September which I have mentioned to Your Majesty will doubtless seem extraordinary. I chose it to mark the same day of last year when the physicians of your country did not hesitate to dishonour on my account one of their colleagues to whom I owe everything. On that day the assembly of the Faculty of Medicine of Paris rejected my propositions. Your Majesty is aware of them. I believed, Madame, and I still do, that after a spectacle so degrading to the physicians of your city of Paris, no enlightened person can any longer avoid examining my discovery, nor can any powerful person refuse it his protection. However that may be, on 18 September next it will be one year since I placed my last remaining hope on the paternal and vigilant care of the government. By that time I hope Your Majesty will judge my sacrifice to have lasted long enough and will see that I have not fixed this limit out of fickleness, temper, inhumanity or caprice. I dare to flatter myself that her protection will follow me to the distant places where my destiny may lead me, and that as a worthy protectress of the truth she will not disdain to use her influence on her brother and her husband to win their good will also.

I am, Madame, with the most profound respect, Your Majesty's most humble and obedient servant, Mesmer. 29 March 1781.[16]

The tone and content of Mesmer's letter have given rise to much subsequent comment. One of Mesmer's biographers, Jean Vinchon, has claimed that if it had been written twenty years earlier it would have led to the writer's incarceration in the Bastille.[17] He based this opinion on Mesmer's comparative disregard for the health of the Queen's friend, the

Duchess de Chaulnes, his comments on the relative importance of public opinion, and his implied criticism of the Queen's brother, the Emperor of the Holy Roman Empire, whom he threatens with the judgment of posterity.

Other critics have remarked on the financial details, believing that Mesmer was taking this opportunity to ask the Queen for a vast sum of money. However, it could well be argued that Mesmer was complaining about the inadequacy of the reward proffered earlier rather than indicating a sum of money that he now wished to negotiate. It is unlikely that he expected a reply to his letter, and he certainly got none.

The letter shows Mesmer in an unfavourable light: as an arrogant man who was making inordinate claims for his discovery and who appeared to be suffering from a persecution complex. He was, in fact, on the verge of a breakdown, and, according to Deslon, he attempted to apply his therapy to himself, having rejected Deslon's aid. How efficacious it was is not known, but he decided to seek a health resort and left Paris for Spa near Liège.

His recovery was rapid, for he stayed only a few weeks in Spa but long enough for him to complete his account of the events of the last three years. The writing of the *Précis historique des faits relatifs au magnétisme animal jusq'en avril 1781* was probably therapeutic in itself.[18] He avoids all discussion of the theory of animal magnetism and concentrates instead on the arguments, betrayals, the blindness of the Parisian savants to the truth, and the indignities heaped on him by their organized bodies. It would be wrong to consider it a biased recapitulation of all his grievances. Mesmer took great pains to get his facts right and to print copies of the more important documents and letters. It was, perhaps, his satisfaction with the accuracy of the account and the belief that it completely justified him that induced him to distribute as many as forty-seven copies to the learned bodies of the principal European countries and to the United States. Certainly the style of the writing is vastly superior to that of his earlier work. Being close to the events he describes leads him to write with passion and sometimes with eloquence; there are even occasional touches of dry humour. In its reference to animal magnetism a subtle difference from his last book is apparent. However difficult the twenty-seven propositions had been to understand, at least they had an apparent scientific respectability. But now Mesmer seems to doubt the possibility of ever explaining the phenomena in a logical manner:

'The subject I treat escapes positive expression. [Animal magnetism] is an artificial sixth sense, only experience can render the theory intelligible to us.'[19]

One is reminded of the many esoteric groups, from Zen Buddhists to psychoanalysts, who argue that experience must precede understanding. Mesmer was taking the first steps into that impasse where the seeking of scientific recognition would be at odds with the unscientific nature of his procedures, and where the need to bring his discovery into the public domain would be impossible to reconcile with his desire to prevent others profiting from his personal secret.

With the Parisian experiences described in print, Mesmer seems to have lost his intention to leave that city for ever. Besides, an event of personal significance required his immediate return: his faithful colleague, Deslon, had apparently betrayed him.

We have an account of the episode in a letter written by Melchior von Grimm, the secretary to the Duke of Orleans, whose vast correspondence contains several references to Mesmer.

> His disciple, Deslon, thought he should console Paris for the loss of his master by setting up an establishment for Mesmeric treatment. A beguiling personality, still possessing the advantages of youth and a pleasing demeanour, had brought Deslon the protection of some literary women of the second rank . . . [who] determined to follow Deslon's treatment and attracted in their turn several young literary novices . . . Mesmer's disciple had the pleasure of seeing his treatment followed by a score of people trying to have convulsions at 10 louis a month . . . As might be expected, Mesmer rushed back to Paris to accuse of infidelity and ignorance a pupil who had dared to magnetize without his approval and off his own bat.[20]

The apparent betrayal was explained by Deslon to be merely an attempt to carry on Mesmer's work in his absence, and it says much for Deslon's tact that he was able to induce Mesmer to co-operate with him again. It is not surprising that their reunion was short-lived. Mesmer's proprietary attitude to his discovery and his ever-present tendency to suspect a plot made it inevitable that he would regard as a traitor a colleague with any independence of spirit. Grimm may also have been right to ascribe importance to the influence of their disciples in bringing about the split:

> It was impossible to reunite and persuade to live in peace the women who had worked together to build Deslon's reputation and Mesmer's; neither side could excuse the pretensions of the other . . . They forced Mesmer and Deslon to separate again, and again the journals were filled with recriminations of the master and the disciple.[21]

Mesmer again abandoned Paris for Spa, taking with him a few patients. Deslon, left behind as master of his own destiny, immediately took the opportunity to reopen his case with the Faculty and this time without reference to Mesmer; but once again he was rebuffed. Meanwhile, Mesmer was taking steps to prevent future dissidence.

The suggestion he adopted came from two of his closest followers, Nicholas Bergasse and Guillaume Kornmann. Bergasse was a lawyer by profession and a philosopher and politician by inclination. He had first consulted Mesmer in 1781 with vague abdominal complaints which had been much improved by the magnetic treatment. Irritated by the bad press Mesmer had been receiving, he had then written a well received pamphlet in defence of the therapy.[22] Now he was one of Mesmer's semi-permanent guests at Spa and anxious to further the causes of animal magnetism which he had already made his own and on which he was to build a philosophical and political superstructure. Kornmann, a successful banker and also one of the group at Spa, had reason to be grateful to Mesmer, who had cured his son of an eye infection and had then helped with Kornmann's own nervous condition brought on by his wife's desertion and the loss of his children.[23]

According to Bergasse, Kornmann first made the proposal to set up a private academy to propagate Mesmer's doctrine.[24] It was called the Society of Universal Harmony and was to be founded by 100 subscribers, each of whom was to pay 100 louis d'or. The total of 10,000 louis would be given to Mesmer, who would give full instructions about his basic theory and methods of treatment. Diplomas would be awarded to qualified pupils, allowing them to set up practice in specified towns. It is clear that the Society, an amalgam of a training course and a secret society, had as its main aims the preservation of Mesmer's doctrines against the depredations of the official learned bodies and his own future schismatics, and the securing of sufficient funds for his comfortable independence.

The enthusiastic Bergasse got busy, the form of contract was drawn up in the March of 1783 and by the end of the year subscriptions numbered forty-eight. Many of the subscribers were of great wealth and high social position: the first list of members contained the names of four dukes and eight marquises, besides other noblemen, doctors, surgeons, bankers, priests, and army officers. Among them was Deslon, still faithful to animal magnetism and probably still harbouring the illusion that there was more to learn from Mesmer and that participation in the Society might lead to the divulgence of Mesmer's final secret.

With the burgeoning success of the Society, it was appropriate for Mesmer to move back to Paris on a more permanent basis. The Hôtel de Coigny, in the same Rue Coq Heron where he had had his former residence, provided the sumptuous setting for the headquarters of the Society. With money beginning to pour in from aspirant members, with several baquets in operation, Mesmer was securing a large income and living in style. He must have thought that he had obtained all the advantages of the rejected arrangements with the Government with none of the disadvantages; he could not foresee that his doctrines were soon to suffer their most serious condemnation and that the coming year of 1784 was to be the most critical in his life.

3

Year of Crisis

The large assembly room at the Hôtel de Coigny was magnificent: chandeliered and mirrored, hung with expensive tapestries, it was a fitting venue for the meetings of the Society of Harmony. To attend these meetings, some of the greatest aristocrats in France had willingly parted with 100 louis and had signed a contract with Mesmer which had not only sworn them to secrecy but had also effectively modified the original prospectus in restricting their future therapeutic practice. Although there were variations in the wording of the contract, that signed by the Marquis de Lafayette on 5 April 1784 was typical:

> We the undersigned, Antoine Mesmer, doctor of medicine, on the one part and M. le Marquis de Lafayette . . . on the other, have mutually agreed on the following:
>
> I, Antoine Mesmer, having always wished to propagate the doctrine of Animal Magnetism among honest and virtuous people, consent and undertake to instruct in all the principles of this doctrine, M. le Marquis de Lafayette, referred to above, on the following conditions:
>
> 1. He will not instruct any pupil, nor transmit directly or indirectly to anyone, either the whole nor the least part of the doctrine of Animal Magnetism, without my written consent.
>
> 2. He will not enter into any negotiation, treaty, or agreement relative to Animal Magnetism with any prince, government or community, this right being exclusively mine.
>
> 3. Without my express written permission, he will not establish any public clinic or bring patients together in order to treat them in a group by my method; he is permitted only to see and treat patients individually and in private.
>
> 4. He undertakes by his sacred word of Honour, both verbal and

written, to conform rigorously and without any restriction to the above conditions, and not to set up, authorize, or favour directly or indirectly, wherever he may happen to live, any establishment without my formal consent.

And I, Marquis de Lafayette, referred to above, considering that the doctrine of Animal Magnetism is the property of M. Mesmer, its originator, and that he alone may determine the conditions under which it shall be propagated, I accept all the conditions laid down in this document and I give in writing, as I have verbally, my most sacred word of honour to observe its conditions in good faith and with the most scrupulous exactitude.

This agreement has been made freely between us and we promise to ratify it in the presence of a notary on the first demand of one of the two parties at his expense.[1]

It is clear that in signing the document Mesmer's pupils were taking a vow of silence; those with the future hope of using their knowledge of animal magnetism in therapy would have to remain content with individual patients; for it seems that Mesmer was determined to keep the baquet to himself. Whether that was to retain the group technique for its financial rewards, or whether, as those more charitably disposed towards him might claim, it was to retain control of the organization of large clinics, is uncertain. Indeed, it is possible that Mesmer believed himself to be the only person who could efficiently manage several patients simultaneously, a feat he was able to accomplish through the possession of a personal secret.

There was much talk of Mesmer's secret in 1784. It was the ostensible reason for Deslon's resignation from the Society at the beginning of the year on the grounds that Mesmer was not divulging all he knew. The probable reason why Mesmer's pupils suspected that there was more to his technique than they were being taught was that their everyday observation would have shown that he was more successful than anyone else in his ability to bring on the crisis. He himself may well have wondered why that was so and would have naturally attributed his success to some personal quality. One of his pupils, the Marquis de Puységur, who was shortly to discover more about the nature of the hypnotic state, was later to claim that Mesmer's secret was none other than the use of will-power, which Puységur mistakenly considered crucial in the induction process. From the vantage point of today, it seems most probable that it was Mesmer's status in the eyes of his patients and pupils that led to their easy acquiescence to his influence. However that may be, Mesmer was not above hinting that he possessed powers greater than other men, powers in which he may have believed, without understanding their nature, the apparent loss of which in the future would inevitably lead to the collapse of his self-confidence and an inability to perform therapeutically or even socially at the level to which he had been accustomed.

Deslon's departure was to be of more importance than Mesmer suspected. For, after having established a private practice in the Rue Montmartre, Deslon began to use his influence at court to persuade the King to initiate an official investigation of the claims of animal magnetism. On this occasion he was successful, and two Royal Commissions were set in train, one from the Royal Academy of Sciences and the Faculty of Medicine, the other from the Royal Society of Medicine. The members of these Commissions were named on 12 March. Four physicians from the Faculty, Sallin, Darcet, Majault and Guillotin, the last giving his name to the device which was to be put to such frequent use in the near future,[2] were at their request joined by five members of the Academy: Franklin, Leroy, Bailly, de Borie and Lavoisier.

Benjamin Franklin was the American Minister to France and in his seventy-eighth year. Although named to head the Commission, Franklin was ill for much of the year and played little part in the experimental work, nor did he draft the report, that task falling to Bailly. Bailly, like Leroy, was well known to Mesmer; he was an eminent astronomer, of whose candour and modesty Mesmer spoke highly in his *Mémoire* of 1779. Lavoisier was at the height of his fame, having recently published with Laplace their memoir on heat.[3]

The Commission from the Royal Society of Medicine also included two acquaintances from Mesmer's recent past, the sceptical Mauduit and Andry. They were joined by Caille, Poissonnier and de Jussieu, the last being an eminent botanist, director of the Botanical Gardens, and famous for his classification of plants.

The report of the first Commission appeared with admirable promptitude on 11 August, to be followed within a week by that from the Royal Society of Medicine. Between the date of formation of the Commissions and the accomplishment of their labours, several events occurred which kept animal magnetism in the forefront of Parisian attention.

Firstly, there was the affair of Father Hervier, one of Mesmer's most active supporters. Hervier, described as fiery-eyed and violent of gesture, was preaching in Bordeaux on the theme of eternal damnation when a young woman in the congregation fell into convulsions. Hervier descended from the pulpit to make magnetic passes over her until the convulsions ceased – whereupon the congregation prostrated themselves in front of this miracle-worker, the women striving to kiss his feet. Hervier resumed his sermon by a logical, if unfortunate, reference to Christ's cures and to the stupidity of the present-day clergy who did not believe in animal magnetism. It is not surprising that he was promptly suspended from preaching, and although his highly placed friends interceded with the King, Louis XVI did nothing. The matter became a *cause célèbre*, with the townsfolk of Bordeaux divided into factions, the doctors, apothecaries and priests on the one hand, the animal magnetists on the other, and hostilities carried on by pamphlet.[4]

More gossip was generated by the visit to Paris of Mesmer's former patient from Vienna, Maria Theresia von Paradis, who was on a European tour. Her Royal concert at the Tuileries brought her wide acclaim. Melchior Grimm noted:

'There is reason to believe that her appearance in Paris at this time has not given Mesmer the most agreeable surprise.'[5]

It is unlikely that Mesmer considered himself in any way responsible for the unsuccessful outcome to this case, but his enemies made the most of it.[6] More grist was added to their mill by the death a few weeks later of Court de Gébelin, an ardent follower of Mesmer. Gébelin was a philosopher and linguist, who was renowned for the eight volumes of his *Monde primitif*, in which he compared ancient and modern cultures, and searched in ancient languages for early forms of scientific thought. Gébelin's interests were aroused by animal magnetism as a primitive therapy, the most likely contender for the 'natural' medicine antedating current practice. In place of the ninth volume of his *magnum opus* he sent subscribers an enthusiastic account of animal magnetism as a modern science and ancient therapeutic. Like Deslon and so many other of the early converts, he had been Mesmer's patient before becoming a pupil. Apparently suffering from a severe kidney disease, of which the symptoms were much alleviated by magnetic therapy, he had unwisely announced his own complete cure and his consequent complete faith in the doctrine. He had moved into the Hôtel de Coigny and was one of Mesmer's most effective publicists. His death in May 1784 is said to have occurred at the baquet; it gave rise to the comment: 'M. Court de Gebélin has just died, cured by animal magnetism.' Or, as one versifier put it:

> Here lies the poor Gébelin,
> Who knew Greek, Hebrew, Latin.
> All should admire his heroism,
> He was a martyr to magnetism.[7]

On the heels of this tragedy came the noisy secession of another savant, Claude Berthollet, a chemist and prominent member of the Academy of Sciences, and thus an important catch for the Society of Harmony. He did not find the trappings surrounding Mesmer's therapeutic regimen to his taste, and when on one occasion Mesmer, sensing Berthollet's critical attitude, pointed his iron wand at him and began to raise his voice, Berthollet lost his temper, shouted furiously at the patients around the baquet, and stormed from the building. When reminded of his oath, he retorted that he had not sworn to keep the secret of a masquerade, and he then made the following written declaration:

After having attended more than half of M. Mesmer's course; after having been admitted to the halls of treatment and of crises, where I have employed myself in making observations and experiments, I declare that I have found no ground for believing in the presence of the agent called by M. Mesmer Animal Magnetism; that I consider the doctrine taught to us in the course irreconcilable with some of the best established facts in the system of the universe and in the animal economy; that I have seen nothing in the convulsions, the spasms – in short, in the cures alleged to be produced by the magnetic causes – which could not be attributed entirely to the imagination, to the mechanical effect of friction on regions well supplied with nerves, and to that law, long since recognized, which causes an animal to tend to imitate, even involuntarily, the movements of another animal which it sees, trying to place itself in the same position – a law so frequently demonstrated by epidemic convulsions. I declare finally that I regard the theory of Animal Magnetism and the practice based upon it as perfectly chimerical; and I am willing that this declaration should be made use of in any way that may be found desirable.[8]

Other members of the Society were as adamant in their belief as Berthollet had been in his rejection. For example, in a letter to the *Mercure de France*, one Mesmerian made the serious suggestion that four baquets should be set up at Chaillot where the Seine had its source. Then the waters of the river and its canals could be thoroughly impregnated with magnetism and the beneficial effects of the universal fluid made available to many, who would undoubtedly pay an extra water rate of fifty livres per household to secure this service. An even more magnanimous gesture would be to operate a type of aerial magnetism towards the four compass points from the towers of Saint-Geneviève so that the whole of the city could be saturated *gratis* with magnetized air.[9]

These logical, if extraordinary, extensions of the mesmeric argument offered little consolation to Mesmer, who was deeply involved in the less than harmonious affairs of the Society of Harmony. From the very first session which Bergasse had opened, he had dominated their proceedings. Mesmer, it was true, was the permanent President, who sat 'mute but with magisterial dignity', his silence being necessitated by his relatively poor fluency in French.[10] Tuition was mainly by lecture given by one or two of the more experienced members, of whom Bergasse was easily the best speaker. Bergasse's lectures, on which he was later to base a book, were of a pseudo-scientific plausibility with diagrammatic representations of colliding molecules and magnetic currents underlying natural phenomena and human interactions. His own interests deflected the centre of gravity of his discourse away from the therapeutic towards the moral, social and political implications of animal magnetism. It was partly this trend, so different from Mesmer's relatively apolitical stance, and partly the influence exerted by Bergasse on his pupils, that led to difficulties between the two men. It was almost a repetition of the Deslon problem, with Bergasse now a rival candidate for adulation. He is said to have had many *femmes d'esprit* enthusiastic over him. The radical politician and editor, Jacques-Pierre Brissot, a recent member and ardent admirer, was apparently told by Bergasse: 'You think you have found a savant; you have found only a simple good man who looks for truth in his heart.'[11] Bergasse was not referring to Mesmer but to himself; he might have added that the 'simple good man' also kept his tongue in his cheek.

In the only direct account of the Society's meetings, the Baron de Corberon makes it clear that from the first lecture he attended – he was inducted at the same time as Lafayette on 5 April 1784 – there was tension between Bergasse and Mesmer.[12] Bergasse, he thought, had more jargon than science and was prone to interrupt Mesmer with a superior air. By 12 April Corberon thought that they were going to break up, and he heard that this was not the first time that Bergasse had considered leaving, because, it was said by his critics, he was finding it difficult to retain a dominant position in the assembly in the presence of Mesmer and Maxime Puységur, brother to the Marquis. Bergasse, indeed, did vacate the position of orator for a few days, but Puységur took over so ineffectually that Bergasse had to be asked to resume the office.

These uneasy bedfellows nevertheless remained together until late in the year, the Bergasse faction not being finally expelled until May 1785. One cause for the prolongation of their association was the appearance of the Royal Commissions' reports, which united them in their belief in animal magnetism against their now more vociferous opponents.

However inwardly rent by schism, outwardly the Society of Harmony was a great success. Besides the mother lodge in Paris, affiliated Societies of Harmony were beginning to spring up in the principal towns of France. In early August Mesmer was invited to attend a meeting of the flourishing Society at Lyons, where Prince Henry of Prussia was on a private visit. Attempts by one of Mesmer's pupils to magnetize a horse and then a company of soldiers were not sufficient to convince the Prince, who volunteered to act as a subject for Mesmer. The combination of his high social status and pronounced scepticism proved too much for Mesmer who failed to produce any effect on the Prince, a result which Mesmer seems to have interpreted as a warning that his own magnetic powers were diminishing. In a more confident vein he would surely have invoked Proposition 18 to claim that Prince Henry must possess the anti-magnetic quality, his insusceptibility then being no reflection on Mesmer. The Lyons Lodge, too, was not to Mesmer's taste, influenced as it was by its founder, Jean-Baptiste Willermoz, a leading mystic, whose inclinations were towards a spiritual mesmerism which was to become the Lodge's characteristic feature. Troubled by his own supposed loss of power and the tendency for his followers to lose sight of the scientific materialistic basis of this theory, Mesmer returned to Paris to be greeted by the publication of the report from the first Royal Commission.[13]

The Commission had interpreted their terms of reference to signify that the chief purpose of their enquiry was to ascertain whether the universal fluid existed. If that were to be established, it would then be in order to examine its possible utility: 'Animal magnetism may indeed exist without being useful, but it cannot be useful if it does not exist.'

Their investigations were directed toward Deslon's clinic as it was Deslon who had initiated the enquiry. Mesmer seems not to have been consulted·at all, the Commissioners apparently considering that Deslon had remained sufficiently loyal to Mesmer's theory and practice for their examination of his claims to be sufficient justification for them to pronounce on Mesmer as well.

Their first experiments involved the baquet itself. By means of an electrometer and an iron needle, they were able to show that the baquet contained no mineral magnetism and possessed no electrical properties. However, the Commissioners were obviously impressed by the variety and extent of the patients' responses when connected to the baquet:

> Some of them are calm, tranquil and unconscious of any sensation; others cough, spit, are affected with a slight degree of pain, a partial or universal burning, and perspiration; a third class are agitated and tormented with convulsions. The convulsions are rendered extraordinary by their frequency, their violence, and their duration. As soon as one person is convulsed, others presently are affected by that symptom . . . These convulsions are remarkable for their number, duration and force, and have been known to persist for more than three hours. They are characterized by involuntary jerking movements in all the limbs, and in the whole body, by contraction of the throat, by twitchings in the hypochondriac and epigastric regions, by dimness and rolling of the eyes, by piercing cries, tears, hiccoughs, and immoderate laughter. They are preceded or followed by a state of languor or dreaminess, by a species of depression, and even by stupor. The slightest sudden noise causes the patient to start, and it has been observed that he is affected by a change of time or tune in the airs performed on the pianoforte, that his agitation is increased by a more lively movement, and that his convulsions then become more violent . . .

Patients are seen to be absorbed in the search for one another, rushing together, smiling, talking affectionately, and endeavouring to modify their crises. They are all so submissive to the magnetizer that even when they appear to be in a stupor, his voice, a glance, or a sigh will rouse them from it. It is impossible not to admit, from all these results, that some great force acts upon and masters the patients, and that this force appears to reside in the magnetizer.

These convulsive seizures are improperly called crises in the theory of animal magnetism; according to this doctrine indeed they are regarded as a salutary crisis, of the same kind as those which nature produces, or of a skilful physician who has the art to facilitate the cure of diseases. The Commissioners will adopt this expression in the following report; and wherever they employ the word crisis, they will always understand it as the convulsive, drowsy, or lethargic symptoms, produced by the means of animal magnetism.

The Commissioners observed that many women and few men are subject to such crises; that they are only established after the lapse of two or three hours, and that when one is established, others soon and successively begin.

Here were the effects that needed to be explained if the baquet were inert. However, the Commissioners decided not to continue their examination of what they called the 'public process', as: 'too many things are seen at once for any one thing to be seen well.' Another cogent reason was political rather than scientific:

'Besides, the patients of rank, who repair hither on account of their health, might be displeased with the investigation of the Commissioners; the very act of watching them might be a nuisance; and the recollection of this might be burdensome and impede the Commissioners in their turn.'

They therefore decided to restrict their enquiry to themselves and to a few other individuals. Their first task was to ascertain if the fluid could be perceived by any of the senses. It did not take them long to discover that it was too subtle for such observation:

'It is not like the electric fluid, luminous and visible; its action is not, like the attraction of the loadstone, the object of one's sight; it has neither taste nor smell, its process is silent, and it surrounds you or penetrates your frame, without your being informed of its presence by the sense of touch.'

They discounted reports from sensitives who claimed that it may be felt during passes of the magnetizer's hands; these reports were based, they presumed, on a failure to identify sensations of warmth or cold. The supposed smell of the fluid was simply the smell of the operator or of the iron rod he was using.

Deslon was not perturbed by these difficulties; he did not think these kinds of observations were very relevant. Instead, he stressed that the only way the Commissioners could observe the action of the fluid would be to direct their enquiry towards the therapeutic results obtained through its use. The Commissioners were firm in their rejection of this approach. They pointed out that too little was known to be able to ascribe a therapeutic effect to a particular cause. Cures of similar illnesses might be produced by different and even contrary regimens. Indeed, Nature herself might be responsible for any improvement. Here they quote with approval Mesmer's own cautionary words:

'It is a mistake to imagine that this kind of proof is unanswerable. It cannot be demonstrated that either the physician or the medicine causes the recovery of the patient.'

To establish anything definite from an examination of cures would, they considered, require 'the experience of several centuries'. As their enquiry was of some urgency, they decided instead to concentrate on the more immediate effects on the body of the application of animal magnetism. A private baquet was set up in Deslon's house and eight of the nine Commissioners, Franklin being absent, attended for sessions of up to three hours. They repeated the experiences weekly for an unspecified period, and also tried repeated magnetization on three successive days. They took one precaution: they determined not to analyse their bodily sensations too minutely on the grounds that they might accentuate the importance of those slight changes of pressure, temperature and the like of which one is normally unaware, and thus attribute them to the magnetic influence.

> Not one of the Commissioners felt any sensation, or at least none which ought to be ascribed to the action of the magnetism. Some of the Commissioners are of a robust constitution. Others have more delicate habits; one of these last was sensible of a slight pain in the pit of the stomach due to considerable pressure that was employed upon that part. The pain continued all that day and the next, and

was accompanied by a sensation of fatigue and dejection. Another one felt a slight irritation of the nerves to which he is very subject. A third, endowed with still greater sensibility and especially with extreme restlessness of the nerves, was subject to a higher degree of pain and a more perceptible irritation.

The Commissioners were struck by the difference between their private experiments and the public proceedings. Here all was orderly and calm, there agitation and tumult were to be observed. And here, apart from the trivial occurrences reported above, no effects were produced on healthy persons.

As Franklin also wanted the experience of being magnetized, Deslon went out to his house at Passy which Franklin had been unable to leave on account of a severe attack of gout. The opportunity was taken for Deslon to operate on Franklin, two of his relatives, his secretary, and an American officer. None of them felt anything, although, besides Franklin, one of his relatives and the officer were not in full health.

The Commissioners decided to complete this section of their enquiry by examining the effects on those who were really diseased. Seven patients 'from the lower classes' were assembled at Passy and Deslon magnetized them in the presence of all the Commissioners. They included:

The widow, Saint-Amand, asthmatic, having swollen body, legs and thighs; Dame Anseaume, who had a swelling on her thighs; the little Claude Renard, a child of six years of age, scrofulous, almost consumptive, having swollen knees, legs bent inwards, the articulation of the knees nearly deprived of motion, a very interesting child possessing a greater degree of understanding than was usual at his age; Geneviève Leroux, nine years of age, subject to convulsions and to a disorder resembling St Vitus' dance; François Genet with a distemper in his eyes, particularly in his right in which he had scarcely any sight, and in which there was a very large tumor; Dame Charpentier, who had been thrown against a log of wood by a cow two years before, the belly so sensitive that she could not stand the pressure of the strings of her petticoat.

A last patient, Joseph Enningi, suffered from an unspecified complaint. Of these seven patients, four felt no sensation at all during the magnetizing. François Genet reported pains in his less afflicted eye, which was observed to water when Deslon's thumb moved across it. Dame Charpentier gave sudden starts of the head and shoulders when Deslon's finger was moved up and down before her face. These occurred even when her eyes were closed. She also complained of feeling faint when the fingers were held under her nose. Joseph Enningi experienced similar but less marked sensations.

To throw further light on the matter the Commissioners selected from 'the polite world those who could not be suspected of sinister views, and whose understanding made them capable of enquiring into and giving a faithful account of their sensations'.

Two ladies and two gentlemen joined the Commissioners at the baquet. The effects were again largely negative, although one gentleman recorded a feeling of heat when Deslon's hand passed over his painful knee, and one of the ladies, suffering from an unspecified nervous disorder, was several times at the point of falling asleep during the operation which was continued for seventy-nine minutes. The other two patients, one with an obstruction to the liver and the other 'severely attacked with obstructions', felt nothing at all. The Commissioners remarked that the latter patient submitted to the operation with 'the highest degree of incredulity'.

Thus out of a total of fourteen sick persons, only five reported any effect at all. The Commissioners discounted the effects produced on the upper-class patients by claiming that the heat reported by one was too slight an effect to be attributed to the operation. The sleepiness of the other was probably a consequence of the fatigue of maintaining a fixed position for such a long period of time. In the case of the lower-class patients the Commissioners drew attention to their probable attitude to the situation:

> The patient is introduced with some degree of ceremony to a large company, partly composed of physicians, and where an experiment is performed upon him which is new to him and from which he persuades himself beforehand that he is about to experience prodigious effects. Let us add to this that he is paid for his co-operation and that he thinks he shall contribute more to our satisfaction by professing to experience sensations of some kind. We shall have definite causes to which to attribute these effects, and we shall at

least have just reason to doubt whether their true cause be the magnetism.

The little Claude Renard, on the other hand, felt nothing, a result the Commissioners attribute to his 'sound understanding'. While Geneviève Leroux's indifference was due to her 'idiotism, which did not permit her to judge whether she ought to have felt anything'. Thus, they conclude, when sensations were reported they were 'the fruits of anticipated persuasion operated by the mere force of imagination'. In their final experiments they put this hypothesis to crucial test.

The most convincing of these experiments involved persons blind-folded or placed behind doors who were asked to report their sensations when the magnetizer operated on them. Sometimes they were misled into believing that he was operating when he was not, while on other occasions he would operate when they did not expect it. In all cases the result was in accordance with the subject's expectations, so that sensations and even a crisis could be produced by the subject's imagination; in no case was the magnetic effect produced when the subject did not expect it.

The matter was clinched for the Commissioners by an ingenious experiment in Franklin's orchard, where Deslon first magnetized an apricot tree, 'considerably distant from any other tree.' A particularly susceptible twelve-year-old boy, a patient of Deslon's, was now blind-folded and led into the orchard. He was required to embrace each tree he was brought to for a period of two minutes. At the first tree he sweated, coughed, spat and complained of headaches; he was in fact 27 feet from the magnetized tree. At the next tree, 36 feet from the target tree, he reported a sense of stupefaction. At the next, now 38 feet away, the stupefaction and headache increased considerably, until at the fourth tree, still 24 feet away, he fainted, his limbs stiffened into a crisis, and he had to be carried out of the orchard.

Deslon was forced to explain this awkward result by claiming that all trees by their very nature possessed a considerable amount of natural magnetism, which in this case had been reinforced by his presence in the orchard, a presence which the Commissioners had been careful to conceal from the boy. As the Commissioners drily commented, if such were indeed the case a sensitive could hardly dare to walk in the garden without the risk of convulsions, an assertion which everyday experience refuted. If Deslon's mere presence was so powerful, why had the boy been able to travel with him in the coach to Passy with no apparent effect?

Deslon now admitted that imagination might indeed be the active agent, 'whose power is as extensive as it is little known.' He pleaded with the Commissioners to embrace the opportunity presented by his practice to investigate further the curative power of the imagination.[14] They, however, declined on the grounds that such an admission entailed the rejection of the fluid hypothesis which it had been their prime object to investigate. Thus, they were led inexorably to their final conclusions, which are worth quotation in full:

> The Commissioners, having found that the animal magnetic fluid cannot be perceived by any of our senses, that it has no action either on themselves or on the patients whom they have presented for treatment; being satisfied that the touches and pressure employed are the causes of changes in the organism which are rarely of a favourable character, and are liable to produce a deplorable effect on the imagination; having finally shown by conclusive experiments that the imagination without the aid of Magnetism can produce convulsions, and that Magnetism without the imagination can produce nothing; they have come to the unanimous conclusion, on the question submitted to them of the existence and utility of Animal Magnetism, that there is no proof of the existence of the Animal Magnetic fluid; that this fluid, having no existence, has in consequence no utility; but that the violent effects which are observed in the public treatment are caused by the touches of the operator, the excited imagination of the patient, and by the involuntary instinct of imitation. At the same time they feel compelled to utter a serious warning: that the touches and the repeated stimulation of the imagination in the production of the crisis may prove harmful; that the spectacle of the crisis is equally dangerous, because of the risk of imitation which seems to be a law of nature; and that in consequence all public treatment by Magnetism must in the long run have deplorable consequences.

The report from the Commission of the Royal Society of Medicine reached much the same conclusions.[15] The primary cause of the crisis, they thought, must lie in the mesmerist's stroking of the patient's body, which would excite the nerves. Secondary causes lay in the patient's imagination, in suggestion and imitation. Great stress was placed on the injurious effects of magnetic treatment, both for the individual and for society in general.

In view of their composition, this group of Commissioners interpreted their task to include an examination of the possible therapeutic effects of animal magnetism. They divided their patients into three classes: melancholics, those with definite maladies of known cause, and those with slight ailments of unknown cause. It was only the last group who appeared to have obtained any relief from animal magnetism. This result was attributed by the Commissioners to hope, regular exercise, and abstinence from the remedies they had previously been taking. As these latter often included cupping (to produce a blister), bleeding, and the moxa (where a substance, such as a cube of agaric is burnt on the surface of the skin), it is not an unlikely conclusion, although a strange reflection on current medical practice.

One of this group of Commissioners dissented from the report's conclusions and issued a minority report of his own.[16] In this respect de Jussieu showed himself a more careful investigator than his colleagues. He had been more assiduous in his attendance at the public sessions, and while agreeing with the majority of his colleagues that repeated crises may be injurious to some patients, he nevertheless recorded one or two cases whose cures were remarkable. In one instance a woman's eyes were covered with a film so thick that the irises could not be distinguished, a condition which had persisted for five years. After a few weeks' treatment the irises became clear and the patient's sight was restored. In another, a washerwoman had strained her arm lifting a heavy tub. The condition had worsened to such an extent that she was unable to move the arm at all. After five weeks' treatment, the pain had gone and she could lift her hand up to her head.

De Jussieu could not accept that the imagination alone was sufficient to account for facts such as these. He implicated instead an agent which he identified as 'animal heat'. This animal heat, he believed, could be directed and intensified by the will. In this respect his theory differed from that of Mesmer, whose animal-magnetic fluid was independent of the operator's willpower, but rather resembled Puységur's future elaboration of the therapeutic process.

The Franklin group also produced a secret report, which was intended only for the eyes of the King.[17] Its object was to draw attention to the dangers to public morality inherent in allowing the practice of animal magnetism. In particular, they remarked on the fact that it was always men who magnetized women. Women have, they maintained, 'more mobile nerves' – that is, they are more susceptible to touch, and their imagination is more readily aroused. Thus, it is not surprising that they more readily achieve a crisis at the hands of the magnetizer. As many of the women who submit themselves to magnetism are not really ill but rather attend for amusement, and as they are often young and in the full bloom of health and attractiveness, the physician himself is also in moral danger:

> The long-continued proximity, the necessary contact, the communication of individual heat, the interchange of looks, are ways and means by which it is well known that nature ever affects the communication of the sensations and the affections.

The medical members of the Franklin committee paid particular attention to the behaviour of the women patients undergoing magnetism. They describe their response in these words:

> When this kind of crisis is approaching, the countenance becomes gradually inflamed, the eye brightens, and this is the sign of natural desire. The woman drops her head, lifts her hand to her forehead and eyes in order to cover them; her habitual modesty is unconsciously aroused, and inspires the desire of concealment. The crisis continues, however, and the eye is obscured, an unequivocal sign of the complete disorder of the senses. This disorder may be wholly unperceived by the woman who experiences it, but it cannot escape the observant eye of the physician. As soon as this sign has been displayed, the eyelids become moist, the respiration is short and interrupted, the chest heaves rapidly, convulsions set in, and either the limbs or the whole body is agitated by sudden movements. In lively and sensitive women this last stage, which terminates the sweetest emotion, is often a convulsion; to this condition there succeed languor, prostration, and a sort of slumber of the senses, which is a repose necessary after strong agitation.

The Lieutenant of Police, Jean-Pierre Lenoir, met Deslon in the presence of the Commissioners and asked him outright if it would be easy to 'outrage' a woman in this condition. Deslon replied in the affirmative, although as the Commissioners fairly pointed out he himself was above suspicion. He had always insisted that magnetism should only be practised by colleagues who were sworn to act with probity. Moreover, although his house contained a room originally intended for individual patients in a crisis, he had never allowed it to be used. By implication, of course, the Commissioners were condemning Mesmer, who used a crisis room in his practice, although he, too, had never been accused of immorality at any time.

It seemed probable to the Mesmerians that the Commissions' reports would be followed by an edict banning the practice of animal magnetism, and Mesmer prepared to flee to England. That their fears were justified was made clear in Lenoir's memoirs where he mentions that the police had received anonymous letters claiming that seditious speeches had been made in the meetings of the Society of Harmony and that at least one minister had proposed the expulsion of Mesmer from the kingdom.[18]

Bergasse now stepped in with a petition to the Parlement of Paris in which he denounced the reports for violating the most basic rules of justice. He requested the Parlement to place animal magnetism under its special protection and to appoint its own investigatory commission, a request to which the Parlement acceded. However, this commission, appointed on 6 September, appears never to have sat, although Bergasse's letter had had the necessary effect. As he was later to write:

'It recalled the authorities to their usual circumspection and caution; and henceforth mesmerism and its founder had no more public persecution to fear.'[19]

The persecution was to be of a different variety: an anti-mesmerist campaign of ridicule in the newspapers, in a flood of pamphlets, and in the Paris theatre. The Mesmerians themselves were equally active in condemning the Royal Commissions, whose arguments they saw as representative of the self-interest of the physicians and the established scientists. Deslon's own response was to produce what he called a supplement to the Commissions' reports, a collection of 115 cases treated mainly by himself.[20]

Noteworthy was the inclusion of twelve cases where children, some being young infants, had been cured by animal magnetism, a result Deslon found difficult to ascribe to their powers of imagination. Many aristocratic patients, contrary to the Commissioners' fears over their possible concern at being observed at the baquet, expressed their pleasure at having the opportunity to place on record the details of their own cures. As one remarked:

> If the health which I believe I now enjoy is an illusion, I humbly beg the clear-sighted savants not to destroy it. Whilst they clarify the nature of the universe, let them leave me to my error, permit me in my simplicity, weakness and ignorance to continue to use this invisible agent, which does not exist, but which cured me.[21]

The medical profession were not slow to produce their own list of apparent therapeutic failures produced by animal magnetism. Thouret read two reports to the Royal Society of Medicine early in November, which were based on communications received from doctors both abroad and in the provinces, where the Societies of Harmony had been spreading the practice.[22] The accounts were no better and no worse than those supplied by Deslon. Patients appeared to be cured and then relapsed or even died. They relinquished orthodox medicine for animal magnetism and when a cure was reported it was ascribed to the later rather than to the earlier treatment. Much of the foreign correspondence emanated from Germany and Holland, where mesmeric practices were evidently prevalent. Nothing was reported from England at this date. Thouret's best critique was based on an investigation in Malta where twenty-five patients undergoing mesmeric treatment had been followed up by a team of six physicians. The patients included those blind from birth, suffering from rheumatism, epilepsy, hypochondria, 'obstructions', paralysis, hysteria and breast cancer. After seventy days of treatment some were found to be worse, some the same, and some were temporarily better but later relapsed.

Well argued defences of magnetism were produced by Bergasse,[23] Bonnefoy, [24] and Servan.[25] The last-named was the radical Advocate General to the Parlement of Grenoble who had suffered for twenty years at the hands of orthodox medical practitioners before finding relief through animal magnetism. His book made the interesting point that convulsive crises were much rarer in the provinces than the Commissioners claimed to have been the case in Paris. Servan claimed that out of every fifty patients not more than five or six would experience convulsions.

Also in his experience all ranks of society mixed freely around the baquet, which was certainly not a haunt of the provincial aristocrat. In a beautifully satirical passage he drew attention to the foolhardiness of entrusting such a delicate enquiry to a cabal of medical men, members of a profession who had in the past obstinately refused to accept the circulation of the blood, rejected the use of emetics, treated quinine as rubbish, a substance for which they now ransacked a continent, had made itself the laughing stock of Europe by opposing inoculation, and which had even condemned the consumption of bread rolls, now to be found on every doctor's breakfast table. Suppose the Commission had been an enquiry into the practice of orthodox medicine, that the doctors had been judged by their own patients, who would then have eliminated all cures due to nature or imagination: 'What a report that would have made!'

These formal attacks and counterattacks seem to have had little impact. In the public arena it was the sheer bulk of the pamphlets, the cartoons, and the letters that took Paris by storm. The mesmerists were at one disadvantage: some newspapers, notably the *Journal de Paris*, refused to publish pro-Mesmer material. When it is realized that 12,000 copies of the Franklin report were printed, it is hard to resist the conclusion that the government were determined to see an end to the practice of mesmerism. In this endeavour they were relatively ineffectual; the far more potent weapon of ridicule was at the service of the anti-mesmerists.

Two burlesques put animal magnetism on the Paris stage. One of the hits of the 1784 season was undoubtedly *Les docteurs modernes*, which opened at the Comédie Italienne on 27 November.[26] Mesmer, as 'Cassandre', was portrayed as a shameless swindler, while Deslon, 'le docteur', helped him to inject credulous patients with animal magnetism and to recover enormous fees. Their followers, played by the chorus, sang the finale linking hands around a baquet. When the author was called upon to receive the tumultuous applause, the actor Rosière stepped forward to announce that he was unfortunately still in the crisis room. As Grimm commented:

> There is reason to believe that this little comedy will do more damage to the new sect than the reports of all the Academies, and all the Faculties, and all the verdicts of the Council or the Parlement that might solemnly proscribe both the doctrine and the practice.[27]

An attempt at a counter-attack by Jean-Jacques d'Eprémesnil, a member of the Paris Parlement, created a stir. D'Eprémesnil denounced the play as slanderous, and went to Versailles to read his pamphlet to the King. But the King refused to see him, and, further attempts to have the play suppressed also failing, he had copies of a manifesto printed in which he expressed his faith in Mesmer, whom he likened to Aristotle. These copies he personally distributed in the Rue Mauconseil outside the theatre while loudly proclaiming that the King was asleep to the public awakening. Not content with this, he attended the play in his full parliamentary regalia and interrupted the performance by showering copies of his document on to the audience from the balcony.

The other and less substantial piece, the *Baquet de Santé*, was written by the same authors to be performed as an epilogue, but as one commentator suggested, it was difficult to find material for satire as powerful as that provided around Mesmer's own baquet.[28]

Animal magnetism was to figure once again on the stage some six years later, but on this occasion in a more gentle guise. Mozart, who appears never to have met Mesmer after their acquaintance in Vienna, introduced a magnetic scene in *Cosi fan tutte*, where Despina, the maid, disguised as a doctor, produces a large magnet from beneath her cloak with which she revives the prostrate lovers while singing that the magnet came from Doctor Mesmer, 'who formerly in Germany and then in France won great fame.' It is unfortunately improbable that Mesmer was ever in a position to appreciate the allusion.[29]

One immediate result of the Royal Commission's findings was the final expulsion of Deslon from the Faculty of Medicine. In company with twenty-one other members who had attended his course of instruction he was required either to renounce magnetism or to lose membership. He and four others remained loyal to magnetism.[30] He was not, however, to enjoy the fruits of his practice much longer: two years later he died while seeking relief at the baquet from the symptoms of the fatal illness which Mesmer had earlier attempted to treat. By that time Mesmer had left Paris and had begun an apparently pointless wandering through Europe, never again to excite the public imagination.

4

The Aftermath

Nicholas Bergasse's book, *Considérations sur le magnétisme animal*, appeared in the year of the Royal Commissions' reports. It can be considered in part as a protest of a loyal Mesmerian at what he saw as a prejudiced response on the part of the medical and scientific establishment to a new order of truth, but it was more than that. In its fluent exposition of Bergasse's own philosophy, it represented a real break from the confines of Mesmer's therapeutic concerns to an extension of magnetism to a social and political system. It was to this book as much as to a dissatisfaction with Mesmer's proprietary attitude to his discovery that we owe the break-up of the Parisian Society of Harmony and the subsequent loss by Mesmer of the control of the movement.

In his book, Bergasse dismisses the Commission's findings as irrelevant; it was only to be expected that they would fail to enquire into the cures produced by animal magnetism, upon which its very existence was predicated. It was only to be expected that their report would be printed in such numbers and circulated so widely, while Mesmer would be prevented from replying. It was all to be expected, but it was immoral. Bergasse himself takes it that the existence and utility of animal magnetism cannot be doubted, nor can it be doubted that a revolution favourable to mankind will be produced if the opportunity is provided for magnetism to affect our ideas, customs and institutions.

The extension of mesmeric theory from the physical to the 'moral' world was in accordance with a fashionable contemporary view of their interaction and reciprocal causality. Bergasse believed that the magnetic fluid was the agent in both the physical and moral spheres, the agent used by nature to bring about harmony. By means of universal physical magnetism all creatures are, or can become, good. Our moral duties can be regarded as the needs of our conscience, as our appetites are the needs of our physical organs. Moral magnetism works through the 'organ of conscience' by means of the sense of remorse, which exercises a normative function in conscience, similar to the way in which a sense of pain shows us that our physical body is in a state of disordered harmony.

In addition to the analogy between the two spheres, it is postulated that there is a very close interaction between their respective organs. Thus, everything that upsets a man's physical equilibrium tends to upset his moral equilibrium, and vice versa. '*L'Homme a donc un interêt à être bon, l'homme a donc un interêt à être sain.*'[1] By putting ourselves into the best physical condition of equilibrium, a condition most perfectly achieved by animal magnetism, we will contribute to the amelioration of the environment. The Good is everything that contributes to the physical and moral harmony of man; Evil is everything that disturbs it. Thus we reach a more just and exact understanding of the institutions of a society. Mesmerism alone provides:

> Simple rules for judging the institutions to which we are enslaved, certain principles for establishing the legislation appropriate for man in all given circumstances.[2]

These rules are nothing less than nature's laws which regulate the movements of the planets, the health of the individual, and the social and political life of a nation. In passages strongly reminiscent of Gébelin and Rousseau, Bergasse extols the virtues of primitive society before man was corrupted by modern customs and institutions. In a primitive state there ruled perfect harmony, and it was to this state that man should now aspire. At present it was the ordinary people, especially those living in the country, who were healthier and who responded to animal magnetism more readily than the individuals constituting the population of the towns, depraved as they had become by contemporary society.

Bergasse's democratic call to improve the health and morals of the population and to reform the institutions of France had an obvious revolutionary tone, even though at the time it seemed to require nothing more of his countrymen than that they should submit themselves to the benevolent influence of the *baquet*. His more influential role as a radical agitator was to lie in the future, but at the time his theoretical revolutionary programme, although confined to the Society of Harmony, was nevertheless of sufficient appeal to attract a sizeable group of supporters, who, in looking to him as a leader, threatened Mesmer's overall control.[3]

The break between the two men became final in May 1785, when a six-month-long struggle by Mesmer to retain the rights to secrecy for his doctrine ended with the secession of Bergasse, in company with Kornmann and a minority of the Paris Society of Harmony. The dispute had arisen in November 1784 when Bergasse demanded a revision of the statutes to provide for the public propagation of the doctrine, a propagation which was obviously essential if the far-reaching effects of animal magnetism envisaged by Bergasse were ever to take place. However, as far as Mesmer was concerned such a move represented a breach of the contract made with his pupils under which he alone had the right to dispense his doctrine. The misunderstanding appears to have arisen over the original agreement between Mesmer on the one hand and Bergasse and Kornmann on the other. While all had agreed that the Society of Harmony was to maintain its secrecy until a total subscription of 240,000 livres had been achieved, which sum was to be a gift to Mesmer, Bergasse and Kornmann saw that amount as the purchase price for the system, while Mesmer saw it as a reward to the discoverer who was still to maintain his proprietary rights. In fact, many more than 100 members had joined and their total contributions had exceeded the prescribed limit to reach some 340,000 livres. According to Bergasse, Mesmer wanted more and argued that they should now demand a half of the original subscription from new members seeking instruction and a proportionate sum from those in the provincial societies, the arrangement being that he should receive half of the total monies received.[4] Puységur put plainly the opposing view in a letter to Mesmer:

> Let no more students be admitted for a fee. Also, the commitment we have made in your name and ours must be honoured, the public must be informed about the merits and applications of your discovery, and the men who wish to be benefactors of humanity must cease to play at your direction the scarcely honorable role of your officers and spoliators of the human race.[5]

The Puységurs were among the largest landowners in France, and

Bergasse had a considerable private fortune; it was easy for them to be critical of Mesmer's avarice. Neither Puységur nor Bergasse appreciated that Mesmer's motives were mixed. He wanted not only the money but also to retain control over the movement. While Puységur's attitude throughout seems to have been one of detached benevolence – he was always to acknowledge Mesmer as his mentor – Bergasse sought fame and public recognition and saw in animal magnetism the means by which to achieve it. He summoned rival meetings under his own direction at Kornmann's house where they were free to disseminate to a wider public the social and political aspects of mesmeric theory. Besides Kornmann and Bergasse, the rebels included Lafayette, Chastellux, Duport, and d'Eprémesnil; they were joined by Jacques-Pierre Brissot, the future leader of the Girondins. The nucleus of the original Society of Harmony retained control of the Hôtel de Coigny, and thus may be said to have won the battle. But by the time of the schism even this nucleus was no longer of the type Mesmer had originally envisaged. Its affairs were to take on an increasingly mystical turn, attracting fewer physicians and more aristocrats whose concerns were less with ministering to the ill than with communicating with spirits and other occult practices.

Relations between Bergasse and Mesmer were by now completely soured. Bergasse had produced a second work expounding his world philosophy, a book which annoyed Mesmer by its use of secret symbols to replace 115 key words in the text, and his anger spilled over into print.[6] Bergasse replied at length, bitterly resentful over what he considered to be Mesmer's ingratitude, a resentment which he seems never to have lost.[7]

Public attention was in any case diverted from Mesmer and his domestic quarrels to a more obvious charlatan, Cagliostro, who arrived in Paris at the beginning of 1785. The infamous affair of the diamond necklace, which Cardinal de Rohan had purchased, as he thought, on the Queen's account, only later to realize that he had been duped, led to Cagliostro's banishment from France and to de Rohan's exile. This nine-month-long trial with its attendant exposure of court scandals intensified popular feeling against the Queen; it also coupled Mesmer with Cagliostro as two renegades who had gained their wealth from their impositions on the credulous.

Whether it was this abyss in public esteem that caused Mesmer to make a decision to leave Paris is not known, but it seems to have been a hasty departure, as he left most of his wealth and belongings behind. He began with a successful tour of the provincial lodges of the Society of Harmony. Despite the satisfaction he must have experienced at seeing the impetus of the movement sustained in many of the societies, he had really lost heart. Abandoning France, he travelled eastwards into Germany and Switzerland, where he lived during the early stages of the French Revolution. Many of his former associates and opponents were to be sucked into that cataclysm.

Lafayette's role in the Revolution is well known, his hazardous career plummeting him from his position as possibly the most powerful man in France to a refugee fleeing from the Reign of Terror, only to suffer imprisonment in Prussia and Austria. His successful later years – in which he would see the restoration of the monarchy – were similar to those enjoyed by Bergasse, who played a significant if less influential part. One of those who persuaded the King to convoke the Estates General, he was duly elected a deputy by the people of Lyons, and was entrusted by the King to draw up a constitution. That act led to his later imprisonment and subsequent condemnation by the Revolutionary Tribunal, when he was fortunate to escape the guillotine by the timely fall of Robespierre. Brissot and d'Eprémesnil did not escape that fate, but Duport managed to leave the country in time.

Among Mesmer's old adversaries, Bailly had served as Mayor of Paris, suppressed a mob of rioting anti-monarchists, lost his popularity and his office, and was condemned to death by the Revolutionary Tribunal. He was executed within a few weeks of Marie Antoinette, at whose trial he had served as a witness. Lavoisier suffered a like fate, largely owing to his unpopularity as a tax-collector, but also, it was said, because: 'the Republic has no need of savants.' His colleague on the Commission, Guillotin, was under arrest at this time; but like Bergasse, he was saved from putting his machine to personal test by Robespierre's overthrow.

During these last dramatic events, Mesmer was far away in Vienna, where he stayed for several months. The reason for his visit is unknown: his wife had died there three years earlier. The evidence for the visit is to be found solely in police reports.[8] The Viennese police appear to have kept him under surveillance, or even imprisoned him, after having made enquiries of the Swiss authorities about his possible connections with secret societies and reactionary organizations in that country. Cleared of such suspicions, he was nevertheless regarded as *persona non grata* and required to leave Vienna, which he did early in 1794. He returned to Switzerland, adopted Swiss nationality, and, apart from a final visit to Paris, remained there inconspicuously until near the end of his life.

His journey to Paris in 1798 had one clear purpose: he wished to reclaim at least part of the fortune and property sequestrated by the government. It took him three years of negotiation to have his claim vindicated, and then the capital sum, reckoned at 400,000 livres, was reduced to one-third of that amount, from which he was to receive a life annuity of 3,000 francs. The franc was the unit of the new currency and roughly equivalent to the livre; so he had enough to live on, but certainly no fortune.

The Mesmer who now quietly accepted the court's ruling was very different from the ebullient personality of some twenty years earlier who had indignantly rejected the Queen's offer. He had become less dominantly self-assured, as convinced as ever that he held the key to the understanding of many natural phenomena, but without the confidence that he could persuade others of the truth. In the book he wrote during his stay in Paris, the polemics were almost absent; instead, he contented himself with a brief exposition of his mature system. What is remarkable about this book lies in Mesmer's ready acceptance of what would now be termed paranormal phenomena.

The work was entitled *Mémoire de F.A. Mesmer, docteur en médecine, sur ses découvertes*, and it was published in 1799.[9] The main interest in the book lies in certain key questions to which he believed he had an answer. The first four questions are sufficient to betray the extent of his credulity:

1   How can a sleeping man diagnose his illnesses and those of others?
2   How can he, independent of all instruction, indicate the best methods to produce a cure?
3   How can he see objects at the greatest distances, and how can he predict future events?
4   How can he receive impressions from a will other than his own?[10]

These supposed abilities were taken by Mesmer as facts to be explained. He obviously accepted telepathy, clairvoyance and precognition. These paranormal phenomena were to be seen, he believed, in their most developed form when the methods of animal magnetism were employed. Thus, the word 'sleeping' would seem to imply that the subject was in a magnetic trance rather than in normal diurnal sleep. There seems little doubt that Mesmer himself had never explored these possibilities during his own practice. It would seem more likely that he had read Puységur's reports on his somnambulistic subjects, to which we shall refer in the next chapter.

Mesmer's acceptance of these paranormal states was not accompanied by any trend towards mysticism on his part: his explanations were still thoroughly mechanistic. They were couched in terms of an inner sense to which the outer senses became subservient when the subject was magnetized. This inner sense was said to become tuned to the objective world and enabled its possessor to see, even though his eyes were closed, because animal magnetism flowed everywhere and the inner sense was its receptor. Thus, the range of inner sense was limitless.

Of course, this lack of specificity in the inner sense is one of the difficulties in understanding Mesmer's theory. Why is it not overwhelmed with its indiscriminate input? Also, Mesmer never satisfactorily explained the possible mechanisms by which the inner sense operated, but it is easy to be critical and more difficult to undertake to construct a plausible physical and physiological basis for paranormal phenomena, a difficulty responsible for the denial of such phenomena by many scientists today.

The inner sense, too, was not constrained by time, which he believed to be a form imposed by the outer senses on their input. For this reason, the inner sense was capable of precognition. Mesmer accepted that such an ability had been recognized throughout the ages, and supplied the reason why people consulted oracles, sibyls, witches and magicians, but it was only now that an explanation could be offered: these special individuals had all learnt to enter, by one means or another, into magnetic states. These states were not accessible to healthy individuals, who were impervious to animal magnetism, which, while it would cure ill-health, would also vouchsafe visions to the patient.

Mesmer closes his monograph with an unusually modest disclaimer: he has neither the time nor inclination to fight further with his critics but only asks for other and greater men than himself to come forward and to search out new facts and to take the science further than he has been able to do. As for himself:

> Already well advanced in years, I want to devote the rest of my time to a practice which I have found eminently useful in the preservation of my fellow-beings, and which will prevent their exposure in the future to the incalculable effects of drugs.[11]

And this, indeed, appears to have been the manner in which he spent his last years, living quietly at Frauenfeld, between Zürich and Lake Konstanz, and treating individual patients, but rarely, if ever, using the baquet. His way of life at this time was described by a Viennese physician who visited him in 1804:

> He lives in Frauenfeld with a female cousin who keeps house for him. His table is always supplied with the best viands, the finest vegetables and choice wines. He loves good company and if he has worries on his mind he unloads them at the table. Usually he is very cheerful and talkative, and takes special pleasure in discussing his ideas. He would often read to me for hours from his manuscripts which are all written in French.[12]

Mesmer consistently refused invitations to return to Paris or to visit other centres of mesmeric practice, such as Berlin. From Berlin he received several letters written by Karl Wolfart, a physician who lectured at the university and who claimed that he had used the baquet with great success. In 1812 Wolfart informed Mesmer that the King of Prussia had authorized a commission to investigate animal magnetism, but, unlike the French Commission, this one was to be composed of men who either practised animal magnetism or who 'understood the truth and importance of the subject'.[13]

In view of the presumed partiality of these investigators, it was perhaps unlucky for Mesmer that his health did not permit him to travel to Berlin to have his work receive some form of official recognition before his death. However, Wolfart was able to come to Frauenfeld, which he did in September 1812, and it is to Wolfart that we owe the retrieval of Mesmer's final manuscript and the following impressions of the master:

> I found him in his advanced age clear in mind and keen in spirit. His
> unwearied vitality showed in his vivacious speech and quick response.
> The breadth of his learning, rare among scholars, was matched by his
> kindheartedness in words and deeds. His marvellous skill in treating
> the sick by his penetrating gaze or merely by his raised hand inspired
> feelings of awe in the beholder.[14]

This somewhat sycophantic description was written for the preface to
Mesmer's last work, which Wolfart edited, and which was published
in Berlin in 1814. Unfortunately, Wolfart was exceedingly careless,
not only losing much of Mesmer's manuscript material, but also even
mistaking his first name and calling him Friedrich. The book, entitled
Mesmerismus, was in fact a poor translation by Wolfart into German
from Mesmer's original French.[15] The contents need not detain us: they
include Mesmer's well known views on astronomy, physics and human
physiology, with an extension in a final section to a consideration of
society, education and law, all treated from an apparently Bergassian
standpoint.

By the time the book appeared, Mesmer, now in his eightieth year, had
moved to Meersburg to be near relatives. It was here, within a few miles
of his birthplace, that he died on 25 February 1815. In his will he had
requested that his body be examined *post mortem* to discover the source
of the bladder pains from which he had suffered in recent years. Autopsy
confirmed a malignant condition of this organ.

Some aspects of Mesmer's life strike one immediately, and in particular the enigma of the man himself. How could he evoke such
contradictory estimates of his worth? Was he a charlatan or a genius?
While it is easy to dismiss the contrasting simplistic and evaluative statements from his sworn enemies and devoted followers, we are without
essential information about his childhood and his relationships – with his
wife, for example – to enable us to reach an adequate understanding.

He was apparently born into relatively humble circumstances and
never lost the concern with material goods common among those
youthfully deprived. His delight in food and comfortable surroundings,
his ability to strike a hard bargain and to pursue the promise of wealth,
all reflect these peasant-like qualities imbued by his early upbringing.
His very physique suggests the pleasure-loving endomorph at odds with
the more Spartan assertiveness of the mesomorph.[16] The mesomorphic

build contains the germs of paranoia, and in his suspiciousness and readiness to take offence Mesmer approximated at times to this pathology. Incipient in the endomorph are the exaggerated mood swings of the manic-depressive, and Mesmer's behaviour was typified by episodes of great activity, flamboyance and self-aggrandizement, followed by periods of inaction and flight, such as those seen after the Vienna and Paris catastrophes.

That Mesmer's impact on others at the height of his mood swings was charismatic in the extreme cannot be doubted. How else could he have risen to his commanding position in the stratified pre-revolutionary society of France? How persuade men as different and capable as Bergasse, Lafayette, Puységur and Deslon that he had such power? How command a baquet of aristocrats to his purpose? His charisma was that of a great religious or political leader, and he had a psychological make-up in common with many such. The desire for loyal followers whose slightest deviance from the doctrine was worthy of expulsion, the suspicion of those outside the group, and the readiness to perceive conspirators among them were all traits well-marked in Mesmer's personality.

The need for followers was not coupled with a need for intimate relationships; he stayed aloof from sexual entanglements, and indeed, he seems to have been, in Darlington's phrase, 'one of nature's celibates'.[17] The sexual implications of his therapeutic practice seem to have escaped him, in spite of the orgasmic experiences of some of his women patients to which the Royal Commission drew attention.

His belief in his own doctrines and, in particular, in the curative powers of animal magnetism never deserted him; it was evident from the time of his first successful treatment in 1764, throughout the relatively short period of public acclaim, and during the longer period of his personal obscurity and retirement. He may have lost confidence in his own power but not in the importance of his discovery. Thus, it is inaccurate to dismiss him as a charlatan who cynically manipulated others for financial gain.[18] However, neither was he the innovator of psychotherapy.[19] Rather than innovator, it is more accurate to describe him as a precursor, for he touched on techniques that were to emerge within a true psychotherapeutic framework a century later.[20] His own framework was of a speculative physical nature, with no theoretical provision for interpersonal dynamics between therapist and patient, or for individual differences among patients, apart from the crude dichotomy between the majority who did and the minority who did not respond to animal magnetism.

In supposing that the efficacy of the treatment depended on the reality of the universal fluid, both Mesmer and the Royal Commission were at one in their approach to animal magnetism. But one cannot avoid the suspicion that the Commissioners were relieved that they were able to extricate themselves from a full investigation of the remarkable phenomena they had observed at the baquet, an investigation for which at that time there was no precedent and no methodology, and that they took refuge in the ill-defined concepts of imagination and imitation. It was Deslon who showed himself a truly pragmatic therapist in his readiness to accept curative factors other than animal magnetism when that explanation was shown to be untenable. Mesmer could hardly be expected to take such a step, which would have entailed the destruction of the whole superstructure of his belief.

After his early observations of the curative powers of the magnet, Mesmer's later use of magnetic passes, the iron wand, and the baquet with its musical accompaniment, represents a logical progression in terms of a plausible theory. He must have been a sensitive observer to note the importance of the general ambience and of the behaviour of himself and his co-therapists in helping to induce crises. He must also have been aware of the differences among patients ignored by his theory, for he adapted his approach in the light of the effect produced on the individual.

It is impossible to be certain about the nature of the crises produced in response to his techniques. It has been supposed by a recent writer, Thornton, that these were true epileptic seizures occasioned in susceptible subjects by sound, light and tactile stimulation.[21] The variety of epilepsy recognized in Mesmer's time consisted of *grand mal* attacks in which the patient fell to the ground with a stiffening of the body (the tonic phase) followed by a general jerking movement of the limbs (the clonic phase) and foaming at the mouth. Epilepsy was still appropriately termed 'the falling sickness', a description of great antiquity. It was not until Hughlings Jackson understood in the late nineteenth century that an involvement of part of the brain in a limited discharge could produce less than a *grand mal* attack, that it began to be realized that other phenomena might be also classified as epileptogenic. In particular, trance-like states with clouding of consciousness and automatic acts, sometimes with hallucinations, and followed by amnesia could occur from temporal lobe attacks. Thus, Thornton argues, all the types of crisis seen around the baquet, and, indeed, all so-called hypnotic phenomena, can be reduced to the various manifestations of epilepsy.

Even as an explanation of the *grand mal* type of crisis produced at the baquet, this formulation appears inadequate. It makes no allowance for the fact noted by the Commissioners and others that women were more likely to be affected in this way than were men, nor does it explain why crises should be much more prevalent around the Parisian baquets than in the provinces. To explain these differences one would have to postulate that epilepsy was more common in women than in men and that the proportion of epileptics was higher in Paris than elsewhere. The former assertion is certainly not valid today and there seems no reason to suppose that it was the case two hundred years ago; the latter supposition is inherently unlikely.[22]

Without denying the possibility that some of Mesmer's clientèle were sent into epileptic states by the physical arrangements in the *salle de baquet*, it seems more probable that the majority of the *grand mal* crises were hysterical attacks of the 'vapours', the fashionable neurosis of the society lady, characterized by fainting and convulsions, which sometimes attained a violence rarely observed today. Patients suffering from hysteria are particularly prone to imitate the symptoms of those in their proximity or of those with whom they identify. It would take only one true epileptic fit to produce a dozen hysterical attacks mimicking it closely, a phenomenon Charcot was to encounter many years later.

The therapeutic value of such an epileptic or hysterical attack might lie in the emotional abreaction provided by the occasion and the solicitude and care evinced by the therapist. Also, one cannot rule out the resemblance of the cerebral storm of epilepsy to the central effects induced by electroconvulsive therapy. In so far as the latter leads to a lifting of depressive mood, so might the former.[23]

However, many crises were not of this kind but involved a state of general drowsiness and sometimes trance. Mesmer's own attitude to these types of passive crisis seems to have been one of condescension.[24] Possibly that arose from his experiences with his very first patient, Fräulein von Oesterlin, whose cure was so definite and whose symptoms were so marked and so dominated by the hysterical fits produced in response to magnetism. In Mesmer's mind, the conjunction of a magnetically induced violent seizure followed by a complete cure, by analogy with the supposed remedial value of the fever in contemporary medical thinking, would have easily led him to suppose that the induction of a violent crisis was essential to a cure, while the appearance of a patient in a passive crisis would seem to be the antithesis of a desirable result. A contributory factor in his neglect of the passive crisis was noted by Wolfart, who claimed that Mesmer feared future interference by the Church if animal magnetizers were to stress the presence of paranormal abilities in such a condition.[25]

However that may have been, Mesmer certainly did not employ the passive crisis in any therapeutic manner. For that crucial development in the history of hypnotism we must now turn to the work of one of his pupils, the Marquis de Puységur.

5

Somnambulism

The Puységurs were scions of the French nobility; immensely wealthy, the family had a long history of service as military commanders and as philanthropists.[1] The three brothers who became Mesmer's disciples were no exception to the tradition.

It was the second brother, Comte Antoine-Hyacinte, who was responsible for the Puységurs taking up the study of mesmerism. He served in the French Navy and had developed an interest in ritualistic practices which he had observed among the natives of the Canary Islands. This fascination with the unusual was probably responsible for his joining the Society of Harmony upon his return to France. He persuaded his somewhat sceptical brothers to join at the same time and they were among the earliest subscribers. It was not long before Antoine was posted to Saint-Domingue, the French slave colony in the West Indies (now Haiti), where he established a Society of Harmony which flourished for a few years before losing its identity when its baquet degenerated into a strange amalgam of mesmerism and voodooism.[2] As we shall see, it was an early observation by Antoine in Mesmer's clinic that was to lead the eldest Puységur to his own formulation of the mesmeric process.

This eldest brother, Armand-Marie-Jacques de Chastenet, the Marquis de Puységur, was to secure for himself a niche in the history of hypnotism, and it is to him that we shall refer when we use the family name of Puységur. Having pursued a successful military career, he enters this narrative at a time when he was maintaining his military duties but combining them with the management of his extensive estates at Buzancy near Soissons.

Puységur tells us that from the very first he was repelled by the sight of the violent crises produced by Mesmer.[3] He thought their violence might arise from the heavy demands on Mesmer's time, which left him

unable to quieten the individual patient and to guide his crisis more
benevolently. He returned to his country seat early in 1784 determined
to try to maintain his patients in a calm frame of mind throughout the
mesmeric induction procedures.

His first two patients were immediately at hand, young women
workers on his estate suffering from toothache. He cured them within
a few minutes without any sign of their entering a violent crisis. He was
thus encouraged to try the procedure on a more serious case, a young
peasant of twenty-three who had been confined to bed for four days with
'inflammation of the lungs'. Puységur describes what happened:

> After having made him get up, I magnetized him. What was my
> surprise after seven or eight minutes to see the man go to sleep
> quietly in my arms, without any convulsion or pain. I accelerated
> the crisis and brought on delirium; he talked, discussed his business
> aloud. When it seemed to me that his thoughts were affecting him for
> the worse, I tried to divert them to lighter themes. The attempt gave
> me no great trouble; I soon saw him quite happy in the belief that he
> was shooting for a prize, dancing at a fête, and so on. I fostered these
> ideas in him and made him move about a lot in his chair as if he were
> dancing to music.[4]

Such talking and clowning about must have been observed around
Mesmer's baquets, because, quite apart from their ready occurrence
through suggestions from the operator, these phenomena are occasionally
produced spontaneously by hypnotized subjects. However, the direction
of the patient's mood by the verbal suggestions of the operator, other
than in expediting and manipulating the crisis, seems never to have
been attempted by Mesmer, and for this novelty Puységur deserves
the credit.[5]

In a series of carefully documented séances with this same young
peasant – whose name, Victor Race, deserves to be recorded alongside
that of Mesmer's first patient, Francisca Oesterlin – Puységur was struck
by the changes induced in his patient's personality and intellect when
he underwent a passive crisis. In his normal state Victor was a simple-
minded man ('*le plus borné du pays*'[6]), who was tongue-tied in trying to
converse with his social superiors. In the crisis he spoke freely, without
embarrassment, and his intelligence appeared to be enhanced. ('*Quand*

*il est en crise, je ne connois rien de plus profond, de plus prudent et de
plus clairvoyant.'*[7])

On one occasion Puységur was mentally rehearsing a song to himself,
when Victor, in a crisis, began to sing the words aloud. Puységur
considered this more than a remarkable coincidence, and before long
had convinced himself that Victor could read his thoughts, because
Victor would reply to his unspoken questions; furthermore, he found
that he apparently had the power, by thinking, to stop Victor's thoughts
whenever he wished, or to change them completely.

Without postulating a telepathic possibility one can only presume
that Puységur was unintentionally giving cues to Victor, either by faint
whispering or by small movements of which he himself was unaware.
The apparent improvement in Victor's intelligence brought about by
magnetism seems likely to have been a consequence of the removal
of the usual inhibitions between servant and master. The Race family
had been in the employ of the Puységurs for several generations; it is
possible that Victor Race's great admiration for his master had led to
some degree of identification with him, and when Victor was in a trance
he found himself able to express himself as Puységur's social equal.[8]

Puységur continued to devote himself to a study of these new marvels.
One of his more substantial findings was that Victor could not recall in
his normal waking state what had occurred during the crisis.[9] On the first
occasion Victor had entrusted Puységur with the deeds of his house while
in a trance, and he was found by Puységur on the subsequent day in a
state of near desperation as he looked everywhere for the documents.
Returned to a trance, he again had access to the forgotten incident.

> The line of demarcation is so complete that these two states may
> almost be described as two different existences. I have noticed that
> in the magnetic state the patients have a clear recollection of all their
> doings in the normal state, but in the normal state, they can recall
> nothing of what has taken place in the magnetic condition.[10]

To this passive magnetic state Puységur now gave the name *somnambulism*, the patients themselves being termed *somnambulists*. Of
course, many patients were unable to manifest what would now be
termed the dissociative phenomena of the deep trance; instead, they
merely became more or less sleepy. But, just as Mesmer worked

to produce convulsions, so Puységur always aimed for the 'perfect crisis', in which the somnambulist, true to his name, walked, talked and manifested unusual abilities whilst apparently sleeping.

It was fortunate for Puységur that he had found in Victor such a gifted somnambulist. Among Victor's many remarkable attributes was the apparent ability to predict the course and duration of his own illness. An instance occurred many years after his respiratory complaint had been cured, when he sustained a fall which left him with severe head pain. He announced in the somnambulistic state that he would be cured of these pains at a particular hour some days later, when 'the blood left in his head' would be discharged through his left nostril. At the appointed hour, the nose-bleed took place.[11]

A more convincing case was provided by another young man, Henri Joly, who consulted Puységur on account of an increasing deafness which had forced him to relinquish his studies. On the second day of treatment he entered a somnambulistic trance, and on the third day was able to tell Puységur about the nature of his complaint. It was, he said, due to a gathering of matter in his head, which if it discharged into his throat would lead to his death, but which if it discharged into his nose would lead to his cure. Two days later he reported that the congestion had divided into two and would be discharged, half on the next day and half sometime later, and that, happily, the route on both occasions would be via the nose!

Puységur was unable to confirm the occurrence of the first discharge, which Joly reported had taken place while he was out riding on the day in question. In the somnambulistic state two days later, Joly predicted more exactly that the second discharge would take place on the next evening and that he would suffer much in the interval, having crises every two hours. Puységur observed somewhat anxiously that the crises, which seem to have been of a painful kind, were occurring as predicted, apart from a period during the night when the patient apparently slept normally. A crisis due at 7 p.m. the following day was noticed to be overdue, and, shortly after its occurrence one hour late, the predicted discharge took place. The patient left treatment cured, resumed his interrupted studies, and obtained the signatures of various dignitaries from his home town to swear that the cure was no illusion and that his hearing had indeed been restored.[12]

One or two points about these cases are of general application in any attempt to assess the claim by Puységur and his followers that somnambulists have the power not only to make these kinds of predictions, but to make them accurately. The description of the excess blood in Victor's head, and the gathering of matter in Joly's head and the consequences of its preferred mode of discharge are obviously unprofessional even by the medical standards of the day, although they do introduce a note of drama which the profession would be wise still to retain. The fanciful anatomy of somnambulists is brought home to us as we read of their self-diagnoses: an abscess of the hand which is discharged through the ear, via a canal linking the little finger to the head; a peasant who sifted wheat, seeing his own stomach full of a caked mass of dust; a young woman whose sufferings were caused by the humours which had accumulated in the umbilical cord, and so on and so on.[13] It is not so much that these patients were being dishonest as that they were expressing in their own vivid terms what they fantasized as the cause of their complaints.

When it came to a prediction of the time and nature of their cure, it is noticeable that the reference is to clock-time, with the cure usually prompt on the hour or half-hour and lasting a certain measure of time. The cure itself was usually a discharge, via ear, nose, mouth or anus, irrespective of the site of the illness. There is no need to invoke a paranormal capacity on the part of the somnambulists when their predictions could themselves have been causative. Joly's prediction of a nasal discharge would be sufficient to make it happen, and in the light of present knowledge, with the physiological consequences of verbal suggestion well documented, such is likely to have been the case.

Puységur's lack of medical training, his transparent honesty and enthusiasm went with a naïve and uncritical attitude towards his somnambulists. Otherwise, he could hardly have maintained in the last major work he was to write:

> If, over the 30 years during which I have been observing them, I had seen, I do not say ten but even a single somnambulist who was once wrong, I should not today have confidence in any of them.[14]

Puységur certainly had no problem in convincing the people of his estates and the neighbouring villages that he was able to perform remarkable cures. They flocked to his château for treatment, and he was forced to adopt the same expedient as Mesmer had done: he magnetized a tree, a beautiful elm in the centre of the village of Buzancy near the source of a spring. Within a week of the inauguration of his group treatment, he was able to write to his youngest brother:

> I continue to make use of the healing power that I have learned about from Mesmer. I bless him every day, for I have the means of healing all the sick in the neighbourhood: they flock around my tree. There were more than 130 this morning, a perpetual procession from the countryside. I spend two hours there every morning, my tree is the best baquet possible – every leaf communicates health.[15]

Fired by Puységur's enthusiasm, the youngest brother came to observe and help him. Jacques Maxime was also a military man, and, it will be recalled, it was he who was prominent in the early meetings of the Paris Society of Harmony. The short period spent at Buzancy soon bore fruit when he came to take up the post of second-in-command of his regiment at Bayonne. He was parading his officers when one, surprised by the sudden order to march, fell over in what was described as an apoplectic fit. Maxime got the bystanders to form a magnetic chain with the officer, who recovered completely. Subsequent cures of an injured pet dog and a cross-country runner's sprained ankle led to public interest in his power, and Maxime was forced to open a public clinic by magnetizing three likely trees.

In the first published account of cures obtained by the brothers Puységur he claimed 60 attested recoveries within a month at Bayonne.[16] He also trained several pupils in the town, who formed the nucleus of the Bayonne Society of Harmony. His pamphlet provides no details of his procedures; it seems likely that they followed those of his eldest brother, who had begun to use the somnambulists themselves as his assistants.

The scene at Buzancy is described by M. Cloquet, a collector of taxes, who was present in June 1784 during Maxime's visit:

> M. Puységur, whom I shall henceforth call the master, chooses among his patients several persons, whom, by the touch of his hands and by presenting his wand (an iron rod about fifteen inches in length), he throws into a perfect crisis. The complete state has an appearance of sleep. They have their eyes shut, their sense

of hearing is gone, they awake only to the voice of the master.

These patients in a state of crisis are called 'physicians'; they have a supernatural power, by means of which, on touching a patient presented to them, by applying their hands even on top of the clothes, they can feel which organ is affected, which part is painful. They declare their diagnosis and almost direct the treatment.

I had myself touched by one of these 'physicians': she was a woman of nearly fifty years of age. I certainly had not told anyone of the nature of my complaint. After her hands had remained for some time particularly in the region of my head, she told me that I had frequent pain and an habitual loud buzzing noise in my ears, which was actually the truth. A young man who had been an incredulous spectator of my experiment then submitted himself for an examination. He was told that he suffered from the stomach, and that he had obstructions in the abdomen arising from an illness which he had had some years previously. All this, he told us, was correct. But not content with this soothsayer, he went straight away to another 'physician', 20 feet distant, and was told exactly the same. I never saw anyone so dumbfounded with astonishment as this young man, who had assuredly come to ridicule rather than to be convinced.[17]

Cloquet explains that the 'physicians' have amnesia for their period of work, which lasts some four hours. Their master is able to direct them to follow him or to go to their homes by merely pointing a finger and without speaking. In contradiction to his earlier assertion, Cloquet claims that they are able to hear at extraordinary distances and to report to Puységur if they hear anything improper:

A circumstance which several times occasioned scenes of confusion among those jesters who indulged in inconsiderate and misplaced sarcasm at M. Puységur's expense.

To bring his helpers out of their trance, or as Cloquet more picturesquely describes it, 'to disenchant the physicians', Puységur would either touch their eyes or tell them to embrace the tree.

Then they arise, go directly to the tree, and soon after, their eyes open, there is a smile on their lips, and a look of satisfaction on their faces.

The possibility that patients in a somnambulistic trance might play some role in the therapeutic process had, strangely enough, been noted quite independently by de Jussieu during the Royal Commission's enquiry:

> A young man, who was frequently in a state of crisis, became in that state quite silent, and would go quickly through the hall, often touching the patients. These regular touches of his often brought about a crisis, of which he would take control without allowing anyone to interfere. When he returned to his normal condition he would talk again, but he did not remember anything that had taken place, and no longer knew how to magnetize. I draw no conclusions from this fact, of which I was a witness on several occasions.[18]

Whether or not Mesmer had seen what was presumably this unique version of somnambulistic behaviour, he made nothing of it. Puységur seems to have been led to the use of somnambulists as helpers through his relationship with Victor who made a chance, and accurate, remark about Puységur's own health. As it was thought to be an ability which a somnambulist possessed only for the duration of his own illness, Puységur could not help almost regretting Victor's cure, since his advice was so valuable for the Marquis' own family, to whom he acted as a personal physician.[19]

Henri Joly, who was so good at predicting the course of his own illness, was also used by Puységur as an assistant physician. In the somnambulistic state he described how he felt when approaching a sick person:

> It is a true sensation that I have in part of my body corresponding to the part which is affected . . . My hand goes naturally to the seat of his pain. I cannot be mistaken, as I am suffering myself.[20]

When asked by Puységur what he should call Joly's ability to predict future suffering and ultimate cure, Joly suggested 'presensing' as the most accurate term, a suggestion which Puységur adopted.

In an endeavour to interest Mesmer in the abilities of somnambulists, Puységur took Victor Race to Paris. He reports:

> Although Mesmer had often had to 'produce' or interact with som-
> nambulists, he thought little of them, and when I went to Paris to
> show him Victor, the first and the most interesting one I had seen,
> he examined him coldly and was not in the least grateful to me for my
> deference.[21]

The public showed much more interest, and when Puységur was posted to take command of his regiment at Strasbourg he acceded to a request to give lectures on his version of animal magnetism. It is clear from the content of this course of instruction, which was to lead to the foundation of the Strasbourg Society of Harmony, that Puységur had by now deviated from Mesmer's teachings.

In his first publication, in 1784, he had done little more than re-state Mesmer's theory. He then accepted the notion of the universal fluid, which he identified with electricity, the human body being described as the most perfect electric machine in existence. The sick person needed to be re-charged by being connected with the universal source of electricity through the medium of the magnetizer. This purely physical theory was now to be modified.

He tells his Strasbourg audience that Mesmer's course of instruction had taught him little. He had learned about the kinship of man with the planets and about other theoretical matters but the real principle at work had not been revealed. It had been his brother, Antoine, who had carefully observed Mesmer with his patients and who had discovered Mesmer's secret on the third or fourth observation. He had discussed his discovery with Mesmer, who was said to have reacted uneasily and who had requested Antoine not to speak of the matter in case premature interpretations were drawn. Antoine had kept the secret until about to embark for Saint-Domingue, when he had told his elder brother. But Puységur's first somnambulist had in any case revealed to him the mystery. It was none other than a belief in the existence of a power within oneself and the will to exert it. Puységur's lectures concluded with this advice:

The entire doctrine of Animal Magnetism is contained in the two words: Believe and Want. I believe that I have the power to set into action the vital principle of my fellow-man; I want to make use of it; this is all my science and all my means.

Believe and want, Sirs, and you will do as much as I.[22]

The published version of the course did not appear until 1807, and by that date Puységur's attitude to the universal fluid was one of indifference: it did not matter whether the fluid existed or not, what was certain was the existence of a force by which the soul can work on the bodily organism.

Animal magnetism does not consist in the action of one body upon another, but in the action of the thought upon the vital principle of the body.[23]

It was necessary for the operator neither to know the nature of the patient's malady nor the anatomy of the human body, he merely had to use his will to reinforce the vital principle within the patient.

The Strasbourg Society of Harmony grew rapidly and had more than 200 members by 1789. It was unique among the provincial Societies of Harmony in that it published annual reports of its cures with details of case histories, all signed and attested.[24] The activities of the Society were entirely therapeutic, with an emphasis on individual treatment. In common with all its sister branches it disappeared in the upheaval of the Revolution.

Puységur himself was imprisoned for two years, and then released to become Mayor of Soissons. His interest in animal magnetism seems to have lapsed and in the next ten years he wrote four plays, all comedies, with the Revolution as their main theme.[25] Around 1805 his interest revived and several of his publications date from the next decade.

The wonderful abilities of somnambulists continued to excite his imagination, and the appearance of a monograph by a well-known physician, J.H.D. Petetin, further accelerated his interest. Petetin's book was published shortly after the author's death; entitled *Electricité animale*, it contained details of observations made on spontaneous cases of catalepsy which the author had sought out over a period of years.[26] These cases were rare, often apparently hysterical in origin, and presented the physician with a state of pseudo-death. Although the patients would not respond when addressed in a normal manner, they would answer if questions were addressed to other regions of the body, such as the pit of the stomach or the toes.

Petetin's discovery of the transposition of hearing occurred by accident. He was sitting beside the bed of a patient who had been mute for days, when, in leaning forward to say something in her ear, he slipped and fell so that his mouth came into contact with her abdomen. To his surprise the patient replied to his question, and from then on he was obliged to speak to her through her belly.

Not only was the sense of hearing transposed, but also apparently the sense of taste, smell and even sight. Petetin gives several instances where his patients were able to describe medals, playing cards, etc., placed on the abdomen. Their clairvoyance sometimes extended to seeing objects secreted on Petetin's person or the activities in another room. Now these were among the very capacities said to be achievable by somnambulists, and it was not long before Puységur was able to match them in semi-public demonstrations with a gifted subject, Madeleine.

These demonstrations typically consisted of a short lecture by Puységur in which he stressed the importance of the magnetizer's will, to which Madeleine was sensitive. For Puységur the peculiarity of the magnetic relationship lay in its exclusivity. The somnambulist responded to the magnetizer as an iron needle responded to a magnet. She shrank from contact with other persons, and would even feel physical pain when approached by dogs or other animals. Madeleine, who was being treated by Puységur for a condition diagnosed as epilepsy, was so sensitive to his wishes that he was able to direct her to a particular chair in the room, or ask her to bring him some object, simply by exercising his willpower and saying nothing. She was said to be able to do these things with her eyes bandaged. Not only the magnetizer, but anyone with whom she was put *en rapport* by the magnetizer was supposedly able to direct her.

One of Madeleine's most convincing demonstrations was at the house of a M. Mitouard, where Mitouard was put *en rapport* with Madeleine. He willed her to walk about, sit down, and pick up various objects in the room, until finally standing before her deep in thought he succeeded in willing her to plunge her hand deep into one of his pockets to remove three small screws he had secreted there. Puységur delights in informing us that this demonstration of Madeleine's powers succeeded in quieting all criticism.[27]

The demonstrations were so lacking in controls that they cannot be seriously considered to provide any evidence for paranormal powers on the part of Madeleine. When she was unsuccessful in divining the wishes of the operator, her lack of success was simply attributed to a lack of concentration on the part of the operator. When she was successful, Puységur was only too ready to invoke telepathy and clairvoyance rather than sensitivity to muscular tensions and other small clues provided by the operator and group of onlookers. Bandaging the eyes so that all vision is occluded is extremely difficult, and these early experiments were notably careless in such respects.

Puységur did not neglect the therapeutic side of magnetism during his last period of involvement with the subject. He undertook the treatment of a twelve-year-old boy, Alexandre Hébert, who suffered from frenzy, delirium, continual crying and severe headaches. In a trance the boy told Puységur that his illness had its origin in a head injury that he had suffered at the age of three, and that it would take six months to cure him, the curative measures to include sleeping in Puységur's room throughout the period. The kindly Marquis devoted much of his time to this treatment, until Hébert discharged himself apparently satisfied that no further good could result. The case received much publicity and probably did more for the cause of magnetism than all the demonstrations of telepathy and clairvoyance.[28]

In his report on Hébert, Puységur broke new ground in his discussion of long-continued somnambulistic states and in the possibility of curing madness by magnetism. However, the difficulties in carrying out long-term magnetic therapy were not minimized. Hébert was particularly prone to imitate others, and Puységur concludes that the Commissioners of 1784 were not mistaken in attributing great importance to this characteristic of the somnambulistic state.[29]

In 1818 Puységur went to see his first and favourite somnambulist, Victor Race. Victor was seriously ill at Buzancy and asking to see his old master. Puységur readily magnetized him and found that he could clearly remember all the details from his earlier somnambulistic trances of over thirty years previously. However, although Victor temporarily recovered, he then relapsed and Puységur was able to do little more than relieve his symptoms, as the illness was terminal.[30]

Another of Puységur's activities was to take on the Presidency of the Société du Magnétisme, an organization founded in 1815 by a group of magnetizers, of whom Deleuze was the best known. A later version of the Society of Harmony, which had collapsed in 1789, its aim was to study and to propagate magnetism. Unlike the earlier society, subscriptions were modest, and its members undertook to treat patients free of charge. Its activities extended to the publication of the first French periodical devoted to animal magnetism, the *Annales du magnétisme animal*. Eight volumes of this journal were published between 1814 and 1816, when it was followed by eight volumes of the *Bibliothèque du magnétisme animal*, edited by much the same committee. The journals contained a mixture of case histories and articles on theoretical issues and technical aspects of magnetism. From reports of foreign correspondents we learn that magnetism had a foothold in Moscow and St Petersburg, that practices had been established in six Dutch towns, that in Berlin Wolfart had constructed a baquet which included woollen cords, mirrors and lamps to propagate the fluid, while in England magnetism had obtained little notice although there were three or four magnetic practices in London.

A further light on Puységur is thrown by a pamphlet he wrote shortly after Mesmer's death.[31] He is here at pains to defend Mesmer's memory as of a great man who had to fight the prejudices of his time. His pupils have built on Mesmer's work and now understand that the will is the essential magnetic agent. Mesmer's disapproval of somnambulism was a consequence of his adoption of a particular system of physics with a mechanical view of the 'automatic animal machine'. Under his theory somnambulism was an undesirable effect of magnetism on the brain rather than on the diseased organ and thus a side-effect of treatment. Now, Puységur claims, magnetism by means of the will has taken over from animal magnetism as Mesmer conceived it, but that fact should not prevent us giving to Mesmer the glory of our present success.

Puységur's loyalty to Mesmer was evident throughout his life. It was coupled with a modesty about his own achievements, which in terms of their impact on the future course of magnetism were considerable. The Revolution and the break-up of the mesmeric movement left Puységur's discovery of the importance of the somnambulistic trance intact. Thus, he served as a bridge from pre- to post-Revolution. The only type of mesmeric crisis with which people were concerned in the early years of the nineteenth century was the somnambulistic crisis of Puységur, although it was Mesmer's name that was retained in that connection and not Puységur's.

One essential difference between Mesmer and Puységur lay in the readiness of the latter to listen and to learn from his somnambulistic patients. Imbued with great patience and with an intuitive understanding that magnetic treatment was a process which required regular sessions, possibly extending over a long period of time, Puységur's resemblance was to a modern psychotherapist – while Mesmer's was closer to a charismatic healer.

Puységur died in 1825, leaving a reputation as a benevolent philanthropist with little knowledge of science or medicine, who had seized upon the most fruitful aspect of the mesmeric crisis and pursued it, albeit uncritically, wherever it had led him. His initial choice of Victor Race as a patient had consequences for him rather as Francisca Oesterlin had had for Mesmer. Suppose Victor had not proved a gifted somnambulist? One wonders if Puységur would still have been led to his life's work.

Puységur's naïveté was to have an unfortunate consequence: through his ready acceptance of paranormal abilities in his somnambulists he led up to the situation of the next few decades when acceptance of the reality of the somnambulistic trance was tantamount to an acceptance of all the miracles claimed to be associated with it, and a critical attitude towards those miracles necessitated a rejection of all the phenomena obtainable in the deep trance.

6

Minor Magnetists

The history of science contains many examples of the persistence of an
inadequate theory in the face of awkward facts. Theories tend to live on
until replaced by more adequate formulations, and to this rule Mesmer's
fluidic hypothesis was no exception. However decisive the Royal Commission's experiments may have been, the failure of those scientists to
provide an adequate alternative explanation led to the continuance of
the fluidic theory in various guises for many years. The modification
in the theory made by Puységur, namely his belief in the ability of
the operator to control the movement of the fluid, was a particularly
robust example, which reached its clearest expression in the work of
J.P.F. Deleuze.

Deleuze was trained in the natural sciences and worked as assistant
naturalist at the Jardin des Plantes and later as librarian of the Museum
of Natural History. His introduction to animal magnetism occurred in
1785 at the house of a friend, where a young woman in the company
succeeded in putting him into a light trance. As he was in poor health
at the time, he decided to repeat the experience as a therapy. Writing of
his magnetist, he remarks:

> After ten or twelve days I became aware that she aroused in me a
> very special affection, and that in spite of myself she preoccupied
> my mind. Two weeks later I felt well, and our relationship ended.
> From then on, the impression which she had made on me gradually
> decreased, and I regarded her as formerly, with a feeling of respectful
> attachment, but devoid of all emotion.[1]

Puységur, as we have seen, emphasized the singular nature of the
rapport between subject and operator in the sense of the exclusive

attention directed by the subject towards the behaviour of the operator. The passage from Deleuze is one among several in which he stresses the emotional aspect of the magnetic relationship, at least as far as the subject is concerned. Although he is a sufficiently careful observer to notice the waning of emotional intensity concomitant with cure, he nowhere concedes any therapeutic value to what a psychoanalyst would term the transference relationship. He also explicitly denies any reciprocal feelings on the part of the operator. The denial is somewhat suspect in view of its intensity and its supplementation with a list of precautions to be taken to prevent the possibility of any impropriety. Thus he considers it best to keep the practice of magnetism within the family:

> The best magnetist for a woman is her husband; for a husband his wife; for a young lady, her sister or her mother.[2]

If, however, a man must magnetize a woman other than his wife, both partners should beware of the dangers involved in prolonged physical contact and sustained gazing, not to mention the possibility of immodest spasmodic movements during a crisis.

These sentiments are typical of Deleuze's whole approach to magnetism, of which the key word was caution: caution in the choice of magnetist, caution in the choice of patient, caution in promising a cure, caution in conducting demonstrations of the phenomena or in believing in anything that one has not seen for oneself. His first book, *Histoire critique du magnétisme animal*, was a model in this respect. First published in 1813, it proved extremely influential and had a wide sale both in France and abroad. As Aubin Gauthier, a later commentator, was to explain, it had been easier to deny theories promulgated by a foreign doctor and a benevolent aristocrat, the former was a charlatan and the latter the dupe of his somnambulists, but Deleuze was a reputable scientist and had to be taken seriously.[3]

The work is in two volumes, of which the second need not be considered here as it is devoted to a review of other writings on magnetism. Volume One begins with a survey of the recent history of animal magnetism, which confronted Deleuze with the problem mentioned by Gautier: the confusion of the theory and practice with the personality of the founder. However self-seeking Mesmer may have been and however obscure his theory, it was impossible not to recognize him as an 'extraordinary man of energetic character with a meditative turn of mind and a strong imagination'.[4] Whatever disputes there may have been over Mesmer's practice, all were now resolved or rendered irrelevant by Puységur's discovery of somnambulism. Deleuze reckoned that there must have been, by the time at which he wrote, at least 1000 published accounts of somnambulism, and yet there were still those who doubted its existence.

> We must dismiss all theories and confine ourselves to ascertaining whether there be a sufficiency of authenticated facts to establish the reality of magnetic effects.[5]

Some of the reports at our disposal must be true unless the narrator is a liar or mad. Often the narrator was a person of some status in society, who had nothing to gain and sometimes much to lose by relating such details. Other reports might or might not be true as the person of integrity who related them might be deceived. The category in which self-deception was common included all cures, where – and one is reminded here of Mesmer's strictures – the original diagnosis might be faulty, and where it was rarely possible to ensure that the treatment was the sole cause of the cure. Other accounts might be true in part, and it was this category which caused the greatest difficulty, as one should ideally exclude the doubtful aspects and admit the remainder.

> Unfortunately this is a distinction which the partisans and antagonists of every new system equally neglect. With the former, the truth of the principal fact entails the credibility of the accessories; with the latter, it is sufficient to recognize some circumstances which are false, to justify a rejection of the whole.[6]

Bearing these precautions in mind, Deleuze examines the evidence for the existence of effects produced by magnetism. (He proposed dropping the word 'animal' from the term 'animal magnetism' on the grounds that it was both disagreeable and unnecessary.[7] This abbreviated expression was generally adopted by subsequent writers in France, especially those favourable to the theory; critics preferred to retain the epithet.) The 1000 published accounts, to which we have referred, were written, he considers, by persons of 'enlightened mind', most of whom were sceptical until convinced by their experience. They are obviously outnumbered by those who have witnessed similar facts but who have not committed their reports to paper. Deleuze had more than 300 such people among his own circle of acquaintances, and estimates that perhaps 50,000 people had seen a somnambulist since Puységur's original discovery of that state.

Furthermore, he finds it impossible to imagine that the 200 members of the Strasbourg Society under Puységur's guidance, who worked for four years with magnetism, were only a set of visionaries, and that the 500 patients, doctors, and notaries who attested the cures were all duped. The same argument can be applied to the members of other Societies of Harmony, and to those magnetizers not so affiliated, who have reported similar effects. Even if nine tenths of the accounts were to be doubted, the proofs would be sufficient to be completely convincing.

Ranged against these facts were the writings of the doubters, who indulged in jests, vague objections and assertions, yet among them there was not one who had attempted to practise magnetism for himself. And it is a practical test of the following kind that Deleuze finally urges upon the sceptical reader – who is to take six weeks in the country and try magnetism with a dozen individuals, touching each of them daily. If, by the end of that period, he has produced no magnetic effects, then he will indeed be justified in condemning magnetizers as visionaries.

In making this suggestion, Deleuze deviated from the teaching of Puységur, for whom belief was the necessary precondition, to be followed by the exercise of the will to direct the fluid at the patient. Deleuze tells his readers first to use their willpower, and a belief in magnetism will follow. He has one simple precept:

> Touch the diseased attentively, with a desire to relieve them; and do not let your desire be distracted by any other idea.[8]

The way in which the patient is to be touched is a matter of experience; Deleuze's advice is to begin with more peripheral contact by holding the thumbs of the patient, to progress to hands on the shoulders and passes down the arms in contact with the clothes, before placing the hands on the stomach and making passes down the legs.[9] The patient will be affected, although not as strongly, even if the magnetizer's hands are kept at a distance from the patient's body.

Deleuze is not as insistent as Puységur on the necessity to produce somnambulism in order to obtain therapeutic effects. Puységur was said to discard patients who did not become somnambulistic: on the ground that he could not then cure them.[10] Deleuze, on the other hand, believes that magnetic treatment can be effective so long as an 'affinity' has been established between magnetizer and patient, a state of affairs which follows from the initial consent to be touched. However, he is much more cautious than Puységur over the therapeutic outcome of treatment; from his own experience he has found that some organic diseases do not respond to magnetism, whether or not somnambulism has been produced.

Thus far Deleuze has written as a practical scientist and therapist reporting his observations from experience. For a theoretical rationale he now resorts to the orthodox fluidic hypothesis:

> I believe in an emanation from myself because magnetic results are produced without my touching the patient; *ex nihilo nil*. I am ignorant of the nature of this emanation. I do not know whether it is material or spiritual, nor to what distance it may be made to extend; but this I know, that it is discharged and directed by my will, for when I cease to will, it ceases to act.[11]

How the will operates in directing the fluid is a mystery to Deleuze, on a par with the mystery of how it operates in general in enabling us to move our bodies. He accepts it as an elementary fact beyond which we are unable to go.

Deleuze's belief in a fluidic hypothesis was bolstered by reports from his somnambulists to the effect that they could perceive a bright light surrounding the magnetizer, a light which seemed to emanate from his hands and head. These reports were common from subjects of magnetic experiments and were thought to occur on account of their unusual perceptual sensitivity. They were to claim that they could see the magnetic fluid impregnate objects touched by the magnetizer, and that the nature of the fluid differed from one magnetizer to another, being more or less luminous, dense and mobile.

> As I have obtained this intelligence from all the somnambulists whom I have consulted, and as similar information has been given by them to magnetizers in every other country, I am compelled to admit the

existence of a magnetic fluid, and to acknowledge that we possess the means of communicating, accumulating, and directing it.[12]

It necessarily follows for Deleuze that Mesmer's baquet and Puységur's tree must have been able to act as accumulators of the magnetic fluid in spite of the Royal Commission's negative findings with regard to the former. Deleuze believes that trees are indeed preferable to manufactured baquets, mainly because they are in the open air, and, with many people around them, the fluid appears to circulate more effectively. He provides instructions for their magnetization:

> A tree is magnetized by first touching it, and then retiring a few paces off; directing the fluid upon it, from the branches to the trunk, and from the trunk towards the roots.[13]

He was even able to distinguish from among the varieties of tree those that were most amenable to the magnetic influence. It was fortunate for Deleuze that he had the Jardin des Plantes at his disposal!

His book continues with a section concerned with the personal qualities of magnetizers and patients. Good magnetizers are rare because they need to possess the sterling qualities of good health, much patience and strong will power, which they have to be able to concentrate without effort; in addition, they need to exude calmness and benevolence. It is, he thinks, due to differences in these characteristics that some individuals prove to be better magnetizers than others. He believes there to be no differences in this regard between the sexes; although women magnetizers are relatively rare, they are just as capable of producing somnambulism in their subjects.

All that is needed of a patient to be a good magnetic subject is for him to have confidence in his magnetizer. It is unnecessary for him to believe in the efficacy of magnetism, although 'absolute incredulity' would be likely to retard the magnetic reaction. This fact explains why simple country folk are magnetized more readily.

He estimates that about one in twenty subjects can achieve the somnambulistic state. He nowhere speculates about the possible reasons for their rarity nor does he ever appear to suspect that personality and attitudinal differences among subjects might play a part in their susceptibility to magnetism. Wedded to the fluidic hypothesis, he naturally concentrates his analysis on the source of the fluid, the magnetizer; it is the magnetizer's characteristics that determine the progress and extent of the magnetic relationship. Uninvolved emotionally with the subject, the magnetizer is the power house, the energy source of the therapeutic fluid. The subject is the essentially passive recipient, who can do little more than delay the progress of magnetization by the degree of his incredulity.

In this concentration on the person of the magnetist, Deleuze followed his mentor, Puységur, who in turn had followed his master, Mesmer. The belief that the operator had the power has proved to be extraordinarily persistent and has even outlived the fluidic theory on which it was based. It is, indeed, commonly accepted today among the uninformed, and it is a belief often fostered by stage hypnotists as part of their preliminary build-up of suggestibility in their audience.

It is at this point that the English translation of Deleuze's book ends. English readers were thus deprived of the unusual facts reported in the eighth chapter, which Dingwall in his review of paranormal hypnotic phenomena has termed 'frankly incredible'.[14] And yet Deleuze tells us that he considered himself constrained throughout the book by an endeavour to convince scientists and doctors, and deliberately refrained from including material which he knew would arouse their scepticism. Nevertheless he states quite confidently that almost all somnambulists are capable of seeing with their eyes closed, of perceiving the interior of their own bodies, and of predicting their next illness. He accepts that somnambulists are not anatomists and may use colourful and imprecise language in describing their organs. In comparison, he cites the case of a medical doctor in a state of somnambulism who gave a description of his complaint in great detail in a way he could not have done in his normal waking state, but the language he used was the language of his training and not that of an uneducated peasant. It is enough for Deleuze, as it was for Puységur, to claim that he has never encountered a somnambulist, whatever his education, who has been wrong in his diagnosis.

These marvels, attributed by the ignorant to the occult, are in Deleuze's opinion explicable by natural causes. Among these natural causes he includes the magnetic fluid, which, he believes, can directly affect the brain without having to go through the usual nervous channels. Thus a somnambulist does not need to have light rays on his eye but receives sensation through the impingement of the fluid on the cerebral organ of vision. Internal organs of the body are presumably seen by the same direct route. Similarly the somnambulist obeys the magnetizer's will without the need for words, because he is like a mobile magnet sensitive to the fluid emanating from the magnetizer's brain.

Predictions of future illnesses are considered by Deleuze to be due to an enhancement of the normal ability to make deductions from present minor symptoms and from likely environmental events. Thus normal perception is intensified in the somnambulistic state. He is at pains to point out that these predictions are sometimes wrong; otherwise he would have been forced to a fatalistic belief in a fixed order of future events, a philosophy contrary to his Roman Catholic convictions. However, he was sufficiently impressed by the phenomena to devote a subsequent monograph to them.[15]

Somnambulists do not possess any more knowledge than they had when awake, except in the sense that they can remember all that they have known and done. A somnambulist can never speak a language he has never heard, but he may speak good French, when he normally speaks patois. He may, too, speak a language he has heard as a child and has subsequently forgotten.

Deleuze is frequently insistent on the need to restrict magnetism to therapeutic purposes and neither to exhibit somnambulists in public nor to conduct experiments with them. He admits that, although many of their abilities appear to be enhanced, the personalities of somnambulists often show a deterioration, in that they become vain and exhibitionistic, desiring to interest and astonish. Dingwall has suggested that Deleuze's caution may also have stemmed in part from a suspicion that he may have been deceived by his somnambulists, and the consequent lack of confidence in his findings would lead him to avoid confrontation with a sceptical audience.[16]

The ninth and final chapter of Deleuze's first volume is an unexpected digression on mystical doctrines and, in particular, a sympathetic account of theosophy, which he completes by suddenly telling his readers that it has nothing in common with magnetism, which deals with natural causes. The belief in a spirit world and in the possibility that somnambulists would be able to communicate with spirits is not, however, rejected outright by Deleuze, although he concludes that it would be more prudent to study more definite and useful matters. Indeed, he believes that it can be harmful to somnambulistic patients to treat them as oracles on account of their spirit messages; it excites their imaginations instead of calming them. The Stockholm Society of Magnetists comes in for his especial criticism in their attempts to communicate with the spirits of the dead.

Further information on Deleuze's views on these matters is provided by his correspondence between 1829 and 1833 with G.P. Billot. Billot was a spiritualist who published their letters after Deleuze's death in an endeavour to 'confound the materialists'.[17]

It seems that by 1830 Deleuze was in broad agreement with Billot that somnambulists were modern examples of visionaries who could indeed communicate with the spirit world. As Deleuze expressed it in one of his letters:

> I am persuaded that in the state of somnambulism one can be *en rapport* with purely spiritual beings, and that the phenomena of magnetism prove the spirituality of the soul.[18]

However, he drew a line at Billot's belief that angels were the agents of magnetic phenomena and directed and controlled the magnetic influence. Thus he refused to entertain Billot's suggestion that the word 'magnétisme' should be replaced by 'magnatisme', after those superior spirits termed 'magnats'!

Billot's book was the first to mention that the 'apport' of objects had occurred during a somnambulistic séance. Branches of thyme and fragments of the supposed bones of martyrs mysteriously fell at the feet of the experimenters. Deleuze was not present, but stated that he did not doubt the truth of the reported facts.

It can be seen that these later writings, which he presumably did not intend for publication, show Deleuze in a different light from that of the cautious natural scientist portrayed in his earlier book. The difference was partly in the *persona* from that which he formerly felt he had to present to have magnetism accepted by its critics, and partly perhaps reflected a real change in his own readiness to accept a spiritual explanation of somnambulistic capacities.

As a modest, lucid and sensible contributor to the literature, Deleuze exercised an influence beyond his capacity for originality. If his training in science had made him more critical than Puységur, it enabled him to go no further in his understanding of magnetism. He was, however, more systematic; he laid down rules for the profession to follow, and described in detail procedures and problems that might be encountered. It was for this reason that his *Histoire critique* and his later practical manual continued to be consulted by magnetists for many years after Mesmer's and Puységur's writings had been forgotten.

It would be difficult to imagine a more striking contrast with Deleuze than the mysterious Portuguese priest, who was to adopt a new approach to magnetism. José Custodio de Faria was born in Goa in 1756 of a Portuguese father and Indian mother.[19] He trained for the priesthood and finally reached Paris in 1788, where he adopted a more worldly life than was usual for a priest.

The first mention of the Abbé Faria's interest in magnetism dates from 1802. Present at a party, he was said to have attempted to kill a canary by staring at it, but claimed that he had to desist as the canary was too strong and might have killed him! There is the suggestion that he obtained a professorship at the Académie de Marseille through the good offices of a gambling associate, brought about, it was said, because the gaming rooms he formerly frequented had become tired of paying him a small weekly stipend on condition that he gambled somewhere else. What is more certain is that he returned to Paris in 1813 and over the next three years became something of a celebrity.

His fame grew with the success of his weekly demonstrations of magnetic phenomena, which, given under the guise of an instructional course in what he termed 'lucid sleep' (*sommeil lucide*), were attended by some hundred persons of whom the majority were elegant women prepared to pay five francs a session.

The demonstrations began with Faria reading from a manuscript, which was chiefly remarkable for its obscurity.[20] He then turned to his subjects and said, 'Sleep . . . ' in a commanding voice, repeating the word possibly twice more. With this simple induction procedure Faria was said to obtain a trance in more than half his subjects within one minute. If subjects proved refractory to this first procedure, they were told to gaze at his open hand, which he then brought close to their eyes until they closed. If that, too, was ineffectual, he would touch them lightly on the top of the head, the temples, the root of the nose, the diaphragm, the heart, knees and feet.

> Experience has shown that a light pressure on these parts . . . pro-
> vokes a sufficient concentration for the abstraction of the senses.[21]

Faria's extraordinary success in inducing somnambulism is attribut-
able to his stage presence, in which he seems to have rivalled Mesmer,
and to his intuitive selection of good subjects. With regard to his
appearance, a contemporary writes:

> He possessed the essential qualities to play his role well; he was
> remarkable for his vivacity and the originality of his physiognomy,
> regular and pleasant in spite of his dark colouring. He had a lively
> and penetrating eye, and he expressed himself well enough in French,
> although with a foreign accent. But the most precious gift for a
> teacher of magnetism was the assurance and imperturbable bearing
> which characterized this charlatan.[22]

Although it is unclear how he selected his subjects in practice, he was
quite definite that somnambulistic ability varied among people:

> One cannot make *époptes* when one wishes, but only when one finds
> subjects who are already *époptes*.[23]

The term *épopte* was coined from the Greek, 'one who sees clearly',
possibly in deference to Puységur's insistence on the clairvoyance of
somnambulists.[24] The predisposing factors that make for an épopte are
the 'liquidity of the blood' and a 'psychological impressionability'.
These terms might be taken for fanciful descriptions of anaemics and
hysterics, and it was perhaps such individuals whom he chose for his
demonstrations. His views on the liquidity of the blood were taken from
contemporary medical thinking on the subject, in which the blood was
thought to be more or less thick, with anaemics having very thin blood.
Women, who were more likely to suffer from anaemia and from hysteria,
were accordingly thought to be more susceptible than men.

Faria claimed experimental proof of the causative role played by the
thickness of the blood in citing as a fact that one could more readily
send a person to sleep if he had been bled within the last twenty-four
hours. Other signs of susceptibility included:

> Everyone to whom sleep is easy, who sweat much and who are very impressionable. Another characteristic, which seems common to all somnambulists, is a rapid and continuous fluttering of the lids when the eyes are lightly closed.[25]

Having chosen his subjects, Faria's demonstrations at their best included practically all the phenomena known to present-day hypnotists. He produced analgesia, negative and positive hallucinations – making, for example, the audience disappear, and conjuring up the spirits of absent friends and dead relatives – amnesia and hypermnesia, and he gave effective posthypnotic suggestions. At their worst, the demonstrations were unsuccessful in convincing the audience that his subjects were unusually accomplished. For example, on one occasion he claimed that his young female subject, who knew no Latin, would possess a knowledge of this language when in a state of lucid sleep. Having put her to sleep, he asked her what 'Ars longa, vita brevis' meant. Her reply that it meant that life was both long and short was greeted with some amusement. The situation deteriorated even further when another subject described, as though with clairvoyant ability, a murder involving two robbers. In fact, the murder had occurred three hours previously and many of the audience knew of it. They became even more sceptical when Faria's subjects claimed to be paralysed at his command, and this particular meeting broke up in some disorder.[26]

Faria's demonstrations were given over a period of three years and ended in his being considered nothing more than a charlatan. A well-known actor, Potier, was instrumental in bringing about this conclusion to Faria's career. Potier volunteered to act as a subject for Faria and feigned lucid sleep. After going along with Faria's suggestions, he suddenly 'woke up' and shouted to the audience that, if Faria magnetized all the others like he had Potier, he had not done a thing. Parisians were soon aware of the fact that at least one of Faria's *époptes* had faked the phenomena of lucid sleep and unfairly concluded that all had.

A playwright, Jules Vernet, now wrote a farce, with Potier in the leading role of Soporito, a magnetizer 'with a colossal reputation but a modest fortune'. Dressed as an abbé with the colouring and mannerisms of Faria, Potier was said to have been superb in his role, and in spite of its lack of literary merit, *Magnetismomania* was a great success.

It opened on 5 September 1816 and Faria gave up his public exhibitions within a few weeks. He retired to a post of chaplain at a girls' school, completed what he envisaged as the first volume of a major work, and died before the end of the year, at the age of 63.

The most important theories expounded in his book relate to the nature of the somnambulistic state. His very term 'lucid sleep' illustrates his view that the condition is allied to normal sleep. Both are caused, he thinks, by the concentration of the senses of the subject, a process which requires calmness:

> One does not sleep when the mind is occupied by the agitation of the blood, by worries or by cares.[27]

The magnetizer, he prefers the term 'concentrator', has a very subsidiary role to play in the induction process. It is only because the particular conditions are insufficient to produce sleep that the concentrator is in any way necessary. His suggestions help the prospective *épopte* to achieve lucid sleep. It is not, however, clear from Faria's exposition how lucid and natural sleep differ and why the subject enters the former rather than the latter state.

Faria's view that the characteristics of the subject and not those of the operator were essential in producing somnambulism was quite new, and a complete inversion of the views of his predecessors. He was able to adopt this new orientation to the magnetic relationship through his dismissal of the fluidic theory, both in its original form and in its modification by Puységur and Deleuze.

> I cannot conceive how human beings were so bizarre as to look for the cause of the phenomenon in a baquet, in an external will, in a magnetic fluid, in an animal warmth, and in a thousand other ridiculous extravagances of this kind.[28]

His confidence that the fluid was non-existent and will-power irrelevant was derived from his own practical experience. He had found magnetic passes to be completely unnecessary; he had conducted experiments in which important persons had become magnetized through staring at the hand of an infant; and he had magnetized subjects as easily when willing them to go to sleep, as when not willing at all, or even when willing them to stay awake.

These experimental results completely contradicted those of Deleuze, who had found that when he ceased to will he could produce no effect. One can only assume that Deleuze's results were obtained by some alteration in his behaviour, perhaps in his technique and in his appearance of confidence, or he may even have communicated more directly to his subject the fact that he was no longer exerting willpower.

Faria also rejected any theory that imagination was involved in attaining lucid sleep. Everyone, he said, has an imagination, but not all can go into lucid sleep. In any case, one can remember everything that one has imagined, but one cannot remember the state of lucid sleep.

This strange argument is not untypical of Faria's reasoning. His book contains many obscurities with occasional flashes of quite exceptional insight. For example, the following passage would seem to describe unconscious thought processes, their cathartic release under hypnosis ('concentration'), and their role in psychosomatic symptom formation:

> Whenever the impressions received by the internal organs from extreme contentment or intense sorrow remain smothered in the depths of the heart, they find in the inner calm induced by concentration the freedom to pursue their original course and to erupt in a violent way.
>
> It is this suppression of anxiety and sorrows, more often than of joy and contentment, which is the usual cause of the formation of those stones that are sometimes found by physicians on opening the bodies of persons of choleric and irascible temperament. I think likewise that a large part of the women who suffer from swellings in the breasts develop these swellings only from this same cause.[29]

At the same time Faria had no idea of scientific method, even the caution of a Deleuze was foreign to him. Thus, he accepted all the paranormal phenomena produced by his subjects, for which he offered a quasi-religious explanation. The soul, he said, is omniscient when freed from the body. In the condition of lucid sleep the soul disengages to various degrees from the body, complete disengagement entailing death. A person in lucid sleep is said to be in: '*un état intermédiaire entre l'homme sensitif et le pur esprit.*'[30] In the state of partial disengagement, the soul possesses only 'mixed intuition', that is, it can receive paranormal information, which may or may not be accurate. Faria's theory, in other words, was incapable of being falsified.

Faria was in many ways an unfortunate man. At the time of his death he was regarded as an atheist by his fellow magnetists, who were all believers in the magnetic fluid. By the time his book appeared he had been largely forgotten, and very few copies of what proved to be an obscure work were ever sold. The novelist Alexandre Dumas incorporated him as a character in *The Count of Monte Cristo*, and if later generations remembered him at all it was as Dumas's old priest of that name who babbled of his secret treasure, but to whom nobody would listen as he was considered mad.[31]

Among the few who were influenced by Faria's contention that the somnambulistic state was brought about by the subject's ability to enter it rather than the operator's ability to induce it was a young physician, Alexandre Bertrand. His interest was originally aroused through conversations with F.J. Noizet, one of the many army officers interested in magnetism. Noizet had been a subject and an assistant at Faria's demonstrations, and he was convinced of Faria's good faith. Bertrand began a course of lectures to the public in 1819, the year of publication of Faria's book. The course was so successful that Bertrand was induced to repeat it the following year. Collecting the substance of the lectures together into essay form, he submitted the result to the Berlin Academy of Sciences who had announced a competition with a prize for the best essay on animal magnetism. Unluckily for Bertrand, his essay arrived too late; instead he undertook to enlarge it to book size. By the time it was ready for publication in 1823, Bertrand had taken part in a variety of interesting experiments in which magnetism was employed for the first time in the Paris hospitals. He postponed any discussion of these experiments until his second book, in 1826, by which time his attitude towards somnambulistic phenomena had become somewhat more critical.

It will be most convenient first to describe these experiments in the Hôtel Dieu, and then to consider Bertrand's two important books.[32] The first experiments were authorized by the superintendent, Dr Husson, who had been requested by his students to allow them to see a demonstration. Husson invited in October 1820 a young and extremely active magnetizer, Jules Denis de Sennevoy, known as the Baron du Potet, to act as his assistant. Du Potet had already acquired a reputation as a remarkably good operator; he was later to acquire one as the turbulent high-priest of magnetism, as a believer in magic, and as the man chiefly responsible for the spread of magnetism to England. He was described by a contemporary as:

> A small spare man with a pale intellectual face . . . The thumb of his right hand was wanting, and to this many attributed the results arrived at by his manipulations on sensitive and hysterical girls.[33]

The subject of the main series of experiments was just such a girl, a seventeen-year-old patient in the hospital, Catherine Samson, who was a domestic servant and who had entered the hospital in May of that year with a variety of symptoms, stomach pains, fever, and vomiting, brought on by a fright. It took Du Potet three sessions to produce somnambulism, and although her vomiting ceased immediately he continued with twenty-four sessions during which various experimental manipulations were attempted.

The first experimental condition was devised to test the possibility that magnetization could occur at a distance and without the patient's knowledge. With Husson's connivance, Du Potet concealed himself in a closet, partitioned off from a larger room, after which a group of doctors entered with Mlle Samson. They awaited Du Potet's arrival, which was overdue, and innocently speculated as to the cause of the delay. Husson then dropped a pair of scissors, which sound was the pre-arranged signal for Du Potet to begin magnetizing. Three minutes later the patient became drowsy and fell into a trance. (It is not stated whether Du Potet subsequently woke her up; he presumably must have done so, and his sudden appearance may well have made Mlle Samson suspicious about future experimental arrangements.)

On the next occasion, a noted surgeon, Professor Récamier, was present, and Mlle Samson was misled by Husson into thinking that Du Potet was not coming at all that day. The signal to Du Potet to begin magnetizing consisted of Récamier's questioning the patient whether she could digest meat, and again it required only three minutes for her to fall asleep.

Bertrand was now invited to attend the sessions. He immediately saw one snag with the experiments: they had taken place at the same time on the same day of the week, which left open the possibility that it was the patient's expectation which had been responsible for her entry into a trance. A control experiment was accordingly run at the same time but without Du Potet; the patient remained awake.

However, Bertrand was unconvinced, and he arranged another control which entailed Du Potet entering the closet some twenty minutes after the patient had been engaged in conversation. During this time various obvious but false signals were given to make her think that magnetization had begun, but these proved completely ineffectual until Du Potet actually started to magnetize, whereupon she became somnambulistic within two minutes.

Bertrand could see a further objection: perhaps Mlle Samson had known all the time that Du Potet was concealed in the closet, and perhaps a little noise was made whenever he began to magnetize, a noise which, although inaudible to the spectators, she, with the increased sensitivity of a nervous patient, might have been able to perceive. A session was therefore arranged in the ward.

> Nearly 7 p.m. We all went to Ward St. Agnes. The patient was in bed 34. Du Potet, preserving the utmost silence, stations himself with two doctors between beds 35 and 36. Husson enters and pretends to visit another patient, saying, 'It's for you that I have come this evening.' He then goes to bed 34 and asks if Mlle Samson is asleep. She replies that she never does go to sleep so early and has no desire to do so. Du Potet begins to magnetize her at exactly 7 p.m., while Husson is several beds away from the patient and out of her view, although near enough to hear what is happening. At 7.08 she says aloud to herself, 'It's astonishing what a pain I have in my eyes; I am falling asleep.' Two minutes later, Husson speaks to her but she does not reply nor respond to his touch. At 7.11 the other observers approach her, and Du Potet asks, 'Are you asleep, Mlle Samson?' She replies, 'Oh dear, how impatient you are!' Du Potet: 'How are you?' Samson: 'I have a pain in my stomach at times.' Du Potet: 'Why are you in a magnetic sleep?' Samson: 'I don't know.' Du Potet: 'Did you know I was there?' Samson: 'No, monsieur.'[34]

Bertrand's objections to this most unconvincing demonstration involved firstly the likelihood that Du Potet's entrance was heard and his presence detected from a shadow he was casting. Secondly, Husson's entry to the ward at this time was contrary to his normal custom and might have alerted the by now sophisticated patient to her environment. It would not be difficult for her to sense that something was expected of her, and her reported comments suggest as much.

Other experiments at the Hôtel Dieu were less open to criticism from a methodological standpoint. These experiments were the first to be published in which analgesia was demonstrated under magnetic suggestion. Surgeon Récamier investigated the apparent insensibility of Mlle Samson when in a trance. According to one report, Récamier: 'lifted her several times from her chair, pinched her, opened her eyes, and she felt nothing.'[35]

As many as twenty-eight doctors, including Bertrand, now signed a statement drawn up by Husson on 10 November to say that Mlle Samson had been calmed by magnetism and had entered a somnambulistic state which was different from normal sleep. Her pulse rate of between 65 and 70 in normal sleep increased to between 115 and 120 in somnambulism, while her rate of breathing decreased from 22–25 in normal sleep to 12–14 in somnambulism. In the somnambulistic state she did not hear noises – the observers were particularly struck by her lack of response to the bells of Notre Dame, which were so loud as almost to stun them – she had no sense of touch or pain, and appeared to respond only to Du Potet's voice and to the movements of his hands, even when she could not see them. She lost her symptoms to some extent after each session, but they returned when the magnetic course of treatment was interrupted.

The reference to an interruption stems from the fact that Husson left the Hôtel Dieu, and a new superintendent, Dr Geoffroy, was appointed. He forbade all treatment of patients by magnetism, the results being a prompt reversal of Mlle Samson's progress. The ban apparently sprang from the insistence of the Duke of Larochefoucauld, who had a strong aversion to magnetism and who was in a position to bring pressure to bear on Geoffroy. Geoffroy, however, confronted with this particular patient who had reverted to her condition on entry, decided to use magnetism secretly, and, fearing the publicity already attendant on Du Potet's activities, he employed another magnetist, Rebouam. Rebouam succeeded in removing Mlle Samson's symptoms, and she was discharged on 20 January 1821.

The analgesia experiments were continued by Récamier and Rebouam using the 'moxa' or cauterization technique. They were able to burn agaric on the upper part of the thigh of a male patient in a somnambulistic trance without his giving 'the slightest sign of any sensation, either by crying out, moving, or by alterations in his pulse rate'.[36] The patient showed pain on awakening and discovering a scar almost 4 cm. long and 2.5 cm. wide. Récamier was apparently still unconvinced by these results, and later became a strong opponent of mesmerism and its therapeutic claims.[37]

In spite of these and similar results obtained with another patient, it was not until 1829 that the first surgical operation was carried out under magnetic analgesia. Jules Cloquet was the surgeon who reported the successful removal of a breast cancer from a 53-year-old woman who had dreaded the operation beforehand but who in the event 'conversed calmly with the surgeon and did not give the slightest sign of sensation'.[38] Cloquet's report to the Royal Academy of Medicine was greeted with derision by most members. The spokesman for the critics, Hippolyte Larrey, former Chief Surgeon to the Army, pointed out that many soldiers were able to withstand great pain without giving any sign of it, an attitude which he attributed to their courage. Similarly, Cloquet's patient had disguised her pain, and Cloquet had been deceived in thinking that the effect had stemmed from magnetism.[39]

The general opposition from the medical profession is not easy to understand in view of the absence of any other form of analgesic agent. However, this theme can best be later explored in the English context where the evidence for magnetically induced analgesia was to become overwhelming although still illogically denied. It can be noted in passing that the treatment of some somnambulists exceeded the bounds of scientific enquiry. The tenth volume of the *Bibliothèque de Médecine* contains the memoirs of a woman somnambulist who was lashed on her bare shoulders and whose back was smeared with honey and then exposed to the stinging of bees in scorching sunlight, ostensibly to make a rigorous check on her insensibility!

One reason why these early claims to have demonstrated analgesia fell on deaf ears lay in the belief of many sceptics that to accept them would be to accept the existence of the magnetic fluid, which was thought in some way to be involved in modifying the sensitivity of the subject. Thus the facts remained subservient to the theory, and to reject the latter meant to deny the former.

However, Bertrand had no such difficulty. He saw that analgesia could prove greatly advantageous to surgeons and to their patients without finding it necessary to pronounce on the existence of the fluid.

> We will not examine here if somnambulism . . . is really produced by the agent recognized by the magnetizers or if it should be attributed to the moral state of certain patients who are predisposed by a quite different cause.[40]

The context of the quotation is his first book, *Traité du somnambulisme*, a work which in many respects bears more resemblance to modern writings on hypnotism than to those of his contemporaries. In spite of the apparently neutral stance he takes towards the existence of the magnetic fluid, the influence of Faria is clear in Bertrand's concentration on the role of the subject in magnetic experiments. And magnetic experiments themselves are placed in the wider context of other types of trance states. To prevent prejudging the matter he drops the term 'magnetic' altogether and refers to 'artificial somnambulism'. Other varieties of somnambulism are called 'essential', i.e., sleepwalking, 'symptomatic', which occur in certain illnesses, and 'ecstatic', those states of ecstasy seen from time to time in religious communities. An examination of these varieties, as they have occurred in various historical contexts and have been reported by witnesses with different belief systems, reveals that they resemble one another and differ from the normal waking state.

His main concern is, of course, with artificial somnambulism; and much of the mystery surrounding the condition is dissipated under Bertrand's penetrating analysis. The various magnetic phenomena observed by his predecessors, such as the potency of the baquet and magnetized trees, the sensations of heat and cold produced by magnetic passes, the perception by somnambulists of the fluid itself, all these he dismisses as products of a heightened imagination in the somnambulist. Whether brought about deliberately by an operator, or whether occurring naturally because of a predisposition and various environmental causes, somnambulism entails an overexcitation of the brain, which leads to an overactive imagination. It also leads to a development and heightening of intellectual faculties in general and of memory in particular. When the brain returns to its normal state as the subject wakes up, it is unable to retain memories of whatever occurred when it was overactive; thus there is no recall of somnambulistic experiences.

However, Bertrand quite clearly recognizes that there is also an inter-action between the two states. It can only be through such interaction that the somnambulist's amazing ability to predict the course of his ill-ness can be understood. For Bertrand believes that it is probable that the somnambulistic prediction itself is the cause of its somatic fulfilment in the waking state. He is even more certain of this interpretation in his later book; on this earlier occasion he also holds open the possibility of an instinctive perception of one's own organic processes in the som-nambulistic state.

Although critical of most of the reports concerning the communica-tion of an illness from a patient to a somnambulist, on the grounds that they are open to the error of asking leading questions of the somnam-bulist, nevertheless he presents examples from his own work which he seems to find convincing.

One case in point is that of a man wounded in the head by a bullet during a duel. Bertrand's somnambulist sat with her eyes closed, *en rapport* with the patient. Bertrand reports his conversation with her:

> 'Well,' I said to her, 'What do you see then?'
>
> '*He* must be wrong,' she said to me. '*He* just says the gentleman has a bullet in his head.' [The *He* here refers to the male voice she would hallucinate, which would give her the necessary information. One is reminded of the spirit guides developed by mediums.]
>
> I answered her that what she said was true and asked her if she could see the point of entry and the trajectory of the bullet. The somnambulist reflected for a moment, then opened her mouth and indicated with her finger that the bullet had entered his mouth and had penetrated to the back of his neck; which was again true. Finally she indicated exactly which of his teeth were missing, destroyed by the bullet.[41]

It is extraordinary in view of Bertrand's critical acumen that he does not point out the obvious means by which his somnambulist could have come to these conclusions: she might have been able to see even though her eyes were apparently closed. If she had caught even a glimpse of the patient's apparently uninjured head and damaged mouth, she might have made an intelligent guess. However, it is not so easy to explain why she suspected a head injury in the first place unless the patient's behaviour made it seem plausible or Bertrand let slip some comment.

Another case, that of an asthmatic patient, is likewise capable of a naturalistic explanation. The somnambulist *en rapport* with the patient firstly presented the symptoms of an asthmatic attack, then described various minor aches and pains, and finally alluded to a skin infection on a part of the body which was covered, an infection of which Bertrand himself was unaware. All these were true indications of the patient's condition. There is no problem in explaining the communication of asthma which might easily have been detected from the patient's breathing difficulties. Bertrand accepts this possibility, and he also rules out anything unusual about the apparent communication of pain. Somnambulists, he claims, are afflicted by a whole gamut of sensations and pains, which, even if only one or two fit the patient, are readily accepted by the credulous as proof of amazing powers. But he does not find it so easy to dismiss the detection of the skin infection, which he thinks must be explained by thought-transference. The simpler explanation lies in the possibility that the patient may have briefly scratched himself or slightly moved his position in some way so as surreptitiously to have indicated the site of the irritation.

In support of his telepathy thesis Bertrand cites several more of his experiments, none of which is convincing. For example. he used to wake one somnambulist by stroking her arm at the end of the session. When he did this during the session, she did not wake. Was the difference due to the fact that he 'willed' the waking up only at the end? To test the possible effect of will, he now performed an experiment similar to Faria's: he stroked her arm as usual at the end of the session and told her to wake up, but willed her to remain asleep. The subject became confused, blushed, and made convulsive movements, but did not fully wake. Bertrand calmed her and asked her to explain why she was upset. It was, she said, because he had told her one thing but had willed another. This is sufficient for Bertrand to believe that thought-transference must have occurred, although he grants that it might have been of a partial kind in which she knew only that he was exerting his

will-power rather than that she was responsive to his particular unspoken thoughts as Puységur would have supposed. The same criticism
may be levelled at Bertrand as at Deleuze: he probably made the somnambulist aware of contradictory cues, the very act of willing having
some physical actions associated with it.

Another and equally unconvincing example of thought-transference
involved an uneducated somnambulist who was asked to define *l'encé-
phale*. Bertrand was sure that she had never even heard of the word
previously, and yet in a trance she was able to define it by tracing a line
with her finger from the root of her nose around to the back of her head.
Bertrand considers the most likely interpretation of this feat to be that
she read his thoughts rather than that she made a lucky guess or knew
it after all.

His belief in telepathy was buttressed by several accounts derived from
early religious chronicles, the ability to read thoughts being regarded by
the church as the touchstone of demoniacal possession. By assimilating
such historical accounts under the rubric of somnambulism Bertrand was
able to show that the association of supposed thought-transference and
trance states was an ancient one.

When he turns to the subject of therapy Bertrand asks magnetists to
realize that whether the fluid exists or not, there is little doubt that in
many circumstances the imagination of the somnambulist is the sole
agent, and that in all circumstances it is involved. As for cures:

> It is chiefly in nervous diseases in general and in hysteria in particu-
> lar that one can expect the greatest success. I regard the success of
> magnetic treatment assured, if it is directed towards this latter type of
> illness, under whatever form it presents itself; when somnambulism
> is obtained, success is even more rapid.[42]

This passage is confined to a footnote, a reflection of Bertrand's opinion that the therapeutic use of magnetism is not the central issue, the
main purpose of his book being to set the phenomenon of magnetically induced trance states within a wider context, and to describe the
peculiarities of these states.

The interest created by the book was immense, yet its reception was
also critical, especially by the medical profession. It seems to have
been on account of the incredulity of this section of his readership that

Bertrand's second book was largely historical. Entitled *Du magnétisme animal en France*, it deals at some length with the history of the mesmeric movement and the opinions of the 1784 Commissioners.[43] Rather less space is devoted to contemporary work, although his account of the experiments at the Hôtel Dieu is detailed and critical.

One can best judge Bertrand's mature conclusions about somnambulism from a list of twelve phenomena considered by him to be characteristic of that state. The items do not appear to be listed in any particular order, and are as follows:

1 Loss of memory for trance events.
2 Ability to estimate time accurately.
3 Changes in bodily sensitivity.
4 'Exaltation' of the imagination.
5 Improvement of the intellect.
6 Ability to prescribe remedies.
7 'Prevision', i.e., the ability to predict future events.
8 Moral inertia.
9 Sensitivity to a patient's symptoms.
10 Thought-transference.
11 Eyeless vision.
12 Ability to influence one's own physiology.

At a glance it can be seen that here is a mixture of paranormal and more readily acceptable characteristics. Amnesia for the trance state was by the time Bertrand wrote a commonly accepted phenomenon, as were those changes in bodily sensitivity such as skin anaesthesia. By 'moral inertia' he is again referring to a well known characteristic of the trance state, the general passivity and lack of initiative typically shown by somnambulists.

Bertrand's inclusion of an awareness of the passage of time arose from the various prevision experiments where patients were able to predict often to the half hour when a curative discharge was to take place. Although prevision itself is included in the list, Bertrand is now more certain than in his earlier book that such an ability should be explained as predetermination. Thus it is linked with the last item on the list, the ability to influence one's own physiology, implying internal processes normally outside conscious control. Although such an interpretation of prevision removes the paranormal aspect, it is still remarkable enough if a person is able to cause, for example, a nose bleed at a particular time of day.

The 'exaltation' of the imagination is considered by Bertrand to be the most characteristic attribute of the somnambulistic state, and, as we saw earlier, it is thought to result from the change in the state of the brain during the trance. It is also invoked by him as an explanation of the occurrence of the trance itself. In a series of neat experiments, reminiscent of the 1784 Commission, he demonstrates the production of somnambulism through the subject's imagination and expectation. In one experiment he sent his subject a magnetized letter which she was to place on her belly. A friend observed that she went into a trance and demonstrated the usual range of phenomena. A second letter sent by Bertrand was similar but had never been magnetized; it produced an identical effect. It was clear to Bertrand that the magnetic agent was irrelevant to the result.

The fifth characteristic, the improvement of the intellect during somnambulism, was widely accepted in Bertrand's time, although the otherwise gullible Deleuze appears to have been more sceptical than Bertrand, whose experiments in this respect leave much to be desired. Any improvement can usually be ascribed to the lifting of social inhibitions similar to that exhibited by Puységur's Victor.

Bertrand is more dubious about the next ability, that of being able to prescribe remedies appropriate to one's own illness. He admits that he has obtained no evidence to this effect among his own somnambulists, but he thinks it probable that an instinctive ability exists in humans similar to that seen in animals who seek out an appropriate food when ill, and it is this ability which may be tapped in a trance state. He is much more certain that symptoms can be communicated to a somnambulist from an ill person, and we have already considered some of the poor evidence for this belief. The occurrence of thought-transference, based on similar weak evidence, is likewise firmly asserted.

The remaining item on Bertrand's list, the ability to see without the use of the eyes, was to lead to a long and fruitless controversy over the next decade. Bertrand's belief stems mainly from his acceptance of reports from earlier workers, such as Deleuze and Petetin, whom he considers careful and above suspicion. Several among his contemporaries had claimed to observe the phenomenon, including Georget at the

Salpêtrière and Rostan, who had recently written on the matter in the great *Dictionnaire de Médecine*, the twenty-one volumes of which were published between 1821 and 1828.[44]

Rostan's experiments had entailed placing a watch a few inches behind a somnambulist's head and asking her first what the object was, and then, when she had correctly identified it as a watch, what the time was. She was correct in her estimation, and several trials were therefore run in which the watch hands were altered, and yet the somnambulist was always correct. The publication of these results some years later in what was generally regarded as a highly orthodox medical directory annoyed many physicians, and the article was removed from the second edition. The magnetists had, of course, been delighted with their initial success in breaching the medical barricade, and Bertrand himself had been impressed by these experiments.

To take them at face value the experimental results might compel belief either in eyeless vision or thought-transference from the operator. However, in common with the several other instances of apparent paranormal powers in somnambulists, the most likely explanation lies in the credulity and lack of experimental sophistication of these early workers. Firstly, the somnambulist was not even blindfolded; Bertrand believed that the observation of the somnambulist's eyes by the operator was sufficient to prevent cheating. Secondly, Rostan had an assistant who could have easily been in league with the somnambulist and who could have provided a code in his questions to supply the correct answer. We have no means of knowing the details of the conversation that took place, and whether, for example, the somnambulist hesitated in her replies, obtained indications from the experimenters as to whether she was approximately right, and so on. In short, the necessary details are lacking for us to evaluate these and most of the other paranormal phenomena claimed to have been observed.

It is ironic that Bertrand, whose re-introduction of imagination to replace magnetism had aroused the wrath of the magnetists, now suffered criticism for his gullibility from fellow physicians. Thus, he was not consulted by the Academy of Medicine when it appointed a Commission in 1826 to re-examine the whole question of somnambulism.

7

Vision Without Eyes

During the 1820s the magnetists began to extend their activities into the major Parisian hospitals. Besides Du Potet and Rebouam at the Hôtel Dieu, work was going on at the Bicêtre and the Salpêtrière, where experiments were being carried out with patients diagnosed as epileptics. The two doctors involved, J.E.D. Esquirol and E.J. Georget, had found that such patients made good subjects for magnetism and responded well to treatment, with a decrease in the severity and frequency of their epileptic attacks.[1]

Some of their patients were fairly obviously hysterics and not epileptics; for example, Georget's best-known somnambulist, Mlle Petronille, who excited much publicity after her spectacular cure. Petronille had become ill after falling into a canal and had prescribed somnambulistically for herself that she should be immersed there again. A bath in cold water was thought to be near enough to the original trauma, and Georget held her under for the length of time she had prescribed. The cure was immediately successful, and Petronille's career as a professional somnambulist began. She performed as well as any of Puységur's 'physicians' in diagnosing and predicting crises and cures. Indeed, she was so convincing that Georget is said to have relinquished his materialistic beliefs in the face of her paranormal powers.[2]

At another hospital, the Hospice de la Charité, a younger doctor, P. Foissac, was drawing public attention by his lecture demonstrations to audiences numbering as many as 300. All this publicity began to alarm the General Council of the Hospitals, who issued a decree forbidding the further practice of magnetism in their hospitals. Foissac determined to bring the matter into the open and approached the Royal Academy of Medicine with the proposal that they should reinvestigate animal magnetism.[3]

The Royal Academy readily assented, for it seemed an opportune moment to initiate such an enquiry. Their conviction was based partly on the grounds that the 1784 Commission had investigated Mesmer's technique rather than contemporary magnetism. But patriotic and professional pride were also evident in their preliminary discussion. It would be, they thought, to the honour of French medicine not to remain behind German physicians in the study of somnambulistic phenomena, and in any case it was the clear duty of the Academy to prevent the possibility of non-physicians abusing the curative arts for financial gain!

A Commission was appointed, composed of eleven members, which included Magendie, discoverer of the function of the spinal nerves, Itard, a specialist in mental deficiency, now best known for his attempts to teach the 'wild boy' of Aveyron, and Laënnec, the botanist, who had to retire on account of illness and who was accordingly replaced by Husson, an ardent magnetist.

The Commissioners began work in 1826, although it was to be 1831 before their report was presented. The slowness of their procedure was occasioned partly by the General Council of the Hospitals, who, abiding by their earlier decision, forbade any magnetic experiments in the hospitals, and partly by the apparent inability of any of the Commissioners to magnetize. They were thus dependent on the assistance of Foissac and Du Potet, who in turn appear to have selected subjects for their sensational value. No more than about a dozen somnambulists appear to have been tested, and in their general approach and procedures the Commissioners seemed to have learned nothing from the writings of their predecessors or from contemporary sources such as the work of Bertrand. In spite of Foissac's own medical training he led the Commissioners to study the miraculous rather than the therapeutic aspects of magnetism. Indeed, the final report is quite frank in its comment that judgment could not be pronounced on magnetic therapy in view of the small number of cases observed.[4] Yet one would have thought that this should have been the prime concern of a medical commission.

However, the Commissioners were not so loath to pronounce on the paranormal powers of one or two somnambulists. Foissac's trained somnambulist, Céline Sauvage, was able clairvoyantly to diagnose complaints in two patients and in one of the Commissioners. These 'diagnoses' were the usual anatomical and physiological rubbish, although her proposed treatment was probably not inappropriate, consisting, as it did, of dietary recommendations and purges. Two other somnambulists correctly predicted the occurrence of their own future epileptic fits and the date of their final cure. One of these people, a M. Petit, was said by his magnetizer, Du Potet, to be able to see without the use of vision, a claim which the Commissioners decided to put to the test.

Petit's first trials were failures. With his eyes closed, he was unable to pick out a coin which Du Potet had previously handled, and he was incorrect in telling the time on a watch when the hands had been moved. He was rather better at playing cards with his eyes closed, in spite of Husson's attempts to mislead him by naming a card other than the one actually played. As soon as a sheet of paper was held in front of his closed eyes, he became unable to play at all.

Nobody was very convinced by these first trials, Du Potet explaining the failures on the grounds that Petit had not been magnetized sufficiently in recent days, a lack which he presumably remedied before the next session. It was only now that the Commissioners became convinced that Petit really was capable of paranormal vision. (The Report of the Commission is confused over dates, stating in one place that Petit was first magnetised on 10 August 1826 and yet reporting a second session on 15 March 1826.[5])

At first his eyes were bandaged, but at his request the blindfold was removed and the Commissioners contented themselves with watching his eyes:

> For this purpose, a candle was almost constantly held during the experiment, before the eyes of M. Petit, at a distance of one or two inches; and several persons had their eyes continually fixed upon his. None of us could perceive the slightest separation of the eyelids. M. Ribes, indeed, remarked that their edges were superimposed so that the eye-lashes crossed each other.
>
> We also examined the state of the eyes, which were forcibly opened without awakening the somnambulist, and we remarked that the pupil was turned downwards, and directed towards the great angle of the eye.
>
> After these preliminary observations, we proceeded to verify the phenomena of vision with the eyes closed.
>
> M. Ribes, Member of the Academy, presented a catalogue which he took from his pocket. The somnambulist, after some efforts which

seemed to fatigue him, read very distinctly the words: '*Lavater: Il est bien difficile de connaître les hommes.*' The last words were printed in very small characters . . .

M. Bourdois took from his pocket a snuff-box, upon which there was a cameo set in gold. At first the somnambulist could not see it distinctly; he said that the gold setting dazzled him. When the setting was covered with the fingers, he said that he saw the emblem of fidelity. When pressed to tell what this emblem was, he added: 'I see a dog, he is as if on his hind legs before an altar.' This, in fact, was what was represented.[6]

The somnambulist again played cards with some facility, while the Commissioners never ceased to watch his closed eyes, which always remained closed. However, they did note a movement of the ball of the eye, which seemed to follow the motions of the hands.

A further somnambulist was a young law student, Paul Villagrand, who had suffered from a paralysis of his left side for a period of nearly two years and who had been cured by Foissac's magnetic treatment. He too was said to be able to read with his eyes closed; on the occasion of his testing by the Commissioners, his eyes were kept closed by pressure on the upper lids from the fingers of one of the investigators. Again, it was noticed that the ball of the eye was in constant motion and 'seemingly directed towards the object presented to his vision'.[7] His reading was fitful, only occasional words or lines being reported correctly, and he could not read at all if the book were placed flat on his stomach instead of in the normal reading position. No experiments were performed in his case with blindfolds or by interposing a screen between his eyes and the reading-matter.

It is obvious that these experiments were ludicrously inadequate. It is difficult to understand why the Commissioners did not persist with bandages and other obstructions to normal sight. They do not even appear to have been suspicious of the eye movements under the closed lids, nor did they appreciate the extent to which an occasional glimpse supplemented by intelligent guesswork might provide the subjects with several consecutive words from a book.

At the same time we find that the Commissioners were able accurately to observe the more mundane changes produced under magnetism. Thus, they describe various physical effects, such as acceleration of the pulse, somnolence, and insensibility to pain, manifested by some subjects. Sometimes, they agree, the effects may have been due to fatigue, monotony, or imagination. Sometimes, no effect at all was produced, and generalizing from those of the Commissioners who had participated as subjects, they consider that this lack of effect is the rule in healthy persons, and is also sometimes true of those who are ill.

They freely admit that it seems to be possible to feign the somnambulistic state, and that it is not always an easy matter to distinguish the genuine from the feigned state on account of the markedly different individual responses to magnetic induction procedures. It was for this reason that the Commissioners seized upon the emergence of new and paranormal powers to serve as the best evidence for the true existence of somnambulism. Unfortunately, as we have seen, only one or two of their somnambulists were willing to demonstrate their powers, and it was perhaps the rarity of the phenomena, coupled with the Commissioners' belief in their significance, which led to scant regard being paid to the most elementary requirements of scientific method.

The Report of the Commission was read before two meetings of the Academy in June 1831 by Husson, who was responsible for the final draft. In spite of the Commissioners' contention that only physicians should be allowed to practice magnetism, and in spite of a final impassioned plea by Husson that the Commissioners should be judged as medical colleagues who had not been swayed by love of the marvellous or by the desire for celebrity, but who had been animated by higher motives, namely the love of science and an anxiety to justify the expectation of the Academy, in spite of these requested concessions the Academicians reacted with astonished scepticism. When their criticisms were voiced and a discussion of the report attempted, it was Husson's turn to object on the grounds that, in view of the rigorous experimental procedures adopted by the Commissioners, there was nothing to discuss, unless the integrity of the Commissioners themselves was to be doubted. The Academy reacted by declining to publish the report, a task which Foissac accordingly undertook, and it is this Foissac report, proof-read by Husson, which provides the semi-official source of the Commission's work.

Notwithstanding the Academy's scorn, a minority of physicians, especially the younger men, retained their interest in magnetism. The Foissae report had mentioned the case of Madame Plantin, whose operation for a breast cancer had seen magnetism employed as an effective analgesic.[8] And now, a few years later, another instance was on hand: the painless removal of a tooth by M.J.E. Oudet, which was reported to the Academy in 1836.[9] During the prolonged discussion of the case, a physician, J. Berna, wrote in with an offer to demonstrate the remarkable phenomena he had observed in his own patients when they had been magnetized. It was resolved to accept the invitation, and the Academy appointed another Commission. On this occasion it consisted of nine members, including Oudet and R. Dubois, later the co-author of the official, and incidentally a most biased, account of the history of magnetism.[10]

The Commission met for the first time in February 1837 under the presidency of F. Roux, a disbeliever in magnetism who had already publicly declared the impossibility of magnetic analgesia. However, analgesia was only one among the many phenomena that Berna hoped to demonstrate.

His first subject was a young woman of seventeen or eighteen years of age, who was magnetized on three occasions. Berna tried to show that his will-power alone was sufficient to remove and to restore sensibility and the power of movement, but his demonstrations were failures. His subject obviously did not pick up his intentions, and the Commissioners thought that she was even feigning the trance state. They asked Berna to obtain another subject for the fourth and, as it was to prove, the final session.

On this occasion a woman of thirty acted as subject. Berna claimed that she had in the past demonstrated clairvoyance and transposition of sensation in the form of eyeless-vision. The Commissioners were very careful in arranging their experimental conditions. The material was written on a card and placed behind the blindfolded subject's head, while the magnetizer, Berna, sat in front of the subject and was kept in ignorance about the writing on the card.

In the first trial, the name 'Pantagruel' was written on the card, but the best the subject could do was to report that the word began with the letter 'M'. The card was then replaced by a blank card, whereupon the subject reported that she could again see only an 'M' although there were two lines of writing on the card. After a few more equally inaccurate attempts at further words, a trial was conducted with a playing card. At least, the subject and her magnetizer thought it was a playing card, although it was in fact a plain white card. After much questioning by Berna, the somnambulist declared that it was a court card, a knave, and finally decided that it was the knave of clubs. Berna was somewhat disconcerted when Dubois, the Secretary, revealed to him the blank face of the card.

These demonstrations seemed to the Commissioners to be conclusive. Berna wrote to them in May 1837 saying that he could offer no further subjects for demonstration. Whereupon the Commissioners advertised in the press for magnetizers and their somnambulists to come forward, but there was no response. They accordingly prepared a report on what they had seen and presented it to the Academy on 17 July.[11]

It was completely damning: not only had no evidence been obtained for eyeless-vision, changes in sensibility, and the effects of the operator's will, but also the Commissioners were dubious about the existence of a state of magnetic somnambulism. They considered that Berna himself had been deceived by his subjects, and although not wishing to pronounce on the credulity of other magnetizers the fact remained that, 'If they have anything to show, they have not ventured to produce it in the full light of day; they have not ventured to challenge the approval or condemnation of the Academy.'[12]

The discussion of the report in the Academy was chiefly noteworthy for the violence of the attack mounted by Husson against the Commissioners.[13] One of his more substantial points was that it was unreasonable to condemn magnetism on the basis of four unsuccessful experimental sessions with one magnetizer and two subjects. To some extent, Berna himself had been irresponsible not to realize the inconsistent nature of the phenomena he had attempted to demonstrate.[14] One might, said Husson, produce a somnambulist capable of eyeless-vision every day for a fortnight but that did not guarantee its production on the next succeeding day.

The sceptical response from the Commissioners was also predictable: how convenient for the magnetizers and their friends that the amazing phenomena they had experienced so often and in which they so fervently continued to believe should be so difficult to produce in front of an impartial scientific enquiry. This argument carried the day, Husson could find few supporters, and the conclusions of the report were adopted by a large majority.

Once again that was not the end of the matter. It seemed unlikely that the thousands of magnetizers now operating in France were all charlatans or dupes. It was clearly difficult to ascertain the reality of subjective states but it would surely be easy enough to test for the paranormal power of eyeless-vision. Even if Berna's subjects had not demonstrated it, were there not others who could? Moved by this type of argument, a member of the Academy, C. Burdin, who was a friend of Dubois, deposited with a notary the sum of 3000 francs to be awarded as a prize to the first person who could prove his ability to read without the use of his eyes and without light. The Academy accepted Burdin's proposal, which was made public in September 1837.

Yet another Commission had now to be nominated. On this occasion it consisted of seven persons, including Dubois and Husson. They met for the first time on 27 January 1838, by which date six letters had been received, mainly from provincial doctors who had seen magnetized patients capable of eyeless-vision. Among the correspondents was J.J.A. Ricard, a well known magnetizer from Bordeaux who edited a magnetic journal, *Le Révélateur*.[15] Ricard claimed to know many somnambulists capable of eyeless-vision, but it turned out that they were all reluctant to come forward. Excuses varied from prohibitions by parents to difficulties in travelling to Paris. The Commissioners were finally left with one immediate possibility in a letter from J. Pigeaire, a physician from Montpellier. In the long account of how his interest in magnetism had been aroused by the Baron Du Potet, who had had a *succès scandal* in Montpellier, Pigeaire described various experiments that he had subsequently carried out with his eleven-year-old daughter, Léonide. The upshot of these experiments was that Léonide appeared to have the sought-after ability.[16]

The Commissioners lost no time in inviting Pigeaire and his daughter to Paris. In his acceptance Pigeaire made one request: that his daughter's fingers should be in the light for she appeared to read with them as normal people used their eyes. Her eyes, on the other hand, should be made completely blind with all light being excluded from them. (It will be noted that these conditions would most readily be met by the illumination of the text to be read and the presence of a blindfold over the eyes. Léonide was probably responsible for arranging matters in such a way that she could most easily cheat.)

Burdin agreed to the necessary alterations in the conditions under which the prize should be awarded, the requirement that there should be no light being dropped.

Having achieved this concession, Pigeaire now went to work as his own publicity agent. Before presenting Léonide to the Commissioners, he arranged for a series of public exhibitions of his daughter's prowess. To these exhibitions he invited various distinguished people, editors of various periodicals, and medical men. Records of the demonstrations were drawn up and the important onlookers pressed for their confirmatory signatures. George Sand's signature was one that was particularly sought, and obtained, to Pigeaire's delight.[17]

The Commissioners do not seem to have been in the least impressed by this public acclaim, and when Pigeaire finally declared himself ready to submit his daughter to the experimental test and described the type of blindfold he was accustomed to use, they were quick to see its inadequacies. Their own equipment was then demonstrated to Pigeaire; it consisted of a screen of black silk, stretched over a wire frame and suspended some 12 cm. in front of the subject's face. Pigeaire immediately protested on the grounds that it was essential that no light at all should fall on his daughter's eyes. The Commissioners thereupon asked him to widen the proposed black silk bandage, which was only about 5 cm. wide. Pigeaire now objected that if this were to be done, light would not fall on his daughter's face, and as, in his opinion, the facial nerve was in some way involved such a measure would prevent success. (A statement that seems to be at variance with his earlier view that she used her fingers.)

The Commissioners very reasonably pointed out that Pigeaire's blindfold was so narrow that the subject might be able to see through gaps at the bottom of the bandage. Nevertheless, they were prepared to accept it if Léonide did not hold the book to be read on her lap, as was her custom; instead, they would hold the book directly in front of her eyes and perpendicular to the blindfold. Pigeaire refused to accept these conditions, and it was regretfully decided not to proceed any further with the experiments.

The one somnambulist actually to be tested by the Commissioners came forward just before the expiry of the term over which the prize was available. In view of the paucity of applicants this period had been extended from two to three years. On this occasion the subject was a Madame Hortense, and her magnetizer was Alphonse Teste, later a well known writer on magnetism.[18] Teste's cardinal fault was one of extreme gullibility, and his belief in Madame Hortense's paranormal capacities was based on the most inadequate evidence. Having learned of the Commissioners' aversion to blindfolds, he proposed a test much more to their liking: a sealed box was to contain some written material which Madame Hortense would then attempt to read; she would need to have prior knowledge of one thing only, the direction in which the lines ran.

The Commissioners arrived at Teste's house promptly at 7 p.m. on 5 September 1840, the somnambulist having indicated this as the exact time at which she could best demonstrate her powers. They brought with them several sealed boxes made of cardboard or wood containing written material. One was chosen at random for Madame Hortense to read. She moved it about nervously from hand to hand, breaking one of the paper bands which had been used to seal it. She appeared embarrassed and grew more and more fatigued as time passed. After an hour of fruitless effort, Teste asked her if she could say how many lines were written on the paper in the box. She replied that there were two and that she could make out the words, 'nous sommes.' She was brought out of her trance, taken to the next room, and the box was opened to reveal six lines of poetry containing neither of the two words.

The Commissioners obviously did not see any necessity for repeated trials, for with this, their one and only experiment, they cancelled their work. Burdin's 3000 francs had never been in serious danger. In his report to the Academy, the President proposed that in view of their findings the Academy should never again bother its head with magnetism but should treat it in the same way as it had treated perpetual motion and the squaring of the circle.[19]

The Academy was obviously still unable to separate the simpler from the paranormal phenomena of the trance, a confusion fostered by the magnetists themselves. In spite of the magnetists' claims that such powers as eyeless-vision were commonly observed among their somnambulists, few had come forward to collect the Burdin prize. It was clear to the Academy that the magnetists were prone to exaggerate and that somnambulists were prone to cheat.

The question of cheating in the case of Léonide Pigeaire was, as we have seen, never established by the Commissioners. Among the audience at the earlier exhibitions of her prowess was P.N. Gerdy, a distinguished Professor of Medicine, who was subsequently to write a very full account of the affair. He described the way in which the girl manipulated her blindfold, pushing her fingers under the upper edge of the material, grimacing, and rubbing her face. When Gerdy later removed her blindfold, he did so from above, and was able to observe cracks of light from between the surface of her skin and the lower edge of the silken material, which had originally been stuck to her face.[20]

The Commissioners were no doubt privy to Gerdy's conclusions, and it was in the light of these previously established facts that they had exercised such caution in devising appropriate conditions. Thus, their rejection of eyeless-vision was not as cavalier as might at first appear, and their protracted involvement with emotional and unscientific magnetists was perhaps justification enough for their further rejection of the whole matter.

Burdin and Dubois now took the opportunity to express their views, which were those of the Academy, in book form. Their *Histoire académique du magnétisme animal* was published in 1841 and consisted of a long and scathing attack on the pretensions of the magnetists from the charlatan Mesmer, the gullible Puységur, and the equally credulous Bertrand to the present time. After 600 pages of text they concluded that the reality of the somnambulistic state still remained in doubt, that although insensibility might be demonstrated during magnetism it was not due to the magnetic procedures but to the will of the subject, and that all the other manifestations of the trance were due to trickery. Much of their criticism was sound but their case was overstated, and in their exaggerated desire to have no truck with magnetism their book did not live up to the promise of its sober title.

The refusal of the French medical profession to concern itself with magnetism was maintained until the 1880s but was not reflected by any change in public opinion. Well known writers, such as Balzac and Dumas, practised magnetism and used it as a theme in some of their work.[21] Among the popular magnetists of the period we find Aubin Gauthier, who wrote a useful history of somnambulism but who was typically uncritical in his acceptance of the magnetic fluid and the paranormal phenomena produced by its means.[22] It is not surprising that he was one of the most prominent in attacking the Academy for its failure to put Léonide Pigeaire to the test.

Alphonse Teste, the one magnetist to present a somnambulist to the Commission, played a more influential role. He began a journal in 1841, *Transactions du magnétisme animal*, which did not, however, survive its first year. More successful was an instructional text book, *Manuel pratique de magnétisme animal*, which went to many subsequent editions.[23] The book somewhat resembles Deleuze's practical handbook but without that author's sobriety. Teste can never refrain from snide remarks about sceptics and his own lack of that quality is only too evident.

For example, in spite of the failure of his own demonstrations before the Commissioners he continues to assert that vision through closed eyelids and through opaque objects is 'not only a real fact but a very frequent fact', and that he himself knew a great number of somnambulists in Paris alone who were capable of it.

His belief in the magnetic fluid and its power was coloured by no qualification. In one amusing episode he relates how, as a guest at a dinner party and without the other diners' knowledge, he had magnetized the drinking water. No effect was produced on the diners until he began to make strongly worded suggestions of sleep to the daughter of the house, Miss Julie, and then explained to the company that the water had been magnetized. The dinner party broke up in confusion when the grandmother began to create a rumpus over the way the fluid was burning her stomach. 'I am satisfied,' Teste concluded, 'that, but for this grotesque episode, Miss Julie would not have been far away from being asleep.'[24]

Teste's use of posthypnotic suggestion led to another embarrassing situation when he gave a somnambulist the suggestion that she would wake up in paradise. As soon as she left the trance state the somnambulist was lost in admiration of a group of beautiful trees, and then, turning to Teste, she started to comment on his nakedness, which led him rapidly to re-magnetize her.[25]

One final example of Teste's naïveté is to be found in his treatment of his young wife, who was an accomplished somnambulist. Suffering from the usual variety of hysterical symptoms she dramatically announced in a trance the time of her own last struggle with her illness: on Saturday next, she reported, at the hour of 8 p.m. she would have a convulsive fit and would remain very ill until 6 a.m. on the Sunday when it would be all over and she would either be cured or she would die. Poor Teste was forced to spend an anxious and sleepless night until, dozing at dawn, he was awakened by his friend, Frappart, who had relieved Teste in watching over his wife. Teste reports their conversation:

Frappart: 'It is over.'

Teste: 'It is over!!! What? Life?'

Frappart: 'No, the crisis!'[26]

In the very next chapter of his book he claims that the magnetist has an 'absolute unlimited power' over the somnambulist, a statement clearly contradicted by his own domestic arrangements.

Frappart was himself an indefatigable supporter of the cause of magnetism, and after the fruitless attempts by the Commissioners to test Léonide Pigeaire it was Frappart who organized further public séances. His book published in 1840 contains his massive correspondence over the Pigeaire affair.[27]

Pre-eminent among this group of uncritical believers was the Baron Du Potet. His involvement in the Hôtel Dieu experiments has been noted in the previous chapter, but these were mere beginnings to a long and ardent advocacy.

Du Potet had become *persona non grata* at the Hôtel Dieu after his demonstration of magnetic insensibility in his patient, Catherine Samson. The surgeon Récamier was convinced that the whole affair had been contrived as a confidence trick by Du Potet, who was accordingly forced to conduct his experiments elsewhere. He promptly opened his own school of magnetic instruction and published courses of instruction for would-be magnetists. It was while conducting such a course in Montpellier in 1836 that he fell foul of the Rector of the University, who forbade him to instruct university students and who brought him before the Justices. The notoriety led, or so he claimed, to a large increase in his clientèle.[28]

In the 1840s Du Potet was established in Paris and holding twice-weekly public demonstrations at the Restaurant des Frères Provençaux near the Palais Royal, editing a new periodical, the *Journal du magnétisme*, and again training students in the art. These attempts to institutionalize magnetism were sufficiently successful to see the continuance on a regular basis of both the periodical and the meetings over a period of some twenty years. It was more on account of this popular and long-continued success than on any theoretical contribution that a contemporary writer termed him the Fourth Pope of Animal Magnetism, the first three being Mesmer, Puységur and Deleuze.[29]

The *Journal du magnétisme* was a somewhat vulgar production which was begun in 1845. It published all kinds of magnetic stories however grotesque, and yet, in spite of its lack of scientific objectivity, it remained systematically hostile to anything of a religious or spiritualistic nature. Du Potet's demonstrations, on the other hand, were becoming more imbued with magic as the years passed. For example, in his *Magie dévoilée* (1852) he describes how he devised a 'Magic Mirror', a circle chalked on the ground and covered with powdered charcoal. The magnetized subject was then able when in this circle to hallucinate a variety of spirit forms, dead relatives, etc. However, Du Potet went further than this, and by the use of certain magical diagrams claimed to be able to affect the life-force of the subject. Thus, by adding a triangle and a double-headed arrow to the circle, a healthy, sceptical, and fully conscious young man was strangely affected. Du Potet reports that in less than two minutes the subject felt a throbbing in his head, his eyes closed, his head bowed, and he fell into a profuse sweat. In typically purple prose Du Potet continues:

Another minute and his body will be an inert mass. We lift his body while it is still warm . . . his terrified parent approaches. I am absolute master of his son's life: another moment and my power of imitating Nature's dread operation will have dissipated the last spark of life.[30]

Of course, the prediction was never put to the test. Lifting the subject on to a different diagram, a square on a straight line, the effect was reversed and the subject revived, no longer a sceptic. Du Potet closes his account of the incident:

I breathe on a candle – I extinguish it, the fact is plain enough. But I breathe a thought, and it will extinguish whatever thoughts or forces are contrary and opposed to it, in spite of the resistance of a being like myself. I rule his life: it is no longer his, but mine. Poor human race! I could laugh at your ignorance, yet it is you who scorn me and my power.

With such supreme confidence in his power it is no wonder that Du Potet was such an excellent operator. He had much of the showman in him and often employed previously magnetized subjects who could dramatically attain instant somnambulism to his signal. He was not above using stage-tricks, as in his apparent demonstration of thought-transference between father and daughter somnambulists. The audience was assembled in a darkened room, from which two identically furnished and darkened rooms led off. Each subject was led to one of these rooms, and, at a signal from Du Potet, began to behave similarly, picking up a particular object and bringing it at exactly the same moment to the entrances to the audience's room, where the objects were illuminated by candles held up by the spectators. Both brought a cup and then a book, and then a fan, and so it went on. A simpler explanation than thought-transference would be to suppose prior instruction by Du Potet or collusion between the subjects, and the possible use of a mnemonic code to remember the order in which the objects were to be picked up.[31]

Du Potet had little appreciation of scientific method, and his belief in the all-pervasive fluid was too strong for him to see any need to conduct control experiments. Thus, in one experiment he demonstrated at least to his own satisfaction that the magnetic fluid could not be destroyed by fire. A magnetized piece of paper was burned to ashes, which were then presented to a trained subject, who promptly fell into a somnambulistic trance.[32]

Although clearly neither a profound nor original thinker, Du Potet succeeded in keeping magnetism in the forefront of public attention for many years. The comments by Elizabeth Blackwell, the pioneer woman doctor, are a testimony to Du Potet's dedication:

> I have a true respect for M. Du Potet. Though he believes in ancient magic, though he lives in the hope of working miracles, I really believe him to be an honest, enthusiastic man, engaged with his whole soul in pursuing what seems to him the most important of all discoveries. His manner is perfectly unpretending, his conversation full of good sense; for twenty-five years he has pursued the same object, through suffering and ridicule and failure. He is honest, I am sure; how much truth he may possess I am at present quite unable to say.[33]

This was the man whose visit to Britain in 1837 was to lead to the magnetic movement gaining real impetus there.

8

The Spread of Magnetism
To Britain and the USA

Prior to Du Potet's visit Britain had remained largely unaffected by the French mesmeric furore. Translations of Mesmer's works and the report of the Franklin Commission had received little notice,[1] and it was not until one or two visitors began to give lectures and practical demonstrations that a mild interest had been aroused.

The first arrival was John Boniot de Mainauduc, a Cork-born physician of French descent, who had visited Mesmer in order to learn his secret. Mesmer apparently refused an offer of 2000 guineas from Mainauduc, who turned to the then rival school of Deslon, from which he learned the techniques of magnetism.[2] Mainauduc arrived in London in 1785 and immediately issued a pamphlet entitled 'A Proposal to the Ladies'. The proposal was that the ladies should learn animal magnetism, the invitation being directed to them because they were: 'the most sympathising part of creation, and most immediately concerned with the health and care of its offspring.' Mainauduc continued:

> I think myself bound in gratitude to you, Ladies, for the partiality you have shown me to contribute, as far as lies in my power, to render you additionally useful and valuable to the community . . . As soon as twenty Ladies have given in their names, the day shall be appointed for the first meeting in my house, where they are to pay fifteen guineas each, which will include the whole expense.[3]

The first group met in April 1786 and Mainauduc proved a success. Applications came in by the dozen and he was 'forced' to raise the fee first to twenty-five guineas, and then, if a contemporary sceptic is to be believed, to 150 guineas.[4] The fees maintained a high proportion of aristocrats among the clientele. According to George Winter, a physician who attended the lectures, the audience included:

> One Duke, one Duchess, one Marchioness, two Countesses, one Earl, one Lord, three Ladies, one Bishop, five Right Honourable Gentlemen and Ladies, two Baronets, seven members of Parliament, one Clergy, two Physicians, seven Surgeons, exclusive of ninety-two gentlemen and ladies of respectability.[5]

Winter took notes of Mainauduc's lectures, but apparently had to desist when Mainauduc objected that they might be lost and the science thereby disclosed to those other than the initiates. For by now Mainauduc had begun to organize his students into a secret society, modelled on the Parisian Society of Harmony. Prospective students had to sign a bond for £10,000 and take an affidavit that they would not divulge what they learned during Mainauduc's lifetime. Winter for one kept his word and did not publish his notes until 1801, after Mainauduc's death.

There seems little doubt that Mainauduc made a lot of money. Hannah More, the religious essayist and diarist, claimed in a letter to Horace Walpole that Mainauduc was getting as much as Mesmer out of animal magnetism and she put the amount at £100,000.[6]

As for his contribution to the theoretical development of the subject it was non-existent. Claiming that he had rejected Mesmer's theory of animal magnetism on the grounds that it had been superseded by that of Deslon, he seems to have preached a gospel more similar to Puységur's. Thus, he insisted on the need for the magnetizer to concentrate hard on the curative task, to possess a sincere intent to cure and a sincere desire to do good.[7] Whether in practice he was an effective therapist is unknown.

With regard to his protégés, the names of Parker, Yedal, Hollaway, Cue and Prescott are recorded as having begun magnetic practices in London and the provinces. Best known of the newly fledged magnetizers were Mr and Mrs de Loutherberg, who were active in the 1780s. We have an account in a pamphlet dedicated to the Archbishop of Canterbury by another of the Mainauduc trainees, a Mary Pratt. Miss Pratt, having attended sessions run by the Loutherbergs at their house in Hammersmith Terrace, felt compelled to inform the public at large of the miracles being wrought there. Described as recipients of 'divine manuductions', the

Loutherbergs were worthy in Miss Pratt's eyes of the assistance of the Archbishop, whom she asked to: 'join in praise and prayer to have this most glorious blessing continued, lest our candlestick be removed from us, which I most ardently pray the Lord Jehovah to avert.'[8]

Miss Pratt lists a remarkable variety of cures effected by the Loutherbergs: blindness, deafness, lameness, cancers, ruptures, palsies in every stage, and so on. Over the six months preceding the publication of her pamphlet they had apparently claimed 2000 cures. Unlike Mainauduc, the Loutherbergs seem to have made no charge for admission to their demonstrations and healings. The result was that they were besieged, on one occasion by as many as 3000 people trying to gain admission to their house. Tickets were issued to maintain some form of order, but were then sold at one or two guineas each. Miss Pratt urged the magistrates to help the Loutherbergs by having a house built for the reception of the sick, but by the time her pamphlet appeared in July 1789 the Loutherbergs had found the pressure of London life too much for them and had retired to the country. They do not appear to have practised magnetism again; Philippe de Loutherberg preferred the less stressful activity of sketching the countryside and published a charming collection of his work in 1805.[9]

It would be wrong to suppose that Mainauduc and his followers escaped criticism. Some, like George Winter, remained sceptics even after attending Mainauduc's lectures:

> Such is the credulity of mankind, that amazing numbers, myself included, were allured to practise this new science, and attempted to effect cures which could not be performed; attempts by silly ridiculous gestures in putting people to sleep, and other useless actions . . . were so extremely wanton and absurd as most justly to merit censure.[10]

Winter kept a register of his own patients and published a list of 100 cures obtained through orthodox medical practice after previous magnetic treatment had failed. The list includes tuberculosis, worms, and dropsy, none of which would seem likely to have a significant psychosomatic component and thus likely to be amenable to magnetic therapy.

Other critics, such as John Martin, a Baptist minister, were more vehement in their attacks. Animal magnetism, he said, was a fraud, devised with the sole objective of giving people 'something for their money'. Magnetizers themselves seemed to agree on nothing except 'to call whatever they please by a new name and of changing their terms as often as it may be found convenient.'[11] Martin's pamphlet concludes in verse, of which two stanzas will give the general impression:

> Spread your hands and dart your eyes,
> With your patient sympathise;
> Catch his pain and hold it fast,
> You can shake it off at last.

> Who for this would vow and pay?
> Who for tricks as these would play?
> Soon the vain and venal scheme
> Must appear a waking dream.

Nevertheless, these tracts and others by pro-magnetists apparently led to no great public interest. Then the discovery of a new therapeutic device completely supplanted animal magnetism in the public imagination.

E. Perkins, an American physician, had found that he could alleviate or cure a variety of disorders if a pair of 'tractors' were rubbed gently over the affected region of the body. These tractors consisted of two 4-inch long needles made of dissimilar metal, brass and iron, one coloured yellow and the other dark blue. Perkins had been granted a patent by the US government and towards the end of the eighteenth century began to advertise his tractors in England at a price of five guineas. Among those who vouched for their efficacy he could claim as signatories three professors, nineteen physicians and seventeen surgeons.[12]

The idea caught on rapidly, to the alarm of the medical profession in general. As John Haygarth, who was soon effectively to kill the vogue, had to admit: 'The tractors have attained such a high reputation at Bath, even among persons of rank and understanding, as to require the particular attention of physicians.'[13]

Haygarth was a physician with some notions as to scientific method, and he devised a series of experiments using imitation tractors made of wood which exactly resembled the real ones. The identity of the fake tractors was to be kept secret from the patient and from everyone else. Not, it would seem, however, from the person conducting the experiments, who was warned by Haygarth to test both types of tractor impartially, beginning always with the false tractors. His instructions to his colleagues conclude: 'The cases should be accurately stated, and the reports of the effects produced by the true and false tractors be fully given, in the words of the patient.'[14]

The experiments were conducted at several centres in London, Hull, Bath and Bristol. Haygarth also enlisted the co-operation of the Professor of Veterinary Science at Trinity College, Dublin, who agreed to test the tractors on a variety of sick animals.

Haygarth had obviously designed the experiment with the hypothesis in mind that people's expectations were instrumental in bringing about the cure. Thus, he presumably expected as many cures with the false as with the true tractors. As he put it: 'The nature of this popular illusion resembles, in a striking manner, that of Animal Magnetism.'[15]

And in both cases Haygarth suspected the importance of the patient's and doctor's imagination. In the experiments on sick animals he expected no examples of cure; such was the case, the report from Dublin concluding that 'these pieces of brass and iron were perfectly inert.'[16] When it came to the human experiments, the real tractors were no better than the fake. However, the fake occasionally did work, especially with rheumatism and gout, Haygarth likening their power to that of highly recommended new drugs which achieve great initial success.

Haygarth's findings received much publicity, even appearing in French translation, and they effectively killed the popularity of the tractors.[17] With the death of the tractors there came, however, no revival of animal magnetism in Britain, and the first two decades of the nineteenth century contain no scientific or literary work of note on the subject. Even the revival of interest in Europe at the close of the Napoleonic wars brought no corresponding wave of popularity in Britain, although it may have been responsible for the increased attention being paid to the subject in literary circles during the 1820s. Most of the interest on the part of writers and poets was theoretical, although Shelley, for one, became directly involved in the practice of animal magnetism.

Thomas Medwin, Shelley's biographer, tells us that at Shelley's request he induced a magnetic trance in the poet in order to cure the paroxysms to which Shelley was subject. Although the therapeutic effect seems to have been slight, Shelley proved to be an excellent somnambulist, composing verses in Italian whilst in a trance, a language in which he was otherwise never known to write poetry. Shelley's wife also successfully magnetized her husband but desisted when she found that he had resumed his old habit of sleep-walking. Shelley himself was extremely impressed by the procedure, believing that it supplied an additional argument for the immortality of the soul, as the mind and body were so clearly separated during the trance, 'the one being most active and the other an inert mass of matter.'[18] He was even moved to dedicate a poem, not apparently of great merit, to a lady magnetist. It begins:

> Sleep on! Sleep on! Forget thy pain;
> My hand is on thy brow,
> My spirit on thy brain;
> My pity on thy heart, poor friend;
> And from my fingers flow
> The powers of life . . .'[19]

It was not until 1829 with the arrival in London of Richard Chenevix, a well known chemist and mineralogist, that animal magnetism again became a subject for scientific debate. Chenevix, a long-time resident in Paris, had by his own confession been a confirmed sceptic until he had attended one of the Abbé Faria's séances.

> I went to laugh; I came away convinced . . . to suspect anything like a trick in the parties concerned was impossible. They were of the highest respectability and distinction, and some of them I had known for many years. The Magnetizer was, indeed, in the frivolous French metropolis, called a charlatan, which made me suppose he was not so . . . But from the hour above alluded to till the period of his death, I remained acquainted with the Abbé Faria, and never knew a man to whom the epithet impostor was less applicable.[20]

Chenevix was so impressed by Faria that he decided to devote his future to the practice of the Faria brand of magnetism, and, recognizing the lack of appreciation shown by French audiences, determined to seek out a more enlightened public.

His first experiments took place in Ireland, where between 23 May 1828 and 20 January 1829 he magnetized 164 people, 98 of whom, according to his own report, showed undeniable effects.[21] Before his departure from Ireland he taught many parents how to magnetize their children, believing that magnetism could be practised by all, and following Faria in denying any special power in the operator. Chenevix claimed some fifty converts in Ireland who had become practitioners, but interest seems to have rapidly faded in that country. In London, Chenevix made the acquaintance of Dr Whymper, the Surgeon-Major of the Coldstream Guards, who gave him permission to work at a military hospital and who acted as an impartial observer at some of the demonstrations. Chenevix was concerned to show that sensations experienced by a subject in the trance were illusory and were the results of the will of the magnetizer acting directly upon the nervous system of the subject. (Chenevix seems here to have departed from Faria's view that the will-power of the operator was irrelevant.) He told Whymper out of the subject's hearing that he would produce sensations of heat and cold in the subject's hand in a predetermined order by the communication of his unexpressed will. Six times he touched the hand with his silver pencil-case, and each time the subject reported the willed sensation. After that the subject occasionally became confused, a result which Chenevix attributed to fatigue of the sense organs, comparable to that seen in physiological experiments with taste, where substances easily distinguishable on the first few trials become confused if there is too much repetition of the experiment.

Similar experiments involved the 'willing' of subjects to become stuck in their chairs, wakening them from their trance without operating on them directly, and sending them to sleep through a closed door. The demonstrations were poorly controlled; for example, in wakening the subject without his knowledge, Chenevix went behind him and made transverse passes behind his head. This, he considered, effectively ruled out collusion between operator and subject and clearly implicated only the power of his will. The experiment through a closed door resembles those of Du Potet at the Hôtel Dieu, where, as we have seen, attitudes of expectation on the part of the onlookers must have played an important role in priming the subject that something was afoot.

Further demonstrations were arranged in May 1829 at St Thomas's Hospital, London, where a distinguished audience of observers assembled. Among them were Professor Michael Faraday, Sir Benjamin Brodie, then President of the Royal Society, Drs Marshall Hall, Prout and Holland, Lord Lansdowne, and Dr John Elliotson, a physician at the hospital. Their attitude in the main was one of interest tempered by scepticism. Brodie watched two sisters, diagnosed as epileptics, being magnetized, and concluded that although they did indeed sleep, their sleep could be explained on already known principles, such as the rocking which sends a child to sleep. Faraday thought that the subject merited 'a fair and candid enquiry', although what he had seen could have been well demonstrated by a gifted actor. Marshall Hall, an authority on the nervous system, considered the patients were impostors who were consciously suppressing reflex responses to stimulation. Elliotson alone seems to have been seriously impressed, although he refused to be entirely won over. He reported:

> The two girls appeared to fall fast asleep by the process; but though I watched them carefully, I might be deceived; and as they were well known to Mr Chenevix, and had been mesmerised before, I drew no inference.[22]

Elliotson now arranged for Chenevix to mesmerize some of Elliotson's own patients who had no knowledge of mesmerism. Results were varied, some went into trance, one had an hysterical fit, and one menstruated two days later for the first time in three months. Elliotson remained unconvinced until an 'ignorant Irish girl' showed paralysis of her arm after Chenevix had made a pass over it. Chenevix then removed the paralysis, and in response to Elliotson's requests, made in French, paralysed and released her various limbs. Elliotson thought deception was impossible (although it need not have been very difficult for the patient to guess what Chenevix was 'willing'), and he concluded that mesmerism was a reality and worthy of his future attention. Chenevix appeared satisfied that he had at least excited the curiosity of some scientists and turned the attention of at least one physician to the possibilities inherent in the mesmeric state. He returned to Paris, where he died suddenly the following year.

The spread of mesmerism to the United States was no more rapid than it had been to Britain. The Marquis de Lafayette made an early visit in 1784 and spoke publicly on the subject. His original plan to establish branches of the Society of Harmony there does not seem to have succeeded. Possibly Thomas Jefferson, who was the American representative in Versailles, counteracted Lafayette's influence when he sent home copies of anti-mesmeric writings.[23]

The best known of a later group of pioneers also came from France; Charles Poyen had as a medical student attended demonstrations by Du Potet in Paris. A visit to Haiti, where the youngest Puységur brother had been active, increased his interest in mesmerism, and when he settled in Providence, Rhode Island, he began lecturing and demonstrating. His discovery of an excellent somnambulist, Cynthia Gleason, marked the beginning of his fame as she accompanied him on highly successful lecture tours throughout the state.[24] Providence became the centre of an active group of mesmerists trained by Poyen. Among them was Thomas Hartshorn who translated Deleuze's practical manual into English which then served as the group's bible.[25] Poyen himself left Providence in 1840 and spent a few years in the West Indies before returning to Paris, where he died in 1844.

By this date many more had followed Poyen's lead in taking up the practice of mesmerism. Writing a decade later, Orestes Brownson, a noted spiritualist, recalled the period:

> Animal magnetism soon became the fashion, in the principal villages of the Eastern and Middle States. Old men and women, young men and maidens, boys and girls, of all classes and ages, were engaged in studying the mesmeric phenomena, and mesmerizing or being mesmerized.[26]

The orthodox views of Deleuze did not last long in the hands of these later mesmerists. La Roy Sunderland, for example, denied the existence of the magnetic fluid and insisted in a manner reminiscent of Faria that the subject was responsible for entering into the somnambulistic state, only then did the will of the operator become critical in implanting ideas in the subject's mind. According to Sunderland, the relationship between operator and subject became at its most developed stage one of complete dominance and submission, with the subject gaining access to extrasensory powers.

A discovery made jointly by J.B. Dods and J.S. Grimes led to a new technique for the induction of a trance state. They had found that a coin, or disc of copper or lead, could produce remarkable effects on a subject if it were held in the hand and stared at fixedly.

It was hypothesized that, although the effects were similar to those produced by mesmerism, they were instead due to an influence from the metal and were independent of any external operator. Various names were given to the practice: Grimes preferred 'etherology' and Dods 'electrical psychology', but it was 'electrobiology' that finally caught on.[27]

The theory behind electrobiology was still a fluidic one, the magnetic fluid having become an ill-defined 'electricity'. Nothing of any significance was achieved by such re-naming, although the technique and the diminution of the role of the operator bore strong resemblances to Braid's discoveries made at about the same time, and to which we shall refer in Chapter 11.

There then occurred an event in 1848 which altered the nature of American mesmerism. In March of that year, the Fox family of Hydesville in New York State were disturbed by apparently inexplicable rappings and other poltergeist phenomena. As it appeared possible to communicate by means of the rappings with a variety of deceased friends and relatives, the family soon achieved notoriety. Other people began to have similar experiences and a new religious movement spread like wildfire throughout the United States.

The seeds of spiritualism had already been sown by Andrew Jackson Davis, the 'Seer of Poughkeepsie', a town also located in New York State. Davis had been magnetized by J.S. Grimes and had become an adept somnambulist. In a similar manner to Puységur's 'physicians' he had set himself up as a travelling diagnostician and healer. But his clairvoyance went further than this, and he believed himself able to see into the past and future of the whole universe and to understand all sciences and philosophies. His dictated insights were put into book form, and under the title of *The Principles of Nature* achieved rapid success.[28] Vaguely Swedenborgian in tone (he had had visions of Swedenborg and of Galen), the book's insistence upon a future spirit life and the possibility of imminent revelation prepared the public for the Hydesville happenings.

Communications with the spirits were at first carried on by rappings and table-tilting. Some sensitives then began to claim that they could see the spirits who caused the rappings. Those able to enter the somnambulistic state were especially gifted in this respect as they could more readily hallucinate. Often they appeared to be taken over by the spirits themselves, and would talk and behave in ways foreign to their normal personalities.

The phenomena produced by somnambulists on these occasions were no more mysterious than they had ever been although they were now given a clearly supernatural explanation. The role of magnetists began to diminish in importance as somnambulists began to induce the trance state in themselves. What had been a magnetic trance became a mediumistic trance in which the medium became open to spiritual influence.

The interest was so great that by 1853 ten spiritualist periodicals had been established in the USA, and one estimate put the number of mediums there at not less than 30,000.[29] The wave of spiritualism reached England and then spread into continental Europe forcing magnetism into the background. The saving of European magnetism from complete subjugation by the powerful spiritualist movement was brought about by a re-recogniton of its possible medical role, either as a diagnostic or as a therapeutic tool. Before that could be achieved, magnetism had to suffer in England almost as controversial and stormy a passage as it had done in France.

9

Elliotson and the Okey Sisters

In England, Elliotson was unable immediately to pursue his enquiries into mesmerism on account of his involvement in a major project, the founding of a hospital in conjunction with London University where he had been appointed as Professor of Medicine in 1831.[1] University College Hospital, or the North London Hospital, as it was first called, opened in 1834 and Elliotson became Senior Physician and resigned his appointment at St Thomas's. During the years 1832–7 Elliotson devoted himself wholeheartedly to the development of the hospital and rapidly acquired a reputation as an outstanding teacher whose lectures were widely attended and frequently reported in the medical journals of the day. A contemporary writer in the *Medical Times* described Elliotson's lectures:

> They were telling things, full of learning, acuteness, careful discrimination, philosophic liberality and daring, and often wonderfully accurate decisiveness. Their interest was quite peculiar. The cases were carefully selected, each stage marked with the greatest nicety, and the principles, whatever they were, on which the patient was treated, recklessly bared to the world. In addition, there was a large dash of novelty, either in the treatment or in its explanation. Elliotson's motto was everlastingly, 'Onward!' If he did not look with hate, he did with distrust, on all that was old . . . With so much of art unexplored before him, and so little of life for the task, his genius strove to reach the goal in leaps, and sought distinction in medicine like a youthful Napoleon in war.[2]

Elliotson was small in stature, barely five feet tall, yet: 'vigorous, unconventional, self-willed and impetuous, with the hand, and something of the disposition, of a pugilist.'[3] With personality characteristics such as these, it was perhaps inevitable that he should have reacted in the way he did to the extraordinary events of the next few years.

Elliotson's main theoretical interest was in physiology, especially in the physiology of the nervous system, which was beginning to yield data under the experimental attack of pioneers such as Magendie. In 1817 Elliotson had translated from the Latin J.F. Blumenbach's *Institutions of Physiology*. Over the next twenty years he extensively revised and added to it, while relegating Blumenbach's contributions to footnotes, until he was justified by the fifth edition in claiming it as his own work. As Elliotson's *Human Physiology* (1840), it became a standard text for medical students. By this time the book included a long section on the truth of mesmerism and its use in medical practice; thus few members of the profession could have remained in ignorance of the mesmeric controversies and of Elliotson's part in them.

It was his physiological interest that led him to found and to become in 1824 the first President of the Phrenological Society of London, an organization less heterodox at the time than it might now appear. If the configuration of the skull did reflect the relative development of areas of the cerebral cortex and if the 'bumps' on the head were related to different psychological 'faculties', then it was obviously the duty of the physiologist to learn more of this approach to an understanding of the functions of the different areas of the brain. Elliotson was thus an earnest advocate of phrenology, impatient with the more cautious of his colleagues.[4]

However strong the interest in physiology, it was subservient to his true physician's desire to cure. It was reported of him that he used to say, 'We know quite enough of physiology and pathology, but we are profoundly ignorant of curative treatment.'[5] Thus, his main research efforts were directed towards therapeutic ends, and he made a number of important contributions to medical knowledge. These included the discovery of pollen as the cause of hay fever, the use of iodine treatment in goitre, and the recognition of the value of prussic acid and quinine. He was also the first in England to adopt the use of a stethoscope. This instrument had been invented by Laënnec in 1819 and was looked upon with some suspicion by the more orthodox English physicians. 'It is just the thing for Elliotson to rave about,' said one of his colleagues, while another remarked that Elliotson would learn nothing from that hocus pocus, and even if he did, he would not be able to treat disease any better.[6]

His innovative approach to medicine certainly seems to have been appreciated by his patients, and he built up a very large and lucrative private practice. He acknowledged himself that his income had increased in one year from £3500 to £35,000 largely through the fame he had achieved from the publication of his clinical lectures in the *Lancet*.[7] Elliotson's unconventionality was reflected in his dress: he discarded the knee breeches and silk stockings still considered *de rigueur* for the physician and walked out resplendent in trousers.

Occupying this considerable position in the medical world, always eager for new discovery and in no way conciliatory towards established opinion, Elliotson seized the opportunity to discover more about mesmerism on the occasion of the Baron Du Potet's visit to London.

Du Potet had arrived in London on 5 June 1837. It had been a bold decision on his part, as he spoke no English, knew nobody, and did not even have a letter of introduction.[8] Not a man to let grass grow under his feet, he had by 20 June produced a prospectus in English for a course of lectures, which he was never in a position to give as nobody attended the first one – perhaps a lucky escape for Du Potet, whose English could hardly have been sufficient after a fortnight's residence. In despair, he advertised free treatment, as he had done at first in Montpellier, but the Londoners were more cautious than the citizens of Montpellier and again he failed to attract any attention. At last he met some physicians from the Middlesex hospital and was invited to give demonstrations there. Hearing of these, Elliotson in turn arranged further demonstrations at University College Hospital.[9]

Du Potet's demonstrations involved patients, students, and non-medical witnesses. The usual variety of responses occurred in reaction to Du Potet's manipulations; some reported no effect at all; the majority, which included Elliotson who had volunteered to act as a subject, reported various tingling, heaviness in the limbs and drowsiness; while a minority went into deep trances and became insensible to sensory stimulation. One epileptic patient fell into a deep coma and was pinched, pricked, and had snuff forced up her nostrils to no avail, until with two or three transverse passes Du Potet awakened her.

Even on these early trials, differences in opinion about their significance were evident. A letter in the *Lancet* from an anonymous 'Eye Witness' stated:

> On the whole, M. Du Potet, leaving entirely out of the question his shiftings from one point to another, and his invariable discovery of exceptions to the rules he lays down, together with the avoidance of direct questions, has adduced nothing as yet in the hospital to prove that animal magnetism is not a fallacy or anything more than a means of producing a peculiar state in very peculiar habits, which state resembles the coma following epilepsy, or the insensibility attendant on hysteria.[10]

Remarkable enough, one would have thought! Elliotson certainly thought so; according to him the phenomena were: 'too striking and invariable for any rational person to disbelieve that some peculiar power had been in operation.' Furthermore, to ascribe the phenomena 'to emotion and fancy, to suppose collusion and deception, would be absurd'.[11]

Elliotson had had an advantage over 'Eyewitness' in observing the many demonstrations which continued throughout the early summer of 1837. He became convinced that the phenomena must be the result of a physical force, which, although strange and as yet unknown, had effects which could be examined systematically. Whatever ideas Elliotson might have picked up from Chenevix's earlier demonstrations it was the orthodox fluidic theory held so adamantly by Du Potet which Elliotson now adopted and which he was so ardently to defend until the end of his life.

However, Du Potet's association with University College Hospital was soon to be terminated. While Elliotson was away on his annual continental holiday, Du Potet began unwisely to invite prospective patients to the hospital in order to treat them himself. The Hospital Medical Committee promptly intervened to prevent him doing so, a decision of which Elliotson approved when he returned. Du Potet had to resort to private demonstrations at the house he had rented not far away in Orchard Street, where many people paid half a crown to witness him at work. Nevertheless, he got into financial difficulties and approached Elliotson, among others, for a loan. Elliotson refused, and Du Potet was finally forced to return to Paris in 1838, where he contented himself with writing an abusive account of his experiences in England.[12]

Before Du Potet's difficulties with the Hospital he had been remarkably successful in inducing trance in a 16-year-old girl, Elizabeth Okey, who was to play a crucial role in Elliotson's professional career.[13] Elizabeth, an undersized domestic servant, had been admitted to hospital in April 1837 after suffering for some time from 'hystero-epileptic' seizures. According to Elliotson, Elizabeth had complained on admission of an almost constant headache, shooting pains, and feelings of coldness and numbness. Her seizures occurred at least weekly, and were severe with loss of consciousness. At first she had been treated in the conventional manner with doses of silver nitrate and copper, and with bleeding, but no change occurred in her condition.[14]

She had been mesmerized by Du Potet for the first time on 28 June, after which she had reported that her headache had improved. Elliotson had then ordered that all medicine be discontinued. From this time onwards she was mesmerized almost daily, often by Du Potet or Elliotson, but also during Elliotson's absence by William Wood, his young clinical clerk. The epileptic seizures ceased; instead, Elizabeth fell into fits of what Elliotson termed 'ecstatic delirium':

> . . . perfectly insensible, though with her eyes open, chattering, mimicking, relating stories, etc. This state could be put an end to by mesmerizing her . . . While sitting before the magnetist looking attentively at him, and saying all sorts of ridiculous, and witty, spiteful things, pale, with the countenance of a maniac, she suddenly seemed lost, her eyes rapidly closed for a moment, then opened, she looked astonished, and was in her perfect senses, smiling amiably, behaving in the most proper manner, in short, in full possession of her intellect and feelings.[15]

It would seem that these 'ecstasies' were spontaneous somnambulistic trances, which were terminated by the operator bringing her back to the waking state. It soon became possible also to induce somnambulism through mesmeric passes, and Elizabeth became more and more expert at slipping from one state of consciousness to another. By the November of 1837 Elliotson had merely to sit on her bed or extend his hand in her direction for her to flip into the mesmeric state. Even hand movements behind her head or reflected in a mirror were effective. She soon became Elliotson's favourite subject not only on account of her extreme susceptibility but also, as we shall see, because she provided a considerable spectacle when in a somnambulistic trance.

Elizabeth's younger sister, Jane, had also been a patient at the hospital from 14 February until 6 June 1837. She suffered from similar fits to her sister and it is perhaps not surprising that her discharge did not mark any permanent cure. She had to be re-admitted on 27 February 1838, by which time her sister was the *prima donna* of the women's ward. Elliotson found Jane to be extraordinarily susceptible to mesmerism, perhaps even more so than her sister. He is at pains to deny that she imitated her sister, although in such a pair of hysterical girls it would seem very likely. Certainly, she had only once visited her sister and seen her mesmerized. Elliotson reports:

> The delirium resembles in many particulars that of her sister . . . During its continuance she is perfectly insensible when any person touches or pinches her. She is conscious, however, of sound . . . if asked if she had any pain in her head, she replied that she had no head, that it is, 'what's, none, when.' She had also a remarkable predilection for the word 'little', applying it to all objects and on every occasion.[16]

Entries in the casebook mention her states of extreme agitation, excitement, violence, etc. Soon after her admission Elliotson began to experiment with both sisters to test if the magnetic influence when directed at one sister could be transmitted to the other. He discovered that when the sisters held hands, the symptoms and behavioural idiosyncrasies of one would pass, generally in a weaker form, to the other. If the operator directed his actions towards a limb of one sister, the resulting movement would be echoed in the same limb of the other girl. When one sister was aroused, the other would wake spontaneously. A difference between the sisters lay in their response to magnetism: Jane's general health improved sufficiently for her to be discharged on 31 July 1838, while Elizabeth stayed on.

It is unclear why Jane responded better to treatment. One possibility is that she had never been as ill as Elizabeth and that her illness had a stronger hysterical component. Another possibility is that Elizabeth was in fact well enough to be discharged at the same time as her sister but was kept on in the hospital to satisfy Elliotson's experimental needs. This view was implicit in the order made by the Hospital Medical Committee at the end of the year that Elizabeth should be discharged, on the grounds that no patient should be allowed to remain in hospital for a period longer than two months without the permission of the Committee.

Before dealing with these events which were directly responsible for Elliotson's resignation, it is important to emphasize that however gullible he may appear to have been from the vantage point of today, he had not achieved his position of eminence in the medical profession without critical acumen and great skill. The very detailed account of patients and their responses, or lack of them, to a variety of drugs and procedures, which are to be found in Elliotson's case registers, supply direct evidence of these qualities. Mesmerism was used as one of several possible therapeutic remedies, most frequently with female patients suffering from fits. Elliotson seems to have been quite willing to accept the fact that some illnesses in some patients did not respond to mesmeric treatment, and he was also aware that the mesmeric trance could be feigned, as the following extracts from one register may show:

> *June 23rd.* Frances Tavistock, aged 15 (chorea). The mesmerism has been tried nearly every day without any evident result. She is better and able to go out. The improvement may or may not have arisen from the mesmerism.
>
> *July 1st.* Brittania Mesnard, aged 17 (epilepsia). Has been mesmerized daily. No visible effect produced.
>
> *July 1st.* Harriet Hancock, aged 17 (epilepsia). She appeared to go to sleep – is easily aroused however, and in all probability merely imitates the girls by whose side she is placed during the process as it has been unsuccessful when tried upon her alone. She is evidently too stupid to wish to deceive.[17]

However, with the Okey sisters Elliotson seems to have had a blind spot; they were firmly established as the Professor's protégées and they guarded their position jealously. Elizabeth on one occasion took a dislike to a young patient, Charlotte Bentley, who appeared to be a good mesmeric subject. Any challenge to Elizabeth's supremacy on that score was soon settled when Elizabeth in her somnambulistic state charged Charlotte with being an impostor and made her drink mesmerized and unmesmerized water in turn. Both drinks produced trance states; the poor girl not having been told that they differed. Thus, she was 'exposed' and discharged.[18] It is ironic to note that a very similar technique was to lead to Elizabeth's discomfiture in the near future.

In the early summer of 1838 Elliotson's demonstrations of the Okey sisters could no longer be accommodated in the wards. Demand to attend these demonstrations had increased enormously, with Elliotson receiving petitions from numbers of eminent people. According to the case register, as early as 4 January 1838, Charles Dickens and his illustrator, George Cruikshank, attended at the bedside of Elizabeth Okey.[19] But in May Elliotson decided that the public theatre of the hospital would be a more suitable venue for the 200 people who wished to attend. The first meeting was held on Thursday, 10 May, and besides Dickens and Cruikshank the audience included various members of the aristocracy, as well as several Members of Parliament, Fellows of the Royal Society, physicians, and literary men. This and subsequent demonstrations and experiments through June and July were reported faithfully in the *Lancet* in a series of articles.[20]

To give the flavour of these very long séances I shall quote from accounts of the first and second public meetings. Elliotson began the first meeting with an opening address in which he referred to the difficulties he was already experiencing with the hospital authorities, who had asked him to conduct his demonstrations in private lodgings or an hotel, as they believed them to be detrimental to the status of the hospital. But he understood that the institution:

. . . was established for the promulgation of truth, and the promotion of education founded on facts, and if the views which he taught were correct, then it was the duty of the other professors also to adopt them, whether the 'institution' was supposed to suffer or not from so doing. For the hospital was not founded in order to fill the pockets of the professors, but to throw light on truth and nature, and to expose fallacies. The question, then, to be decided was this, 'Is animal magnetism based on facts or fallacies?'

Elliotson now turned his attention to the first subject of his demonstration, Elizabeth, who had been brought by Wood from the wards and who had remained impassive throughout Elliotson's address. George Mills, the reporter from the *Lancet*, was amazed at the rapidity with which Elliotson induced trance, Elizabeth's expression changing from one of dullness to one of mingled archness and simplicity. So marked and rapid was the change, that:

> The question of deception was at once met by a conviction, derived from appearances, that the most accomplished actor that ever trod the stage could not have presented the change with a truer show of reality.

Catching sight of the Marquis of Anglesey who was sitting in the front row, she said: 'Oh, how do ye do, white trowsers. Dear! You do look so tidy, you do. What nice things. You *are* a nice man.'

Turning to Sir Charles Paget she asked him why he was wearing his hat, and then took hold of his hand. Elliotson was standing behind her, and now, apparently unseen by the girl, made a downward pass with his hand, whereupon she fell backwards into his arms and was lowered to the ground. She recovered spontaneously in half a minute and again approached the audience and diverted them with her remarks. Her interaction with the audience was child-like and spontaneous, as she commented on their looks and their clothes, borrowed their sticks and opera glasses, held hands and even sat on their laps when she wanted to avoid another of Elliotson's experiments.

Mills points out that her recognition of objects now appeared to become faulty. She referred to the buttons on Elliotson's coat as 'beauty oysters'. When Elliotson placed a board under her chin to prevent her from seeing anything that occurred below, she called it a 'dirty beast' and asked it, 'Does your mother know you're out?' But, from the context, these and other examples appear to be part of her general childish behaviour rather than misperceptions of real objects.

Elliotson now demonstrated catalepsy, with Elizabeth maintaining a rigid and awkward pose with all four limbs extended for some minutes until he blew in her face. He then moved on to what he termed one of his most important mesmeric discoveries, the effect of 'mass' or 'surface' in inducing trance. He began by making a mesmeric pass using one finger only. Mills reports that the subject instantly 'evinced temporary "stupidity" and then awoke herself'. When two fingers were used, the "stupidity" was more marked and of longer duration. With three fingers, deep trance occurred.

Elizabeth frequently imitated Elliotson's movements even when these were made behind her back. When Elliotson silently opened and closed his mouth, Elizabeth did the same. She seemed compelled to make the same response in unison with his hands when he clapped them in front of her. She then spoke to him saying: 'Poor Dr Ellisson, would you like some sop, with some milk in it? You've got some beauty oysters there . . . Oh! Dr Ellison, you poor thing, an't you? How do you? Aye?'

She continued talking nonsense, speaking to her fingers as if they were people: 'Come, talk to me. Why don't you talk? Speak, I say. You're not good for that. Would you like to be happy, my dears? Oh, pray tell me, do.'

Upon Elliotson asking her to make bows with her fingers in front of her face, Elizabeth succeeded in mesmerizing herself into a deep trance, a feat greeted by murmurs of 'marvellous' from the audience. She now whistled and sang psalms and snatches, and then volunteered to 'wheel about and turn about', but was prevented, to 'the manifest disappointment of the spectators'.

Eventually another child patient was brought in and placed on a stool in front of Elizabeth. The child attempted to mesmerize Elizabeth and succeeded in doing so in 45 passes of her hands. Elizabeth came out of the trance of her own accord. Next, Elliotson placed his hand on the shoulder of the child, who again began to make mesmeric passes. Again Elizabeth fell asleep, but after only 21 passes. Members of the audience were now called up to lay their hands on the child mesmerist, and upon each individual hand being laid on, the time lapse between the onset of the passes and the induction of Elizabeth's trance decreased. This phenomenon was termed the 'effect of numbers' by Elliotson.

Jane Okey was now brought in, two hours after the beginning of the demonstrations. She appeared to Mills to shrink away in terror from Elliotson's gaze, which he had only to fix sternly upon her for her to fall into a trance. Mills was unable to observe clearly the experiments with Jane as the crowd was now so dense, and after another half hour Elliotson decided to bring the session to a close. Unfortunately, it proved impossible to awaken Elizabeth – who was obviously enjoying herself! Eventually he had to ask her to predict when she would awaken.

Elizabeth said it would occur in five minutes if her neck were rubbed, a prophesy which was accurately fulfilled after Elliotson and then Wood had complied.

The public's reaction to the proceedings was one of astonishment and admiration, much of it directed to the brave little housemaid. Mills tells us:

> On proceeding to leave, as the throng of persons opened to let her pass, many gentlemen, won by her apparent amiability, shook hands with her, which compliment she engagingly acknowledged by a slight curtesy, seemingly greatly wearied, depressed, and much abashed at her situation.

In his concluding address to the assembly Elliotson gave it as his opinion that:

> In the circumstances respecting the influences of 'mass', 'surface', and 'numbers', in magnetism, he recognized the existence of a law which permitted him to believe that this 'science' would, at some future day, be reducible to certain fixed principles.

The second meeting in the public theatre took place on 2 June and was so crowded that the Bishop of Norwich was forced to stand during the three-hour demonstrations, while Thomas Moore, the poet, had to crouch on a small shelf from which he descended covered with whitewash. Firstly, two young male patients were shown, one of whom was impervious to mesmerism, and then two girls, apparently cured of 'hysterical lock-jaw' and of epilepsy by magnetic treatment. As in all the cases treated by Elliotson, the therapy had consisted merely of 'doses' of magnetism repeated several times a day. Both of these girls were very susceptible and entered a sleep-like state immediately when passes were made. Elliotson was at pains to point out that such a response was not necessary in curing mental diseases of these kinds, the mere application of mesmeric passes having a salutary effect. The demonstration thus far had been rather dull, and the audience must have been impatiently waiting for the entrance of the Okeys.

Elliotson introduced their cases. Elizabeth, he claimed, exhibited four distinct states of mind and body: her normal state, when she was reserved and quiet, and perfectly rational; a delirious state in which she was vivacious, talkative and familiar, a condition exhibited in response to mesmeric passes, and maintained, as we saw, during most of the first public demonstration; a third state could be induced by passing a finger before her face when she was in the delirious state, when she was immediately fixed in position for about half a minute, until spontaneously returning to the delirious state, invariably saying, 'Ah! how do ye?' If this mesmeric pass was continued downwards, the stupor lasted longer; while if the passes were repeated, she went into a deeper comatose-like state from which she had to be aroused by rubbing her eyebrows or blowing into her eyes.

Jane likewise manifested these four states and was so constantly in the delirious state that spectators thought it her natural condition. When she returned from the third stuporous state into delirium, she also had her pet phrase, 'Oh, God bless at my soul!'

While Elliotson was talking, Wood brought the two girls in and began magnetizing Elizabeth. The lack of care in preventing hints and suggestions being given to the girls as to how they were expected to behave is very evident on this occasion. During this period, when the whole explanatory emphasis was placed on the magnetic fluid, the idea of any implicit agreement between operator and subject would not have been entertained, although fraud was a very obvious alternative. Thus the early magnetists, and Elliotson can here be seen to be no exception, would discuss in front of their subjects the very behaviour they would later elicit.

Elizabeth, now in a trance, began her usual nonsensical chat to the audience. 'Oh, don't sit that way!' she said to some gentlemen sitting on the floor. 'Your name isn't Norval if you sit in that poor place.' Looking up at the crowd, she said, 'Oh, what a many white ones. Why, where the devil did you all come from?'

Then she began to skip and sing:

> I went into a tailor's shop,
> To buy a suit of clothes,
> But where the money came from,
> God Almighty knows.

Much laughter followed and Elizabeth became too excited for Elliotson to conduct any experiments, a situation he remedied by telling the audience that he 'must stupefy her', an action accomplished by the usual pass with one finger before her face.

She was now asked to try to lift a weight of 84 lb but appeared to find this impossible, both in the normal and somnambulistic states. Her arm was then bandaged to a splint from palm to elbow to prevent injury to her wrist, a procedure of which she seemed to be insensible as it occurred while she was in a trance and she was busy whistling and singing. Catching sight of her arm she said, 'Oh look here! What the devil's that?' Elliotson said she mustn't use such words as they would frighten the hospital chaplain, Mr Stebbing. Elizabeth replied, 'I don't care for Mr Stebbing, nor the devil neither, my dear. I only care for Mr Wood and Dr Elliotson.'

The weight was reduced to 70 lb after she reported that 'the Negro' – a spirit whom she consulted on various occasions – had said that she could manage as much as 80 lb but that it would hurt her ribs. Wood now held his hand above her splinted arm while she grasped the weight. He then made drawing movements upwards as though to help her and she succeeded in clumsily lifting the weight three or four inches from the floor. Restored to her waking state after this unsatisfactory demonstration, which was intended to show increased strength when 'drawn' by the magnetizer, she had no memory of the event.

Her sister Jane had been taken out of the theatre some time earlier and was now brought back in. She embraced her sister joyfully, but Elizabeth in her waking state disapproved of such a show of affection in front of strangers and pushed her away. Elliotson now put Elizabeth into a trance and placed Jane's hand in hers, whereupon Jane fell asleep also, 'so highly sensitive was she of the magnetic influence,' as Elliotson explained it.

A few similar demonstrations concluded the meeting and most of the audience left. Elliotson now engaged Elizabeth in conversation, of which the following is a sample reported in the *Lancet*:

> 'Have you done any naughty things to-day?'
> 'I'm solly to say I'm always doing naughty things.'
> 'Then you're a great sinner?'
> 'No, that's *tic douloureux*. [A patient in the next bed.] She's the
> sinner. She says so all day. Dr Elliotson goes and feels her puzzle

[pulse] every day, but I think he'll soon catch her sins, and be as wicked too, and then he'll be a gard [blackguard] in the streets. Oh, pray don't look at me so fierce. I can't bear it. It do so disfigure you. I won't stay if you do. There, now you don't look slavage [savage].'

And in delight at the change of countenance she threw her arms round the Doctor's neck. She constantly mispronounced words: whiskers she called *wickspers*, and waistcoat, *wickscoat*; teeth, *tiffs*; appetite, *acketite*.

Mills claimed that in her ordinary waking state she never mispronounced words. The mispronunciations and silly talk seem to indicate a regression to behaviour typical of a younger age. The consistency of her actions when mesmerized might suggest the appearance of another 'personality', and Elliotson did refer to the case as one of double consciousness in which there was no transfer of knowledge from one state to the other; they were psychologically quite distinct.

The language used by the Okey sisters had a stronger impact than might easily be imagined today. Their mild swearing, 'blast', 'damn', 'devil', etc., was regarded as particularly heinous in front of clergymen, and the *Lancet* took care not to spell the words out. Even some of Elliotson's students were later to draw attention to the girls' language as deserving of censure.

It can be seen that many of these demonstrations were puerile. Far from having scientific or medical value, their main interest was in the histrionic abilities of the Okey sisters and in the expectation that they might do something unexpected and shocking. In particular, their overfamiliar attitude with the gentlemen of high social rank was a source of great amusement. It was also according to Mills, convincing evidence that the girls really were mesmerized to see them unconcernedly curl up on the lap of a stranger, only to be overcome with embarrassment if they were suddenly to regain normal consciousness while still in that position.

The later experiments, reported in the third to seventh *Lancet* articles, did not take place in the public theatre, owing to pressure from the College authorities, and were of a less sensational kind. In them, for example, Elliotson tried to discover some laws for the time of occurrence and duration of a trance.

It seemed to Elliotson that mucous membrane was more sensitive to the magnetic influence than normal skin. Thus, experiments were run timing the onset and duration of the trance when the operator's finger was placed near the lips, near the open lips, near the everted underlip, when the lip was touched, when it was touched hard, when both lips were touched, and when both were touched hard. Sleep occurred more rapidly and for a longer period as more contact was made, a result Elizabeth presumably produced to confirm Elliotson's predictions made to the observers in front of the girl. A second series of experiments on the same day investigated the effect of the position of the eyes; another series involved passes behind the back with the neck covered and with the neck exposed. In all, Elizabeth seems to have been put into a trance at least sixty times during this session.

Another session was devoted to the effect of magnetized water and was chiefly remarkable for the efforts made by Elliotson and the other experimenters (with Elizabeth's help) to rationalize the confusing results. In one experiment the third and fifth glass of a series of six glasses of water had been magnetized by dipping the magnetist's fingers into them. Elizabeth went into a trance after sipping the contents of the second, third and fifth. Put into a trance at the conclusion of this experiment she was asked why she had responded in a similar manner to the second and third glasses. Her reply, that she still had the water from the second in her mouth when she drank from the third, satisfied all the experimenters, although Mills ruefully comments that the need to take these experiments slowly was often forgotten in an anxiety to obtain results. However, it is obvious that Elizabeth's answer was satisfactory only on the supposition that it was the second glass that was mesmerized; Mills and the others appeared to forget that her response to this glass was to ordinary unmagnetized water.

On another occasion when she went into a trance upon drinking unmagnetized water, the result was explained by her as due to the magnetizing of the glass by the hand of the experimenter who handed her the water, an explanation seized upon by the experimenters. Elliotson's reluctance to adopt a really critical attitude to the Okeys' behaviour was to be the root cause of his subsequent embarrassment at the hands of his critics. It seems, though, that he was not alone in his beliefs; a group of members belonging to the Royal Society were present at some of the Okey demonstrations and were unequivocally in favour of the view that their somnambulism was genuine. This group of experimenters could see the girls' trance behaviour and could attribute it only to the magnetic fluid. They therefore went to extraordinary lengths to sustain this explanatory principle when the girls 'made a mistake' and went into trance at the wrong time. Elliotson must have been carried along by group pressure and by the affection he seems to have had for the Okey girls, an affection which was obviously reciprocated.

Experiments with various chemical substances were conducted with similarly uncertain results, but to metals the Okeys seemed to react in a more consistent manner. Elliotson's purpose in running these experiments was to discover more about the nature of the magnetic fluid through a study of the substances which appeared best to conduct it. Thus, magnetized gold, silver, platinum and water were found to transmit it, whilst copper, tin, zinc, and lead were non-conductors. Of the conducting substances, gold and nickel were found to be the best, but they differed between themselves in that mesmerized nickel produced a violent and even dangerous trance state. Gold was a reliable producer of cramps and general trance, the strength of the effect being found to depend on the strength of the 'dose' of magnetism previously imparted to the metal by the operator's hand. If a mesmerized sovereign was placed on the floor, the Okeys would suddenly become cataleptic as their hands approached the coin, and they would remain fixed in a stooping position until released by the operator.

By 7 July 1838 one senses that a defensive tone was creeping into Mills' accounts:

> It ought to be demanded of sceptical observers, either that they acknowledge that the *sleep* is real, or demonstrate that it is affected, or point out reasons for believing that an imposition is practised; for, of course, if the somnambulism be deceptive, everything that is performed during that state is a deception also.[21]

In his next report, Mills claims that the phenomena 'are singularly impressive as illustrations of insanity, producible at will, by any operator, lasting almost at his pleasure and developing rare forms and peculiarities of mental alienation.'

But if feigned, 'they are equally remarkable as instances of perfection in acting and deception which defy the most vigilant scrutiny to detect proofs of the imposition.'[22]

And on 21 July he writes:

> To continue these reports without distinctly avowing either an entire
> credence or a total disbelief in the somnambulism and other phe-
> nomena . . . might seem to be uncandid and disrespectful, without
> considering two exculpatory circumstances. Firstly, that to declare
> the latter . . . would amount to a confession of time and labour
> wastefully employed in indefensible intrusions on the attention of
> scientific men, . . . secondly, a declaration in the affirmative would
> express a single opinion, wanting authority, and therefore properly
> withheld.[23]

Nevertheless, Mills now felt obliged to assure his readers that he was
completely convinced that no fraud was being practised by the Okey
sisters, and that those critics who impugned the girls' honesty were
lacking the moral courage necessary to accept Elliotson's startling
discoveries.

However, in spite of their reporter's conviction, the editorial policy
of the *Lancet* now began to change, and articles openly critical of
mesmerism began to appear. Shortly after Elliotson's work with metals
and liquids was published in August 1838, a letter from a surgeon, John
Leeson, described a more likely means by which the Okeys might be
sensitized to magnetized objects. Leeson had attended a demonstration
on 27 July in which he had noticed that Elliotson had magnetized water
by placing his finger in it. It was possible, he thought, that the subject had
responded to the slight change in temperature rather than to any magnetic
quality in the water. Similarly, when eight sovereigns were placed on a
stone mantel shelf, some of them, unknown to the subject, having been
magnetized beforehand, it might have been the warmth of the relevant
coins that enabled the subject to 'go into a trance' only when she picked
them up, while the unmagnetized, and therefore cooler, coins produced
no effect.

Leeson ran the experiment in his own house on a number of occasions
and obtained results exactly in line with his suppositions. He concluded
his letter, that, if temperature were the crucial variable, then: 'all
those experiments, hitherto so much talked of, must go for nothing,
leaving only for reflection the most extraordinary cunning and ability
of Okey.'[24]

In the same issue of the *Lancet*, there appeared an article on the exposure of the pretensions of animal magnetists in France. The editor, Thomas Wakley, was beginning to reconsider his attitude.

Wakley was the founder and first editor of the *Lancet*.[25] Since it had first appeared in 1823, with William Cobbett as one of its supporters, the journal had been remarkable for its exposure of pretensions, and its witty and often scurrilous attacks on rival publications. Particular targets for attack were the *London Medical and Physical Journal*, termed by Wakley 'the Yellow Fungus' on account of its yellow cover, and the *Medico-Chirurgical Review* edited by James Johnson, the former physician to William IV. The 'Post-Office M.D.' was Wakley's nickname for Johnson, referring to the fact that he had obtained his medical degree from a Scottish university without taking an examination. In the first ten years of the *Lancet*'s existence, Wakley was involved in no less than ten libel actions. These were mainly with these and other editors, although he also succeeded in offending many leading members of the medical profession by having reporters record their lectures for publication in the *Lancet*, a service much appreciated by students who could buy the periodical for 6d., but one less congenial to the lecturers who received a £35 fee from each student for a session's lectures.

A leading surgeon, John Abernethy from St Bartholomew's Hospital, took legal action to prevent the *Lancet* publishing his lectures. He even tried putting out the lamps in the lecture theatre to prevent the shorthand reporter making a copy! But Wakley won the battle, and saw the circulation figures for the *Lancet* reach 4500 copies a week.

Wakley's campaigning zeal and hatred of what he considered quackery had led him to seek public office and he had become a radical Member of Parliament in 1835. He made his political reputation with an inspired speech championing the cause of the Tolpuddle martyrs, and he was largely responsible for their later pardon. He used the House to attack homeopathic medicine, whose practitioners he termed 'an audacious set of quacks'. He acted as a coroner and attended as many as thirty inquests a week. Dickens, a member of the jury on one occasion, found him 'nobly patient and humane', but others accused him of acting more as an advocate than a judge. This tall portly man with a rolling gait and hearty manner was incredibly energetic, aggressive and prejudiced. He was also a friend of Elliotson's, who had never objected to his own lectures being made available to a wide public, and who, as we have seen, owed much of his success and popularity to Wakley's policy. He was now, some ten years later, to find that same journal doing its best to effect his ruin.

Wakley's regard for Elliotson was not to deter him from sniffing out any quackery involved in mesmerism, and when Mills enthusiastically proposed that Wakley should personally witness a test of the Okey girls, Wakley arranged for the parties to meet at his house in Bedford Square. Two meetings took place in the early August of 1838, but were discounted by Wakley as inadequate tests owing to the fact that the demonstrations were all conducted by Elliotson. A third test was arranged by Elliotson for 16 August, but Wakley had inadequate notice and was unable to invite anyone apart from George Mills to witness the experiments. Elliotson however brought Du Potet, Dr Richardson, Mr Herring, and Mr Clarke, who was also a *Lancet* reporter. Wakley appeared satisfied, and took over the role of experimenter for the session.

It was to be a long day: the experiments began at 9 a.m. and were not discontinued until 10 p.m. The first experiments were designed to discover the effects of magnetized nickel on Elizabeth Okey. She sat, with a pasteboard screen held under her chin, opposite and close to Wakley who applied the discs of metal to her hands. He began by applying the lead disc alternately to each hand. No effect was produced. Elliotson now held the nickel disc to 'charge' it with the mesmeric fluid; Wakley had taken the precaution of holding the lead disc in order to warm it with his hand until it was of the same temperature as the nickel. Wakley then applied the nickel, but no effect was produced. Twice more the lead was tried, but Elizabeth showed no change in her behaviour. Then, some minutes after the original application of the nickel, the expected result occurred, with Elizabeth falling back in her chair with rigid limbs, flushed face, and arched back, a position she maintained for a quarter of an hour.

These results were obviously not clear-cut, and Elliotson proposed that trials should be run using mesmerized nickel alone. Wakley, however, decided on a stratagem and consulted with Clarke, who, unseen by the others, pocketed the nickel disc and went about 18 feet away to stand by the window. Wakley then applied the lead disc to Elizabeth's hand, while Herring, who was also a party to the trick whispered to Wakley, loudly enough for Elizabeth to hear, 'Take care, don't apply the nickel too strongly.'

Scarcely had these words escaped from his lips, when the face of the girl again became violently red; her eyes were fixed with an intense squint, she fell back in the chair, a more evident distortion of the body ensued than in the previous paroxysm, the contractions of the voluntary muscles were more strongly marked, producing a striking rigidity of the frame and limbs, and the shoulders were thrown back to the utmost, the spine displaying as complete a bow as in an attack of opisthotonos. In a word, the severity of all the symptoms appeared to have undergone marked increase. Dr Elliotson again observed that 'no metal other than nickel had ever produced these effects; that they were most extraordinary'; in fact, that 'they presented a beautiful series of phenomena.'[26]

The experimenters now went into an adjoining room where Wakley disclosed the trick, to Elliotson's discomfiture. Experiments were resumed with everyone except the Okeys knowing what was happening. Three times more Elizabeth went into a paroxysm to the lead. Wakley then tried nickel, to which she failed to react. Elliotson was quite frank in his admission that he could not explain these results, although he believed that an explanation would be found.

Further trials with similar procedures were made on a second day before more witnesses invited by Wakley. Elliotson on this occasion was accompanied by Wood, with whom he had discussed the matter. He now proposed to Wakley that an explanation must lie in the fact that the lead and nickel were touching the same portion of skin and one metal was therefore affecting the other. Wakley replied that Okey could give a better explanation and that further experiments were of no interest to him. However, he agreed to conduct the proceedings and began by inducing a somnambulistic trance with the lead disc. Elliotson had to admit that his theory about the inertness of lead would have to be revised. Nickel was now applied, and an identical trance occurred, without the convulsions and rigidity expected from the impact of that metal.

Elliotson suggested that the metals should be applied to the inside of the lips. Nickel had no effect; then lead was applied several times and a violent paroxysm ensued. Elliotson now complained that it was not fair to apply the lead more frequently than the nickel nor so soon after it that the nickel had not had time to operate. Wakley was not impressed by the argument, contending that one could test the theory by using lead all day; he then left the house for an engagement. Elliotson and Wood also left, taking the metals with them. Upon Wakley's return, further experiments were conducted with a piece of nickel and some lead which he had just bought. It was also decided in Elliotson's absence to repeat the tests with mesmerized water, gold, etc., which had been previously reported in the *Lancet*.

As Elizabeth was exhausted following her last paroxysm, the next series of experiments, which lasted five hours, were all conducted by Wakley with Jane as his subject. Seven trials were run, in each of which six glasses of water were used. On all seven trials Jane drank from all six glasses. On trials 2, 3, 5 and 7, one or all of the glasses were 'mesmerized' by placing fingers in them. Jane was completely unaffected throughout the experiment and reacted no differently to mesmerized than to normal water.

Wakley claimed that these experiments were quite conclusive and that it was useless to continue to investigate mesmerized water any further. This opinion was shared by all present.

The next series was run with gold sovereigns, which were sometimes mesmerized by the experimenters holding hands to form a 'battery' to 'charge' the sovereigns, or were sometimes warmed with hot water to mislead Jane and lead her to think the sovereigns had been handled. She showed the rigidity of the hand and arm, produced in Elliotson's demonstrations by the mesmerized coins, when she handled unmesmerized sovereigns, and she did not react at all to mesmerized sovereigns. Wakley and the others agreed that it was unnecessary to pursue any further experiments with gold.

He now returned to trials with nickel and lead rubbed on the inside of the lips. In no instance did Jane react at all to these metals, and it was decided to discontinue experiments with her. It was not denied that she apparently went to sleep when manipulations were made before her eyes, but when, as in the experiments with water and metals, she was kept in another room and only allowed in after the magnetization of these objects had occurred, very little in the way of response was obtained.

As we have reported, her sister, Elizabeth, had been less cautious, and it was agreed to run further trials with magnetized water using her as a subject. She was now well enough to take part, although it was late in the evening. The results of the experiment were completely damning:

Six glasses of water, which had been strongly impregnated with the subtle and marvellous 'magnetic' fluid, had produced no effect on the patient, while in two other instances, mere sippings of the unmesmerized drink, appeared to produce stupefaction, sleep, rigidity, and, ultimately, in one case, prostration on the floor and snoring.

There was no doubt in Wakley's mind, when he concluded the session, that: 'the effects which were said to arise from what has been denominated "animal magnetism", constituted one of the completest delusions that the human mind ever entertained.'[27]

Of course we can now see that both parties to the dispute were in the wrong: Elliotson was wrong to believe in the existence of the magnetic fluid as the only cause of the phenomena, and not to have checked on its existence by proper control experiments before submitting himself to Wakley's examination; Wakley was wrong in thinking that if the magnetic fluid could be shown to be a chimera then the only other possible explanation was that the Okeys were impostors. Neither could be expected to see that the Okeys' expectations were critical in triggering off their dissociative condition, and that an explanation of their behaviour lay in a more sophisticated psychology than the investigators had at their disposal. However, Wakley's experiments are so reminiscent of those employed by the French Commissioners of 1784 that it is hard to see why he could not have given the Okey sisters credit for using their 'imagination' rather than rush to the conclusion that they were frauds. It is also unfortunate that he directed his attention only to the supposed effects of magnetized objects, rather than to the trance state itself and what occurred in it.

The *Lancet* now campaigned most vigorously against animal magnetism, and subjected its practitioners to extreme ridicule. So extreme was the transition in the journal's attitude from positive to negative that one could be excused for suspecting Wakley of trying to exonerate himself for his own credulity by projecting it on to others.

On 8 September Wakley wrote:

Careful investigation and a consideration of all experiments have convinced us that the phenomena are not real, and that animal magnetism is a delusion; we shall, therefore, lose no opportunity of extirpating an error, which in its nature, applications, and consequences, is pernicious.[28]

Turning to the practitioners of the art he was content with generalized remarks:

> The 'science' of mesmerism, like the 'science' of fortune telling, will always carry on a precarious existence wherever there are clever girls, philosophic bohemians, weak women, and weaker men, but it can no longer affront the common sense of the medical profession, or dare to show its face in the scientific societies after the late exposure.[29]

He was more direct in his reference to the Okeys: while Jane was 'but a tame copy of her sister', Elizabeth was 'a genius in her line' similar to 'the licensed fool of the old comedy'. Indeed, he thought that 'some of the minor theatres may find it no bad speculation to set up a mesmeric farce, in which Okey, with a little training, would appear with advantage.'[30]

Wakley believed that it was Elizabeth's natural cunning and insight that had enabled her to manipulate and fool scientific men of the highest calibre. Her motives were those that 'few uneducated girls could resist'.

A possibly more objective description of Elizabeth Okey was given by J.F. Clarke, one of the observers at the Wakley experiments. He considered her:

> A girl of extraordinary cleverness and shrewdness. She was below the middle height, indeed rather diminutive, but she had a fine expression of features and a well-formed head. She had full dark eyes, with long black lashes, 'the jetty fringe' falling upon her cheek in such a manner that it was sometimes quite impossible to tell whether she was asleep or not. That this peculiarity gave her immense power in appearing to be asleep when she was not, I am quite convinced. I am, moreover, convinced that she feigned some of the phenomena that were exhibited, while I feel as certain that others were really the production of mesmerism.[31]

It would have been of interest to have had Elliotson's own considered views of Elizabeth and Jane, but he did not publish them, although he

was said to have taken voluminous notes on the two cases with a view
to ultimate publication. Neither did he ever mention any suspicions
that he might have entertained and that might have been responsible
for the termination of his experiments with them three years later.
Indeed, his only comment suggests his complete, although possibly
overstated, conviction of their innocence. This occurred in the context
of a criticism of Wakley's cruelty in slandering:

> . . . two perfectly virtuous and afflicted female children, who had
> been carefully brought up and had lived only with their parents
> and afterwards in a respectable family till they were seized with
> epilepsy . . . Everything stated or ever printed to their disadvantage
> was an absolute falsehood.[32]

Elliotson had left for his usual continental holiday immediately after
Wakley's investigation, and was shocked to learn on his return that
Wakley had conducted the further experiment with Elizabeth Okey and
had publicly condemned mesmerism in his *Lancet* articles.

As Elliotson wrote later, he had left: 'the poor little girl in an
intense coma, with occasional violent tetanic spasms . . . little imagining
that any farther experiments would be attempted, especially in my
absence, by a person ignorant of the subject and altogether incapable
of making experiments.' As for the *Lancet* critique, it reflected: 'that
gentlemanly delicacy for which he and his friends are so remarkable.'[33]

It can be seen that Elliotson could give as good as he got. But
before describing his defence of his theory in the face of the Wakley
experiments, a defence he must have thought through during his month
abroad, it is necessary to consider the situation that had arisen at
University College Hospital during these events.

There were two factions among the medical staff of the hospital, one
headed by Elliotson and the other by Robert Liston. Liston had been
forced to leave the Edinburgh Royal Infirmary because of quarrels with
his colleagues. He was hot-tempered and impetuous, and had been at
daggers drawn with Elliotson for three or four years. Both were popular
with the students and each was jealous of the other's success. As a
surgeon, Liston was very dexterous. It was said that when he amputated
a limb – the most common surgical operation at that time – 'the gleam

of his knife was followed so instantaneously by the sound of sawing as to make the two actions almost instantaneous.'[34]

As a lecturer, Liston could be uncivil to his colleagues: on one occasion he ridiculed Elliotson's treatment of erysipelas by describing it as 'turning a white man into a nigger'. Elliotson, on the other hand, might make sly allusions to treatments other than his own but never criticized his colleagues in front of the students. However, he does seem to have delighted in provoking Liston at committee meetings, Liston threatening never to enter the hospital again, or, on one occasion, to thrash 'Elliotson Cantab.', as he called him.[35]

Liston's part in these arguments was generally taken by Anthony Todd Thomson, a man who also disliked Elliotson. He too had had no university education; he was more of a pharmacologist than a physician and well known for his hesitancy, with none of Elliotson's decisiveness. Against these two were ranged with Elliotson, Samuel Cooper and Richard Quain, both surgeons; thus, Elliotson was just in a majority and his party won every vote.

However, Cooper and Quain were becoming disillusioned with Elliotson's advocacy of mesmerism and its effect on the reputation of the hospital, especially among their professional colleagues. For example, Sir Astley Cooper refused to witness mesmerism 'because he had a character to lose', while Sir Benjamin Brodie used to say that he disliked turning his horses' heads towards Russell Square to visit a patient lest people should think he was going to 'that scene of humbug, University College Hospital'. Matters came to a head with the public demonstrations: as early as 6 June the Medical Committee had held a special meeting to consider the two demonstrations which had already been given. They had previously communicated their disquiet to Elliotson, as we saw in his opening address at the first demonstration. They now wrote to him saying that while they did not wish to interfere with his right to use animal magnetism as a remedial agent in the wards, they did wish to know if he was going to discontinue the public demonstrations.

The Committee met again three days later when they had Elliotson's reply. It began:

> Gentlemen, I am so deeply impressed with the importance of the
> facts of mesmerism, and its utility as a remedy, that no consideration

of pecuniary interest or personal arrogance could induce me to discontinue my investigation of its employment.[36]

He continued by saying that he considered it his duty also to teach it and that he had received petitions from medical and scientific men and from men of high rank to observe the phenomena, whom he could not refuse without leading them to doubt the truth of mesmerism. Since the majority of his colleagues thought he was wrong to invite them, he would in future send a list of their names to the Committee which could have the responsibility of making the decision.

He now sent the Committee the list of names with another letter in which he again stressed the importance of his work:

> These phenomena [of mesmerism], I know to be real, to be independent of imagination or any other cause to which ignorant persons are pleased to ascribe them, to be of the most interesting, most extraordinary and most important character in a mental, physiological, therapeutical and physical point of view. To be such that the knowledge of the circulation of the blood and the distinct offices of different nerves in physiology which attract ordinary attention are the merest trifles in comparison. I say all this boldly and sincerely, but soberly and advisedly, after the most laborious and careful examination.[37]

As it was his duty to communicate the knowledge to others and as everyone had a right to demand demonstration and not mere description, he had informed these gentlemen that he would provide such a demonstration; it would be up to the Committee to permit or to refuse.

No decision was taken immediately by the Committee, but after further consideration the next meeting on 13 July came out more strongly against Elliotson: they could not consent 'to sanction public exhibition of animal magnetism in the hospital to any parties whatsoever.'[38] However, there was nothing to stop Elliotson using mesmerism in the wards, and his experiments there were, as we have seen, reported in the *Lancet*. After the Wakley fiasco, and his annual holiday, Elliotson resumed the private experiments. The *London Medical Gazette* commented:

> We thought that Mesmerism had received its death blow, and was defunct, but we understand that since Dr Elliotson's return to town,

the Madames Okey have made their appearance at the University
College Hospital, and that the learned professor declares his faith in
the science to be quite unimpaired. Now, with Dr Elliotson's opinions,
as a private individual, we have nothing to do, but if it be intended
to resume exhibitions of these accomplished performances either at
College or at the hospital, we think the other medical men owe it to
themselves and to their school to take immediate steps for putting an
end to all such mummeries.'[39]

The *Lancet* was of course not to be outdone, and in the issue of
1 December Wakley accused physicians who employed mesmerism of:
'insulting public decency and abusing the confidence which has been
reposed in them by parents and guardians.'[40] Turning to the medical
schools in general, although the reference was clearly to University
College Hospital in particular, he made the point that: 'the sooner the
Governors take serious notice of what is passing in their institutions,
the better will it be for the interests of charity and the reputation of the
science of medicine in this country.'

In an attempt to add more fuel to the fire he again implied that some
immoral advantage was being derived from the practice of magnetism:

> The medical schools with which it [mesmerism] is connected must
> be speedily and irreparably ruined, unless the immoral quackery is
> at once put down by the Governors or other controlling body of the
> institutions, in which this heinous enormity against common sense and
> female delicacy is perpetrated.

The mounting tension between Elliotson and his colleagues was
further aggravated by Wakley's editorial on 15 December. In it, he
describes the case of a French magnetist who had 'effected the ruin
of a young and artless female through the "mighty magic" of animal
magnetism'.[41] Such a case should serve as a warning:

> If a few passes of the hand can veil the eyes in profound sleep and
> deprive an individual of consciousness, who could shut his eyes
> against the dreadful consequences to society of the existence of such
> an agent.

Alluding to the mesmerists' claim that nervous and impressionable women were the most easily magnetized, Wakley addressed himself to the fathers of the country and with heated Victorian indignation asked:

> What father of a family then would admit even the shadow of a mesmerizer within his threshold? Who would expose his wife, or his sister, his daughter, or his orphan ward to the contact of an animal magnetizer? If the volition of an ill-intentioned person be sufficient to prostrate his victim at his feet, should we not shun such pretenders more than lepers, or the unclean?

And yet, Wakley's tirade continued, opportunities were provided for instruction in 'this scandalous science' in the private wards of one of our public hospitals, where 'wealthy and, perhaps, libidinous men are daily invited to witness the easy mode of producing "sleep" which has been invented by one of the physicians'.

The sentiments are strange, coming from a person who believes mesmerism to be a hoax and whose object is to expose the humbug of its practice. One can only presume that Wakley was carried away by his indignation and did not stop to consider that he had recently shown mesmerism to be a delusion. The implication that Elliotson himself may not have been above moral reproach was completely unjustified. No breath of scandal ever touched Elliotson's private life either before or after his involvement with mesmerism; in this respect he was a true disciple of Anton Mesmer.[42] Elliotson's lack of heterosexual interest was well known, a fact which made Wakley's attack foolishly ineffectual. As events turned out it was also unnecessary, for Elliotson's experiments now took a turn which supplied the hospital authorities with an adequate reason for them to take the final step and to ban mesmerism within their walls.

Increasingly, Elliotson had become convinced that the Okey sisters were capable of diagnosis and prognosis whilst in a trance. There was nothing new in this idea; as we have seen, much use was made of it by Puységur. Elizabeth Okey, in particular, manifested the ability in an idiosyncratic manner. She had, writes Elliotson,

> a wonderful susceptibility of unpleasant feeling from the influence of persons seriously ill: a feeling of weakness, oppression, and distress;

and such an effect on her mind that she, being in her delirium, fancied an image of death wrapped in white clothes, standing by the side of the patient. The more adult the patient, and the more violent the disease, the more intense were the distressing feelings, and the taller the fancied spectre.[43]

Elliotson had formerly believed that whereas a somnambulist could predict morbid changes within himself, this ability did not extend to other individuals. Now there seemed an opportunity for further investigation. He began taking the girls from ward to ward in order to test the accuracy of their prognoses. The patients began to grow wary of the diminutive sisters. On one occasion while in a male ward at dusk, Elizabeth was overheard by a patient to say that she saw 'Great Jackey' sitting on the bed of the patient in the adjoining bed. Some days later the relevant patient died, an event which caused great alarm in the men's ward and which spread consternation throughout the hospital.

The matter was referred immediately to the University Council, who at a meeting on 22 December 1838 decided to instruct the Hospital Committee to have Elizabeth Okey immediately discharged and to take steps to prevent the future practice of mesmerism, or animal magnetism, within the hospital. The Hospital Committee held a special meeting soon after Christmas (27 December) at which Elliotson was 'respectfully requested to cause Elizabeth Okey to be discharged forthwith'. Elliotson responded in writing to the Secretary of the Council:

I have just received information, that the Council, *without any interview or communication with me*, has ordered my patient, Elizabeth Okey, to be instantly discharged, and forbidden me to cure my patients with mesmerism. I *only* am the proper person to judge when my patients are in a fit state to be discharged, and what treatment is proper for their cases.

As a gentleman in the first place, and as a physician in the next, I feel myself compelled at once to resign my office of Professor of the Principles and Practice of Medicine, and of Clinical Medicine in the College, and of Physician to the Hospital; and hereby resign them all, and will *never enter either building* again.

When I was made Professor I received a class of 90, – the class is now 197, – even 13 more than at Christmas last year: and, as there

were 24 entries after Christmas then, the whole number of the present
session would, no doubt, have been above 220.

I have not received my fees this session. It is my wish that they be
all refunded to the young gentlemen, who are perfectly welcome to the
lectures which I have already delivered.[44]

However relieved the hospital authorities might have been and however triumphant the Liston party, the student body was not so compla-
cent. Elliotson was a very popular figure and an admirable teacher, and
when he invited a number of students to a dinner party the evening
following his resignation it was thought that he was trying to enlist
student support, which could have proved a powerful bargaining counter
at that time when medical schools were competing to attract students. It
is not known exactly what ensued at the party, although Dickens, who
was present, reported that: 'Elliotson addressed them very energetically
on the step he had taken.'[45] At the beginning of the lecture term
the students held a mass meeting in the Anatomy Theatre to discuss
appropriate action. It became clear that the pro-Elliotson group, in spite
of William Wood's ardent advocacy, were only just in a majority, and it
was by a vote of 124 to 113 that it was decided to send a resolution to
the Council regretting the circumstances 'which had necessarily led to Dr
Elliotson's resignation'.[46] The Council, however, had already accepted
his resignation and were not moved to reconsider their verdict.

A presentation of a silver plate was made to Elliotson by the students
on 15 April 1840 inscribed with the words: 'from the grateful and
admiring students of the eminent and magnanimous professor.' In his
reply, a formidable composition of 36 pages, Elliotson expressed his
gratitude, describing the occasion as 'the most gratifying day of my
existence.' Most of the document consisted of a justification of his own
conduct and critical comments on the behaviour of former colleagues,
comments that were too personal for the manuscript to be read publicly,
according to the student to whom this task had been delegated. Elliotson
later reprinted much of this Farewell Address in the 1840 edition of his
Human Physiology, and the London Medical Gazette also printed it.[47]

It was here that he gave his considered reasons for discounting
Wakley's counter-experiments. Firstly, he pointed out that mesmeric
susceptibility fluctuates, not only from person to person but also over
time. Thus, a person might be high or low in susceptibility for days, or

might vary continually during the one day. He also thought it certain that susceptibility could be exhausted by excess experimentation, especially when metals are used. So great was the Okeys' sensitivity to some metals, that once they had been applied they left mesmeric traces, which could then be activated by any substance, even lead. In addition, there was the possibility that if the experimenter held in his hand a highly efficacious metal, such as nickel, and subsequently handled a less efficacious one, the latter would become 'nickelized' and possess stronger mesmeric powers than normal.

When these possibilities were taken in conjunction with Wakley's approach, all could be understood. Wakley, it was implied, was 'an ignorant person, determined to make experiments at all hazards, as though he had inanimate matter before him'.[48] With regard to Wakley's own experiments during Elliotson's absence:

> For an ignorant man to take the matter in hand himself, as though he had made himself master of the subject, is as absurd and disgusting as if a countryman should push aside a chemical lecturer and mix acids, alkalis, and salts from various bottles, and declare because things did not happen as he expected, that chemistry was fudge.[49]

In short, Wakley had performed poorly controlled experiments and by frequent repetition had exhausted the Okey girls' susceptibility. Prior to his experiments Wakley had formed a strong friendship with Liston and therefore knew at first hand the political situation in the hospital and that he could count on the support of the hospital authorities if he were able to injure Elliotson. He was motivated by jealousy and not by a regard for the truth. Furthermore, Wakley had told Elliotson that the *Lancet* had been pestered with letters on the subject of mesmerism and nineteen out of twenty were unfavourable: 'nineteen persons of course purchase more *Lancets* than one, and I fancied I already saw his rejection of the evidence.'[50]

Elliotson visited University College only once more: on the occasion when he was invited to deliver the Harveian Oration of 1846. There was much opposition to the invitation, and indeed this must have been the only occasion on which the police were present during the Harveian Oration in case of audience unrest. The *London Medical Gazette* expressed the opinion that the College should have had the

courage of its convictions and should have denied Elliotson this opportunity to expound mesmeric doctrine. In any case, they thought Elliotson
should have had the discretion and good taste to refuse. The *Lancet* was
more violent, referring to Elliotson as:

> The visionary follower of Mesmer, the bitter enemy of legitimate
> medicine, the professional pariah – he who for years has been per-
> forming such fantastic tricks as might well make the angels weep.
> [Elliotson's oration would] strike a vital blow at legitimate medi-
> cine, and would be a black infamy degrading the arms of the
> College.[51]

Nothing daunted, Elliotson delivered the oration on 27 June; he
spoke in Latin, as was usual, but then broke with tradition in having
the text printed in English in order to ensure that a wide public
learned from it. Much of the oration was historical, very little was
devoted to mesmerism, and none of it was really controversial. He
asked his listeners to preserve an open mind in view of our ignorance of natural phenomena. He reminded them of the opposition
with which new discoveries had been greeted by the medical profession. He instanced the discovery of the lacteal vessels, the circulation of the blood, the sounds of the chest and their relation to
diseases of the heart and lungs, the use of vaccination in smallpox,
the ligature of bleeding vessels after operation, instead of the application of burning pitch or red-hot irons. He appealed to the College never to forget these things, nor to 'allow authority, conceit,
habit, or the fear of ridicule, to make us indifferent, much less hostile, to truth'.[52] They should particularly bear them in mind when
examining mesmerism. For ten years he had shown how mesmerism
could prevent pain, produce sleep and ease in sickness, and even cure
many diseases that could not be relieved by ordinary methods. He
concluded:

> In the name, therefore, of the love of truth, in the name of the
> dignity of our profession, in the name of the good of all man-
> kind, I implore you carefully to investigate this important sub-
> ject.[53]

The plea fell on deaf ears. The *Lancet* had long since closed its columns to partisans of mesmerism, an example which had been followed by other medical periodicals. As a body, the British medical profession continued to exhibit an intolerance towards mesmerism remarkable for its persistence over many years.

10

The Mesmeric Campaign

Elliotson's departure from University College Hospital did not mark the end of his mesmeric practice; on the contrary, he now began to support his cause with all the zeal of a missionary. With the assistance of William Wood, his faithful clinical clerk, he continued daily experiments and demonstrations with the Okey sisters for the next three years, on one occasion having the girls live in his own house for a period of four months.

His elegant mansion in Conduit Street could accommodate up to 40 visitors, and Elliotson was not slow to issue invitations as a means of spreading the gospel.[1] As the mesmeric movement began to catch on and as Elliotson found himself leader of the new cult, it became necessary to find a better forum for the presentation of his views. The launching of a new periodical seemed to be the answer, and in 1843 he and his sympathizers produced the first issue of the *Zoist*, subtitled *A Journal of Cerebral Physiology and Mesmerism, and their Application to Human Welfare.*

The peculiar title was derived from the Greek *zoon* and *zoe*, thus expressing the dual concern of the journal with (a) the animal body, the domain of cerebral physiology, by which was meant phrenology, and (b) with life in general, with which mesmerism was involved. The journal can be seen to be a direct expression of Elliotson's two scientific interests; it provoked the comment from Johnson, the editor of the *Medico-Chirurgical Review*, that: 'a marriage extraordinary has lately taken place between phrenology and mesmerism, to the great scandal and indignation of the rational and sober advocates of the former science.'[2]

If the phrenologists were scandalized it did not show in the pages of the *Zoist*, although it is true that they contributed fewer articles than the mesmerists, a difference which became more noticeable in later issues when phrenology had begun to lose its impetus. For Johnson, even the cover of the new journal was provocative:

> The *Zoist* is ornamented with a neat vignette representing a venerable man, intended no doubt for Dr Elliotson, poring over a volume opened on his knee, while two females of prepossessing mien, but remarkably loose habits, support the Doctor upon either side, and compose a striking and interesting group. The ladies, of course, are the Okeys, and though we are aware that such gifted individuals are far above what are vulgarly called the decencies of life, yet we would venture, with great diffidence, to hint that their petticoats are rather scant.[3]

Neither Johnson's veiled sexual allusions nor the *Lancet*'s lack of notice were effective in dissuading prospective subscribers, who were largely drawn from professions other than medicine. The prospectus had emphasized that the editors hoped to provide a medium for 'the freest expression of thought on questions of social, moral and intellectual progress', and the journal did indeed present a progressive view on social problems, an attitude commonly found in phrenological circles. The first copy of the *Zoist* was sold out before the second issue appeared, and the venture seemed set for success. Articles appeared in the early issues on education, crime, sanitation and overcrowding.

According to one contributor, an enquiry at Bristol had shown that only one half of the children between the ages of five and fifteen were attending school. It was, he maintained, a duty of the state to provide a training so that every member could have his faculties and powers developed, and especially his moral faculties. If this were not done, many would fall into criminal habits.[4]

With regard to the treatment of the criminal, the *Zoist* was implacably set against capital punishment for murder, and regimes of punishment for lesser crimes.[5] Prisons should be institutions of reform and re-education. A regular contributor, the Rev. C.H. Townshend, reported favourably on the Munich prison where library facilities and free beer were provided.[6]

As well as indicating the latent powers of an individual which could be developed by training, phrenological analysis could be used in screening those who sought public office. As T.S. Prideaux proposed, the application of phrenology in the choice of parliamentary candidates might lead to MPs of strong character and high moral worth. Unfortunately,

Prideaux decided to omit any attempt to assess a candidate's intellectual capacity, on the grounds that it would be better to keep the examination simple.[7]

Among the well-known contributors were the philosopher Herbert Spencer, the orientalist and explorer Sir Richard Burton, and the writer Harriet Martineau. As a believer in phrenology, Spencer wrote two articles in which he speculated about the physical proximity of the organs of benevolence and imitation, and wondered about the function of the organ of wonder.[8] Burton wrote to Elliotson from Bombay and described the induction of trance by having the subject stare at a pool of ink in a magician's hand, a practice common in Eastern Countries where clairvoyant subjects could be led to see the King of the Jinns, who would supposedly guide them to recover lost or stolen objects. Burton believed that it was the dry climate and 'pure electric air' of these countries which was favourable to mesmerism. In addition, the Eastern magician practised concentration and had piercing eyes and a dignified air, which helped to render the inhabitants susceptible to his procedures.[9]

Harriet Martineau's contributions were of a more personal nature: she had become an ardent convert to mesmerism after having been cured of an unspecified female complaint which had incapacitated her for five years. She had published a collection of her letters on this cure and associated topics in 1845, which had shown her to be a sensible, if uncritical, disciple of Elliotson. She now contributed to the *Zoist* an account of the cure of her cow, which had been given up for dead by the 'cow doctor' but which recovered after a night of mesmeric stroking. Martineau accepted that her story might be ridiculed but pointed out that it was important to discover more about the effects of mesmerism on animals in order to deal with the objection that the patient's imagination was responsible for mesmeric effects. As she concluded: 'I am fond of my cow, and stand up for her good qualities, but I cannot boast of any imaginative faculty in her.'[10]

One man who had done just what Martineau suggested was John Wilson, Physician to the Middlesex Hospital. In a book which received little notice, he had reported trials with a great variety of animals: domestic animals, including dogs, cats, ducks, hens, geese, pigs and calves, and wild animals at the Zoological Gardens in Surrey, which included leopards, elephants and a lioness. His technique was to make magnetic passes as close as he dared; it thus differed from the more usual type of animal control, long practised by country people in bringing fowl to market, whereby the animal is quickly inverted and held pinioned.[11] Wilson had varying degrees of success in making the animals drowsy, although he admits that many animals doze during the day and his passes may have coincided with a sleepy period. Perhaps his most impressive result was obtained with a lioness:

> As I stopped before a lioness, lying down tearing a half-devoured joint, which she held between her paws, and growling at me, I began making passes towards her head; she very soon, almost immediately, ceased eating, grasped the joint between her jaws, and ceased growling; her eyes began to twinkle, and soon closed at times, for short intervals; when some strangers came up, and asked me how it was that I seemed to affect the lioness, I gave them an evasive reply, in hopes of their going away, and ceased the passes, but held my hands a little out towards her, as she continued in the same position; but her eyes were much less closed than when I made the passes; when other visitors came, and again I ceased, and held my hands out steadily before me; then she got up and walked about, and then lay down again. As the company remained standing there, I ceased all trials and retired, as the lioness began to tear the joint, after having retained it full twenty minutes in her mouth without once relaxing hold of it.'[12]

Presumably any result that Wilson may have achieved must have been due to the animal's curiosity having been aroused by the unusual spectacle of an arm-waving man.

Elliotson himself decided to try whether animals could be used in mesmeric induction. He took Elizabeth Okey to the zoo, and found that the rapidity with which she went into a trance depended on the size of the animal with which she made hand contact. Thus the muzzle of a large deer mesmerized by Elliotson was more effective than that of a small deer. Strangely enough, no effect was produced by the top of an elephant's trunk, although contact with the mucous membrane made her drop senseless to the ground! However, Elliotson did not report any effects of mesmerism on the animals themselves.[13]

Better evidence for the existence of the mesmeric fluid seemed to come from the work of Baron von Reichenbach, a well known chemist and the discoverer of creosote, who claimed to have discovered that physical effects could be produced on the human organism by magnets and various inorganic substances. The Baron's results were certainly startling: subjects, some of whom were in the somnambulistic state, reported sensations of warmth, cold, prickling, and headache, and sometimes fainted when a large magnet with a supporting power of 10 lb. was drawn along their bodies. Some of the subjects reported seeing an aura around the poles of an 80 lb. magnet, and the Baron's hands themselves seemed to some sensitives to emanate a luminous force. Plants and human bodies varied in the 'warmth' of their parts, some parts representing particularly intense concentrations of animal magnetism.

> As it appears that the lips are a focus of concentration for the new force, the author hazards the conjecture that the true theory of kissing with the lips may depend on this circumstance. He states that the flames depicted on the lovers' lips by poets, do really and truly burn there for those who can perceive them.[14]

Some subjects found that they were irresistibly drawn to follow the pole of the magnet with their hands. Other substances were found to have various effects: gold and silver coins and copper were inert, but fine crystals of gold and of copper sulphate caused mild finger closure when applied to the hand. Rock salt and crystals caused spasmodic closure, while fluor, heavy spar and gypsum produced violent spasmodic closure. These effects were produced on some subjects in the waking state, although they were much more pronounced if the subject and the substances were previously magnetized. Reichenbach concluded that:

> This force, which has been called animal magnetism, has the following properties: it is, namely, conductible through other bodies; it may be communicated to other bodies either by directly charging them or by its dispersion. It soon disappears, but not immediately, from bodies charged with it. It has no marked relation to the earth's magnetism. It attracts mechanically the hands of cataleptic patients, and its presence is associated with luminous phenomena.[15]

Like Mesmer before him, Reichenbach succumbed to the view that this force was of no mere terrestrial origin. When a plate of copper was exposed to the sun's rays, a connecting wire being taken to a sick person's hand, the patient immediately gave vent to a cry of pleasure, likening the refreshing sensation to the fresh air of a fine May morning. Weak magnets were strengthened in their animal magnetic effects when placed in the sun, and the Baron's own hands were likewise recharged with the force.

The night sky itself possessed different degrees of warmth to a sensitive subject, the major planets being warm, while the Milky Way was cool. Believing the objectivity of his subjects, Reichenbach thought that he might have found the true basis of astrology, a force from the stars affecting the workings of the human brain. To this force he later gave the name 'Od'; in England it was more often referred to as the 'odic' or 'odyllic' force and achieved some currency during the 1850s as an alternative to animal magnetism.

In common with many before him and since, the Baron could not resist prescribing a regimen based on his discoveries. For health, one must rise no later than dawn, because the magnetism in the forehead was then at its peak, eat one's main meal no later than 1 p.m., and retire to bed in the evening twilight, in order, like the beasts and the savages who were supposed to follow such a routine, to be spared the diseases of civilization.

It says much for the scientific status achieved by Reichenbach as a chemist that his speculations were taken seriously. Elliotson, for his part, welcomed them enthusiastically and took three long articles in the *Zoist* to describe them and to compare them with his own findings with the Okey sisters and other patients. Indeed, his response was so enthusiastic that he lost all his critical faculties. In spite of the fact that Reichenbach had found gold coins to be inert and Elliotson had found them extraordinarily effective in producing trance, in spite of these and many other discrepancies, he claims that his own: 'observations in mesmerism made eight years ago coincide in every point with those of another which are analogous. Every one of his observations I feel must be true.'[16]

Because Elliotson too had had subjects report luminous streams of light from his fingers he believed that their reality could not be doubted and that such statements 'may be relied upon as securely as the phenomena in the chemist's laboratory'.[17]

A few years after his review of Reichenbach's work, Elliotson's enthusiasm was again aroused; this time it was in response to the appearance of a book by a French doctor, Victor Burq, who had developed a metallic therapy. In his sixty-page review of Burq's work Elliotson explains how Burq had found mesmerized patients responded differently to different metals and how Burq had taken his 'metallic arsenal' to the Salpêtrière. In that huge Parisian hospital where hundreds of women were subsisting on public charity, scenes reminiscent of the years before Pinel struck off the chains of lunatics were enacted daily. It was, said Burq,

> lamentable to see sometimes 10 to 20 of these wretched beings confined by strong bands to which they are accustomed early to submit, all calling at once, roaring, foaming, twisting themselves about, and struggling against the resistance which is opposed to them, and frequently in vain.[18]

Straitjackets and other restraints were replaced at Burq's request by metal bands worn around the limbs, and he was gratified to see convulsions cease in three out of five severe hysterics, although no effect was produced in epileptics. Having to leave the Salpêtrière, owing, it was said, to the jealousy of a colleague, he now went to the Hôtel Dieu where he was less successful. Burq attributed his lack of success to the deficiency in his knowledge of metals: one had to find the right metal for the right patient. His new technique, as applied to patients having anaesthetic regions of the body, now consisted of putting various metals on the affected region until sensibility was restored, the patient typically reporting sensations of tingling, twitching, and fatigue. Then Burq loaded the patient with bands on the limbs, plates on the trunk, a crown for the head, and rings for the fingers, all made from the successful metal. The patient was required to wear this 'armour' throughout the night. More elegant corsets, collars and chains were devised for daily wear, and patients were also given baths of copper and steel filings.

Burq reported many cures, which were attested by the Academy of Medicine, who affirmed that 'no medical novelty was ever made known with greater authenticity and proofs'. All this was, of course, grist for Elliotson's own metallic convictions. He explains in the course of his review how as long ago as 1827 he had experimented with acupuncture using gold or silver needles which were left in place for an hour. He had succeeded in curing 30 out of 42 cases of 'uninflammatory rheumatism'. In a comment, which is as appropriate today as it was then, he declares:

> The *modus operandi* is unknown. It is neither fear nor confidence:
> since those who care nothing about acupuncture, and those who laugh
> at their medical attendant for proposing such a remedy, derive the
> same benefit if their case is suitable as those who are alarmed or who
> submit to it with faith.'[19]

Having had this early experience with metals, it was only natural for him to experiment with them with the Okeys. The Wakley fiasco had apparently been followed by further trials with rods of supposedly inert lead or iron. Elliotson claims that he had rubbed such rods as many as 500 times on the girls' palms and no effect had ever been produced in thousands of experiments. Yet if he put the extremity of the rod against a sovereign or shilling held behind his back and then applied it to the subject's hand, it would close with a strong spasm. And, as a control, when he had taken the rod behind his back and avoided contact with the coin, the manoeuvre led to no effect being produced on the subject's hand.

One can only presume that in these control experiments the subject had somehow realized that no contact with the supposedly exciting metal had occurred, Elliotson possibly having betrayed the fact by his demeanour, or by the small noise of contact being absent.

The Burq and Reichenbach investigations, taken with Wilson's occasional success with animals, all supplied evidence for the fluidic hypothesis. Difficulties had, however, been created for that theory by some of Elliotson's own observations as well as those of others. It will be remembered that during the University College Hospital demonstrations Elizabeth Okey had shown the ability to send herself into a trance by waving her fingers in front of her face. The fact was not easy to explain unless in some way the magnetic fluid could act back upon the agent. However, Elliotson never referred to it. Similarly, he never seems to have been troubled by the difficulties involved in explaining, by the fluidic theory, paranormal phenomena which he had come to accept.

The crucial observations in this respect were made on the celebrated clairvoyant, Alexis Didier, who gave some séances at Elliotson's house in 1844. In his reports on the séances in the *Zoist* Elliotson claims that he had been trying for six years to obtain 'higher phenomena' but without success. Presumably, he was referring to trials with the Okeys, who manifested apparent increases in sensory acuity but nothing else – until in a series of experiments in July 1838 Elizabeth appeared to be able to see with the back of her left hand. The experiments were typically inadequate: they involved her ability to pick up pieces of bread without using her vision and were obviously difficult to monitor; even Elliotson was chary of believing in them.[20]

Alexis specialized in 'travelling clairvoyance', in reporting what was going on at a great distance and in relating future or past events in his sitters' lives. Elliotson now became completely convinced: 'This year I have met with exquisite clairvoyance of the highest kind for the first time, and its truth I will now fearlessly maintain as I originally did the production of simple sleep.'[21]

However, if the mesmeric fluid were the agent of such powers, how did it function at such distances and through buildings, etc? Perhaps wisely, Elliotson remained silent on this point.

His editorial silence on another matter was more reprehensible. In 1843, the year of the first issue of the *Zoist*, a book had appeared by a Scottish physician, James Braid. Entitled *Neurypnology*, it described a method for inducing a trance and a theory as to how that method worked which were revolutionary, although in essence the theory harked back to Faria in its rejection of supposed influences from the mesmerist. Braid was, as we shall see in the next chapter, to proceed beyond his early theory and to become a crucial figure for the development of a medically and scientifically respectable theory. His early view that eye fixation and concentration on the part of the subject without any direct participation by an operator were sufficient to produce a trance state obviously created problems for fluidic theory. That is hardly sufficient reason for Elliotson with his professed belief in the importance of practical experiment to ignore those demonstrations that did not fit his preconceived theory. For Braid was largely ignored by the *Zoist*, and when it noticed him on one or two later occasions it dismissed him briefly.[22]

A less formidable challenge came from another mesmerist, Spencer T. Hall, who had treated Harriet Martineau, and who, also in 1843, produced his own journal, *The Phreno-Magnet and Mirror of Nature* in competition with the *Zoist*. It contained a similar mixture of phrenology and mesmerism, although Hall's contributors were less distinguished and he wrote most of it himself. His attitude to Elliotson and to Braid, whose first book he reviewed, was scrupulously fair and he advised the reader to consult the writings of these gentlemen. His enthusiasm for phrenology knew no bounds, and the *Zoist* seized on the following passage with delight:

> It was little more than a fortnight ago that we discovered a most important class of mechanical faculties . . . We find in the eyebrows special faculties not only for walking, riding, swimming, driving, sailing, rowing, climbing, descending, aerostation, evolution, convolution, extension, and contraction, for pulling, pushing, lifting, dropping, various modes of gyration, leverage, etc., and in the region of the outer angle of the eyebrow which has hitherto been appropriated to Order, besides one for velocity, and another for retrogressive motion, we find shooting, spearing, crouching, springing, striking (or smiting, as with a battleaxe), slinging, and other belligerent faculties.[23]

Elliotson reproduced the passage with the comment that: 'Mr Hall, not having enjoyed the advantage of a scientific education, is evidently inclined to follow the promptings of an imaginative brain.'[24] But the threat was short-lived: the *Phreno-Magnet* went no further than its first volume and Spencer Hall died soon after.

Elliotson's most savage attacks were reserved for those outside the mesmerist camp. As the leader of the mesmeric movement, Elliotson used the *Zoist* as a propaganda machine. He also had personal axes to grind, and through the pages of his journal he kept up a running fight with Wakley and those whom he termed the Anti-Mesmeric Crusaders. He took to publishing the more outrageous diatribe of his opponents without comment before his own articles. He lost no opportunity to revert to his own research with the Okeys and to the personal rivalries within the hospital prior to his resignation; he continually harked back to these events as though to purge them from his memory. His more general counterattack was directed at any periodical which published anything critical of mesmerism. It is apparent from the index to the *Zoist* which periodicals came in for Elliotson's disapproval:

Blackwood's Magazine – exposed; *Quarterly Review* – its anti-mes-
merism; *Medical Times* – its folly; *British and Foreign Medical
Review* – its appalling dishonesty, etc., etc.

John Forbes, the editor of the last of these, was second only to Wakley
as a target for Elliotson's wrath. In an attempt to submit Alexis Didier
to scientific investigation, Forbes considered that he had demonstrated
the fraudulent nature of the séances. Elliotson, having been thoroughly
convinced of their paranormal nature, must have been struck by the
similarity of the episode to that of Wakley's clumsy intervention in the
Okey case and over-reacted in his attitude to Forbes.[25] Forbes' own
attitude to mesmerism was, in any case, to change dramatically, and he
was forced to resign his editorship in 1847 after writing a paper in which
he recommended the trial of mesmeric anaesthesia in surgical operations.
As he wrote:

> If insensibility can be produced artificially, surely the immense
> acquisition both to operator and patient is obvious at once. We
> hesitate not to assert, that the testimony is now of so varied and
> extensive a kind, so strong, and in a certain proportion of cases
> so seemingly unexceptionable, as to authorize us, nay, in honesty,
> to compel us to recommend that an immediate and complete trial of
> the practice be made in surgical cases.[26]

By this date evidence had indeed accumulated that the use of mesmerism permitted apparently painless surgical operations, and over the next
few years the *Zoist* devoted many pages to accounts of such operations.
Elliotson had noted insensibility in Elizabeth Okey early in her mesmeric
career: she was wont to take hot coals from the fire in spite of protests
from other patients, and upon wakening would wonder why her hands
were blistered. During his treatment of her headaches he prescribed a
seton (a thread passed through the skin to promote drainage):

> She was not apprised at all of it; and was standing before me and
> several others chatting wittily and deliriously, when Mr Wood, who
> was behind her, suddenly took up the flesh of the back of her neck, ran
> a large seton needle with a skein of silk into it, and put on the plaster,
> without a moment's check to her chattering and fun, or any sign of

her noticing it, though I watched her most minutely. On dissipating the state, and bringing her to her natural condition, she soon found there was something wrong at the part, and put her hand to it, saying someone must have pinched the back of her neck. In her deep coma, and in that of her sister, there was always insensibility of touch, and cupping and the severest blistering were perfectly unnoticed.[27]

The first major surgical operation under mesmeric anaesthesia in Britain took place in 1842 when W. Squire Ward, the former house surgeon at St Bartholomew's, amputated the thigh of a 42-year-old labourer, with the trance state being induced by W. Topham, a barrister and amateur mesmerist. The report of the case was read to the Royal Medical and Chirurgical Society and led to a lively debate. The patient had moaned at intervals, but reported upon awakening that he had never felt any pain at all. Topham had watched him throughout, and claimed that:

> The placid look of his countenance never changed for an instant; his whole frame rested, uncontrolled, in perfect stillness and repose; not a muscle was seen to twitch. To the end of the operation, including the sawing of the bone, securing the arteries, and applying the bandages, occupying a period of upwards of twenty minutes, he lay like a statue.[28]

The reception of the paper was mostly hostile and resembled that given to the first French report of the mastectomy performed by Cloquet. Some objected that the patient either had been trained not to feel pain or belonged to a group of persons who were by nature insensible to it. Johnson said he would not have believed it even if he had seen it! Marshall Hall, one of the more critical observers of the early Chenevix demonstrations, who had continued to remain an opponent of the 'trumpery that polluted the temple of science',[29] by which he meant mesmerism, thought that the sound leg should have reflexly contracted, and the fact that it had not implied that the patient was an impostor. Liston thought it physiologically absurd for the patient to have reported that he had heard the sawing of the bone but not to have flinched when the divided end of the sciatic nerve had been pricked by the surgeon's forceps. He rose once again during the meeting to ask: 'if the interesting patient had sufficiently advanced in education since the operation to be able to read with the back of his neck or his belly?'[30]

The critical disbelief may have been expressed so strongly because Elliotson had played a part in advising the operation and was present in the audience. He was finally prevailed upon to speak and contented himself with mentioning a case published in the *Lancet* of spontaneous somnambulism with complete insensibility, in which the surgeon had experimented by tearing two pieces of skin from the patient's hand, an action termed 'wanton and barbarous' by Wakley.[31] The surgeon on that occasion had been Liston, who kept very quiet during Elliotson's comment.

When the Society adjourned, Topham withdrew his paper and published it as a pamphlet. It remained only for Dr Copland, who had replaced Elliotson for a time at University College Hospital, to propose at the next meeting of the Society that the reading of the paper should be removed from the records. In his view it should never have been read in the first place because the main author was not medically qualified, and, in any case, 'pain is a wise provision of nature, and patients ought to suffer pain while their surgeon is operating; they are all the better for it, and recover better.'[32]

Elliotson contemplated resignation from the Society, of which he had been President when it had received its Royal Charter, but thought better of it. Instead he brought together as many accounts of mesmerically induced analgesia as he could find and published them under the title *Numerous Cases of Surgical Operations without Pain in the Mesmeric State.*

This pamphlet was largely taken up with a very full description of the Topham and Ward amputation, to which he added the first English account of the Cloquet case and of numerous dental operations. The collection of cases of amputations, excisions and extractions was continued in the *Zoist*, and the list was extended to include venesection and childbirth. Then in 1845 the most remarkable reports began to appear from a Scottish surgeon with the East India Company, James Esdaile, who was in charge of the Native Hospital at Hooghly, Bengal.[33]

Without ever having seen a demonstration of mesmerism himself, going on the basis of a conversation with a friend who had witnessed it, Esdaile had succeeded in inducing such a profound stupor in a patient that he had remained unconscious for three hours during which time an operation for hydrocele had been successfully performed. That was on 4 April; by January of the following year Esdaile was able to report in a letter to Elliotson that he had performed 73 surgical operations while employing mesmerism as the anaesthetic.[34] Some of these operations were of a major kind, such as arm and breast amputations and the removal of large tumors. The comparatively large number of scrotal tumors, weighing from 8 to 80 lb., represented a condition endemic in the native population at that time, and one with which Esdaile was to obtain his most dramatic successes. Later in the year another letter to Elliotson contained the offer to send to him a recently extirpated and gigantic scrotal tumor. Esdaile's account of the operation is worth quoting:

> S., aged 27, came to the Native Hospital with an immense scrotal tumor as heavy as his whole body. He was mesmerized for the first time on October 10th, 1846, then on the 11th and 13th, on which latter day he was ready for operation. The operation was performed on the 14th. The tumor was tied up in a sheet to which a rope was attached, and passed through a pulley in the rafter. The colis was dissected out, and the mattress then hauled down to the end of the bed; his legs were held asunder, and the pulley put in motion to support the mass and develop its neck. It was transfixed with the longest two-edged knife, which was found to be too short, as I had to dig the haft in the mass to make the point appear below it, and it was removed by two semicircular incisions right and left. The flow of venous blood was prodigious, but soon moderated under pressure of the hand; the vessels being picked up as fast as possible. The tumor, after half an hour, weighed 103 pounds, and was as heavy as the man's body. During the whole operation, I was not sensible of a quiver of his flesh. The patient made a good recovery.[35]

These successes formed the basis of Esdaile's appeal to the Deputy Governor of Bengal that an official investigation should be carried out. This was agreed to, and Esdaile was given charge of a unit in a Calcutta hospital where for two weeks he demonstrated his techniques before a committee of seven doctors. Ten native patients were selected, all males, aged 18-40. Three had later to be rejected: one for drinking, one because he suffered from bouts of coughing, and one because he was not mesmerizable. The remaining seven were mesmerized by Esdaile's assistants, young native workers recruited from the Hooghly Hospital. The procedure was peculiar to Esdaile and somewhat different from that practised in Europe:

> To each patient a separate mesmerizer was assigned. The room in which they operated was darkened, but from time to time the Committee were enabled to witness, through small apertures made in the door panels, the manner in which the processes were carried on. The patient lay on his back, the body naked from the waist upwards, and the thighs and legs bare; the mesmerizer seated behind him at the head of the bed, leaning over him, the faces of both nearly in contact, the right hand being generally placed on the pit of the stomach and passes made with one or both hands along the face, chiefly over the eyes. The mesmerizer breathed frequently and gently over the patient's lips, eyes and nostrils. Profound silence was observed.[36]

The average length of the induction period was two hours, but in some cases it was continued for as long as eight hours without interruption. It is possible that Esdaile was influenced by local informants who had some knowledge of Jar-Phoonka, an ancient Yogic breathing and stroking technique used to induce trance states, and that he based his induction procedures on that practice.

The Committee were agreed that insensitivity was brought about by these procedures, even the pupillary reflex to the noonday Indian sun having been abolished. With regard to the surgical operations it was clear to the Committee that four of the seven patients had shown no signs of pain at all, and in three of these cases the operations had been severe enough for this fact to be quite extraordinary. The remaining three patients had been observed to writhe their bodies, move their arms, and control their faces as though suppressing pain, although the patients themselves were adamant that they had felt nothing and did not even remember the operation. Esdaile's explanation was that these were instinctive movements not indicative of the experience of pain. The Committee did not comment, although they were curious about the pulse rates of these patients compared with the rates of the three who had not shown signs of pain in spite of their major surgery. In fact the pulse rates of those patients who behaved as though they were suffering did not increase, and, indeed, remained extraordinarily steady throughout the operation. In contrast, those patients who had remained still during the operation produced large increases in their pulse rates, although they rapidly reverted to normal upon awakening. The Committee attempted no explanation of this interesting finding, but contented themselves with noting that the amount of bleeding and the post-operative recovery rates were similar to those found with the usual operative procedures.[37]

Esdaile was now asked to take at random one hundred patients from the wards and to mesmerize them in front of the Committee to ascertain the incidence of anaesthesia, but he refused to comply on the grounds that the request was outside the Committee's terms of reference. The Committee were sufficiently impressed by what they had already seen, and, although concerned that mesmerism might be of limited utility in view of the protracted induction period, they were unanimously of the opinion that:

> Great credit is due to Dr Esdaile, for the zeal, ability and boldness with which he has taken up and pursued this enquiry. His sphere, however, has been hitherto limited but the Committee hope that his further investigation may be extended to medical as well as surgical cases, to European as well as native patients, and to the elucidation of the several questions, which have been adverted to in the course of this report.[38]

The Governor, in turn, saw the need for further research and put Esdaile in charge of a small experimental hospital in Calcutta. In his first monthly report Esdaile included the results of a trial he had made with ether as a surgical anaesthetic. Robert Liston had performed the first operation with ether in Britain at University College Hospital on 21 December 1846, and Esdaile's report is dated January 1847. It would seem that Esdaile must have seized on the idea with equally immediate enthusiasm. He got his patients to smoke a hookah and to inhale the ether fumes. The resultant state he found to be indistinguishable from that induced by mesmerism, although the chemical agent produced a more profound trance which would yield only to long-continued affusions of cold water. He concluded:

> By cautious and graduated doses, and with a knowledge of the

best antidotes, I think it extremely probable that this power will soon become a safe means of procuring insensibility, for the most formidable operations even.

All mesmerists, who are lovers of truth, and not mere traders, will rejoice at having been the means of bringing to light one truth more, especially as it will free them from the drudgery required to induce mesmeric insensibility to pain, which, although the most striking, is the least important branch of the subject.

It is only of late years that the application of mesmerism to surgery has been prominently brought forward, principally with the view of affording an ocular demonstration of this great vital agent. But the great field for a display of its usefulness is in the treatment of medical diseases, where it often comes to our aid when all other resources have failed.[39]

As the passage reveals, Esdaile was already working with mesmerism in situations other than surgery. Thus he continued until the end of 1847, when, despite a favourable report by the inspectors, the experimental hospital was closed. Esdaile received promotion to the rank of Presidency Surgeon, a much sought-after post to which he was the youngest-ever appointee. However, Government support did not extend to the establishment of an official mesmeric hospital, in spite of a petition by '300 native gentlemen of Calcutta', and funds had to be raised by private subscription. Within three months enough money was raised to establish the Calcutta Mesmeric Hospital with Esdaile as Superintendent. Here he stayed for 18 months until further promotion to Superintendent of Government Hospitals meant that he was forced to discontinue most of his practice. He finally left India and the prospects of a considerable fortune in June 1851 to return to semi-retirement in Scotland at the age of 43.

Despite the favourable attitude of the Bengal government, Esdaile considered that he had suffered much at the hands of his medical colleagues. Although the original Committee of Enquiry appear to have been scrupulously fair in their report, Esdaile considered that he had been 'sorely tried and tortured to the utmost of human endurance' by their later attempts to gag him and to bring failure to his experimental hospital by refusing him patients.[40] One of the signatories to the report, a Dr Thompson, later denied that the operations were painless and said that he had only signed out of pity for poor Esdaile, whom the Committee could easily have crushed.[41]

Indian medical journals consistently refused to publish his reports, and whatever coverage he did receive was negative. The usual criticisms were made here, as in the European context, namely the untrustworthy nature of the patients, who were considered by the *Calcutta Medical Journal* to be 'a set of hardened and determined impostors'.[42] In retaliation, Esdaile submitted reports to the daily newspapers, whose reaction was for the most part favourable. This move infuriated the medical profession, Esdaile's conduct being variously described as 'unprecedented – undignified – unprofessional – only worthy of an advertising quack'.[43]

During the six years Esdaile lived in India he claimed to have performed several thousand operations on mesmerized patients, of which 261 were major. Two hundred of these major operations were for the removal of scrotal tumors, and among these there were only sixteen deaths, although the previous incidence of mortality had been between 40 and 50 per cent. In spite of these results the use of chemical anaesthetics spread through India as it had through Britain. Two years after he had expressed his initial enthusiasm for ether, Esdaile completely changed his view:

> The indiscriminate use of ether and chloroform in surgery will prove anything but a blessing to Europe, and its general use here is a positive evil to the poor Natives who are generally independent of such violent measures.[44]

However, he was willing to grant that a harmless anaesthetic might be found without the dangers of ether and chloroform, which, being new and little understood, occasionally had disastrous consequences. Even so, mesmerism could be used to relieve post-operative pain and discomfort, and it had all its medical uses in disorders ranging from gout to insanity. He returned to Scotland convinced on these matters and began to submit accounts of his Indian work to the medical journals. He can hardly have been surprised by their negative response, although it must have been galling to have had his paper on the 'Anaesthetic and curative powers of mesmerism' rejected after an editor had particularly requested it. Even worse, the same journal then published a long contribution by Braid, which covered much of the same ground. Esdaile regretted that he had not followed Braid's example and replaced the word 'mesmerism' with 'the unknown power' or something equally innocuous.[45]

The *Zoist*, of course, continued to carry his correspondence with Elliotson and reports of his now more limited activities. From his letters it appears that Esdaile left India because he had come to hate the country and found it injurious to his health.[46] A Dr Alan Webb continued to run the Mesmeric Hospital after his departure, and *Zoist* readers were indebted to him for the picture of the 5 lb. tumor he had removed under mesmeric anaesthesia.

In Scotland, Esdaile's practice was at first confined to his own family, and he successfully treated his sister-in-law and a niece for hysterical symptoms. He then opened a small private surgery and had some success with what would appear to have been psychosomatic and hysterical cases, including the abolition of a paralysis of twenty years' duration.[47] However, he was adamant that he would not do any surgical operations in order to convince anyone, even if he were asked, which he was not. In any case, he was finding it much more difficult to induce trance among his Scottish patients than among the natives of Bengal, and this in spite of his adoption of the more usual European induction technique. Factors responsible for his comparative failure may have included the more critical attitude prevalent in Scotland, cultural differences in the ability to dissociate, and the relative loss of prestige suffered by Esdaile in his transition from a high-ranking British surgeon in India to a small-town Scottish surgeon with curious views at variance with those of most of his medical colleagues.

When in 1853 the U.S. Congress offered a prize of $100,000 to the true discoverer of the anaesthetic property of ether, which they described as the earliest anaesthetic, Esdaile protested that:

> Painless surgery by means of mesmerism, years before ether was heard of, was as common in my hospitals, as it has since become in Europe under the influence of chloroform, and nearly 300 capital mesmeric operations had been performed by me before leaving India, two years ago.[48]

Esdaile gradually faded from public view. His last contribution to the *Zoist* was in 1854, and he died in 1859 at the early age of 50. Throughout his practice he seems to have held a simple belief in the magnetic fluid.

He was never an experimentalist, and his requirements with regard to scientific method seem to have been even more lax than those of Elliotson. Thus he considered that he had conclusively demonstrated the existence of the magnetic fluid when he was able to abolish pain in a patient by having him drink previously mesmerized water. According to the *Zoist* he used to carry about with him a variety of small objects previously 'charged' with the magnetic fluid for the use of any of his friends who might be ill.[49] His credulity was very apparent when confronted with a patient in a spontaneous coma, who, like Petetin's cataleptics, could see and hear only through the stomach. Esdaile was completely convinced of her clairvoyance and the transference of her senses, although her eyes were wide open during her successful attempts to 'see' objects with her stomach, and when they were bandaged her accuracy fell away dramatically.[50]

Esdaile's importance lay in the massive statistics he was able to bring to bear to support the mesmeric cause. The one spectacular proof of the reality of the mesmeric influence lay in the insensibility of the magnetized patient under gross physical assault. In spite of the extreme opposition's view that all was feigned, people were, and still are, amazed at the lack of reported pain in deep trance states. The advent of chemical anaesthesia destroyed the mesmerists' best evidence; as Liston put it, 'This Yankee dodge beats mesmerism hollow.'[51] Not for long could Esdaile maintain the identity of the chemically and mesmerically induced states. Thus, when both Esdaile and Elliotson became increasingly hostile to the use of chemical anaesthesia, it is not difficult to read between the lines and to see in their obvious concern for the safety of their patients a deeper worry with regard to the future utility and public image of their science.

But nothing could stop the progress of the more efficient and certain chemical agents. Mesmerism was obviously unsuitable for emergencies in view of the usually slow induction period.[52] Not everyone was susceptible, while everyone responded to the drugs, even the Queen, whose enthusiastic response to chloroform – 'soothing, quieting and delightful' – removed the ground not only from under the mesmerists' feet but also from under those of the religious rearguard who considered pain a divine requisite of childbirth.[53]

From 1850 until it ceased publication at the end of 1855, few operations under mesmeric anaesthesia, and most of them minor ones, were recorded in the *Zoist*. Yet Elliotson searched out and published every account that he could find. It was apparent that the cause was a lost one. Such operations had always been rare in the regular hospitals, where mesmerism was generally excluded, a fact which had led to earlier discussion among Elliotson and his supporters about the feasibility of setting up Mesmeric Infirmaries where all treatment would be conducted by mesmerism. The first steps had been taken at a meeting held at the home of the Earl of Ducie on 9 July 1846 when it was resolved to establish a Mesmeric Infirmary by voluntary contribution 'for the cure of diseases and the prevention of pain in surgical operations.'[54] It was not, however, until March 1850, with the example of Esdaile's Calcutta Mesmeric Hospital as a successful forerunner, that the London Mesmeric Infirmary opened its door to patients at premises at 9 Bedford Street.

The *Lancet* reacted with one of its rare excursions into verse:

> Dr E. will of course be the leading physician!
> A man of acknowledged and vast erudition,
> Well versed in the art; and the cream of the joke is,
> He has booked for the nurses the two little Okeys.
>
> Then away with examiners, drugs and degrees;
> Away with old fashions, excepting the fees;
> Away with the Hall, and away with the College;
> Away with chirurgo-medical knowledge;
>
> No more will we hear the afflicted complain,
> Operations will give more of pleasure than pain;
> And ladies will smile in their mesmerized trance
> As the pangs of their uterine efforts advance.[55]

Elliotson did not act as physician to the infirmary; two mesmerists were appointed at 16 shillings a week salary.[56] He did however join the Committee of Management which met weekly to review cases and general progress. The Earl of Ducie was President, with the Earl of Stanhope and Archbishop Richard Whately of Dublin as Vice Presidents. Ducie seems never to have played any active part, and the Rev. Sandby, a well known writer on mesmerism, conducted the early meetings. Stanhope was said to be an able man but eccentric, believing in the prophetic powers of mesmerism, and disbelieving in all remedies except herbal ones.[57] Whately, a considerable scholar, was of sounder judgment and had himself used mesmerism to remove the pain of toothache.[58] He was to give active support to the founding of the Dublin Mesmeric Infirmary in 1852.

Patients began to arrive at the rate of twenty a day and it was soon necessary to engage four full-time mesmerists. Successes were reported with paralyses, epilepsy, chorea, pericarditis, and burns. After the first year it was estimated that 50% of patients had been cured, 25% were still under treatment, and 25% had not been helped. It is not clear whether there was a selection on admission of those patients most likely to profit from mesmerism.

Meanwhile infirmaries began to spring up elsewhere. Bristol and Exeter closely followed London, the mesmerist J.B. Parker reporting as many as 200 surgical operations in the Exeter infirmary's first year of existence, plus 40 tooth extractions in front of audiences of from 10 to 70 witnesses. In spite of these figures neither Bristol nor Exeter lasted longer than two years. Infirmaries at Leeds, Edinburgh, where Esdaile was a Vice President, and Dublin were short-lived. In Dublin, treatment was free, and the other infirmaries also acted largely as charitable institutions. They all closed from lack of funds.

The London Infirmary had twice to move its premises on account of opposition from other inhabitants of the houses they had rented. It remained at 36 Weymouth Street in the West End until its final demise in 1868. Failures occurred, it was said, because patients wanted rapid results and when these were not forthcoming they tended to break off treatment. It, too, ran into serious financial difficulties which were responsible for its closure.

The last number of the *Zoist* had appeared in December 1856. Dwindling subscriptions had made it impossible to continue. Elliotson, nevertheless, wrote a courageous if unduly optimistic finale, in which he claimed that the object for which the periodical had been undertaken was now obtained:

> That object was neither pecuniary gain, nor worldly reputation: for loss was very nearly certain; contempt, ridicule, virulent abuse, and serious injury, were all inevitable. It was the establishment of truths, splendid, exquisite, extensive in their bearings, and of

the highest importance to the moral and corporeal wellbeing of mankind.[59]

It was not true that mesmerism had won the day; it was merely that the crusade had run out of steam and the opposition had become more muted. Elliotson's life was marked by a physical and mental decline from this date until his death. He had maintained a private practice, which had been reduced by two thirds after his resignation and which was to continue to shrink. However, his income was probably sufficient for his needs; although in the depressive state into which he now fell he was to exaggerate his many difficulties.

Our best source of evidence from 1862 onwards is provided by the correspondence of Charles Dickens. Dickens went to considerable trouble to help out his old friend. Aware that he was depressed and had mentioned suicide, Dickens returned from Paris to look after Elliotson's money matters, only to find that they appeared to be in a healthier state than he had feared:

> Unless the entries from day to day, with varying pens and in varying shades of ink were all made fraudulently or maniacally it is impossible to doubt that he realizes in his practice in this present year more than one thousand gns.[60]

Even so, Elliotson was claiming that it was impossible to renew the lease on his Conduit Street house and he had already had to mortgage his sisters' house in Chatham to alleviate his financial problems. Dickens proposed that his friends should raise a fund to pay off the mortgage, but Elliotson declined their assistance and the project was left in abeyance. However, as Dickens wrote to Elliotson:

> If it should become necessary, it is ready for us to resume it at an hour's warning, always on our own responsibility, and with as true a delicacy and sensitiveness for your own great name and fame, as we could possibly have if they were our own.[61]

Apparently it was never considered necessary, by Elliotson at any rate. He died at the age of 77 in the house of a former student on 29 July 1868, the same year in which the London Mesmeric Infirmary closed its doors.

His friend, Townshend, also died in that year, and Dickens was to survive them for only two more.

It would be wrong to dismiss Elliotson's contributions to mesmerism as solely those of a successful practitioner and publicist. While his kindness and persistence as a physician were legendary – in one case he attended a patient three times a day for the greater part of five years – and while his role as the leader of British mesmerists was unquestioned, his careful observation of his patients and his many experimental investigations were not without value. Thus, he noted strong transference reactions in some patients; he was often led to distinguish between genuine mesmeric phenomena and attempts at deception; he recognized that the imagination of the patient rather than the actions of the mesmerist was often the crucial variable. But he never went so far as to reject the existence of the mesmeric fluid and continued to base his interpretations on this faulty premise. This physicalist stance was understandable in a man used to the methods of enquiry in the physical and medical sciences. His intransigence in the face of contradictory evidence was more difficult to reconcile with that type of training. Perhaps it stemmed from his earlier successes with unconventional approaches to medical practice. Elliotson had never had a real failure: ridicule and disapproval were not unknown to him before his involvement with mesmerism, but these had always given way to ultimate triumph. Consequently he had no reason to believe that he would not finally see the general acceptance of mesmerism. He was as convinced by mesmeric phenomena as he had been convinced by the auscultatory data. His natural antagonism sustained him in his belief, now as it had then. Indeed, the fiercer the attacks, the stronger his belief and the greater the evangelical zeal with which Elliotson infused his campaign. He finally suffered the fate of many an evangelist and became a martyr to his cause.

11

Braid and Hypnotism

During the years when Elliotson and Wakley were first locked in combat, there seemed to be no choice between the view that the animal magnetic fluid existed and produced the extraordinary mesmeric phenomena and the opposing view that these phenomena were the product either of fraud or of that ill-defined concept, the 'imagination'. But, of course, other possibilities did exist: for example, the phenomena might be genuine enough, and yet not produced by the agency of the supposed fluid but by some other physiological means as yet undiscovered. This view was that initially adopted by James Braid on the basis of his observations made during a demonstration by Charles Lafontaine, an itinerant Swiss magnetist.

Lafontaine was described by Spencer Hall, who had himself been led to magnetism after seeing Lafontaine perform in Sheffield, as having an appearance 'calculated to awaken curiosity and wonder in a high degree'. Hall continues:

> He was about middle age, slightly above middle size, with a well-set muscular frame, and was clothed in black. His hair was dark, his eye bold, powerful, and steady; and his beard, which was very profuse, descended to his breast.[1]

Lafontaine took with him on his travels two young women somnambulists who were subjected to considerable ordeals during their stage appearances, having snuff pushed up their nostrils, lighted matches and candles applied to their lips and noses, and needles inserted right through their eyelids, cheeks, eyebrows, and hands. These demonstrations of insensibility proved very popular among English and Irish audiences, although on occasions Lafontaine's poor command of English and his reliance on an interpreter created problems.

It was at Manchester on 13 November 1841 that Braid first saw Lafontaine in action. Braid was a surgeon by training and a sceptic by nature, and he went to Lafontaine's demonstration prepared for a fraudulent display. According to Professor Williamson, an eyewitness on that occasion, Braid was loud in his denunciation of the whole performance, and in this he was joined by an eminent Manchester ophthalmist, Mr Wilson, who claimed that it was all humbug. The indignant Lafontaine excitedly replied that it was not 'Bog' and there was no 'Bog' in it at all, and invited the sceptical doctors to examine his somnambulist. Williamson, Wilson and Braid took the girl's pulse, which was raised, examined her eyes and found the pupil contracted, and Braid forced a pin behind her fingernail but produced no response. They were forced to conclude that whatever it was it was not humbug.[2]

A week later Braid returned, determined to watch the induction procedure more closely. Lafontaine held the subject's hand and stared steadily into her eyes until she seemed unable to sustain his gaze any longer and dropped her head. He then made slow passes from head to foot, and straightened her limbs until they became rigid, a posture which she then maintained for as long as he required.

Braid's attention was particularly drawn to the apparent inability of the subject to open her eyelids, and on his third visit to Lafontaine he believed that he had discovered the cause: it must be the continuous fixed stare required of the subject that paralysed the levator muscles of the eyelids and rendered it physically impossible to open them.

Two days later, during a dinner party, Braid conducted his first experiments to test the theory he had developed. A guest was induced to maintain a fixed gaze at the top of a wine bottle placed somewhat above his eye level. In three minutes his eyelids closed, his head drooped, and he fell into a profound sleep marked by slow deep breathing. After four minutes' trance Braid woke him up and the company were surprised to see the man's consternation. Braid's wife volunteered to try the procedure and began to gaze at an ornament on a sugar bowl. In two-and-a-half minutes her eyelids closed, her mouth twisted, her bosom heaved, and she fell back as though passing into an hysterical fit. Braid quickly aroused her and found her pulse rate to be 180 per minute. Further trials with a man-servant, and then using Lafontaine's technique of eye-to-eye fixation, were equally successful.

Braid considered his theory was now fully proved: the disturbances in the nervous, circulatory, respiratory and muscular systems were induced by 'a fixed stare, absolute repose of the body, fixed attention, and suppressed respiration, concomitant with that fixity of attention'.[3] The physical and psychological condition of the subject was considered paramount, no importance being attributed to the will-power or behaviour of the operator.

Within a month Braid began to give public lectures on his discovery, an impetuous act in view of his inexperience and the incomplete proof of his theory. On one occasion Lafontaine turned the tables on Braid and attended Braid's demonstration, which does not seem to have been wholly successful. However, Braid rapidly began to make an impact and travelled to London to lecture and demonstrate in March 1842.

In April he was back in Manchester and competing with Lafontaine for public attention. In the midst of their debate, a Liverpool clergyman, Rev. James McNeile, gave a sermon in which he claimed that mesmeric phenomena were of a diabolic nature, a not uncommon accusation at that time.[4] Braid replied in the first written statement of his views, which makes it clear that he believes it to be the exhaustion of nervous centres due to continuous monotonous stimulation of the eye that is responsible for the trance state. He admits that his theory does not explain all the mesmeric phenomena and that his procedure does not guarantee the occurrence of a trance. It was this latter point that McNeile had taken up, claiming that if Braid were dealing with a natural phenomenon it would occur uniformly and not capriciously: 'If it operates capriciously, then there is some mischievous agent at work; and we are not ignorant of the devices of the devil.'[5] As Braid replied, it would be as reasonable to accuse the captain of a ship of acting by satanic agency because he set sail in rough weather and only some of his passengers became sick instead of them all. And just as the cause of sea-sickness was unknown, so we also had incomplete knowledge of the trance state.

A more formal statement of his views was now sent as a paper to the Medical Section of the British Association which was meeting in Manchester in June 1842. The paper was rejected, but the interest on the part of the members was so great that Braid was induced to hold a private meeting in parallel to the Association at which he read his rejected essay and gave a demonstration. He particularly asked his medical audience to think of a possible explanation for the fact that when a subject showed catalepsy of a limb it was possible to change its state, with almost the rapidity of thought, to the extreme opposite condition by a simple puff of air on to the surface of the affected part. No one ventured an opinion, and Braid was left with this problem for as long as he held his physiological theory.

That theory was now given a full exposition in his first book, *Neurypnology* (1843), which sold 800 copies in a few months. In the Introduction Braid explains the title and proposes a new terminology; derived from the Greek, the title can be translated as the 'rationale of nervous sleep', which he defines as 'a peculiar condition of the nervous system induced by a fixed and abstracted attention of the mental and visual eye, on one object, not of an exciting nature'.[6] Nervous sleep is to be termed 'neurohypnotism', and the now familiar derivatives are obtainable by dropping the prefix, viz. 'hypnotism', 'hypnotist', and 'hypnotize'. (The one term of Braid's that has not survived in its original form is 'hypnotic' used as a noun referring to 'the state of nervous sleep'; today, the more recent form 'hypnosis' is used in that context, and, often, as a preferred synonym for hypnotism.)

In spite of the proposed change in terminology, Braid believes that the condition of the nervous system in hypnotism and in mesmerism is similar. Whenever mesmeric induction is successful it is because the monotonous movements of the mesmerist succeed in bringing about a fixation of the eyes and of the mind. His own success, which he now claims is general, is due to his insistence on such fixation; failure in the past has been due to people talking in the audience and other noises, distractions preventing the necessary concentration by the subject.

However, certain phenomena are said to have been produced under the mesmeric influence which he admits he has never been able to produce by hypnotism. These are the paranormal capacities of clairvoyance, diagnosis and prognosis of disease, and the influence of the operator at a distance. He leaves open the possibility at this time that these really do occur, although if they do, he thinks a naturalistic explanation will ultimately be found. For the moment he offers a tentative explanation of the supposed ability to see without the use of the eyes by invoking the idea that in a trance subjects have very acute sensory capacities. Thus, when blindfolded, they may be able to feel the warmth from an object held close to the skin and identify its shape. Demonstrations of mesmerizing at a distance may be explicable by virtue of the subject's increased skin sensitivity to the currents of air created by the mesmerist's passes. This enhancement of sensory acuity occurs, Braid thinks, early in the process of induction.

His own technique now consists of holding a bright object above the forehead and about twelve inches from the eyes until the pupils begin to dilate. He then moves two fingers of his free hand from the object towards the eyes until they automatically close. Then, and he appears to have followed Lafontaine in this procedure, the arms and legs of the subject are lifted to an extended position, which is maintained if the subject is now in a trance. If the subject drops his limbs, Braid asks him to keep them there by voluntary effort, and, he claims, in time they will become rigid and immovable. This cataleptic condition is considered a requirement for therapy, because it leads to an 100% increase in heart rate, which in turn, he thinks, leads to an exaltation of the muscular and sensory capacities, and of certain mental faculties, owing to the restriction of blood flow to the limbs and the increased blood flow to the relevant parts of the brain.

He considers that the sequence of events under hypnotism is similar to that experienced by those using opium or drinking alcohol, for in all these cases after an early stage of exaltation comes a state of depression of function. Under hypnotism this is much greater than the torpor of natural sleep, with which he compares the state. The most marked difference between natural and hypnotic sleep lies in their respective curative powers. For example, a patient with torticollis, which had lasted for six months and had obviously, therefore, not been cured by the normal amount of sleep she had had during this period, was cured in five minutes of hypnotism. More dubious are Braid's claims to have cured congenital deaf mutes after ten minutes of hypnosis, although the eight years of their lives spent in natural sleep had done nothing to alleviate their condition. One can only presume that these cases were hysterical rather than congenital.

It is clear from Braid's comments that he did not use any verbal suggestion at this time, but followed the example of Elliotson and others in thinking that the mere placing of a patient in an altered state of consciousness had a therapeutic effect. However, in the case of the torticollis patient, he did manipulate the neck and head, and may thus have made implicit suggestions that she could turn her head voluntarily.

Braid conducted a series of experiments which proved to his own satisfaction that whereas monotonous stimulation of the senses other than vision could produce normal sleep, it was only with visual fixation that hypnotic sleep occurred. However, if a subject had been previously hypnotized, then his 'imagination' could come into play to produce the hypnotic state when the other senses were stimulated. Indeed, the more often the subject was hypnotized, the more susceptible he became, until he might go into a hypnotic trance merely because he thought that some relevant induction procedure was being carried out. On the other hand, an expert hypnotist was powerless if the subject did not expect to be hypnotized and had not agreed to comply.

Thus, already, Braid had begun to modify his original purely physiological theory. Normally, the most rapid induction procedure involved the visual fixation of a near object, but he had found that it was perfectly possible to hypnotize subjects in the dark and those who were blind. He had not, however, succeeded with very young children, or with persons of weak intellect or restless minds who were unable to follow his simple rules. It was to be only a few years later that Braid was to put forward his revised theory which stressed mental rather than visual fixation.

These observations on the ways in which subjects could be hypnotized, coupled with demonstrations of self-hypnosis in the absence of the operator, convinced Braid that he had destroyed the grounds for the mesmerists' belief in the magnetic fluid. Also, the fact that the subject would be affected by hypnotism only if the subject himself desired it removed any criticism that hypnotism could be used for immoral purposes. The medical profession could feel free to use the technique without fear of exciting popular prejudice against them. Indeed, Braid thought that only doctors should be allowed to use hypnotism, as only they were in a position to use it to the patient's best advantage. It was not a universal remedy, but an important means of curing a certain class of illness, examples of which are given in the second part of *Neurypnology*.

The 56 cases recorded there were all treated by Braid himself. The cases are grouped into those of sensory deficit, particularly of vision and hearing, paralyses, rheumatism, epilepsy, palpitations, headache, and muscular spasm. He notes that in those cases where there was no improvement, the heart rate did not change, whereas beneficial results followed increases in blood pressure and heart rate: it is these changes in the circulatory systems which he thinks are responsible for the benefits of hypnotherapy. Thus, his therapeutic rationale is a purely physiological one.

The most unusual section of the book is devoted to 'phrenohypnotism'. Although, as we have mentioned, it was common practice among the magnetists of the period to attempt to excite a particular cerebral 'faculty' by the touch of a finger on the scalp, their theory entailed the excitation of the appropriate region of the brain by means of the magnetic fluid flowing from the finger. Braid's view is that any such effect results from the mechanical pressure exerted by the finger on nerve trunks running over the scalp. These nerves excite muscles in the face involved in emotional expression; they also affect respiration. These physiological changes are in turn responsible for exciting in the mind the particular emotions associated with the phrenological map of the head. (Readers familiar with the James-Lange theory of emotion will be struck by the similarities with this earlier version.) Again, the theory is of a physiological nature with no place for any magnetic emanation from the operator; the changes are the necessary internal consequences of external sensory stimulation.

It may be wondered why Braid found it necessary to involve phrenology in his hypnotism at all. The reason is that it seemed to him the only possible explanation of a series of experimental demonstrations. Braid had worked with 45 subjects, most of whom were said to have been ignorant of phrenology, and had obtained very similar results when he had pressed on similar regions of their scalps. For example, a well educated lady, the wife of a regimental colonel, who assured Braid that she knew nothing of phrenology, and who was unable to locate a single phrenological 'organ' on her head, was hypnotized:

> In about three minutes after she was asleep, I placed two fingers over the point named 'veneration'; instantly the aspect of her countenance changed, in a little while she slowly, and solemnly, and majestically arose from her chair, advanced towards a table in the middle of the room, and softly sank on her knees, and exhibited such a picture of devout adoration as can never be forgotten by any who had the gratification to witness it . . .

When awakened, this lady was quite unconscious of all which had happened.[7]

Another subject had her region of 'imitation' accidentally touched by Braid, whereupon she imitated everything said or done by a scholarly member of the party, even when he spoke French, Italian, Spanish, German, Latin and Greek, every word of the imitation being rendered with great precision, a standard, it was said, that she could not approach in her normal waking state.

Even more curious were Braid's experiments in stimulating antagonistic points on opposite sides of the head, the result being the exhibition of correspondingly antagonistic feelings on opposite sides of the body. Thus, one young woman, who knew nothing of phrenology, had the regions for 'friendship' and 'adhesiveness' touched on one side of her head; the result being that she embraced a female friend in a most affectionate manner. Now Braid pressed the area for 'destructiveness' on the other side of her head, and the result was dramatic:

> She rushed forward with great impetuosity to repel some imaginary adversary, whilst, with her other arm and hand, she contrived to shield her friend. Had I not laid hold of her, she would most certainly have rushed through the window. On being roused she was quite oblivious of all she had done.[8]

Spencer Hall visited Braid on one occasion and was able to locate new phrenological faculties on the heads of his hypnotized subjects. He demonstrated the organ for 'acquisitiveness' by pressing on the appropriate spot, which led the subject to remove a silver snuff-box from one of the bystanders. Then, shifting his finger to 'conscientiousness', Hall was able to stop and then reverse the movement of the subject's arm, while she evinced great anxiety to return the object to its owner.

Braid claims that he was alert to observe that Hall did not prompt the subject in any way, while collusion he rules out in view of the smallness of the areas of the head stimulated in order to elicit the appropriate behaviour. But nowhere does he give us details of the conversation, nor does he seem to have been aware that the operator's movements and the attitudes of expectancy on the part of the spectators may have helped to indicate to the subject what was required. Yet, as we have seen, he was earlier insistent on the heightened sensory acuity of the subject providing a basis for some of his apparent supranormal capacities; it is difficult to understand why he does not invoke a similar explanation for phrenohypnotism. Instead, he concludes:

> If I am to believe the evidence of my senses, therefore, *in anything*, I cannot see how I can doubt that some relation subsists between certain points of the cranium, and the mental manifestations, which we excited by acting on them during Hypnotism.[9]

Braid's acceptance of phrenology is tempered by qualifications, for he cannot see that the size of a cerebral organ is necessarily related to its activity, just as a large eye is not necessarily more acute than a small one. Thus, he thinks it improbable that a true delineation of character can be made from mapping the relative size of areas of the skull. However, by phrenohypnotism it appears to be possible to stimulate particular phrenological organs, and one might thereby correct the malfunction of an organ, or by stimulating the antagonistic function one might reduce an overactive organ. The value of phrenology, he believes, lies in this: its therapeutic aspect.

Another difficulty lies in the inexact mapping of the skull, and the tendency for different ideas and emotions to be excited in different subjects when the same point on their heads is touched. Braid thinks that this variation is due to the condition of the subject in the hypnotic trance, i.e., whether he is in the initial excitable or later torpid condition. Braid warns prospective hypnotists that they will have to try the procedure again and again, as it is impossible to tell beforehand the exact moment when their expectations will be fulfilled and the subject will manifest the appropriate behaviour. (Of course, this repetition of procedure is one way in which the operator might unintentionally suggest to the subject what was expected of him. Secondly, we might note the circularity of the argument, in that we only know for certain that we have stimulated the organ of, say, acquisitiveness, when the subject shows acquisitive behaviour.)

The publication of *Neurypnology* was immediately followed by a paper on phrenohypnotism which appeared to cast more doubt on phrenology as a basis for character delineation.[10] However, even now Braid found it impossible to shake off his belief in what was at that time still a respectable science. And that is how he left the matter; he appears to have done no more work in phrenohypnotism, and a promised version of his mature views on the subject never appeared. Instead, he turned his critical attention to the Reichenbach phenomena, and in this line of enquiry his experiments were much more conclusive.

His work was published during 1846 in three papers in the *Medical Times*, a periodical which had already accepted his previous articles on phrenohypnotism.[11] The interest aroused was great enough for Braid to republish his account as a pamphlet entitled, *The Power of the Mind over the Body*. The title was apposite, for Braid's argument was simple and was supported by devastating evidence: the Reichenbach phenomena were all due to suggestions and expectations.

> It is an undoubted fact that with many individuals, and especially of the highly nervous, and imaginative, and abstractive classes, a strong direction of inward consciousness to any part of the body, especially if attended with the expectation or belief of something being about to happen, is quite sufficient to change the physical action of the part, and to produce such impressions from this cause alone, as Baron Reichenbach attributes to his new force. Thus every variety of feeling may be excited from an internal or mental cause – such as heat or cold, pricking, creeping, tingling, spasmodic twitching of muscles, catalepsy, a feeling of attraction or repulsion, sights of every form or hue, odours, tastes, and sounds, in endless variety, and so on, according as accident or intention may have suggested.[12]

Braid's first experiments were with magnets applied close to the skin of subjects in the waking state, who typically reported the physical effects claimed by Reichenbach. By blocking the subject's vision, and doing nothing himself, while leading the subject to believe he was again using the magnet, Braid obtained the same, or even more intense, responses as he had on the previous trials with the magnet.

Other experiments were conducted in darkened rooms with the subjects being instructed to stare at large horseshoe magnets, which, Braid suggested, would be seen to produce flames. The subjects, some in the waking state, others under hypnosis, were speedily convinced that they did indeed see red flames, sparks, etc., emanating from the magnet. They continued to see them when Braid covered the magnet or even took it out of the room and they were in fact staring at a blank wall.

In an amusing account of a visit to a London physician, who had obtained wonderful results with magnets applied to mesmerized patients, Braid clearly demonstrated the effects of indirect suggestion. The physician described to Braid how a magnet would produce catalepsy of the limbs in a patient who, in a mesmeric state, was in the same room, and who had presumably overheard their conversation. After the physician had applied the magnet and obtained the desired effect, Braid, in turn, stated that he had an instrument in his pocket which was quite as powerful. The instrument was about three inches long and attached to a ring. He told the doctor that it would produce catalepsy in the patient's arms and legs; it did. Having removed the catalepsy by wafting air over the afflicted parts, he explained that his instrument would now have the opposite effect and that the patient would be unable to grasp it; again, the effect was as predicted. Now he made her limbs rise and stiffen when they were touched with the instrument; next he made them drop and become flaccid. He woke her up, and sent her back into a trance by applying the ring of the instrument to the third finger of her right hand. He then woke her again, put the ring on the second finger of her left hand and told the doctor that now he would be unable to mesmerize her. These and other effects were readily produced so long as the patient overheard Braid's predictions, for the magical instrument was nothing more than the key to Braid's portmanteau.

Braid's explanation of the Reichenbach phenomena was well received by the medical and scientific world, and his reputation was much enhanced by this short pamphlet.[13] In his rejection of any new imponderable force, as in the rejection of animal magnetism, we see his preference for parsimonious explanation in terms of a person's physical and mental capacities. In his clear demonstrations of the effects of directing attention to parts or functions of the body, he also saw how such a power could be of curative value in disease.

Braid's cautious and careful assessment of Reichenbach's claims was in remarkable contrast to Elliotson's uncritical enthusiasm. The difference in their reactions was no doubt a reflection of their natures and attitudes towards findings apparently supportive of the fluidic theory. However, their antagonism went further. The *Zoist*'s neglect of Braid's work has already been noted. When he was mentioned in its pages, it was with something like scorn. Thus, he is referred to as 'the renowned Mr Braid of Manchester', and the sarcasm is evident in the context.[14] On another occasion, when Elliotson completed the cure of a patient previously hypnotized by Braid, the hypnotic procedure is described as 'the coarse method practised by Mr Braid'.[15]

Braid himself was not without aggression, and it would seem likely that he is referring to Elliotson in the following passage:

> In consequence of my *hypnotic heresy*, and my honest endeavours to protect myself and hypnotism against the most unfair and wilfull misrepresentation by a chief in the mesmeric school, this gentleman, who as well as his friends, had raised a mighty outcry against the cruelty and injustice, illiberality and persecution which the medical profession had manifested towards *him*, in consequence of his having adopted the mesmeric notions and practice in some cases, carried his spleen and persecuting spirit against me to such a pitch, that he raised such determined opposition at headquarters as deprived me of an official appointment which had been most kindly and voluntarily offered to be secured for me by the chairman of a public board; and which election, I would have good reason to believe, would have been decided in my favour, but for the implacable opposition to me, for the above-named cause, of this illiberal, vindictive, and persecuting mesmeric autocrat.[16]

Apart from his personal animosity with Elliotson, Braid encountered strong opposition from both medical and mesmeric establishments. He attributed this antagonism to his role as an originator:

> Like the originators of all new views, however, hypnotism has subjected me to much contention; for the sceptics, from not perceiving the difference between my method and that of the mesmerists, and the limited extent of my own pretensions, were equally hostile to hypnotism as they had been to mesmerism; and the mesmerists, thinking their craft was in danger – that their mystical idol was threatened to be shorn of some of its glory by the advent of a new rival – buckled on their armour, and soon proved that *odium mesmericum* was as inveterate as the *odium theologicum*.[17]

The *Lancet*'s ban on all mesmeric submissions extended to Braid's work, and no notice was taken of his publications during his lifetime.[18] The fact that the *Medical Times* accepted Braid's papers was to be attributed to its rivalry with the *Lancet* and its endeavour to attract readers, rather than to any editorial commitment to Braid's views. It continued hostile towards mesmerism in general, although that hostility was muted in comparison with the *Lancet*'s. Apart from the *Medical Times*, Braid found that only the *Edinburgh Medical and Surgical Journal* was open to him. Here he published an article on mesmeric anaesthesia but not without dissension among the editors, which led to the resignation of one of them.[19]

Generally, however, Braid was content to produce his work in pamphlet or book form. And it was in similar format that he was attacked by leading mesmerists. One example will suffice. J.C. Colquhoun, a lawyer and well known as the writer of *Isis Revelata*, an early and credulous account of mesmerism, devoted some space in his final work to what he considered to be Braid's pretensions. The book, *An History of Magic, Witchcraft and Animal Magnetism*, appeared in two volumes in 1851, soon after Braid had published a pamphlet on human hibernation, based on reports of Indian fakirs. While welcoming Braid's observations in this respect, Colquhoun accused him in general of being 'uncandid, uncourteous, and unjust towards fellow-labourers in the magnetic mine.'[20] Braid, he believed, was seeking to supplant mesmerism by hypnotism so that he could become entitled to be considered as the inventor of a new science. However, all that he had done was to adopt a portion of the mesmerists' discoveries and to depreciate the remainder, in particular the reality of clairvoyance and higher phenomena, which to Braid were 'a mockery of the human understanding.'

Braid, who was of orthodox Christian belief, took Colquhoun's criticisms to imply that he was a materialist and replied heatedly in his next major publication. Before consideration of that work, the 72-page pamphlet on hibernation is worthy of mention. Entitled *Observations on Trance: or, Human Hybernation*, it appeared in 1850, and consisted largely of recorded and well authenticated cases in which Indian fakirs had survived burial and entombment over a period of days. Braid drew the analogy with the hibernation of animals, and explained the achievements in terms of an ability voluntarily to enter a trance state in which the vital functions were reduced to a minimum compatible with the continuance of life. So impressed was Braid by these accounts that he concluded his work with a list of precautions that should be taken to prevent damage to any patient who is apparently unconscious. It was possible, he thought, for tissue damage, produced for experimental or surgical reasons, in an hypnotized, drugged or anaesthetized person to have a psychological effect after the patient had been restored to his normal state.[21] Also, as there was no certain sign of death, he recommended that patients who were apparently dead should not be interred until unmistakable signs of bodily decomposition were observed.

Braid had made no apparent theoretical advance in his views on trance induction at this time. The preface to his pamphlet contains an identical statement to that in *Neurypnology* as to how the hypnotic state could be obtained. Dissatisfaction with his early theory and nomenclature was first expressed in his next book, *Magic, Witchcraft, Animal Magnetism, Hypnotism and Electro-biology* (1852).[22] It was incorrect, he now thought, to use the term 'hypnotism' to describe conditions which varied widely; only the one in ten of his patients who passed into a state resembling sleep and who were amnesic upon awakening could strictly be described as having been 'hypnotized'.

> The real origin and essence of the hypnotic condition is the induction of a habit of abstraction or mental concentration, in which, as in reverie or spontaneous abstraction, the powers of the mind are so much engrossed with a single idea or train of thought, as, for the nonce, to render the individual unconscious of, or indifferently conscious to, all other ideas, impressions, or trains of thought.[23]

He was now convinced that all hypnotic phenomena were the result of mental concentration. The fixed gazing and the concentration of attention tended to produce 'monoideism'. An individual in the normal waking state might be led to fix his attention on one part or function of his body, and to withdraw it from other parts, as a result of impressions received from without, either in the form of verbal suggestions or physical manipulations. In this way, 'dominant ideas' were produced, which reacted on the body.

A new terminology was necessary to replace the old hypnotic terms. 'Monoideism' was suggested as an alternative to 'hypnotism', with 'monoideize' to replace 'hypnotize', 'monoideizer' for 'hypnotist', and so on. These rather awkward terms never caught on, and Braid himself was forced to continue to use the original terms which had been such popular successes.

The mental and physical phenomena of hypnotism resulted from the presence of dominant ideas. These might already exist in the subject's mind before trance occurred, or might be produced through suggestions on the part of the operator. The operator was like an engineer, who activated the forces in the subject's own organism and directed them by his suggestions.

Braid was now able to explain his previously mysterious finding that a catalepsy induced under hypnotism could be instantly abolished by a current of air over the limb. The whole attention of the subject had been directed to the muscles of the limb, but the current of air suddenly called the attention to the surface of the skin; as it was only possible when hypnotized to attend to one function at a time, the muscular rigidity was lost when the attention was withdrawn and directed elsewhere.

What was previously called hypnotic sleep was in fact the antithesis of ordinary sleep, because the latter condition arose from 'a diffusive state of mind, or complete loss of power of fixing the attention', while the state of concentration, which was the basis of hypnotic sleep, enabled the subject to develop rigidity, agility, insensibility, etc., according to the ideas which passed successively through his mind. Thus, if the attention was directed towards a particular movement, the nervous force was sent into the relevant muscles, often without the subject's volition, because he had lost the power to neutralize the dominant idea introduced by the hypnotist.

Part of Braid's book is taken up with an answer to Colquhoun's strictures, which need not delay us here. It is interesting to note in passing that Braid had attended séances, in which paranormal capacities were supposed to be exhibited, only to be confirmed in his scepticism. For example, Mlle Prudence Bernard gave a demonstration of eyeless vision in Manchester in 1852, and in Braid's account of the proceedings it is clear that he considered the bandaging of her eyes to be inadequate, and was unable to prevail upon her manager to introduce more rigorous controls.[24] Apart from these cases of apparent fraud, his experiences had led him to conclude that:

The whole of the really striking achievements of mesmeric

clairvoyants – which are not simply occasional coincidences and
shrewd guesses – are merely results of concentrated attention,
quickened memory, exaltation of the natural organs of special
sense, with self-confidence, and accurate deductions as to what
might be calculated upon regarding the future, from contemplation
of the circumstances in the existing case, compared with what was
known from past experience.[25]

Having disposed of the paranormal aspects of mesmerism, Braid
claims for hypnotism everything that mesmerism has achieved, and
more. His induction procedure is more rapid and he has never had
any difficulty in waking his patients, nor do they ever experience any
annoyance from being touched by persons other than the operator, a
common phenomenon with mesmerized subjects. It would seem from
these remarks that Braid believed that the hypnotic and mesmeric states
were different, although in *Neurypnology* he had written of them as
though they were identical; an uncertainty on this issue is apparent in
much of his writing and he appears never to have come to a definite
conclusion.

In one other respect Braid differed from Colquhoun and the mesmerists: he refused to regard mesmerism or hypnotism as a medical panacea.
Colquhoun took this view to such lengths that he regarded the 'magnetic
temperament' of the prescriber of a drug as more important than the drug
itself. Braid pointed out that there was sufficient proof of the efficacy
of some medicines for Colquhoun's view to be fallacious, although
he accepted that the manner of the doctor and his confidence in his
prescription might well be contributory factors. Here Braid seems at his
judicious best.

In his approach to electrobiology one can sense Braid's concern that
the exponents of this new American technique should not be allowed
to take the credit for a discovery which was essentially his. The
resemblance of the electrobiologists' procedures to those of Braid was
remarkable, and, as the first publications of the electrobiologists dated
from the 1850s and as Grimes actually referred to Braid in his main
work, it seemed to Braid very probable that the idea had been pirated.
It was certainly a commercial success, as the metal discs were saleable
in a way that the magnetic fluid was not.

Two exponents of the system visited England in 1851, and the demonstrations by Darling and by Stone led to large gatherings, so much so that one critic entitled his pamphlet *The Mesmeric Mania of 1851*, and he included Darling's procedures under this heading.[26] According to one participant – William Gregory, Professor of Chemistry at Edinburgh, and the translator of Reichenbach – Darling used a coin to obtain concentration of the subject's thoughts. Fixation of the object was required for a period as long as 15 minutes, Darling then closed the subject's eyes and told him that he could not open them. If he could, Darling would stare at him, holding his hand, and repeat the attempt. A second failure led to the subject being dismissed.

It is clear that the procedure had nothing 'electrical' about it, and, as Braid comments, there should have been no need for suggestions by the operator, any more than one needed to speak to an electric telegraph in order for it to convey a message. The electrobiologists' claim that unspoken thoughts could be communicated by the power of the will were readily dismissed by Braid as yet another instance of unconscious suggestion by the operator and spectators, who imply by their speech and movements what they require of the subject. As in hypnotism, the changes in a subject's muscular and sensory systems resulted from an over-excited imagination and a fixed concentration on a single idea.

Braid's later writings on hypnosis include a treatment of fascination, which he explains as similar to hypnosis in the disturbance caused in nervous centres originating from the presence of a prevailing idea.[27] Sometimes a complete suspension of movement is produced, as when a snake fascinates its prey, and sometimes a continued movement, as when a person is drawn into danger without being able to prevent it. This kind of non-volitional movement is the reason why tables tilt in séances, a phenomenon which has deceived many, 'who thought the tables drew them, but it was they who pushed the tables.'

The comments on table-turning were printed as an appendix to a collection of cases published under the title *Hypnotic Therapeutics* in 1853. It is apparent here, as in his later publication on paralyses in 1855, that he has not developed his views beyond the theory of monoideism. However, he now makes it clear that he thinks therapeutic suggestions can be effective in the waking state, although they are much more effective during nervous sleep when the attention is so much more concentrated, and when the 'imagination and faith, or expectant ideas in the mind of the patient, are so much more intense than in the ordinary waking condition'.[28]

He provides a very good example of the way in which an 'idea' in the patient's mind can bring about a change in the function of an organ: he hypnotized a nursing mother and by touching her left breast and having her think of her baby and the fullness of her breast, produced an augmented flow of milk in that breast. Upon her later complaining that he had made her lop-sided, as her left breast was now over-large, he told her that he would reduce it under hypnotism. Instead, by the same procedure as before, he enlarged her right breast, which also began to produce such a copious flow of milk that the mother was able to feed her infant for another six months, although, before being hypnotized, she had complained of having very little milk left.

In his *Physiology of Fascination* Braid had promised to produce an account of the whole of his research in a volume to be entitled *Psycho-Physiology: embracing Hypnotism, Monoideism and Mesmerism*. The work never appeared, nor did a revised edition of *Neurypnology* intended for the French market. Braid died suddenly in 1860, leaving some work in manuscript to his daughter. She in turn bequeathed it to her brother, who gave it to Wilhelm Preyer, Braid's German translator, and it was in Preyer's translation that it first appeared in 1890.[29]

On the Distinctive Conditions of Natural and Nervous Sleep contains Braid's final thoughts on the nature of the hypnotic state. In it he rejects the theory of monoideism because he has found that it is not the case that a hypnotic subject can attend to only one point at a time. Indeed, the hypnotic state is not very different from the waking state after all: it is essentially another state of consciousness. One does not have to go through a condition resembling sleep in order to enter the hypnotic state. Volition is unimpaired, and it is not true that subjects can be made to perform acts against their will or moral judgment. The loss of memory which follows on awakening from the hypnotic state can always be restored by subsequent hypnotism. Thus, a better descriptive term than monoideism is 'double consciousness'.

In view of its obscure origin and very late publication, Braid's final theory had no impact, and it was his first hypnotic theory that remained associated with his name, his theoretical advances from that position not being generally recognized. A frequent criticism of Braid, found particularly in the French literature, to the effect that he made no advance on Faria, seems to be based on just such a truncated knowledge of his publications. For example, Bernheim attributes to Faria the discovery of hypnosis by suggestion, while to Braid he allows little more than the coining of a new term, although he accepts that Braid's experiments and case studies were meritorious.[30] His argument would seem to turn on Braid's failure to give direct spoken suggestions in his earlier work. At that time Braid's use of suggestion was indirect, with eye fixation to produce the hypnotic state and with manipulation of the body to effect therapeutic change. According to Bernheim, making the patient's limbs cataleptic does not produce the circulatory changes claimed by Braid, and the success of such a procedure must have depended on indirect suggestion – the patient knowing what was intended and expecting it to work. Faria used speech to induce hypnosis and to bring about various hypnotic phenomena; he should therefore deserve to be credited with priority. However, Braid did use verbal suggestion in his later therapy, as reported in *Hypnotic Therapeutics*; but even there it does not enjoy the fundamental role ascribed to it by Liébault and Bernheim (see Chapter 13).

In a careful comparison of Faria and Braid, a later writer, Dalgado, finds that nearly all Braid's discoveries were anticipated by Faria.[31] He merely grants to Braid the discovery of a type of echolalia where the subject does not just imitate another's speech but another's song. (Braid once had a hypnotized girl, ignorant of music, copy the singer Jenny Lind in the most complex vocal exercises, a feat of which she was said to be completely incapable in the waking state.[32])

The difficulty in making any comparison between Faria and Braid lies in the very obscure and unscientific nature of Faria's single volume. Braid, also, did not express himself clearly in his writing and was frequently misunderstood. His confusion with regard to the separation of the mesmeric and hypnotic states has been mentioned, and his attitude to phrenology was similarly left uncertain. His experiments and demonstrations, on the other hand, were generally straightforward and apparently conclusive. His therapeutic work, too, seems to have been a model.

Braid was certainly very concerned to maintain the priority of his discovery and he could be over-sensitive and over-assertive in response to criticism. His forceful dogmatic manner was associated with a burly frame, and his extraordinary success in inducing trance states by his method may have been more dependent on his appearance and behaviour than he was prepared to admit. After all, he had directed attention away from the mesmerist's personal powers to physiological and psychological processes in the subject himself. It would have been difficult to reintroduce the characteristics of the operator into his theory without weakening it. Although he was able to accept the operator as one source of suggestion, that was a far cry from the notion of rapport long held by the mesmerists.

A practical, somewhat unimaginative man, whose respect for the medical science of the day led him to seek explanations of a limited, yet rigorous and parsimonious kind, Braid's approach made hypnotism more scientifically respectable than mesmerism had ever been. It did not immediately supplant the older doctrine; however, it did weaken the little support there was for mesmerism in medical and scientific circles.

Braid's death made one fact apparent: he had no disciples and had developed no school. In Great Britain interest dwindled rapidly, and publications in the 1860s and 1870s were few. It was not until the formation of the Society for Psychical Research in 1882 that serious research into hypnotism was resumed. In the meantime Braid's work had been taken up in France, and it was in that country that the death throes of animal magnetism were to be witnessed, at the great Salpêtrière hospital.

12

Charcot at the Salpêtrière

Situated in grounds of 100 acres on the left bank of the Seine near the Quai d'Austerlitz and the Jardin des Plantes, the hospital of the Salpêtrière takes its name from its original use as a powder magazine in the reign of Louis XIII. The beginnings of the charitable movement led by Vincent de Paul coupled with the administrative efforts of Cardinal Mazarin led to new buildings on the site, which was converted to a hospice for women, the neighbouring Bicêtre being reserved for men. By the end of the seventeenth century it held 3000 persons: vagabonds, beggars, prostitutes, the mentally defective, the paralytic, the old and the mad. A hundred years later it had grown to be the largest hospice in Europe, with a population of 8000. It was here and at the Bicêtre that Pinel liberated the insane from their chains; the painting by Fleury of the event hangs in the Charcot library there today. Pinel's attempts to reorganize the Salpêtrière as an asylum were continued by Esquirol and other distinguished superintendents, and yet at the date of Jean-Martin Charcot's appointment in 1862 this '*ville des femmes incurables*' still held 5000 inmates of the most varied types.[1] No longer chained, nor sleeping on straw and plagued by rats, but still a diagnostic pandemonium.

Charcot had been born in 1825, the son of an exceptionally artistic coachbuilder. He had served his internship at the Salpêtrière, where, having seen all 'the wilderness of paralyses, tremors, and spasms, for which no name or proper understanding existed', he is said to have commented, '*Faudrait y retourner et y rester.*'[2] Return he did at the age of thirty-six, to the post of chief physician and with the opportunity to bring diagnostic clarity into the confusion surrounding him.

He began by examining every patient in every ward. This gigantic undertaking was probably responsible for a diagnostic method which became peculiar to Charcot. Instead of examining patients in the wards, he had them brought to him in a small room furnished with nothing more than a wardrobe, a table and a few chairs. The room and its furniture were all painted black, which must have produced a sombre effect. The patient stripped naked while an intern gave a summary of the case.

> Then there was a long silence, during which Charcot looked, and kept looking at the patient while tapping his hand on the table. His assistants, standing close together, waited anxiously for a word of enlightenment. Charcot continued to keep silent. After a while he would ask the patient to make a movement, induce him to speak, ask that his reflexes be tested and that his sensory capacities be examined. And again there would be silence, Charcot's mysterious silence. Finally, he would call for a second patient, examine him like the preceding one, call for a third patient, and always without saying a word while making comparisons among them.
>
> This meticulous observation, particularly of a visual type, is at the root of all Charcot's discoveries. The artist in him, who went hand in hand with the physician, played an important role in these discoveries.[3]

Charcot was an extreme visualizer who was accustomed to look repeatedly at incomprehensible conditions until suddenly he reached an understanding. His method of diagnosis and his method of teaching both illustrated this strong visual component in his thinking. For example, in his Friday lectures, which were to become famous, he would introduce one patient after another, sufferers from the same or similar conditions, to allow the audience to compare and contrast their demeanours. When he was lecturing on tremor, several women patients wearing hats with long feathers enabled the audience to see the differences necessary for diagnosis. He used diagrams, models and a photographic projector. His interest in photography led him to build a photographic studio at the Salpêtrière and to encourage the photographic recording of patients.

Charcot used his eye like a camera producing composite portraits: a large number of individual cases superimposed one on another led to a strengthening of their similarities and to an omission of their peculiarities on the final image. Above all he searched for patients with major symptoms to serve as model types. Having found the model types and having discerned there the essence of the disease, he could move on to those with lesser symptoms, to what he termed blurred or incomplete forms of the disease ('*formes frustes*').

Other aspects of Charcot's diagnostic procedure must have caught the attention of the reader, such as the explicit dehumanizing of the doctor-patient relationship, with the patient standing naked before the chief physician, who uttered no word of sympathy or interest. It might seem that the writer-physician Axel Munthe was right when he claimed that Charcot was interested only in the diagnosis and its subsequent confirmation at autopsy.[4] Perhaps it was the magnitude of his initial task which allowed little time for courtesy. However, the avoidance of ward rounds and the lack of knowledge of his patients, while of little significance in the scientific understanding of incurable neurological disorders, were to prove Charcot's undoing when he turned his attention to hysteria and hypnotism.

The air of mystery was assiduously cultivated by Charcot, of whom it was said that he liked to exaggerate his physical resemblance to Napoleon. He was as small as Elliotson, pale, clean-shaven with straight black hair, a hard mouth and remarkably sad dark eyes. He was described by Léon Daudet as the most authoritarian man he had ever known, who would brook no contradiction and who would go so far as to wreck the career of any young doctor who persisted in a disagreement with him.[5]

He was impatient of stupidity, and attracted a circle of brilliant men, but his desire for domination created difficulties for those of independent mind. Nevertheless, the Salpêtrière was destined to become the first neurological centre in Europe, with Charcot its premier neurologist.

The Salpêtrière needed much more than a photographic studio to become a research and teaching hospital. It had no laboratories, no examination rooms, and no teaching facilities. Charcot installed workshops, a histological laboratory, a museum of pathological anatomy, consulting rooms for ophthalmology and otolaryngology; he bought microscopes, electrical and laboratory equipment; later he added an outpatient department where men were also treated, and a large auditorium.

He was pushed by his own ambition and helped by the influential circles in which he now moved. Early in his career he had been recommended as personal physician to the Minister of Finance and his private practice was soon to attract patients of the highest social standing from all over the world. He had married a rich widow, he charged high fees, and he lived in style – with a villa at Neuilly and a veritable palace on the Boulevard Saint-Germain, where his Tuesday night receptions attracted a galaxy of politicians, artists and scientists. He travelled extensively, collected paintings, books and antiques, and was well informed in literature and in the history of art.

It was between 1862 and 1870 that he made the discoveries which brought him fame as a neurologist and which enabled him to live in this fashion. His first major piece of research entailed the differentiation of a disease, which had previously been confused with Parkinsonism as it also evoked tremors. He named it 'multiple sclerosis', and showed that the abnormal structures found in the nervous system, and known to anatomists as 'pathological plaques', were characteristic of the disease. Another new clinical entity, amyotrophic lateral sclerosis, was described in 1865, and subsequently named Charcot's Disease. In conjunction with a team of collaborators Charcot demonstrated that the anatomical lesions in poliomyelitis were in the anterior horn cells of the spinal cord. These were his more easily appreciated discoveries, and we have omitted his work on locomotor ataxia, aphasia, cerebral localization especially of the motor areas, and the rarer neuropathological conditions. No wonder Freud likened him to Adam, an Adam before whom God displayed the varieties of neurological disease for him to name them.[6]

Academic preferment followed this period of productive research: he was elected to a Chair of Pathological Anatomy in 1872, and ten years later the Chamber of Deputies voted 200,000 francs to establish a Chair of Diseases of the Nervous System, the first recognition anywhere of neurology as an autonomous discipline. Charcot, who was by then recognized by the French government as a national asset – '*un prince de la science*' – accepted the new Chair, which he held at the Salpêtrière until his death in 1893.

An accidental cause was probably responsible for Charcot's shift of interest from the organic neurological disorders to those for which no organic basis can be found, viz., the neuroses. By 1870 one of the buildings in the Salpêtrière complex had become so dilapidated that it became necessary to evacuate its heterogeneous collection of epileptics, hysterics and psychotics. It was decided to separate the psychotics – mainly, it would appear, depressives and schizophrenics – from those with episodic convulsions, i.e., the hysterics and epileptics. The latter two groups were housed in a new Quarter for Pure

Epileptics, and, as Senior Physician, Charcot assumed charge of this department.

His valued technique of searching for a lesion at autopsy was now useless, the causes of these illnesses were dynamic or 'functional', that is, the causes lay in the inappropriate functioning of the nervous tissue rather than in damage to its anatomy. Charcot likened hysteria and epilepsy to sphinxes, because symptoms without an anatomical substratum were to the mind of the physician lacking in that appearance of solidity and objectivity possessed by those with appreciable organic lesions. That did not mean, however, that such illnesses were inaccessible to analysis. Referring to Pierre Briquet, a senior physician at the Paris Faculty, who had written an extensive work on hysteria in 1859, Charcot claimed that he had: 'established beyond dispute, that hysteria is governed in the same way as other morbid conditions by *rules* and *laws*, which attentive and sufficiently numerous observations always permit us to establish.'[7]

Charcot's first task was to bring his objective neurological analysis to bear on hysteria, to describe these rules and laws, and then to see if he could distinguish the condition from epilepsy. His approach was still that of the neuropathologist, whose interest was in sensory capacities and motor functioning, and not that of a psychologist wishing to understand hysteria in terms of its psychological function. It was also still his endeavour to find perfect full-blown examples of the disease, and to work from that basis towards the incomplete forms.

The perfect examples of what became known as 'major hysteria' (*la grande hystérie*) showed four stages in their hysterical attacks. The attack began with an epileptoid stage, in which the patient lost consciousness and fell to the ground. A premonitory 'aura' heralded this event and took a variety of forms, e.g., the patient might experience palpitations, tremors, pains in the body, especially in the ovarian region, a lump in the throat (so common as to be designated *globus hystericus*), hallucinations, involuntary coughing and yawning. After loss of consciousness a tonic phase ensued in which the limbs jerked in violent oscillations, and that in turn was followed by a phase of muscular relaxation. The whole epileptoid stage lasted a few minutes and there was considerable variation in the duration and intensity of the symptoms.

The second stage was sometimes known as 'clownism' on account of the gymnastic movements of a quite surprising nature, which would often appear to be impossible for untrained bodies. Typically, the patient would move rapidly from a lying to a sitting posture and continually repeat these sit-ups – or *salutations*, as they were called. Sometimes the body would be arched as in a wrestler's bridge, supported by the top of the head and the feet, the famous *arc-en-cercle*. A large drawing of this posture adorned the walls of the Salpêtrière lecture room and is to be seen in Brouillet's well known painting of a Charcot lecture.

The third stage was much more variable than the preceding ones and was termed by Charcot *attitudes passionnelles*. The patient now appeared to go through a variety of emotional states – such as fear, love, rapture, hatred – which were acted out with great expressiveness. Sometimes a scene from earlier experience, often a scene related to the genesis of the illness, would be re-lived. The patient might scream, have imaginary conversations, or make long declamatory speeches.

The classical fourth stage of post-hysterical derangement involved a confused delirium in which the patient might remain for several hours or even days. More usually, the first three stages completed the attack, although it might immediately recycle and begin again with the epileptoid collapse.

Many patients did not exhibit major hysteria; their attacks were limited to one or two stages or were more muted in form. Thus, they might jerk their limbs and weep and little more. These *formes frustes* of the disease were known as 'minor hysteria' (*la petite hystérie*). Charcot claimed that throughout the wards one could observe all transitions between the scantiest symptom complex and the fullest attack, but they were all essentially forms of the same disease, manifested in various ways on account of the various derangements in cerebral functioning.

Differences from epileptic seizures were of major diagnostic significance. Charcot was well aware of the tendency for the hysteric to imitate the seizure of the epileptic patient, especially when both types of patient were housed together, but he believed that careful observation could distinguish them. The hysteric was given more warning of an attack by the aura preceding the epileptoid stage, and thus was usually able to avoid injury in falling. The hysteric struggled violently and spoke or shouted, while the epileptic did no more than groan; the hysteric could have numerous attacks during the day, and yet his temperature, unlike that of the epileptic, was not raised, nor was there any intellectual impairment. While the administration of bromide to some extent inhibited an epileptic fit, it had no effect on hysteria. Furthermore, one could frequently distinguish hysterical patients by their possession of stigmata, namely, anaesthesias and other sensory deficits.

The search for stigmata was reminiscent of a medieval witch hunt.[8] Patients were pricked all over their bodies to discover any localized areas of anaesthesia, in very much the same way that witches had been identified. The comparison with the witch hunt pleased Charcot, who was glad to be able to affirm the antiquity of his procedures, for hysteria was not an illness limited to his time, and had not witches often been hysterical women?[9]

Typical of the anaesthesias were those of the 'glove and stocking' type, with clear-cut boundaries which were anatomically meaningless in terms of the distribution of the sensory nerves, but which were psychologically meaningful in terms of a person's conceptualization of his or her body and its functions. Deficits in the special senses were also common, especially visual defects of various kinds. Loss of colour vision, restrictions in the extent of the visual field, loss of acuity in one or both eyes, such defects could even occur without the patient's awareness and were revealed only upon ophthalmological examination.

The motor paralyses were, of course, apparent to the patient and were not usually difficult to distinguish from simulated illness, in that the hysterical variety did not disappear during sleep, although deep anaesthesia would abolish them too. In an experimental demonstration, Charcot showed how a slight young girl suffering from hysteria could sustain a weight with her paralysed thumb over the course of half an hour with no apparent effort, as indicated by her regular moderate breathing. In comparison, a vigorous young man performed the feat only with difficulty and great respiratory effort.[10]

Hysterical paralyses could also be of the flaccid kind where the limb hung uselessly, and they were often accompanied by anaesthesia of the affected part. The grosser varieties might lead to the patient being unable to stand or walk, in spite of no defect being discoverable when the patient was examined in a recumbent position.

The photographic laboratory of the Salpêtrière did its best to record these numerous manifestations of hysterical behaviour. With Charcot's guidance, the photographs and text by two of his pupils, Bourneville and Régnard, appeared in three volumes between 1876 and 1880.[11] This iconography of the Salpêtrière attempted to capture photographically the characteristic and often dramatic postures adopted by patients during their attacks and in response to various stimuli. A star and much photographed performer was the young woman given the various pseudonyms of *Augustine, Louise Glaiz, X, L* and *G.* She entered the Salpêtrière at the age of 15, and 5 years later served as the first subject for Bourneville and Régnard. They describe her as 'coquettish, spending much time on her appearance, arranging her abundant hair in various styles'.[12] She was an excellent example of a sufferer from major hysteria with four 'hysterogenic zones', i.e., pressure over the right ovarian region, the umbilicus, the breasts or the spine would trigger an hysterical attack. She would experience a premonitory aura, beginning with pain over the right ovarian region and the sensation of a lump moving from there to the throat, accompanied by palpitations and headache. She would then have time to lie down before the epileptoid stage began. Strangely enough, pressure on the ovarian region would also terminate an attack, a general finding with these patients. Bourneville even had an ovarian 'compressor' made as a therapeutic aid.[13]

With no male in-patients at the Salpêtrière it is not perhaps surprising that the iconography is limited to depictions of females. However, Charcot did not accept the then current view that hysteria was limited to women; on the contrary he was responsible for bringing his authority behind the view that men also could show this type of reaction; indeed, among the poorer section of the community the incidence among males was greater than among females, a fact Charcot ascribed to 'traumatism and intoxication'.[14]

Charcot's work on the traumatic paralyses was revolutionary. It was generally thought that paralyses following a physical shock were due to lesions in the nervous system, but Charcot demonstrated conclusively that some of these paralyses were functional. Thus, in the case of a young stonemason, *Pin,* who was bruised slightly in a fall, a partial paralysis of the left arm appeared three days later. Three weeks later, the paralysis of the arm was complete and accompanied by anaesthesia of that limb. The anaesthesia had a clearly hysterical demarcation, extending neatly from the shoulder to the wrist. A similar case, *Porcz,* had a flaccid paralysis of the right arm following a fall on to his right shoulder from a coach which he was driving. Again the anaesthesia was of the glove and sleeve variety. Another male example was the patient, *Lys,* also a young stonemason, who had been involved in a quarrel in which his adversary had thrown a large stone which narrowly missed him. Hysterical convulsions began 15 days later, together with tremor of the limbs.

This last case illustrated the fact that the trauma could be of a psychological kind; as Charcot described this type of case in one of his lectures:

> I want to speak about these strange paralyses that have been designated as psychic paralyses, paralyses arising from an idea, and paralyses resulting from imagination. I did not say, and make note of this, 'imaginary paralyses', because, in short, these motor weaknesses that develop as a result of a psychic disturbance are just as real as those arising from an organic lesion.[15]

The importance of psychological causes in bringing about conditions that more or less mimicked those resulting from organic lesions was illustrated most vividly by the new experimental technique introduced by Charcot into his Salpêtrière clinic in 1878. Thirty-five years had elapsed since the publication of Braid's *Neurypnology*, and French interest in hypnotism had been slow to develop. According to his first biographer, Guillain, Charcot was familiar with Braid's book – he was certainly a voracious reader of medical and scientific publications in the main European languages – but it is not clear when he read the book. Certainly, it was E. Azam of Bordeaux who first drew French attention to Braid's work in 1858 and who communicated the results of some preliminary experiments of his own to Paul Broca.[16] Broca decided to use the technique to induce analgesia in a young woman who was to be operated on for an anal abscess. Although she cried out when the surgeon made the initial incision, she gave no other signs of pain, and when awakened fifteen minutes later she recollected nothing. Broca reported the case to the Academy of Sciences on 7 December 1859, giving appropriate credit to Azam.[17]

Broca, whose work on cerebral localization had brought him international fame, knew Charcot, as, indeed, did Azam, and it is possible that Charcot received his first intimation of Braid's work from these men.

In the following year, a course on 'Braidisme' was published by Philips, the pseudonym of Durand de Gros who had returned to France after living in America where he had been impressed by Grimes' discovery of 'electrobiology'. Durand de Gros realized that the induction techniques of Grimes and Braid were similar and that Braid's theory was more adequate. His own theory was similar to the second version of Braid's in that it stressed that the purpose of fixating a bright object was not just to fatigue the eye muscles but to restrict sensory input and to concentrate the thoughts. Similar to Braid in his stress on the efficacy of therapeutic suggestions made during hypnotic sleep, he differed from him sharply in accepting a telepathic link between operator and subject.[18]

Another and later user of Braid's technique was Lasègue, one of Charcot's predecessors at the Salpêtrière. He had employed the method to bring about catalepsy, which, he pointed out, was normally found in hysterical attacks.[19] However, his 1865 paper attracted little attention, and it was not until another physician, Charles Richet (a subsequent Nobel Prize laureate in physiology), began to publish a series of papers in the next few years that greater interest was aroused. Richet had been convinced by a stage hypnotist of the genuineness of hypnotic phenomena, and his own experiments had confirmed him in this belief. In his writings he argued skilfully for the importance of the psychological changes that could be brought about under hypnotic influence, while the physical changes appeared to him to be more variable and of less interest, a viewpoint he was to change in the light of Charcot's subsequent work.[20]

It is probable too that Charcot was mentally prepared to use hypnotism after he had become convinced of the efficacy of metallotherapy in removing anaesthesias in hysterical patients. Burq's work in this field dated back to 1851 and had been favourably viewed by Elliotson. Burq's claims were now based upon twenty-five years' experience, and when Charcot was nominated as the President of a Commission of Enquiry to investigate these claims he decided to repeat Burq's experiments at the Salpêtrière. Bourneville, the co-author of the 'iconography', and his colleague, Paul Richer, became enthusiastic proponents of the therapy when they found that anaesthesias did respond to metallic contact, but only if the appropriate metal was used. Most striking was the phenomenon of 'transfer', whereby when a function had been restored to one side of the body, the other side would acquire the original disability. Thus, feeling would be restored to the right leg by contact with a metal, only for it to be lost in the left leg. Magnets were found to be particularly efficacious in producing transfer, and Charcot noted that some amelioration in symptoms might be produced by repeated applications of a magnet, as the symptoms tended to weaken as they went from one side to the other![21]

Charcot's error, as in Burq's own work and in Elliotson's experiments, lay, of course, in supposing a direct physical influence from the metal or magnet; the role of suggestion was completely overlooked, an ominous harbinger of errors to come.[22]

Whoever the precursors and whatever the channels of influence, Charcot published in 1878 a first preliminary communication on the use of Braid's method.[23] Although he avoided the use of the word 'hypnotism', he described how two young hysterical women, *Alphonsine Bar* and *Louise Glaiz*, to whom we have referred, became cataleptic after fixating a bright light. By cutting off the source of light, or by closing the patient's eyes, the operator induced a state of lethargy; this state could in turn be changed into one of somnambulism if the subject were spoken to in a peremptory fashion.

Further papers in the same year repeated the view that three states were involved in hypnotism, and Charcot now adopted this term. He also now described the phenomenon of muscular hyperexcitability, which appeared to accompany the lethargic state. Mechanical pressure on a muscle or nerve had much the same effect as electrical stimulation in the normal state: the relevant muscle would contract strongly and independently.

Bourneville lost no time in incorporating photographs of hypnotized patients in succeeding volumes of the iconography, and it was no secret that Charcot was working intensively with hypnotism. However, one has to wait until 1882 for a full description of the hypnotic condition. In that year Charcot applied for membership of the Academy of Sciences, a vacancy having occurred through the death of Professor Cloquet. In pursuit of his aim, Charcot presented a famous paper, 'On the various nervous states determined by hypnotization in hysterics', a paper which purported to give an objective description of the hypnotic condition in purely neurological terms. As Pierre Janet was later to remind his readers: 'It must not be forgotten that the Academy had already thrice condemned all researches into animal magnetism, and that it was a signal exploit to make this learned assembly listen to a lengthy description of kindred phenomena.'[24]

Charcot's investigations into what he now termed 'major hypnotism' (*grand hypnotisme*) had convinced him of the truth of his early observations: hypnotism was made up of a series of nervous states which were distinguishable by particular symptoms. He summarized his findings for the Academy:

> In the *cataleptic state*, the patient holds his limbs in whatever position they have been placed, tendon reflexes are abolished or are very weak; there are long respiratory pauses, and various automatic impulses may be provoked.
>
> In the *lethargic state*, muscles are flaccid, respiration is deep and rapid, tendon reflexes are remarkably exaggerated, and the patient shows 'neuromuscular hyperexcitability', that is, an aptitude of the muscles to contract strongly if the tendon, muscle, or corresponding nerve is touched.
>
> In the third, *somnambulistic state*, tendon reflexes are normal, there is no neuromuscular hyperexcitability, although certain slight stimulation causes a state of rigidity in the limbs; there is usually an exaltation of certain little-known varieties of cutaneous sensitivity, of the muscular sense, of certain special senses, and it is usually easy to bring about, on demand, the most complicated automatic acts.[25]

All Puységur's somnambulistic marvels were encompassed in that last line of Charcot's description! Equally remote from animal magnetism, or so it seemed to his audience, were Charcot's methods for inducing these states in his hysterical patients. Catalepsy in a waking subject was produced by the fixation of a bright light, or by a loud and sudden noise, such as a blow on the Chinese gong used for this purpose at the Salpêtrière.[26] In some patients catalepsy could occur in response to pressure on certain areas of the body, 'hypnogenic zones', analogous to the hysterogenic zones.

Lethargy was produced by prolonged fixation, or by continuous pressure on the eyeballs, or simply by closing the subject's eyelids if he were in the cataleptic state. To transfer the patient back to catalepsy, one merely had forcibly to open his eyes. Curiously enough, it was possible to maintain one side of the body in catalepsy and one side in lethargy, by having one eye open and one closed!

The somnambulistic state sometimes resulted directly from prolonged fixation of the eyes or through continued monotonous stimulation of the other senses, but the usual procedure was to induce it from the cataleptic or lethargic states by the surprising expedient of rubbing the top of the subject's head.

As in his approach to hysteria, Charcot once again restricted himself to the study of reflexes and movements. Such behaviour could not, he thought, be simulated, as it arose from theoretically localizable functional 'lesions' in the nervous system. In his view it was only after having learned to understand the simpler changes characteristic of the hypnotic condition that one should proceed to investigate the psychological intricacies. Earlier investigators had made the mistake of being fascinated by the marvellous without ever having looked scientifically at their subjects. The methods Charcot had used so successfully in the past were now once more to be used to elicit the simple fundamental changes that occurred in the nervous system when susceptible patients were subjected to hypnotic procedures.

Charcot's belief in his method must have been strengthened by the unilateral effects shown by patients such as *Louise Glaiz*, effects which were analogous to the paralyses and other disturbances seen in many organic conditions. Resemblances with hysterical symptoms were also very apparent: the magnet was found to be equally effective in transferring an hypnotically induced symptom from one side of the body to the other as it had been in hysterical states. This discovery was made by Alfred Binet, who was later to become identified with the first successful attempt to scale mental ability. He had joined the Salpêtrière in 1884 at the youthful age of 28, and with a colleague, Charles Féré, had confirmed all of Charcot's major findings with regard to hypnotism. In 1885 they had used a magnet to transfer movements and perceptions from one side of the body to the other when the patient was hypnotized. They cite the somewhat absurd example provided by one patient, *Witt*, who having obeyed the order to use her left hand in order to thumb her nose at a bust of Franz Gall, was induced to change hands and to use her right hand when a magnet was secretly placed near the right side of her head and apparently out of her sight. Magnets also seemed to be able to 'polarize' perceptions and emotions. Thus, an hallucinated red cross on a white background would under the influence of an apparently unseen magnet develop green rays, and then change colour to rose and to white. An emotion of fear expressed towards an hallucinated snake would be changed by the magnet into a caressing approach, and likewise with other 'opposite' emotions.[27]

These transfer phenomena helped to make the assimilation of hypnotism and hysteria almost complete. Both were abnormal mental conditions consequent upon dynamic (functional) rather than structural lesions. Hypnotism was an experimentally induced neurosis that could be brought about only in hysterical patients or in those with an hysterical predisposition. Thus, it also had a diagnostic value in its power to discriminate these patients from epileptics and from those with organic conditions.

Charcot's demonstrations, always of a dramatic variety, now broke new ground. By 1885 he was demonstrating in two young hypnotized hysterical women, exactly similar anaesthesias and paralyses to those of post-traumatic origin suffered by the male patients, *Porcz* and *Pin*, mentioned earlier. By verbal suggestions to the hypnotized subjects, Charcot was able to produce artificially and in a piecemeal fashion anaesthesias from the shoulder to the elbow, the elbow to the wrist, the wrist to the fingers, and finally of the whole arm. Then he was able to undo them systematically. A final demonstration involved the use of the posthypnotic suggestion, that, after awakening, a slap on the back would be sufficient to re-induce paralysis and anaesthesia of the arm. Having demonstrated this effect, Charcot drew the parallel with the shock in the natural environment that had produced the symptoms in the male hysterical patients.

> No doubt the men were not in an hypnotic sleep when they had their falls or when later their paralysis came on. But in this respect it may be enquired whether the mental condition occasioned by the emotion, by the nervous shock experienced at the moment of the accident and for some time after, is not equivalent in a certain measure, in subjects predisposed as *Porcz* and *Pin* were, to the cerebral condition which is determined in hysterics by hypnotism.[28]

It must now seem to us surprising that Charcot seems not to have taken the next apparently obvious step and to have attempted to remove the naturally occurring hysterical symptoms in the same way that he was able to remove the hypnotically induced ones, that is, by hypnotic suggestion. Apparently attempts were made to hypnotize *Porcz* and *Pin*. Charcot alludes briefly to the fact that if these attempts had succeeded it would have 'lightened the therapeutic task', but he explains no further.[29] His faith was put in physical treatments, electrotherapy, massage, cold baths and exercise, and in exhortation and attempts at re-education. These were the routine therapies at the Salpêtrière, coupled with isolation from the parents in the case of young patients, who were rewarded by visits whenever their symptoms ameliorated.

Charcot's lack of interest in therapy has already been noted; he avoided reference to therapeutic suggestion in his lecture courses, and the Salpêtrière's failure to use such a demonstrably powerful technique can be attributed to Charcot's avoidance of what he must have seen as psychological methods, whose uncertainty and lack of precision did not appeal to him as a neurologist; he may also have been afraid of what he might uncover. Instead, he was content to employ hypnotism as an investigatory tool and by its means to reveal the mechanism of the hysterical symptom, work which Freud was later to describe as 'an incomparably fine piece of clinical research'.[30]

By the date of Freud's visit to the Salpêtrière (1885-86), Charcot's Friday morning lectures were attracting large crowds. Open to many professions other than doctors, the audience often contained writers, dramatists, magistrates and philosophers. The resemblance to Elliotson's lecture demonstrations was remarkable, and it was perhaps inevitable that they should have taken on some of the former's theatricality. However, unlike Elliotson, Charcot's position was secure, perhaps too secure, in that as the 'Caesar of the Salpêtrière' little criticism was offered him from within its walls.

As in hysteria, there were rudimentary and less distinct versions of major hypnotism. These *formes frustes* were of little interest to Charcot, and the study of minor hypnotism (*petit hypnotisme*) was left to others. The strategy, which had worked so well with the organic conditions, was maintained with hypnotism as it had been with hysteria: the search for the most perfectly developed examples of this experimental neurosis.

Such examples were not too difficult to find: in addition to *Louise Glaiz* and *Alphonsine Bar*, on whom he had based his preliminary observations, Bourneville and Richer brought a third patient to his notice. *Witt.* (Blanche Wittman) was admitted to the hospital as an adolescent; she was capable of exhibiting full-fledged convulsions, vivid emotional displays, and dramatic hallucinations, as well as anaesthesias and paralyses to order. Apparently a capricious and bossy young woman, she was unpopular with the other patients and went to extreme lengths to maintain her dominant position and to live up to her nickname as '*la reine des hystériques*'. She is portrayed as the patient in Brouillet's painting of a Charcot lecture.[31]

According to Frederick Myers,[32] Blanche was in fact the prototype for the three classical stages of major hypnotism, but as these were established before she became a subject for Charcot's investigations, it seems more probable that she refined them and learned to reproduce them repeatedly and exactly. She and her two colleagues were soon joined by others, and it was on observations and experiments with perhaps a dozen such women that Charcot's discoveries were confirmed. As they were so few in number, it became necessary to employ these gifted performers repeatedly for experimental work and for demonstration purposes. It was a narrow basis on which to build a theoretical structure, and yet Charcot's certainty was understandable. After all, there was so little variation among these patients: they all went regularly into the stages of major hypnotism in response to similar stimuli. If there had been more variation, there might well have been more uncertainty on his part. He was convinced of his meticulous methodology, and as the world's leading neurologist he convinced many others of the scientific respectability of his work.

Hypnotism was rapidly to become an appropriate subject of study by members of the medical profession, after having been proscribed as animal magnetism. In a count of relevant European publications during the decades from 1840 to 1880 an average of less than 30 publications per decade is obtained; during the 1880s, 1030 publications appeared.[33] Without attributing this huge increase solely to Charcot's influence, there is no doubt that his great prestige triggered a change in professional attitudes and in scientific concern.

Charcot was not, however, to remain for long above the reaches of criticism. He had made enemies as well as loyal followers, and the dramatic productions by Blanche and her colleagues were beginning to arouse some disquiet. When a scholarly book by Hippolyte Bernheim, Professor of Medicine at the new University of Nancy, appeared in 1884, the first disagreements with Charcot became manifest; soon the rival schools of Paris and Nancy were to make the differences irreconcilable.

13

The Triumph of Suggestion

Bernheim's interest in hypnotism dated from 1882 when he heard of the local celebrity enjoyed by a country doctor, working in a village outside Nancy, who employed hypnotism in his daily practice. Auguste Liébault was then fifty-five years old, a man of humble origin, who after training at the University of Strasbourg had worked all his life as a general practitioner with a clientèle mainly of peasants. Liébault had long been fascinated by the works of the old magnetists, and when he finally dared to introduce hypnotism into his own practice it was as a free alternative to the orthodox methods for which his patients paid the normal fee. The free treatment proved so popular and so effective that in a few years Liébault found himself with an immense practice and little income.

The results of his practical experience were incorporated in a book which had the distinction of selling five copies in five years.[1] In spite of its lack of popular success the book is important as the source of many of Bernheim's early ideas. Its title, *Du sommeil et des états analogues*, expresses the fundamental theoretical position taken by Liébault, that is, that the somnambulistic state is similar to ordinary sleep. The hypnotist's endeavour is to put the patient in the physiological condition of pre-sleep. This he does by constricting the subject's attention through eye fixation – Liébault knew of Braid's work – and by telling him to think only of sleep.

Attention, conceptualized as nervous energy, is a key factor in Liébault's theorizing. In the waking state, attention is diffuse, with one idea following another. In the sleeping states, there is little attention available to be directed towards the sense organs; instead, it is immobilized in the brain. Thus, the sleeping person is unaware of his surroundings and neither does rational thinking occur.

In the hypnotic state, attention is not subject to any self-regulatory control; instead it can be influenced by suggestions from without. The hypnotist is able to direct it to one or other of the senses to produce anaesthesias, hallucinations, etc., or he can excite particular ideas and emotions and influence memory.

The hypnotist's influence is exerted on the sleeping subject because the subject has entered sleep whilst thinking of the hypnotist. This *rapport* is not peculiar to hypnosis: it can occur in ordinary sleep, for example, when a mother sleeps near her child and will awake at his least cry while remaining asleep during much louder irrelevant noises.

On waking from sleep, the nervous force which has been accumulated in the brain is again diffused throughout the organism. Since it is accordingly diminished in the brain, it becomes impossible for the subject to remember what has happened during hypnotic sleep. According to Liébault, a similar process underlies one's poor recall of dreams after ordinary sleep.

Therapeutic results can be obtained by spoken suggestion, the hypnotized subject being nothing more than an automaton controlled by the hypnotist's suggestions. Posthypnotic suggestions are given pride of place in Liébault's therapy; such therapeutic suggestions are comparable in their persistence to the patient's own memories, but unlike ordinary memories they have to be acted upon as soon as they become conscious. Their strength, he thinks, originates from the accumulation of attention during hypnotic sleep, an accumulation available for discharge posthypnotically through the verbal suggestion of the hypnotist.

Although suggestion was thus given a crucial role in Liébault's theory, he did not consider it to be involved in the induction of the hypnotic state but only when utilized by the hypnotist for therapeutic ends. As we shall see, Bernheim was to extend the explanatory role of suggestion to encompass all hypnotic phenomena, including the induction process.

Just as everyone has the ability to enter ordinary sleep, so, Liébault claims, can everyone under favourable conditions be put into that state of artificial sleep called hypnosis. The great majority will enter a more or less superficial passive state, becoming drowsy or even going into a sleep; only a minority can reach the deeper state of somnambulism. In his own practice Liébault has observed 385 somnambulists out of 2534 patients, the more gifted in this respect being drawn from hysterics, anaemics, those with nervous tics, and women subject to 'the vapours'.

(It will be noted that most of these susceptibles have hysterical-type symptoms.)

Descriptions of Liébault's clinic have been furnished by some of the many visitors who went there after he had achieved a belated fame through Bernheim's writings. An early Dutch visitor, Van Renterghem, described the clinic as an old shed in the corner of Liébault's garden, with whitewashed walls and a stone floor. Liébault treated between 25 and 40 patients in the course of a morning, the treatment being carried out singly but in public with no concern at all for the surrounding noise.[2]

> After asking, if necessary, the patient's complaint and without making any medical examination whatever, he seats the patient, puts his hand on his forehead and, without even looking at him, says, 'You are going to sleep.' Then he closes the patient's eyes at once while assuring him that he is sleeping. He lifts his arm, saying, 'You cannot lower your arm.' If he does lower it, M. Liébault does not seem to notice it. He then asks the patient to rotate his arms and tells him that he cannot stop this movement; while saying this he rotates his own arms vigorously, the patient having his eyes closed all the time.[3]

The patient now received his dose of curative suggestions which were directed towards the negation of the symptoms of which he had complained, together with suggestions for general well-being, such that he would sleep well, feel more energetic, have good digestion, etc.

Milne Bramwell, a British physician, noted that the patients chattered freely with one another and questioned the doctor in a more familiar way than they did in England: 'The quiet ordinary everyday tone of the whole performance formed a marked contrast to the picture drawn by Binet and Féré of the morbid excitement shown at the Salpêtrière.'[4]

Liébault seems not to have prescribed medicines, his reluctance stemming from a belief that it was premature to do so before their action on the body was properly understood. In any case, he had found that suggestions could sometimes be powerful enough to mimic, or even to neutralize the effects of medicine, although he never went so far as to consider them a panacea.

From a theoretical point of view it is not difficult to see in Liébault's book the substance of the teaching of Bertrand, Faria, Noizet and Braid; he was clearly in this tradition, with its refusal to admit a fluidic influence from the operator. Liébault's predilection, described by Bramwell, for giving mothers magnetized water for their infants seems to have arisen not from any conviction on his part that the water was therapeutically 'charged' but rather from the fact that the mothers themselves believed in it and that it was therefore good suggestive practice to use it.[5]

Liébault's suggestive brand of therapy came in for particular praise from the Belgian psychologist, Delboeuf, who visited Nancy in 1888. He describes Liébault's tone as: 'so ardent, so penetrating and so sympathetic, that I have never once listened to it without a feeling of admiration.'[6]

Thus it was as a practitioner that Liébault owed his subsequent fame and achieved his status as the spiritual father of the Nancy School. For the polemicist and active leader of that group we must turn to the younger man, Hippolyte Bernheim. Bernheim had held a position in the medical school at Strasbourg until Alsace-Lorraine had been annexed by the Germans in 1871. He had then moved to the newly founded University of Nancy, where he established a reputation through his research into heart disease and typhoid fever, and where he was appointed to the Chair of Medicine.[7] Of a similar cast of mind to Braid, he had little time for the fantasies of the old magnetists. More critical than Liébault, energetic and tending toward authoritarianism, he was more suited to the role he now assumed as the principle opponent to Charcot.

His first meeting with Liébault in 1882 arose out of curiosity. Having unsuccessfully treated a patient with a persistent neuralgia who had subsequently obtained immediate relief at Liébault's clinic, Bernheim paid him a visit. Sceptical at first, he was soon convinced that he should try Liébault's method with his own patients. After two years' practice he considered he had acquired enough experience to propound his own theory, which he proceeded to do in a slim volume of 110 pages.

The book, *De la suggestion dans l'état hypnotique et dans l'état de veille*, was dedicated to Liébault, although it was Faria, and to a lesser extent Durand de Gros, who came in for Bernheim's particular commendation as the originators of the view that the trance state was not dependent on the power of the operator but on the ability of the subject. Braid who, of course, held strongly to this position was dismissed by Bernheim as of little significance other than as the coiner of the term 'hypnotism'. One can detect here a possible instance of Bernheim's chauvinism, a characteristic which mars the discussion of several French writers of this epoch.[8]

Bernheim's method for inducing the hypnotic state was modelled on that of Liébault, although it seems to have been generally more prolonged and assertive. He describes it thus:

> I say, 'Look at me and think of nothing but sleep. Your eyelids begin to feel heavy, your eyes are tired. They begin to blink, they are becoming moist, you cannot see distinctly. Your eyes are closing.' Some patients close their eyes and go to sleep immediately. With others, I have to repeat these instructions more forcibly and even accompany them with gestures. It makes little difference what sort of gesture is made. I hold up two fingers of my right hand before the patient's eyes, or persuade him to fix his eyes on mine, endeavouring at the same time to concentrate all his attention on the idea of sleep. I say, 'Your eyelids are closing, you cannot keep them open any longer. Your arms feel heavy, so do your legs. You cannot feel anything. Your hands remain motionless. You see nothing, you are going to sleep.' And I add in a commanding tone, 'Sleep!' This word often turns the scales. The patient's eyes close and he goes to sleep or is at least influenced.[9]

In its essentials this technique of Bernheim's is that of the authoritarian type of modern operator; it differs from Braid's in omitting the latter's insistence on catalepsy of the limbs. According to Bernheim, this and all other hypnotic phenomena are produced through suggestion, none of them will occur spontaneously.

Suggestion, then, is given pride of place in his analysis. Suggestions can be classified into positive and negative: positive suggestions are those which bring about actions and cause sensations, including hallucinations, while negative suggestions stop actions and prevent sensations, as in paralyses and anaesthesias.

Bernheim provides a picturesque illustration of the effects of positive suggestions:

> I put a pencil in his mouth, telling him that it is a cigar; he puffs out the smoke . . . I tell him the cigar is too strong and that he will feel ill: he is affected by bouts of coughing and spitting, he feels sick, looks pale, and feels dizzy. I get him to swallow a glass of water,

telling him it is champagne. He thinks it is strong. I give him more: he becomes drunk and staggers about. I say drunkenness is gay: he sings, hiccoughs, and laughs in a silly way. I say drunkenness is sad: he weeps and wails.[10]

And so on. Never, however, was the subject seen to perform acts of which he was normally incapable, and no trace of paranormal powers was ever exhibited. Neither was the subject necessarily forced to act as a blind automaton, a fact most easily noted when posthypnotic suggestions were given. For example, a patient told to walk three times around the room after he had woken up, did it once only. A young hysterical girl told either to walk around the room or to read a prayer, did neither, and then showed extreme astonishment at Bernheim's ability to read her mind when he told her that he knew what she was thinking about at that moment, namely, whether to walk around the room or to read a prayer.

Bernheim provides many examples of experiments employing posthypnotic suggestions, some apparently modifying the patient's physiological function, and making him, for example, suffer from thirst or the need to urinate, and some creating hallucinatory scenes, such as in one case where the patient awoke from hypnosis in his hospital bed to find the other beds in the ward apparently occupied by large dogs instead of people.

One effect of having been hypnotized was to make the patient more compliant and amenable to suggestions when returned to the waking state. In his later work, Bernheim was to emphasize the use of suggestion in the waking state. He is frank in his acknowledgement that it was Braid who first discovered the variety of responses that can be obtained by suggestions made to some subjects when they are wide awake, but, as we have seen, Braid seems rarely to have employed verbal suggestion for therapeutic ends. This Bernheim did, and he was also the first to notice that it was possible to produce anaesthesia and analgesia in the waking state through suggestion.

Not only are all the phenomena of hypnosis brought about by suggestion, but so is the state itself. There is nothing mysterious about the condition, it is merely an exaggeration of what we experience in our everyday lives. We often perform an action immediately after the idea of the action comes to mind. Indeed, there is, Bernheim believes, a natural tendency for such 'ideo-motor' action. 'Ideo-sensory' effects also occur;

for example, when we think of the clock in the room and become aware of its ticking.

In certain circumstances and in some persons these natural tendencies are further developed so that there is no intervention by the intellect. Everyday examples of yawning and falling into step with a companion are cited. An enhancement of the tendency is especially evident in somnolent and sleep states where the subject will not think about a suggestion before obeying it. These states can in turn be brought about by suggestions given in the waking state. Thus the hypnotic state is nothing more than a sleep produced by suggestion.

It follows for Bernheim, as it did for Liébault, that everybody must be capable of entering the hypnotic state. Hypnotizability does not imply hysterical illness; it is found to a greater or lesser degree in all. The most impressionable are those ordinary folk with docile natures, old soldiers, peasants and other manual workers; the least impressionable are the more refined people, especially preoccupied thinkers, who are critical and who resist the process often without being aware of so doing. The really difficult subjects are hypochondriacs, melancholics and insane persons where there is no desire to cooperate. Most of Bernheim's patients were hypnotized on their first visit to his clinic, although he was not quite able to match Liébault's statistic of less than 3% refractory.

To say that so many were hypnotizable is not to say that they all were capable of exhibiting similar phenomena. Bernheim follows Liébault in distinguishing various levels of hypnotic depth. These range from mere sleepiness and loss of initiative, through responsiveness to various simple suggestions, to all kinds of hallucinations and profound somnambulisms with complete amnesia. This scheme, which he was soon to extend to one encompassing nine degrees of hypnotic depth, was the first clear attempt to put hypnotic phenomena on a scale; in common with many later workers Bernheim was well aware that the scale was somewhat arbitrary in view of the many individual differences in responsiveness to various suggestions. Thus, one person might easily respond to a 'difficult' suggestion while an 'easier' suggestion earlier on the scale would not produce an effect. In this connection he mentions the dubious nature of the claim that hypnotic analgesia might one day replace chloroform: he thought it too hit-and-miss ever to serve as a general anaesthetic.

There was little in this first book to which Charcot and his pupils could object. Admittedly Bernheim had not found hypnotism to be a

technique applicable only to hysterical patients, although his more vivid
experiments were performed with such patients, and it would not have
been difficult for Charcot to maintain his position that it was only in these
cases that true examples of major hypnotism were being encountered.
It was, however, noticeable that Bernheim never mentioned having
found the spontaneous neuromuscular hyperexcitability discovered by
the Salpêtrière school; indeed, he did not appear to have found the three
fundamental stages at all. On the other hand, many of Charcot's own
demonstrations came in for Bernheim's approval, and he was frank in
acknowledging the importance of Charcot's influence in overcoming the
general prejudice that had previously prevailed.

Two years later Bernheim's second book appeared. *De la suggestion
et ses applications à la thérapeutique* was in part a revised edition of
his first book. In it he took into account the criticisms he had received
and provided more evidence to support his viewpoint. The second part
of the book is devoted to what he calls 'suggestive therapeutics' and in
it he details the results of his therapy with more than 100 cases.

It is here that he mounts his first clear attack on Charcot's teaching:

> If, in our researches, we failed to take as our starting point the
> three states of hysterical hypnotism described by Charcot, this
> was because we were unable, by our own observations, to
> confirm their existence . . . We could not detect either neuromuscular
> hyperexcitability, or exaggeration of the reflexes . . . In all the states,
> and I insist on this fact, the subject hears the operator, he has his
> attention and his hearing fixed on him. He often answers questions;
> indeed, this is nearly always the case if one insists and he is told he
> can speak. Even when he remains motionless and insensible, with his
> face as expressionless as a mask, apparently detached from the outer
> world, he hears everything. Upon awakening, later, he may or may not
> remember all that has happened.[11]

In addition, Charcot's use of physical stimuli could not be shown to
have the effects claimed for them:

> We have not observed that the action of opening or closing the sub-
> ject's eyes, or friction on the top of the head, modified the phenomena
> in any way; or that these actions develop the phenomena in subjects

incapable of manifesting them by suggestion alone. Conversely, all the phenomena can be readily obtained when they are described in the subject's presence, and when the idea of them is allowed to permeate his mind.[12]

Bernheim continues:

> If I am mistaken, if these phenomena can occur as primary manifestations, in the entire absence of suggestion, then it must be admitted that this major hypnotism is exceedingly rare. Binet and Féré tell us that during a decade there have been only a dozen such cases at the Salpêtrière. Should these cases, in comparison with thousands in which the phenomena have not been noted, serve as a basis for a theory of hypnosis?[13]

Only once did Bernheim come across a case who exhibited Charcot's three states. It was that of a young woman who had been a patient at the Salpêtrière for three years. In his opinion she was imitating the behaviour of the other somnambulists at that institution who had been unwittingly drilled to reproduce the phenomena in the typical order.

As for the use of the magnet by Binet and Féré, Bernheim has found that he can reproduce all their transfer effects so long as the subject is told what is expected. Furthermore, if the subject is misled and the magnet is replaced without his knowledge by a pencil or other non-magnetic object, the phenomena will occur as before.

It will be remembered that a similar sequence of events led Mesmer to postulate the existence of animal magnetism as distinct from mineral magnetism. The lapse of a century had rendered a psychological explanation possible, if not completely acceptable to those tied to a physiological point of view.

In addition to his critical commentary on Charcot's procedures, Bernheim reported two new hypnotic discoveries. In what he termed 'retroactive hallucination', a subject was induced to believe a scene had been enacted in the past although it had actually been suggested in the present. He provides an example of a hypnotized subject who was told that three-and-a-half months previously she had seen in an adjoining apartment an old man raping a young girl. He had gagged the girl, who was bleeding from his assault. Three days after hypnosis a lawyer was brought in to question the subject, who swore to the truth of her account in spite of Bernheim's attempts to persuade her that she had imagined it all. Bernheim now hypnotized her again and 'wiped out' his previous suggestion. She was now adamant that she had seen nothing and had made no statement to the lawyer. She became agitated by his constant assertions to the contrary, until Bernheim re-hypnotized her, calmed her, and removed all memory of the complete episode.

Such 'retroactive hallucinations' would seem to have therapeutic application, and they obviously also have legal implications, a topic to which we shall shortly return.

Bernheim's second discovery was really a case of re-discovery, as the facts had been noted by some of the early magnetists. They concern the amnesia following hypnosis for the events of the trance. Such posthypnotic amnesia appears to be relative rather than absolute. That is to say, the amnesia will yield to a prior suggestion to the subject that he will remember everything. This suggestion, often coupled with a physical sign, such as the operator's hand on the subject's forehead, can also be effective after the subject has come out of the hypnotic state and after he has maintained that he can remember nothing of what has transpired.[14]

In his theorizing on this matter, which bears a strong resemblance to what Liébault had said, Bernheim describes an imaginary cerebral train of events: the superior part of the brain, which normally intervenes to control the lower automatic and imaginative actions is 'benumbed' during sleep. All, or nearly all, nervous activity is concentrated in the lower centres, which therefore react promptly and vividly to the operator's commands. Upon awakening, this activity now diffuses back to the superior centres and to the peripheral sense organs:

> The impressions received during sleep can be said to have evaporated, they are latent like a faint image . . . but each of these memories can be reborn when the same state of consciousness in which they were produced is reinstated.[15]

Thus, the operator's task, if he wishes the subject to recall events that have occurred in the trance, is to insist that the subject concentrates his attention on what has happened, withdraws his attention from the world around him, and tries to re-enter his earlier state of altered consciousness. Many somnambulists are very suggestible in their waking state, and, on the operator's insistence, can return to an approximation of their hypnotic state. Often, too, they may themselves spontaneously enter a withdrawn state in which the latent memories of trance events are revived.

Turning to the subject of cures, Bernheim mentions the convincing evidence for cures through religious faith activated at grottoes such as Lourdes. Not all patients are so highly suggestible; some lack the imaginative powers necessary for shocks of this nature to prove effective, the intellectual aspects of their minds retaining control. However, hypnotism, like natural sleep, exalts the imagination and renders everyone more susceptible to suggestion:

> The strongest minds cannot escape from the hallucinatory suggestions of their dreams. It is a physiological law that sleep induces in the brain a mental state in which the imagination accepts and recognizes as real the impressions which are received by it. To provoke this special mental condition by hypnotism and to cultivate the suggestibility thus artificially increased in order to cure or to relieve, that is the role of hypnotic psychotherapeutics.[16]

He proceeds to discuss some of his own therapeutic successes with hysterical patients where he has produced by suggestion rapid cures of hysterical blindness, aphonia, anaesthesia, and lameness. Apart from these hysterical conditions, he has also successfully treated insomnia, menstrual disturbances, incontinence, gastro-intestinal conditions, writer's cramp, sleep-walking, loss of appetite, rheumatism, and a variety of chronic pains and neuralgias. Even in cases of organic lesions of the central nervous system, suggestions can be effective in helping recovery and restoring movement.

However, Bernheim's remarkable therapeutic successes did not arouse as much interest as his criticisms of the Salpêtrière, which marked the beginning of the war between Paris and Nancy. Some of the first return of fire came from Binet, who pointed out that Bernheim had performed very few experiments compared with the thousands undertaken at the Salpêtrière. Thus he was unjustified in claiming that the three stages of hypnotism did not exist; he had not had access to the *grandes hypnotiques* of the Salpêtrière but only to common-or-garden somnambulists. As Delboeuf ironically commented, it was only in Paris that you got major hypnotism; those in the provinces had to make do with the minor variety.[17]

Furthermore Bernheim had overextended the notion of suggestibility and had denied the importance of physical stimuli. The action of the magnet on the body was not mysterious; it was similar to that of a weak electric current. 'To deny the action of the magnet on the organism would be to deny the action of electricity. Will M. Bernheim go so far?'[18]

Bernheim's rebuttal of these charges was lucid and uncompromising: at Nancy the three supposed stages of major hypnotism had never been obtained; all procedures for inducing hypnosis could be reduced to suggestion, which was also the key to all the phenomena observed during hypnosis; hypnosis was manifested in a similar way in those suffering from major hysteria and in other subjects, and it could not be regarded as an experimentally induced neurosis; indeed, it was no easier to obtain the condition in neurotic than in normal subjects.[19]

Bernheim's criticisms of the Salpêtrière workers had not entailed any direct reference to faults in their procedures; he had remained largely content to describe the Nancy findings, which were robust enough to cast considerable doubt on the extent to which Charcot's findings were generalizable. A first-hand if belated account of the ways in which Binet and Féré had done some of their experiments was furnished by Delboeuf, who visited the Salpêtrière in 1886 and reported three years later what he had observed in connection with their experiments on the transfer of symptoms with a magnet.

> When I saw how they did these last experiments; when I saw that they neglected elementary precautions, for example, not to talk in front of the subjects, announcing in fact aloud what was going to happen; that, instead of working with an electromagnet activated without the knowledge of either the subject or the experimenter, the latter was satisfied to draw from his pocket a heavy horseshoe; when I saw that there was not even a *machine-électrique* in the laboratory, I was assailed with doubts which, insensibly, undermined my faith in all the rest.[20]

In an earlier publication Delboeuf had described Blanche Wittman, who served as Binet and Féré's chief subject:

> Between them [Binet and Féré] sat the placid and 'appetizing' Alsacienne *Witt.*, not only wearing a complacent look, but finding visible pleasure in getting ready to do anything that should be asked of her. Féré played *Witt.* as if playing on a piano . . . a light touch on any muscle – or even pointing to it without touching – made *Witt.* contract any muscle even in her ear.[21]

Only Blanche Wittman was a completely successful subject in the transfer experiments, and Delboeuf was obviously suspicious that she was playing more the part of a collaborator than of a subject. However, these criticisms evoked no response from the Salpêtrière school, and it is possible that their publication escaped the notice of Charcot and his colleagues.

Binet and Féré's major joint publication was a book curiously entitled *Le magnétisme animal.* Much of the volume is taken up with long and meticulous accounts of their various experimental investigations at the Salpêtrière. They are still convinced of the soundness of their transfer experiments, although they inject a note of caution:

> Only the first experiments are convincing, since, strictly speaking, only those are safe from unconscious suggestion. Every time an experiment is repeated there are some spectators who comment aloud. Moreover at the second experiment the subject may recall the first, and so contaminate the experiment.[22]

They seem by now to have become aware of the snags in using Blanche more than once in the same experimental demonstration, although there is no indication that they were not continuing to use her for many different demonstrations.

Binet seems to have become less certain than formerly about the limitation of hypnotic ability to hysterical patients. Although hysterics are still regarded as the best subjects, others could be susceptible if they were in a state of fatigue. He is still adamant on the efficacy of physical stimuli in producing the various hypnotic states; if the Nancy workers could not confirm these findings, their subjects were not hypnotized. This is one of the rare references to the work at Nancy, the few criticisms of Bernheim being very muted.

Charcot's own response to Bernheim's work was also comparatively mild. He appealed to common sense and to his own observations to reject Bernheim's contention that 90% of a normal population were hypnotizable. Addressing his audience on a Friday evening he pointed out that although there might well be one or two neurotics among them he hardly thought that there were 90%. He warned his listeners against the misuse of the term 'suggestion', which had become a sort of *deus ex machina*, but which was not an adequate explanation of all hypnotic phenomena.[23]

Apart from a reiteration of his views Charcot remained aloof from the controversy, leaving it to his junior colleagues to defend the Salpêtrière. Besides Binet and Féré, the neurologists Richer and Gilles de la Tourette kept strictly to the dogma that the only truly scientific studies were those that followed the methods of Charcot.[24]

Others went further, and their efforts to produce more evidence to support Charcot's cause led them into absurdity. Thus Luys reported a series of experiments intended to demonstrate a 'special hyperexcitability' found only in subjects under major hypnotism.[25] A chemical substance in a sealed tube held behind the subject's neck would produce effects in conformity with its normal pharmacological properties. For example, a tube containing brandy would make the subject drunk, chloral make her sleepy, and other substances would produce vomiting, make her happy, sad, and so on.

Although at first sight Luys' experiments seemed well designed and although he repeated them and obtained similar results, Bernheim was not impressed and refused even to investigate the matter. His refusal was vindicated when Luys' assistant, Marrin, dissociated himself from Luys' conclusions on the grounds that they had been reached from a series of experiments on only two hysterical women. Marrin now asserted that the women were 'two pretty practical jokers who made fun of the professor and of the public'.[26] One is left to presume that Luys must somehow have made obvious the response he was expecting from the girls, who were only too keen to oblige.

Another extremist was Pitres, a former student of Charcot's and now the chief neurologist in Bordeaux. Adhering resolutely to the three stages of major hypnotism, Pitres found he could distinguish finer gradations within each stage. Greater or lesser pressure on the various hypnogenic zones of the body would produce one or other of the various subdivisions of the cataleptic, lethargic or somnambulistic states. He even went so far as to describe unilateral hypnotism obtained through monocular fixation:

> I say to the patient, speaking into her right ear, 'You are in a country garden, gather a bouquet.' She looks astonished, because on that side she has not been hypnotized, nor is she suggestible. I repeat the same phrase in her other ear, she bends down and makes the movement of picking flowers with her left hand.[27]

Following Binet and Féré's lead, Pitres then found that he could transfer the hypnotism to the other side of the body with a magnet or other metal object, the delay in the process being dependent on the nature of the metal.

Bernheim took no more notice of Pitres than he had of Luys. By now he was not alone at Nancy; not, like Charcot, the centre of a clique of enthusiastic followers, but with two colleagues, men of some seniority in their own specialities. Henri-Etienne Beaunis held the Chair of Physiology at the University of Nancy and Jules Liégois the Chair of Law. Their professional interests helped to widen the area of controversy, and as both were ardent men they threw themselves into the battle.

Beaunis' main contributions were to document the physiological effects produced by hypnotic suggestion.[28] For example, he was able to record changes in heart rate consequent upon suggestions to that effect. By suggestion alone he was able to produce blisters, to alter various bodily secretions, to increase auditory acuity. Whenever he could, he recorded and measured, and his work was therefore valuable in advancing the scientific acceptability of Bernheim's views. It also, of course, incidentally implied that the Salpêtrière demonstrations of the various physical symptoms of hypnotism could well be the results of suggestions made sometimes implicitly and sometimes quite explicitly during periods when the subject was falsely assumed by Charcot to be unresponsive to spoken words.

Liégois' main interest was in the relevance of hypnotic suggestion to the criminal law. The question had arisen, it may be remembered, as long ago as 1784 when Deslon had been asked if it would be possible to violate a woman in a crisis. Over the intervening century other magnetists had extended the question to cover all incitement to crime. Bernheim himself had conducted an experiment with an hypnotized subject which he had reported in his first book:

> Wishing to ascertain how far the power of suggestion could go, I one day staged a little drama for this subject. I showed him an imaginary person standing in front of the door, and said this person had insulted him; I then gave him a paper-knife, telling him it was a dagger, and ordering him to stab the offender. He leapt forward and stabbed fiercely at the door, and then stood rigid, wild-eyed, and trembling violently.[29]

Liégois went further. His experiments succeeded admirably in persuading subjects to commit a variety of imaginary crimes: one was persuaded to shoot her mother with a pistol she thought was loaded; another thought there was arsenic in a drink he gave to his aunt, although later before a tribunal he denied having given a drink to anyone; others signed cheques of large value payable to Liégois, or donated vast sums of money to various causes; others confessed posthypnotically to the police to imaginary thefts. From all this evidence Liégois concluded:

> All conscience has disappeared in an hypnotized subject who has been forced to commit a criminal act; he is accordingly irresponsible and should be acquitted. Only he who has given the suggestion is guilty, and only he should be pursued and punished. The somnambulist has been a simple instrument in his hands, like the pistol which holds the bullet or the flask which holds the poison.[30]

This extreme view of the power of suggestion came under immediate attack from the Salpêtrière; Gilles de la Tourette drew attention to the important distinction between real-life crimes and the play-acting which went on in these typical experiments, where the subject knew very well that it was only an experiment, often having nothing more than a wooden knife or imitation pistol with which to commit the crime. Even when the weapons were real, the subject knew that the operator would never allow the experiments to exceed certain bounds.

As an instance Gilles de la Tourette cited a demonstration with Blanche Wittman as subject given at the Salpêtrière before magistrates and academics. Blanche had most realistically stabbed, shot, and poisoned a variety of people at a simple command or sign. The demonstration being over and the distinguished audience having withdrawn, Blanche, still under hypnosis, was left at the mercy of a group of young doctors. She was told that she was alone and should strip naked in order to take a bath. In spite of having acceded to all the previous suggestions, this one angered her greatly, she refused to comply, and went into a violent hysterical attack. Thus, Gilles de la Tourette concluded, it was dangerous to generalize from fictitious to real situations and to draw conclusions about the subject's inability to withstand suggestions.[31]

The possibility of criminal acts under hypnosis continued to excite much debate, to figure as themes in novels, and to enter the courts where experts from the Salpêtrière and from Nancy were to express opposing views.[32]

There was little doubt that the Nancy School had gone too far in their assumption of almost automatic obedience to suggestions, including those of an anti-social kind. As Bramwell was later to express it:

> While Bernheim considers the Salpêtrière subjects so abnormally acute that they can catch the slightest indications of the thoughts of the operator . . . he, on the other hand, supposes the Nancy subjects to be so abnormally devoid of intelligence as to be unable to understand when a palpable farce is played before them.[33]

Although on this issue a small victory had been gained by the Salpêtrière, the major battles of the campaign were clearly being won by the Nancy School. This fact became obvious at two of the congresses held in Paris at the time of the Universal Exhibition of 1889.

In the first of these, the International Congress of Physiological Psychology, one of the four sections was devoted to hypnotism.[34] Although Charcot was nominated as Congress President he failed to put in an appearance. The chairman of the section was Delboeuf, whose sympathies were with the Nancy School. Bernheim spoke on the general question of hypnotizability and maintained that everyone could be hypnotized provided a certain 'impressionability' was present. Babinski defended the Salpêtrière position that a pathological state was a necessary precondition and that such individuals became hypnotized through particular physical stimuli and not through suggestion. Although Richet spoke of the coming together of the rival schools, in William

James' view the Salpêtrière doctrine appeared already to be a thing of the past, and the Nancy workers dominated the discussions.[35]

It was much the same story at the second congress, which was concerned solely with hypnotism. The First International Congress of Experimental and Therapeutic Hypnotism was held at the Hôtel Dieu. Charcot was again nominated as one of the Congress Presidents and again he did not take office. The Salpêtrière was well represented on this occasion by Babinski, Binet, Janet and Gilles de la Tourette, while the full complement of the Nancy School was there, including Liébault; among other distinguished visitors were Sigmund Freud, William James and Frederic Myers.[36]

In opening the Congress, and perhaps in the hope of preventing sterile controversy, Dumontpallier expressed the view that some truth lay with both schools of thought: one could not deny the action of physical stimuli in bringing about the stages of hypnotism, nor could one doubt the therapeutic potentiality of hypnotism and its application in forensic medicine.

Bernheim, of course, did deny the former assertion, and in his paper he described the various ways of procuring hypnosis through suggestion and then employing the heightened suggestibility for therapeutic ends. The paper was well received by the majority of the delegates, although Gilles de la Tourette claimed that he was unable to reply because his own conception of hypnotism was so different, it being a true neurosis with established laws. Pierre Janet produced the by now usual criticism of Bernheim's unscientific procedures and then went further in claiming that Bernheim's methods were even anti-psychological, for psychology had its laws just as physiology had. Bernheim rejoined that there was one fundamental psychological law in this area: an idea implanted in the brain tends to be acted upon.

The influence of the Nancy School had clearly spread to Holland, a fact which became apparent when Van Renterghem, the early visitor to Liébault, and his colleague, Van Eeden, described their clinic of suggestive psychotherapy at Amsterdam which had been modelled on the Liébault and Bernheim model.

Legal problems and the responsibility issue were not ignored by the Congress, Liégois' paper on criminal suggestion leading to a heated discussion. Other sessions were devoted to case studies and hospital visits, including one to the Salpêtrière. Not, however, to Charcot's clinic, but to that of Auguste Voisin, who demonstrated his work with psychotic patients with whom he had claimed occasional therapeutic success with hypnotism.

Apart from Janet and Gilles de la Tourette, the delegates from the Salpêtrière were strangely silent, and the Congress was again dominated by Bernheim and his colleagues. After the Congress, Bernheim was invited to demonstrate at the Hôtel Dieu and was inundated with offers of help, including one from the novelist Alexandre Dumas.

The wave of enthusiasm for the Nancy approach was strengthened by the re-issue of Liébault's book followed by another volume from Bernheim in 1891 entitled *Hypnotisme, suggestion, psychothérapie.* Bernheim regarded the book as complementary to his 1886 work; there he had reviewed the facts and had provided an interpretation, now he was to expound in more detail his theory of suggestibility and to discuss its role in hypnosis and in the therapeutic process.

He defines suggestion very broadly as 'the act by which an idea is introduced into the brain and accepted by it'.[37] The acceptance of a suggestion depends on the 'credivity' of the individual patient. The term *credivité* had been coined by Durand de Gros to indicate a limited form of credulity.[38] Whilst a young child might be said to be naturally and generally credulous, as he matures he will learn to discriminate and will show credivity only towards certain sources of information, such as his parents. In the normal adult state credivity is limited by the 'higher' faculties of attention and judgment. Thus it follows that anything which diminishes the action of the intellect and lessens cerebral control will augment credivity.

Bernheim believes that certain environments will have this effect; he instances the ambience at Lourdes and other shrines, the hospital setting, the use of clinical instruments and other medical procedures. Hypnosis, in particular, is a most efficacious method towards this end.

After the stage when an idea is accepted, which Bernheim describes as a 'centripetal phenomenon', there follows the output, or 'centrifugal phenomenon.' Here we are concerned with the operation of an ideodynamism: 'All cerebral cells activated by an idea act on nervous fibres for the realization of that idea.'[39]

As we have seen, an idea can give rise to a sensation, an image, or a visceral reaction, such as the purgative effect produced by a placebo; it can produce a movement, as when a subject unconsciously makes a table turn at a séance; it can neutralize a sensation, as when it produces analgesia, or it can prevent a function, as in psychological impotence. Ideodynamisms are utilized by the physician in rendering his therapeutic suggestions operative.

In the case of the hypnotic situation the subject's credivity is directed towards the operator and is normally limited to the hypnotic session. Here Bernheim comes close to the old magnetists' idea of rapport. He does not strictly follow Liébault; unlike his mentor, who thought sleep and hypnosis were similar in this respect, Bernheim considers normal sleep entails the subject being *en rapport*, not with another person as in hypnosis, but with himself alone.

Another reason for rejecting the view that hypnosis and ordinary sleep are identical lies in the variety of response to hypnotic suggestions of sleep. Bernheim's nine stages of hypnotic depth bear witness to this variety. Can it, he asks, be maintained that only those subjects have been hypnotized who appear to have slept soundly and who subsequently have no recollection of their trance? He thinks not, and in any case he believes it to be irrelevant from the point of view of therapy. Not only does Bernheim now reiterate his opinion of the value of therapeutic suggestions made in all the varieties of conditions produced in response to suggestions of sleep, but he also denies any specific therapeutic virtue inherent in the hypnotic state itself: 'The hypnotic state is nothing other than a state of exalted suggestibility; we have seen that it can be produced with or without sleep.'[40]

All the methods of producing hypnosis reduce to suggestion. Sleep is unnecessary, although one may as well try to produce it because it helps to increase suggestibility and may accordingly make the therapeutic task easier. The subject may say he has not slept and yet may have exhibited the catalepsies, the analgesias, the automatic obedience and all the other phenomena of another subject who can remember nothing of what has occurred. The operator, in short, can influence the subject whether or not the latter considers himself to have been hypnotized.

Bernheim's view was later to become more extreme until in the following year he even appeared to reject the existence of hypnosis itself. This extreme stance was to lose him future support and to deny him influence as one of the important instigators of psychotherapy. In 1891, however, he was still riding the crest of the wave.

One among his former opponents at the Salpêtrière now grudgingly admitted his error. Binet, who was no longer associated with that hospital, completed a book, *Les altérations de la personnalité*, in that same year; it contains an admission that the enthusiasm engendered by Charcot's first experiments had now waned. Even the most careful experimenters, among whom he presumably includes Féré and himself, had been misled, and the cause of their error lay in 'suggestion'.

Binet employs the term to refer to 'the influence of the operator by his words, gestures, attitudes, and even silences' – what psychologists would now call the 'experimenter effect'.[41] In future he was to treat suggestion as the greatest source of error in psychological investigation and to go to great lengths to guard against it. That he was somewhat scarred by his Salpêtrière experiences seems implied by his reported reluctance ever to talk about his work there. According to his later co-worker, Simon, he considered that he had been led astray by Charcot's prestige – an indication of his own suggestibility.[42]

Those members of the Salpêtrière school who had not modified their views preferred to keep silent, no longer keen to take on their increasing number of critics. Their presence was barely felt at the next Congress of Experimental Psychology, the word 'experimental' having replaced 'physiological' at the request of several members. The Congress was held in London in 1892, the venue being University College, the scene of Elliotson's debacle over fifty years before. No demonstrations of mesmerism or hypnotism had been permitted by the College in the interval, but now Bramwell was able to demonstrate hypnotically induced analgesia and other phenomena to a packed audience.[43]

The main interest of the participants, however, was in hypnosis as a therapy, and Van Eeden again reported progress from his Amsterdam clinic, while Janet, who had also now left the Salpêtrière, discussed various psychological techniques for recovering lost memories and modifying them by suggestion. Nothing was heard of Charcot's stages nor of his limitation of hypnotism to hysterics.

In fact it was at this time that Charcot was in the process of assembling his papers in order to revise his whole conception of hysteria, a revision which must surely have entailed a radical alteration in his views on hypnotism.[44] Before that step could be taken, he died suddenly of a heart attack on 16 August 1893. With his death, the life went out of the Salpêtrière. Hysteria and hypnotism were dropped from the agenda of most of his staff's clinical work. The neurologists returned to pure neurology and turned their backs on psychology. There were two notable exceptions. Gilles de la Tourette was deep into his magnum opus, a three-volume work on hysteria, which, when it appeared in 1895, was seen to reiterate Charcot's view that hypnotism had little if any therapeutic value.[45] The same conclusion was held by Babinski, who continued to attack the Nancy view and to defend Charcot's theories until the turn of the century. His change of heart was late in coming but when it did in 1901 it entailed a complete reversal of his views, with the demolition of hysteria as a clinical entity, the totality of symptoms being produced by suggestion and removed by persuasion.[46] By that date Babinski would therefore seem to have transferred himself into Bernheim's camp, but, as we shall see, there was no longer any such camp.

The evidence was certainly overwhelming that Charcot had fallen prey to a series of extraordinary mistakes. There was his failure to adapt his peculiar mode of work to the different circumstances encountered in dealing with hysterical and with hypnotized subjects. By distancing himself from individual patients, by not visiting them in the wards, by leaving it to his junior colleagues to select those patients who were to be hypnotized and even to rely on them to induce the trance state, Charcot was left with the end result of what turned out to be a training procedure. The dozen hysterical women were selected for experimental work and demonstrations because they were 'good hypnotic subjects', that is, they could be relied upon to give vivid displays of the various phenomena thought to be associated with the three stages of hypnotism.

We are still left with the problem of the origin of these stages. Janet was able to throw light on the matter when he later encountered a patient who had never attended the Salpêtrière and yet who manifested various stages of hypnotic trance. The stages were not quite concordant with those described by Charcot, different stimuli were effective and intermediate phases could be observed. This patient had had a history of hysteria and in her youth had been magnetized by a well known practitioner, Perrier. From Perrier's notebooks, Janet discovered that before 1860 Perrier had distinguished stages in the magnetized state. Janet concluded that his patient was now recreating in 1884 the stages she had demonstrated under Perrier's guidance some twenty years earlier.[47]

Perrier was by no means unique in his approach. Alphonse Teste had distinguished three stages associated with different sensory and motor conditions. Earlier still, Elliotson had noted different stages in the Okey sisters' mesmeric condition, for example, the state of rapture which followed upon catalepsy.[48] Others, such as Despine and Du Potet, had described the physical stimuli effective in transferring the subject from one state to another and had included rubbing the top of the head as a preferred technique.

Although Charcot was not exactly anticipated by his magnetic forebears, there is enough to lead us to conclude that his three stages and their concomitant physical modifications were derived from them. The reasons why these earlier magnetists reached their particular classificatory systems need not detain us. Undoubtedly, much must have been due to unconscious suggestions on their part, which the patient would have found rewarding to confirm. Presumably, too, the patients' own preconceptions of somnambulism played a part. These may well have been based on their notions of demonic possession retained from an earlier age.[49]

What makes Janet's contention more certain is the presence of magnetizers in the great Parisian hospitals earlier in the century. Also, Du Potet's regular demonstrations at the Palais Royal had attracted many medical students. Charcot's own colleagues had invited a well known magnetist, the Marquis de Puyfontaine, into the Salpêtrière to teach them technique, and it was under his direction that their first experiments were carried out. It is ironic that the breakthrough in scientific acceptance made by Charcot was based on a perpetuation of the errors of those from whom he wished most clearly to be distinguished.

In any case Charcot compounded their errors. Convinced that patients were oblivious to his voice except in the somnambulistic stage, he would discuss with his audience the effects he would expect to obtain, prophecies which were naturally fulfilled by his highly suggestible and obliging hysterical patients. Even Richer's drawing on the back wall of the lecture theatre of the *arc-en-cercle* position must have provided an additional cue as to how an hysterical attack was expected to proceed.

Charcot's lack of empathy with his patients has already been noted. Without understanding or feeling for them, he was also without the sensitivity to understand what they were making of the hypnotic situation. He was not, of course, alone in this; he carried the staff of the Salpêtrière with him. And they too were not alone in their somewhat derogatory attitude towards patients, especially towards hysterical women.[50] The medical profession was beginning to assume a new assurance, and

Puységur's diagnostic consultations with his somnambulists represented one aspect of the magnetic tradition from which the break had been decisive.

Charcot's rejection of the ubiquity of suggestion may have also been a refusal to allow Bernheim any credit for its emphasis. Yet suggestion riddled the whole of Charcot's approach to hysteria and to hypnotism. Hysterical stigmata, neuromuscular hyperexcitability, hysterogenic and hypnogenic zones, the various physical stimuli thought to produce the various stages of hypnotism, the stages themselves whether of hysteria or of hypnotism, the whole vast edifice had been built upon an implicit denial of suggestion or indeed of any psychological factor at all.

In a more open environment than the Salpêtrière the theoretical formulations would not have hardened so rapidly nor would they have lasted as long as they did. But with Charcot's high status and dislike of criticism, those few of his colleagues who were not his admirers kept silent.

Charcot's theoretical downfall and the disintegration of the Salpêtrière School left the Nancy School somewhat at a loss. Never a school in the sense of the Salpêtrière, but rather a small group united in their opposition to Charcot, the removal of the opposition removed their *raison d'être*. Beaunis had taken up the directorship of the Laboratory of Physiological Psychology at the Sorbonne in 1889 and he retired in 1894. In that same year Liébault dissociated himself from Bernheim. It had been apparent that Bernheim's change of emphasis and his denial of the identicality of sleep and hypnosis were not congenial to the older man, who retained his early theory. But it was Bernheim's love of paradox which seems finally to have exasperated Liébault to the extent that they fell out. It had been at the London Conference of 1892 that Bernheim had first put into words what became a famous and repeated utterance: 'There is no hypnotism; there is only suggestion.'[51]

He was slow to explain what he meant; apparently he did not mean to repudiate the existence of the hypnotic state, but to stress that there was a continuum of suggestibility from that which exists in the normal waking state. For therapy it did not matter much where one was along that continuum and there was nothing very special about those positions towards one end which were termed hypnotic. Thus, hypnotism was a product of suggestion, and suggestion was the primary agent. However, he was as misunderstood by his colleagues as by those less close to him, and most of the partisans of the Nancy School continued to follow Liébault in stressing the singularity of the hypnotic state. Liébault himself retired to his country practice, where Bramwell visited him in 1899, to find him still at work hypnotizing for five hours every morning.[52]

Bernheim's isolation became more marked over the last period of his life. He suffered personally from being a Jew at a time of strong anti-Semitic sentiment in France which culminated with the Dreyfus affair.[53] There were quarrels with such men as Edgar Bérillon, the influential editor of the *Revue de l'hypnotisme*.[54]

The medical and scientific establishments did not regard him with any favour, seeming rather to blame him for his demolition of Charcot. After all, Charcot had had such admirable intentions in his desire to put hypnotism on a scientific basis with a physiological explanation. So many who had been convinced by Charcot now had their convictions overturned. Bernheim had been responsible, a man whose own theory was psychological in nature and which dealt with such immeasurables as suggestion and 'credivity'. If this was what hypnotism was, medical science wanted nothing to do with it. Bernheim may have won a victory, but it was unwelcome to those who sought a place for hypnotism within contemporary science.

14

The Twentieth Century

By the turn of the century it became evident that interest in hypnotism was declining. The decline began in France, where, in Janet's words, it was not that hypnotism had been repudiated or the power of suggestion denied; it was simply that people had ceased to talk about them.[1] Fewer publications devoted to the topics appeared; those periodicals that survived dropped 'hypnotism' and similar words from their titles, even the *Revue de l'hypnotisme* becoming the *Revue de psychothérapie et de psychologie appliquée*. Medical practitioners began to stress the dangers of hypnosis, how it lowered the moral standards of patients by appealing to their less rational, more primitive selves, how it was really the province of the quack.

Significant work continued for a time to appear from German sources, notably in the *Zeitschrift für Hypnotismus*, a periodical published under the editorship of Auguste Forel and Oskar Vogt. Forel was Professor of Psychiatry at the University of Zürich and one of the first to introduce the Nancy view of hypnotism to the German-speaking world. Vogt, a much younger man of considerable energy and wide interests, was in practice in Leipzig and later in Berlin. He was a very effective hypnotist and collected a group of enthusiastic clinical workers around him. Between them, Forel and Vogt established a reputation for their journal which quite eclipsed the French *Revue*. They published case reports with different therapeutic procedures and outcomes. The emphasis throughout was much more on hypnotism as a medical therapeutic aid rather than on theoretical or experimental writing.

The shift in interest in hypnotism from France to Germany, although marked during the 1890s, was short-lived. In Germany too, apart from rare exceptions, the medical profession did not embrace hypnosis as a useful tool even for blatantly psychological disturbances. Other forms of psychotherapy seemed to hold more promise than the Nancy type of suggestive therapy which had a misleadingly simplistic air about it. It did not seek the causation of a symptom but merely sought to suggest it away. In fact there proved to be more to it than that, as Bernheim went on to develop an active psychotherapy in which the patient was encouraged to try out new ways of behaving in an attempt to overcome his contemporary problems. However, in its earlier versions it did seem superficial to those seeking a causal explanation; foremost among these was Sigmund Freud.

Freud had mainly used hypnosis to recover the patient's forgotten memories rather than as a suggestive technique. But he had found it an unreliable procedure in that some patients proved unresponsive to his attempts at hypnotic induction. It was also unreliable in another sense: symptoms removed by suggestion seemed to return or to be replaced by different symptoms.

An embarrassing scene on the therapeutic couch seems to have been the final straw as far as Freud was concerned:

> It related to one of my most acquiescent patients, with whom hypnotism had enabled me to bring about the most marvellous results, and whom I was engaged in relieving of her suffering by tracing back her attacks of pain to their origins. As she woke up on one occasion, she threw her arms round my neck. The unexpected entrance of a servant relieved us from a painful discussion, but from that time onwards there was a tacit understanding between us that the hypnotic treatment should be discontinued. I was modest enough not to attribute the event to my own irresistible personal attraction, and I felt that I had now grasped the nature of the mysterious element that was at work behind hypnotism. In order to exclude it, or at all events to isolate it, it was necessary to abandon hypnotism.[2]

This episode during one of his early analyses seems to have been the origin of Freud's discovery of the 'transference'.[3] With his refusal to attribute the patient's response to his own 'animal magnetism', Freud necessarily had to assume the existence in the relationship of a fantasy figure introduced from the patient's past to whom her response was appropriate in a way it was not vis-à-vis himself, the unknown physician and relative stranger.

While Freud thought that Bernheim was right to consider the phenomena of hypnosis as responses to the suggestions of the hypnotist, he could not accept that suggestion was a sufficient explanation in itself; it also required explanation, and Freud offered one in terms of the transference, which he considered the primary cause of the subject's susceptibility to the influence of the hypnotist.[4] Thus he assumed that the subject was reacting inappropriately to the actual hypnotist, but because he or she had invested the hypnotist with qualities of knowledge and power, probably derived from a parental figure, the subject would uncritically accept suggestions from this source.

However, Freud knew that there was more to explain. In particular, there was the altered state of consciousness of the hypnotized subject, accompanied by access to physiological processes normally outside voluntary control, which lent an air of strangeness to the hypnotic relationship, unlike other therapeutic relationships in which transference also played a part. His mature view of the matter entailed a phylogenetic hypothesis: that we were witnessing in hypnosis a re-emergence of a state found in the pre-history of mankind, which lived on in nascent form in every individual's constitution.[5] The hypnotized subject reacted to the hypnotist as a member of the first group formed by man, the primal horde, reacted to his leader, the horde father: without criticism, with dependence and complete obedience. The subject's psychological and physiological state were then distinct from those of his normal waking life.

Freud was aware of the great differences in hypnotic susceptibility which were not well explained by this hypothesis. One would have to assume incomplete acceptance of the dependent role, with an awareness of the play-acting involved, to account for the reluctance of some subjects to carry out their hypnotist's requests. However, Freud always regarded his explanatory attempts as tentative, and although he ceased to practise hypnosis after his discovery of the slower but non-directive technique of free association, nevertheless he continued to theorize about it.

Freud's rejection of hypnotherapy and his adoption of psychoanalysis led to his followers doing likewise. As his fame grew, psychoanalysis became the preferred method of 'deep' psychotherapy, and hypnosis was relegated to the background. Only a few therapists continued to use hypnosis, notably Pierre Janet in France and Milne Bramwell in England.

During Janet's lifetime he was overshadowed by Freud, and it is only recently that he has begun to attract renewed attention, probably because his theories lend themselves more readily to contemporary neurological understanding.[6] Even before joining Charcot at the Salpêtrière, Janet had studied the behaviour of hysterical patients under hypnosis and had come to the conception of dissociation as an explanatory principle.

It is assumed that normal remembering is the result of association, and that therefore the failure to recall what should normally be recalled must be due to an interruption in the associative process which is thus termed 'dissociation.' Hysterics suffer from an inherited 'general cerebral exhaustion' which leads to an inability to hold many associations together and their field of consciousness is restricted. Traumatic events in their past will tend to be split off from consciousness to form isolated and self-integrated groups of memories to which normal access is denied. These active centres can lead a life of their own and disturb ongoing behaviour, by, for example, causing physical symptoms or a split in consciousness which might in rare instances become a secondary personality.

In his therapeutic practice Janet showed great ingenuity in his use of suggestion and hypnosis. The endeavour to reintegrate the dissociated memories after strengthening the field of consciousness so that it could bear them was the preferred method, but other possibilities included either eradicating the memories altogether, or modifying them into a more innocuous form. The wealth of therapeutic techniques described in Janet's writings has never been fully exploited, and yet, great therapist though he was, Janet never quite shook off the influence of Charcot with regard to his views on the nature of hypnosis. For him, hypnosis continued to be a state of artificial somnambulism which could be produced only in those with an hysterical disposition.

Cases of spontaneous somnambulism, hysterical fugue states, where patients have complete amnesia for a period in their lives, and other examples of split personality had been recorded from the earliest times. It was only when the interpretation of these phenomena in terms of spirit possession became unfashionable that accounts began to appear in the medical literature of what was to become known as 'multiple personality'. Towards the end of the nineteenth century the topic began to catch the public imagination and many novelists and playwrights employed the theme, notably Robert Louis Stevenson in *The Strange Case of Dr Jekyll and Mr Hyde* (1886).

Early in his career Janet had encountered a celebrated somnambulist, Léonie, who under hypnosis spontaneously produced a secondary personality of a childish kind (Léontine). Behind the hypnotic personality Janet found it possible to uncover a third personality by the use of mesmeric passes. This last personality (Léonore) had been elicited twenty years earlier when Léonie had been the subject of experiments by the magnetizers but had never appeared in the interval. Léonore had access to the memories of the other two personalities, Léontine had access to Léonie's, whilst the normally prevalent personality, Léonie, was amnesic to the others.

The account of Léonie appeared in Janet's first book, *L'automatisme psychologique* (1889).[7] Here he discusses two broad classes of automatisms, total and partial. In the first case we are dealing with the fugue states and alternating personalities such as Léonie. In the partial automatisms a small group of phenomena are split off from consciousness, such as is the case with hysterical paralyses, anaesthesias, water divining and automatic writing. Janet describes a number of ingenious ways of communicating with hypnotized and hysterical patients by inducing automatic writing. Often he would arrange for the patient to become absorbed in an activity and would then slip a pencil into the hand and whisper questions to which an answer would be written while the patient seemed to be fully absorbed in talking or even calculating. By this means he was able to communicate with Léontine without Léonie's knowledge and induce her to perform actions to Léonie's surprise.

However, it was the American psychiatrist, Morton Prince, who presented the first book-length account of a multiple personality. 'Miss Beauchamp' was first treated by Prince in 1898 and the details of her treatment published in full in 1906.[8] A sufferer from 'neurasthenia' (persistent fatigue, insomnia and a variety of physical pains), brought about by an emotional shock received five years previously, she presented a picture of extreme reticence and prim rectitude. After some weeks of hypnotic treatment, during which she was less inhibited but not otherwise very different from her waking self, a new personality suddenly appeared who called herself 'Sally'. Sally formed a strong contrast with 'Christine', (as Prince called the original personality) being lively, childishly mischievous and strongly critical of the dull Christine whom she tried to trick and embarrass whenever possible. This she could do because Christine was not aware of Sally's existence whereas Sally had access to Christine's thoughts. Thus she could intrude into Christine's activities and consciousness and force her to behave untypically.

To complicate matters still further, another personality appeared after Miss Beauchamp received another emotional shock, similar in some ways to the trauma that had predated her neurasthenic symptoms. This new personality was a different sort of contrast to Christine, being, for example, irritable and irreligious, to the extent that Prince dubbed her 'The Devil'. Christine was also amnesic for this personality, whilst The Devil had no knowledge of Sally. Unlike Sally she had no memory of any events prior to the original trauma, whereas Sally claimed that she had always been present from childhood. Prince used the hypnotic sessions to try to amalgamate these personalities, and finally succeeded in producing what he called the 'real' Miss Beauchamp, who was largely an amalgam of Christine and The Devil, with Sally no longer apparent.

It may have been the case that these personalities were produced unwittingly by suggestions made by Prince during hypnosis. However, he seems to have been surprised by the emergence of Sally and to have actively discouraged her; also, there seems to have been a clearly traumatic origin for the emergence of The Devil. The other possibility, that Miss Beauchamp deliberately deceived Prince for private reasons of her own, seems to be unlikely, as she was ignorant of the psychological literature and suffered much from the depredations caused by Sally.

Prince persuaded Sally to write her autobiography, from which it became clear that she had gradually become more separate from Christine as Miss Beauchamp had grown up. In childhood the two personalities had thought about the same things at the same time, although they might think differently about them. Later, different thoughts occupied the two consciousnesses, especially when Miss Beauchamp was doing something which Sally considered uninteresting. This resulted, for example, in Sally having no knowledge of French, while Christine could read it fluently. It is also fascinating to read how Sally was able to force Christine to perform actions against her will, and how she could even cause her to have an hallucination.

From a theoretical point of view, this very full and well documented case lends itself to an interpretation in terms of dissociation and subconscious trains of thought. This fact may explain why numerous cases were found in the late nineteenth and early twentieth centuries when Janet's theorizing was popular; after about 1910 there was a wave of reaction against the concept of multiple personality. At about that time Janet's theories were being displaced by those of Freud, who provided no simple explanation of – or, indeed, showed any interest in – cases of multiple personality.[9]

In recent years the incidence of these cases has dramatically increased, especially in the USA, where one author has been led to entitle his 1982 paper on the topic, 'The multiple personality epidemic.'[10] As some therapists appear to encounter the condition very frequently whilst others never see an example at all, it seems likely that in the former case there is a strong influence from the therapist who typically uses hypnosis and who may well encourage, albeit unintentionally, the emergence of secondary personalities by giving them names.[11]

Turning now to the use of hypnosis as a more general therapy, we find it remained little utilized until the period of the Second World War when there was a renewal of interest. Hypnosis appeared to offer a comparatively rapid therapy for battle-stressed combatants, whose traumata were recent, and for whom psychoanalytic exploration of childhood seemed irrelevant. The renaissance of hypnotic therapy originated then and seems to have been sustained until the present day. Bernheim's forgotten techniques have also now been resuscitated and incorporated among the plethora of modern behavioural therapies; thus one finds extensive use of relaxation and suggestion, although explanations of their efficacy are usually proffered in terms of theories of learning derived from laboratory psychologists.[12]

One hypnotherapist who stood apart from the mid-century mainstream was an American physician, Milton Erickson.[13] The extent of his divergence from the orthodox can be appreciated by the fact that there is still debate as to whether 'Ericksonian hypnotism' is really hypnotism as it is generally understood. One reason for this confusion lies in his very varied and individual methods of trance induction, the situation being further complicated by the intertwining of hypnotic and psychotherapeutic procedures to the extent that it is impossible to tell one from the other. From Erickson's own therapeutic point of view it was immaterial whether a patient was hypnotized or not, and in this he resembled Bernheim.

Erickson also added to the confusion by drawing a distinction between the 'therapeutic trance' and the 'laboratory trance'. By the latter term he seems to have meant the hypnosis produced by research workers such as Clark Hull, with whom he studied as a postgraduate. As we shall see, Hull regarded hypersuggestibility as the main criterion of the hypnotic state; this Erickson rejected and used the presence of certain clinical signs to indicate the trance state. Erickson believed that the laboratory setting was not conducive to the full manifestation of hypnotic phenomena, but that seems an insufficient reason to make such a fundamental distinction.

Erickson is best known today for his techniques of indirect suggestion, making use of non-verbal communication, apparently allowing the subject much freedom, and always being extremely attentive to the moment-by-moment interaction. Accounts of Erickson's induction procedures often give the impression that every word has been carefully selected and tailored for a particular patient. The very sensitive use of words and the full appreciation of their symbolic meanings is the hallmark of the Ericksonian approach, and it is impossible to do justice to his work in short compass.[14]

Erickson's early research contributions in the field of experimental hypnotism are now almost forgotten in the light of his later therapeutic reputation.[15] They form part of what is by now a vast data bank of experimental findings produced mainly from laboratories in North America.

The attempts of such men as Braid and Charcot to devise experiments to test their theories now seem naïve. There have been great advances in experimental sophistication and methods of measurement since their day, and it would not be inappropriate to have entitled the present chapter the Century of Experiment. During this century the centre of gravity of hypnosis research has shifted quite decisively away from Europe, largely because the experimental approach to hypnosis has gone hand-in-hand with developments in the scope and application of psychology, and these developments have been a North American phenomenon.

The first major advance was taken in 1933 when the psychologist Clark Hull published the outcome of a series of experimental studies conducted by his research team.[16] Hull's early education had been in mining engineering and his approach to psychology was of the hard-headed no-nonsense variety in which overt behaviour was the focus of attention. Tasks were chosen at which performance could be measured, and any differences between hypnotic and control conditions subjected to statistical test.

Writing in 1961, Ernest Hilgard, a leading contributor to the experimental approach, said of Hull's book, *Hypnosis and Suggestibility*, that: 'It still stands as a model of clarity and objectivity in the approach to what remain even today puzzling and unresolved problems.'[17]

Among such problems one might include the role of suggestibility in hypnosis, the relationship between hypnosis and sleep, the possible transcendence of normal capacities under hypnosis, e.g., in memory, in strength, and in sensory abilities, and the nature of posthypnotic suggestions. All these and several more became the subject matter for Hull's experimental approach.

As an example of that approach let us look at his work on the supposed improvements in muscular power obtainable under hypnosis. Demonstrations of this phenomenon have always been popular as, in common with exhibitions of analgesia, they seem to preclude any faking on the part of the hypnotized subject. Charcot, for one, was impressed by his own demonstration of the lack of muscular fatigue in a patient under hypnosis.[18] The patient was a young woman diagnosed as hystero-epileptic whose hand, whilst she was in the cataleptic state, was connected to an apparatus designed to register tremors when the arm was extended horizontally at shoulder height. The record obtained over a 15-minute period was perfectly smooth with hardly a tremor, whereas the record obtained from a healthy man for purposes of comparison was marked by irregularities which increased as time passed and he became fatigued. Even more impressive was a comparison of their breathing records, with the healthy man being unable to sustain the smooth normal breathing rhythm recorded from the hypnotized patient. Binet and Féré were as impressed as their chief, writing of this demonstration that it served as proof that simulation could not have occurred, for nobody could voluntarily imitate such effects as these brought about by hypnotism.[19] Hull was not convinced:

> Such a display of uncritical cocksureness on the part of a person who later attained the scientific eminence of Alfred Binet is all but inexplicable, for it would be difficult to imagine a more thoroughly bad experiment.[20]

The experiment was bad chiefly for the reason that we have no means of knowing what the woman patient might have been able to achieve in her normal waking state. An attempt to remedy this and other deficiencies was made by one of Hull's research team, G.W. Williams, who employed eight subjects in both trance and waking states. Using a more sensitive measuring apparatus to record the tremors of the outstretched arm, he obtained results that did not differ significantly between the two conditions. Hull concluded that hypnosis was unable to increase resistance to muscular fatigue.

In spite of the apparent advance in experimental sophistication, Williams's experiment also has its flaws. Subjects were apparently hypnotized by staring at one of the experimenter's eyes, and when their own eyes closed were given verbal suggestions to the effect that they were in a deep trance and that their arms were becoming rigid. As described, this process of hypnotic induction appears to have been somewhat cursory. While we remain unsure whether a subject is hypnotized or not, it becomes impossible to claim that negative results such as those of Williams demonstrate conclusively that hypnosis does not affect muscular tremor. This general problem vitiates many of the experimental demonstrations in Hull's book, most of which reach similar negative conclusions. It is a problem, which as we shall see, has exercised the ingenuity of later investigators.

However, not all Hull's research came to the conclusion that subjects under hypnosis were incapable of transcending their normal abilities. In the case of long-term memory it was demonstrated by Stalnaker and Riddle that the recall of material learnt at least one year previously was much better when the subjects were hypnotized when they attempted the recall than when they tried in their normal waking state. In this experiment more care seems to have been taken to ensure that the twelve subjects were well hypnotized as they were able to demonstrate such hypnotic phenomena as analgesia and negative hallucinations. This finding is, of course, consistent with the many clinical observations to the effect that hypnosis may aid the recall of early memories.

A different methodological snag detracts from the value of this experiment. When subjects act as their own controls, that is, when the same subjects perform a task under the hypnotic and waking conditions, it is possible that they may, consciously or unconsciously, affect the outcome by not trying as hard as possible when awake in order to demonstrate an improvement under hypnosis. Thus, we reach the conclusion that if a negative result is obtained, as in Williams's research, it may be that the subjects were not sufficiently hypnotized; if a positive result is obtained, as in this case, it may be due to the normal base line having been lowered. It seems clear that experimental rigour demands the use of different subjects under hypnosis and waking conditions, and some external criterion to ensure that they are really 'hypnotized' in the hypnotic condition. In general, Hull's work suffers from insufficient attention being paid to these requirements.

In a lucid conclusion to his book, Hull insists that any adequate theory of hypnosis must await a fuller knowledge of suggestibility in the context of a developed theory of human behaviour. Nevertheless, he felt confident enough in his research findings to reject what he calls 'pseudo-difficulties' in reaching this goal. Among these he mentions the beliefs that rapport is an essential characteristic of hypnosis, that hypnosis is a form of sleep, or dissociation, that hypnotized subjects are super-sensitive to faint stimuli, that catalepsy is peculiar to hypnosis, and that hypnosis is a pathological condition, presumably allied to hysteria.

Hypersuggestibility seemed to Hull to be the sole characteristic of hypnosis and the only justification for calling it a 'state'. Any difference between the hypnotic state and the normal waking state was a quantitative and not a qualitative one:

> Despite the widespread and long-standing belief to the contrary, the author is convinced that no phenomenon whatever can be produced in hypnosis that cannot be produced to lesser degrees by suggestions given in the normal waking condition.[21]

The nub of Hull's argument is here: upon entering the hypnotic trance an increase occurs in one's suggestibility, and it is this change which is the defining characteristic of hypnosis. Thus if a subject shows no shift in the direction of increased suggestibility after submitting to a hypnotic induction procedure, he should not be regarded as being hypnotized. The question why induction procedures should have the effects they often do is left unanswered by Hull, although he speculates that the muscular relaxation ordinarily suggested during induction may be responsible.

Hull's removal of most of the criteria of hypnosis, leaving only an increase in suggestibility, remained the dominant view for a quarter of a century. It was not until Ernest Hilgard began an intensive research programme at Stanford University in the early 1950s that an alternative theory began to gain ground. Hilgard was an experimental psychologist with a reputation as a leading learning theorist.[22] The transformation of his laboratory from this mainstream academic field to a concern with what was, in spite of Hull's pioneering efforts, academically still barely respectable represented a major decision on his part. Nevertheless, he obtained research funding and was successful in attracting many scholars to what became a major centre for hypnotic research.

One of Hilgard's first problems was to define what he called the 'domain of hypnosis', that is, which aspects of behaviour and experience were generally agreed to constitute hypnosis and which problems should therefore be the target of experimental attack. To help in this endeavour, he and André Weitzenhoffer developed the Stanford Hypnotic Susceptibility Scale (SHSS). This was not the first attempt to obtain a measure of hypnotic susceptibility; we have mentioned Bernheim's rough attempt to scale the depth of hypnosis which his patients achieved, and an improved scale had been developed by two American psychologists, Friedlander and Sarbin, in 1938.[23]

The SHSS in its developed form was a more sophisticated instrument than these earlier attempts.[24] It consisted of a standard induction procedure and a graded series of suggestions ranging from the inhibition of muscular movement and sensory distortion to hallucinations and posthypnotic amnesia. Having such a scale at their disposal, researchers could now investigate the characteristics of those people highly susceptible to hypnosis and compare them with those of low susceptibility. Furthermore, they could increase the precision of their experiments by matching control and experimental subjects for their degree of hypnotic susceptibility, or 'hypnotizability' as it came to be called.

A great deal of modern work has resulted from these refinements. Hilgard's research team carried out detailed studies of the personality characteristics of good hypnotic subjects.[25] Little was found to characterize them on standard personality inventories, but in a later search for childhood antecedents Josephine Hilgard drew attention to the ease with which the highly hypnotizable had shown an imaginative involvement in activities such as reading and play.[26] This finding had theoretical links with the work of her husband on hypnotic analgesia.[27] In these experiments, subjects selected for high hypnotizability were rendered insensible to pain in a hand and arm. When the arm was immersed in ice water they seemed able to keep it there with little or no pain being reported. However, when they were asked to signal simultaneously the intensity of the pain by pressing a switch, a process similar to automatic writing, they indicated that the cold was in fact extremely painful. In further experiments with hypnotically induced blindness and deafness and with positive hallucinations, Hilgard was able to obtain similar reports from what he termed 'the hidden observer', a part of the person constantly monitoring the reality of the situation. The whole person was simultaneously feeling and not feeling pain, hearing and not hearing a sound, and so on; parallel processing of information seemed to be occurring.

As an explanation of these findings Hilgard was led to modify the classical dissociation theory of Janet and Morton Prince. In his 'neodissociation' theory no assumptions are made about the pathological nature of dissociation. Dissociative abilities vary among the normal population and individual differences are marked. Josephine Hilgard's highly hypnotizable people had shown their dissociative ability in their absorption in their childhood activities, and the hidden observer in the analgesic and other experiments had also borne witness to a dissociative process.

Hilgard rejects the idea that consciousness is a unity: there are too many everyday shifts or lapses in consciousness to make that plausible. For example, how often have we driven a car whilst thinking of something else other than the road conditions? Any overlearnt activity, such as driving, seems able to proceed automatically without conscious control. Thus, Hilgard believes that there must be subordinate cognitive systems which can become autonomous. However, there cannot be a free-for-all among all the different competing and interacting cognitive systems, so they must be organized in some sort of hierarchical structure and there must be a monitoring and controlling of this structure.

The theory is potentially much wider than just a theory of hypnosis, and it has been extended by later theorists to the wider realms of modern cognitive psychology.[28] From the narrower focus of hypnotic theory it entails a clear rejection of Hull's conclusion that hypnosis is nothing more than hypersuggestibility. For Hilgard, suggestibility is only one component in the hypnotic process. Responsiveness to hypnotic suggestions is seen as similar to the responsiveness to waking suggestions. The first items on the SHSS entail the ability to relax and to respond to simple suggestions. But the hypnotically talented then go beyond that to experience a state of dissociation in which the phenomena of deep hypnosis occur. Such dissociation is not in his view brought about by suggestion; it simply occurs in those so prepared by constitution and experience.

It would be misleading to give the impression that neodissociation theory has gained general acceptance. In recent years sophisticated attempts have also been made to incorporate hypnotic phenomena within the mainstream of social psychology and to use known psychological processes to understand hypnotic behaviour and experience. The origins of this perspective lie in the theorizing of R.W. White and T.R. Sarbin in the 1940s and 1950s.[29] These earlier theorists rejected the idea that hypnotic subjects were passive recipients of suggestion; on the contrary, they were seen as actively striving to produce the behaviour and the subjective experiences which they considered appropriate for the role of the hypnotized subject. Sarbin was more radical than White as he rejected completely the notion of an altered state of consciousness; for him, all the manifestations of deep hypnosis were the consequences of the enactment by the subject of the hypnotic role. This role was defined partly by the hypnotist and partly by the prevalent cultural assumptions of what was involved in hypnosis. Some subjects would be more adept than others in playing this role and would therefore appear to be 'better' subjects. Sometimes subjects might become completely immersed in their role and lose awareness of themselves in the part they were playing.

Sarbin carried out little experimental work himself, a deficiency which was to be made good by T.X. Barber whose extensive work throughout the 1960s was clearly influenced by Sarbin. Barber and his associates conducted many investigations in which they demonstrated that under certain instructions non-hypnotized subjects could achieve everything claimed for hypnotized subjects.[30] Under these special 'task-motivation' instructions subjects were told that they could, for example, experience hallucinations 'if they really tried'. The results were convincing, but perhaps better conceptualized as demonstrations of the effectiveness of persuasion in bringing about overt acquiescence. Later work revealed that when subjects were asked to report truthfully to someone other than the hypnotist they admitted that their earlier show of acquiescence had not reflected their inner experience.[31]

Another researcher, Martin Orne, produced an interesting refinement in experimental technique when he began the use of 'simulators' as control subjects.[32] Subjects who were low in hypnotizability went through the usual induction procedures, pretended that they were hypnotized, and acted accordingly. It was found that experienced hypnotists were unable to detect the more skilled simulators. By keeping the hypnotists 'blind' as to the status of their subjects it was possible to make experimental comparisons between hypnotized subjects and those simulating hypnosis which would not be contaminated by the hypnotist's preconceptions.

By such a technique it was hoped to distinguish the essence of hypnosis from the social demands implicit in the situation. Subsequent work has made it clear that there are many problems of interpretation involved in the use of simulators.[33] The methodological complexities may outweigh apparent advantages and fail to lead to the resolution of theoretical issues. It seems more likely that the intensive study of the characteristics of these various groups may prove of greater value for social psychology in general than for hypnosis in particular.

Nicholas Spanos has proved to be a most prolific exponent of what he has called the 'sociocognitive' approach.[34] In a series of papers he has taken up a theoretical position which is as extreme as Barber's:

> Despite more than a century of empirical research, there is no convincing evidence to support the contention that hypnotic subjects enact behavior, process information, or develop experiences in ways different from those of nonhypnotic control subjects.[35]

Hypnotic subjects are thought to use whatever 'cognitive strategies' they have at their disposal in order to maintain the requirements of the hypnotic role. In responding hypnotically, subjects actively seek to play the role as they conceive it, and those conceptions will be historically and culturally rooted. Thus, hypnosis cannot be considered a condition that can be traced from one era or society to another. It is not so much an entity as a social construction, and it cannot, like a physical disease such as tuberculosis, be shown to exist across the ages.

Spanos elaborates this notion by attempting to show that the social roles played by the early magnetizers and their patients evolved out of the earlier roles of exorcist and the demonically possessed. In the nineteenth century these roles were again modified through the progress of medical science, and neurological explanations such as those of Braid and Charcot were provided to explain hypnotic behaviour. We are still left with the remains of this medical influence in the ways in which hypnotic behaviour is usually conceptualized today, when we speak of 'amnesia' instead of motivated forgetting, and 'hallucination' instead of imagining.

Examples of what would seem to be clear instances of dissociated behaviour, such as multiple personality, are considered by Spanos to be the results of suggestion on the part of the therapist, a view which accords well with the recent increase in the numbers of such patients, although it seems a very forced explanation of those cases where more than one personality developed in childhood. Hilgard's 'hidden observer' is likewise dismissed as a function of suggestion, Spanos claiming that the phenomenon occurs only when the hypnotist has alerted the subject to this possibility. The subject then proceeds to enact the role expected of him in the context of the social demands inherent in the situation; thus there is no reason to suppose that analgesia is a function of dissociation.

To support this latter point, Spanos and his colleagues have conducted several studies in which control subjects were as successful as hypnotized subjects in exhibiting analgesia.[36] This result was achieved by the control subjects using such cognitive strategies as imagery, self-distraction, and coping remarks to the effect that the pain was not bad at all. Of course, this does not imply that hypnotized subjects use similar techniques to cope with pain, although it leaves open that possibility. This particular controversy has become extremely involved, with different experimental designs leading as yet to no clear conclusion.[37] One common characteristic of these experiments is their continued use of the standardized painful stimulus used by Hilgard, the immersion of the hand in iced water. The comparative mildness of this pain may be one reason why Spanos has been able to maintain his interpretation of analgesia. It is difficult to believe that cognitive strategies could be as effective under major surgery without anaesthetic, such as was commonplace in Esdaile's time.

The experimental manoeuvres devised by Spanos and his colleagues to clarify the cognitive strategies underlying hypnotic amnesia are even more complex than in the case of analgesia, and it is unnecessary to detail them here. Suffice it to say that Spanos interprets amnesia as a goal-directed attempt by attending elsewhere to ignore the normally relevant cues that would trigger recall. It is consistent with his theoretical position that this attempt to forget is a voluntary act consistent with the subject's desire to play the role of a deeply hypnotized person. His opponents believe that this does not get to the essence of hypnotic amnesia which they think represents a temporary breakdown in memory mechanisms outside the subject's conscious control.[38] The controversy continues.

It follows from Spanos's views that it should be possible to teach the sociocognitive strategies involved in being a good hypnotic subject. In particular, it should be possible to train those of low susceptibility so that they become highly susceptible. To this end, Spanos devised the Carleton Skills Training programme, named after his university.[39] Trainees were given information about hypnosis to remove their misconceptions, they were told that they should become imaginatively absorbed in the suggestions they were to be given, and they were taught to behave as though a suggestion was an instruction which at first they should simply obey. Having obeyed it, they should then try to imagine that it had occurred spontaneously without conscious control. Measures of hypnotic susceptibility on a scale devised by Spanos were taken before and after this training, and it was found that between 50% and 80% of low susceptibles became highly susceptible.

Spanos considers that the apparent success of his programme throws considerable doubt on the views of Hilgard that hypnotic susceptibility is a relatively stable trait. His conclusion is open to a similar objection made to Barber's research, namely that outward compliance may not reflect inward conviction. However, even the trait theorists accept that some modification in susceptibility can occur with practice, and many clinicians have testified to their subsequent success in hypnotizing originally insusceptible patients, although this change is usually ascribed to the removal of pre-existing anxieties about hypnosis rather than to the acquisition of a skill.[40]

Perhaps the greatest difficulty for role-taking explanations of hypnosis lies in the reports of hypnotic subjects that their responses are involuntary. Spanos accepts that these may be honest accounts of the manner in which subjects interpret their experiences but also argues that they must be deceiving themselves.[41] He does not accept that behaviour can be purposeful and goal-directed if it is involuntary. There is semantic confusion here, because behaviour can have a purpose, in the sense that it is directed towards some goal, without being performed 'on purpose'. The neodissociationists would argue that this is exactly what happens when the higher levels of planning function are cut off and lower levels of the hierarchy become autonomous.

It is hard not to admire the ingenuity of the social psychologists in devising experiments and in seeking alternative explanations for the classical 'deep' hypnotic phenomena. However, admiration of their ingenuity does not necessarily imply acceptance of the correctness of their interpretations. Their appeal is largely limited to those from the more orthodox experimental tradition in academic psychology who are typically sceptical about phenomena which seem to require novel interpretations. The neodissociationists, although springing from a similar background, can draw on the support of most clinicians and neurophysiologists; the former find the theory fits well with their clinical observations, while the latter are able to envisage a possible neural substrate for the dissociative process.

Experimental results are open to a variety of interpretations and it has proved more difficult to devise decisive experiments in hypnosis than the earlier experimenters believed. In addition, there is the ever-present difficulty that the objectivity inherent in the scientifically impeccable experimental approach may actually serve to destroy the very phenomena the hypnotist has set out to investigate.[42] The attitude of disciplined scepticism in the laboratory setting is not one calculated to allow the emergence of the dramatic and bizarre phenomena produced in response to the vivid urgings of the committed charismatic, such as a Du Potet. The really effective hypnotist has to exude confidence, enthusiasm, and certainty; in so doing, he will find it difficult to maintain the objective stance necessary for the scientist.

It may be that currently antagonistic theories will come together in some future synthesis. Or it may be, as the British psychologist Graham Wagstaff has proposed, that a variety of explanations will be necessary for the different parts of the hypnotic domain.[43] What is clear at the moment is that the nature of hypnosis continues to elude us, as the study of any contemporary textbook will confirm.[44]

The lack of agreement on theoretical matters has had little effect on the ways in which hypnotic techniques are being used in practice. A brief survey of these practical applications may help to conclude this historical account by providing a truer picture of the state of hypnotism today.[45]

Hypnotic therapy comprises a wide variety of techniques; it is commonly classified as one of the various treatments considered as alternatives or adjuncts to orthodox medicine. To that extent it is accepted by the public, although its retention of an air of mystery may be responsible for its inappropriate position as a last-ditch or magical solution. Thus, there is a heavy demand on hypnotic practitioners from those wishing to stop smoking or drinking, to lose weight, or to change what they regard as an undesirable habit which they have been unable to relinquish. However, research into the efficacy of hypnosis in leading to permanent change in habitual behaviour is not encouraging, with a fairly low success rate. Much more seems to depend on non-hypnotic factors, such as the person's motivation, than to their susceptibility to hypnotic suggestion. In this context it is interesting to note that in the case of smoking, one or two sessions of hypnosis have been found to be sufficient to bring about cessation of the habit in 98% of those who were successfully treated.[46]

As an alternative therapy, hypnosis is often chosen by those suffering from chronic conditions which have not yielded to medical intervention. Sufferers from asthma, rheumatism, skin disorders, and lower back pain are among the more common of those attending hypnotists. It is difficult to generalize about the therapeutic outcome even within any one such ailment. So much seems to depend on the belief in and rapport with the hypnotist. The depth of trance attained and the frequency and duration of treatment may also be of significance in determining the result.

As a general statement, it would be true to say that where the psychological component in the condition is strong – where, for example, stress and anxiety are clearly involved – hypnosis can be a very effective treatment. However, this does not exclude the use of hypnosis in many cases where psychological concerns appear to be minimal. There is good evidence that hypnotic suggestion can have a direct physiological effect, at the very least in altering blood flow to an affected part of the body.

One of the most remarkable cures of this kind was reported by A.A. Mason in 1952.[47] The patient had suffered for many years from ichthyosis, a rare skin disease in which the sweat and sebaceous glands in the skin were unable to function normally, leading to an appearance of being covered in fish scales. The disease was hereditary and there was no known cure. Using direct suggestion, and with the patient in a deep trance, Mason was able to clear the skin progressively from limbs and trunk. There was no recurrence of the disease over a five-year follow-up.

Such therapeutic 'miracles' are naturally very rare, and Mason's subsequent trials with other sufferers from this disease were unsuccessful. Without further research, leading to deeper understanding of the physiological processes involved, hypnotic treatment will continue to have a hit-or-miss character in organic conditions of this kind.

Only a minority of patients need, or can achieve, sufficient levels of hypnotically induced anaesthesia to enable major surgical operations to be carried out. But for the relief of chronic pain, hypnosis is often a very effective alternative to drugs. Research has shown that this relief is not simply the result of a placebo effect; the hypnotic alleviation of pain is separate and distinct from that brought about by placebo alone.[48]

The various strategies used to alleviate pain range from direct suggestion – e.g., that the part affected has become numb – to complex procedures, such as having the patient regress in age to a period before the onset of pain. Transforming the pain into another type of sensation, relocating it into another part of the body where it is less troublesome, distracting the patient from absorption in the pain . . . these are only some of the possibilities that are being successfully explored.

Pain reduction is only one of a number of potential uses for hypnosis in dental practice. These include the relaxation of the patient and the removal of fears about treatment; fears which can be of phobic intensity, leading to fainting in the dental chair or refusal to contemplate any treatment at all. Apart from these psychological problems there are what might be called purely dental problems, such as the prevention of gagging, and the control of bleeding and salivary flow. The scope for the use of hypnosis in dentistry has only recently been appreciated.[49]

In psychiatric disorders hypnosis can be variously used, although it is surprising that so few psychiatrists and clinical psychologists are trained in its use. As we have seen, in the course of its history hypnosis was employed extensively in cases of hysteria, which were so much more prevalent in the Europe of previous centuries. Today, gross hysterical cases are rare and there is also a general dissatisfaction with the notion of hysteria as a diagnostic entity, but these facts do not mean that hysterical mechanisms have fallen into disuse. Disorders of memory and conversion reactions (e.g., paralyses and sensory defects) still occur, although usually in less blatant form than in the past. Hypnosis is now probably under-used for these problems, as it can remove symptoms, explore causative conflicts, and reduce evident anxiety.

In other psychiatric illnesses, particularly obsessive-compulsive disorders, phobias, and some depressions, hypnosis has been found to be a useful adjunct to certain types of psychotherapy, especially cognitive-behavioural interventions.[50] However, in cases of schizophrenia and other severe psychoses, it is unlikely to have any therapeutic value so long as the patient is inaccessible and unresponsive to social interaction.

There is a current tendency to attribute many adult difficulties to sexual or physical abuse in childhood, abuse which has in many cases been forgotten. Some therapists may employ hypnosis to lift this amnesia, uncover the trauma, and hopefully relieve the symptoms. The technique and theorizing is remarkably similar to that used by Freud in his early analytical practice before he came to consider the majority of such memories to be childhood fantasies.[51]

Leaving aside the theoretical issue of the nature of the forgetting involved in these cases, a major concern has been expressed over the possible role of the hypnotherapist in suggesting, explicitly or implicitly, that abuse must have occurred, and requiring the patient to recall it. Memories retrieved under hypnosis are often accompanied by a great feeling of confidence, but can they be relied upon as veridical?[52]

Earlier in this chapter we reported an experiment in Hull's laboratory that supported what many clinicians believe, namely, that hypnosis can indeed aid recall. However, even that claim has not achieved universal support. What does seem certain is that although 'memories' may be recovered from a total amnesia, and may sometimes be accurate, they may sometimes be inaccurate, and there is no way of ascertaining their truth from the memories themselves; corroborative external evidence is always necessary.[53] This fact necessitates great care not only in therapeutic but also in forensic situations. The memories of witnesses enhanced by hypnosis are too unreliable to be used in court unsupported, nor can hypnosis be used with any confidence to explore the mental state of a defendant.

The old controversy about the supposed power of hypnotic suggestion to overcome a person's will, and to lead him to act as an automaton, is another area of forensic interest which has still not been laid to rest. Indeed, until recently much of the detailed debate between the Salpêtrière and Nancy Schools was overlooked, and repetition and rediscovery occurred.

In their extensive review of the historical and contemporary evidence on these issues, Jean-Roch Lawrence and Campbell Perry make the interesting point that many hypnotized individuals believe that the hypnotist can coerce them to act contrary to their normal behaviour.[54] This belief may often have been derived from watching hypnotists on stage, where the hypnotist's powers appear unlimited as his subjects perform bizarre acts at his command. With such a mind-set, persons put into coercive situations may make few attempts at resistance, labouring as they do under the misapprehension that such resistance would be futile – the conclusion being that it is not the condition of hypnosis that forces compliance; compliance occurs during hypnosis because of the previous beliefs held by hypnotized persons. Whether this view is an adequate explanation of all such cases seems dubious when we take into account the power of hypnotic suggestion to distort a deeply hypnotized subject's perception of reality.

The more successful stage hypnotists are competent showmen who build up expectations in their audience that they possess unusual and often paranormal powers. Volunteers of high suggestibilty are usually chosen from the audience by means of preliminary tests, and the pressures on them, when on stage, to fulfil the expectations of the hypnotist and of the audience are very high. Compliance with the demands of the situation is probably less stressful than withstanding them, even when those demands require the volunteer to behave in ridiculous and degrading ways.

The main dangers in stage performances arise from the carelessness of some hypnotists in ensuring the subsequent well-being of their subjects. Age regression may be upsetting if a 'return' is made to a traumatic past period; a bizarre suggestion to be carried out posthypnotically may cause embarrassment and even physical danger; sometimes subjects are not fully awakened after hypnosis, and occasionally they return spontaneously to a trance-like state. In the one study of individuals who had participated in a stage show it was found that four out of eighteen volunteers described the experience in unequivocally negative terms.[55] Whether this would be generally true and not peculiar to the university students involved in this study is unknown, but it would seem reasonable to assume that stage hypnotism is an unpleasant and possibly dangerous experience for some of those who volunteer to participate. In some countries these negative aspects have been considered sufficiently serious for a ban to be imposed, but such a step is generally ineffectual in view of the difficulty in coming to an agreed definition of hypnosis.[56]

Other non-clinical uses of hypnosis are more benign; they centre around attempts to improve a person's present condition. This improvement may be limited to a particular direction, such as to the playing of a sport, or be manifested in a more general approach to 'personal growth'.

In the case of sport, hypnosis is most often used to allay anxiety and to enable the achievement of optimal performance.[57] Mental rehearsal beforehand of the physical actions involved can also be helpful, although this does not necessitate hypnosis but merely a relaxed attitude on the part of the player, who then uses imagery to play through the future performance.[58] Intellectual and artistic work have also been shown to be susceptible to improvement through the skilful use of hypnosis, the emphasis here being on the removal of blocks to creative achievement.[59]

Perhaps the best-known use of suggestion for general well-being was that developed by Emil Coué, who followed Bernheim in what was sometimes called the New Nancy School. The essence of Coué's practice was to repeat to oneself a very general formula over and over again during the period preceding sleep. This procedure was based on the premise that self-suggestion could be powerful especially if the subject was drowsy and did not have to pay undue attention to the meaning of the words used. During the 1920s the method became popular and exaggerated claims were made for its efficacy.[60] It has been followed by many variations of positive-thinking programmes which, without using hypnosis, may succeed in altering a person's perceptions of their own worth. There is a dearth of hard data here and for the moment it is impossible to come to any firm conclusion about the merits of these techniques.

Some popular systems of meditation, such as transcendental meditation and autogenic training, have an unacknowledged hypnotic component, and practice of these techniques may involve entering stages of autohypnosis. The benefits that accrue for many people have been widely attested but may have been wrongly attributed by their enthusiastic practitioners to the peculiarities of a particular technique rather than to that which is common to them all, namely the relaxing and calming effect of self-induced hypnosis.[61]

The more directed use of autohypnosis, preferably learned from a skilled hypnotist, can help to deal with the minor problems of everyday life. For example, it can be used to instil confidence and poise in a forthcoming social encounter; it can reduce the effects of jetlag[62] and enable one to sleep when biorhythms have been disturbed; it can reduce distraction and improve concentration on a task at hand.

Perhaps enough has been said for the numerous possible applications of hypnosis to be appreciated. For these and as yet undiscovered possibilities to be fully explored will require changes in public and professional understanding as well as research by the scientific and medical communities. Our debt to Mesmer, who secularized his discovery and who tried to make it part of science will perhaps only then have been fully discharged. And not only to Mesmer, but also to those other pioneers who so often suffered for their advocacy.

Notes & References

Chapter 1: The Discovery

1 There are many biographies of Mesmer, of which the following is a selection. The earliest was that by Justinus Kerner: *Franz Anton Mesmer aus Schwaben, Entdecker des thierischen Magnetismus* (Frankfurt, 1856). A more recent biography in the German language with a fuller account of Mesmer's period in Vienna was written by F. Schürer-Waldheim: *Anton Mesmer. Ein Naturforscher ersten Ranges* (Vienna, 1930). A more substantial work is Karl Bittel & Rudolf Tischner: *Mesmer und sein Problem: Magnetismus – Suggestion – Hypnose* (Stuttgart, 1941). An account in French, with a heavy psychoanalytic slant, was provided by Jean Vinchon: *Mesmer et son secret* (Paris, 1936), and this book has appeared in a new edition by R. de Saussure (Toulouse, 1971). More recently, also in French, is Jean Thuillier: *Franz Anton Mesmer, ou l'extase magnétique* (Paris, 1988). In English, a racy account by Stephan Zweig: *Mental Healers* (London, 1933) needs more accurate supplementation by Margaret Goldsmith: *Franz Anton Mesmer: the History of an Idea* (London, 1934), and better still by the standard biography, D.M. Walmsley: *Anton Mesmer* (London, 1967). Vincent Buranelli in *The Wizard from Vienna* (London, 1976) has written a good biography for the general reader.

All references to Mesmer's writings are to: Robert Amadou (ed.): *Franz-Anton Mesmer: Le magnétisme animal* (Paris, 1971) in the present author's translation. An English translation by George J. Bloch is also available under the title *Mesmerism* (Los Altos, Calif., 1980).

2 Frank A. Pattie: 'Mesmer's medical dissertation and its debt to Mead's De Imperio Solis ac Lunae', *Journal of the History of Medicine and Allied Sciences* (1956) *XI*, pp.275–87.

3 Leopold Mozart to his wife, 21 July 1773: In Emily Anderson (tr.): *The Letters of Mozart and his Family*, second edition, (London, 1966) Vol.I, p.235.

4 F.A. Mesmer: *Schreiben über die Magnetkur an einen auswärtigen Arzt* (Vienna, 1775), in Robert Amadou (ed.): *op. cit.*, p.50.

5 Emily Anderson: *op. cit.*, pp.235, 236, 239, 244.

6 F.A. Mesmer: *op.cit . . .* , p.51.

278

7 M. Hell: In F.A. Mesmer: *Mémoire sur la découverte du magnétisme animal* (Geneva, Paris, 1779), in Robert Amadou (ed.), *op. cit.*, p.64. An English translation, under the title *Mesmerism by Doctor Mesmer* (1779) by V.R Myers, with an introduction by Gilbert Frankau, was published in London in 1948.

8 F.A. Mesmer: *Schreiben* . . .

9 F.A. Mesmer: *Mémoire* . . . , pp.66–7.

10 Wolfgang Mozart to Leopold Mozart, 17 March 1781, in Emily Anderson: *op. cit.*, Vol.II, p.713. Fraülein Franzl had married Mesmer's stepson, Franz de Paula von Bosch.

11 J.C. Unzer: In D.M. Walmsley: *op. cit.*, pp.60–3.

12 According to D.M. Walmsley: *op. cit.*, p.63.

13 Johann Sulzer: Berlin Academy of Sciences, Report of 24 March 1775.

14 Ernst Seyfert (article in *Asklepieion*, April 1812), in Julius Kerner, *op. cit.*, tr. D.M. Walmsley: *op. cit.*, pp.69–70.

15 Letter dated 20 November 1775 (Hegau, Switzerland), in Karl Bittel: *Der berühmte Hr. Doct. Mesmer, 1734–1815* (Überlingen, 1939).

16 F.A. Mesmer: *Mémoire* . . . p.69.

17 Johann Joseph Gassner: *Weise, fromm und gesund zu leben, auch gottselig zu sterben, oder nützlicher Unterricht wider den Teufel zu streiten* (Kemptem, 1774).

18 J.A. Zimmerman: *Johann Joseph Gassner, der berühmte Exorzist. Sein Leben und wundersames Wirken* (Kempten, 1879).

19 F.A. Mesmer: *Mémoire* . . . , p.74.

20 Mesmer's account of this case is contained both in the *Mémoire* . . . , pp.71–4, and in his later *Précis historique des faits relatifs au magnétisme animal jusqu'en avril 1781* (London, 1781), in Robert Amadou: *op. cit.*, pp.89–202.

21 The version by Herr Paradis is given by Julius Kerner, *op. cit.*, pp.61–71, and in French translation as a footnote in F.A. Mesmer, *Mémoire* . . . , also, as an Appendix to the English translation of this work by V.R. Myers, *op. cit.*

22 F.A. Mesmer: *Mémoire* . . . , p.73.

23 A comparison of this case of Mesmer's with those of patients who regain

their sight after an operation for congenital cataract is most instructive. In a 1932 compilation of cases by M. Von Senden: *Raum- und Gestaltauffassung bei operierten Blindgeborenen* (translated by P. Heath, London, 1960), the Paradis case is included and the text implies that she had been blind from birth. The confusion is understandable as her progress bears striking resemblance to those organically blind for a long time. Colours are discriminated relatively quickly after sight has been regained but colour names are difficult to learn. Fräulein Paradis' difficulties in distance perception and in retaining size constancy and the resulting unstable nature of the visual world are also found in cataract patients. Her rapid loss of confidence in movement when muscular and tactile cues are abandoned in preference for visual ones has also been reported of other patients. The similarities lend credence to the view that her visual deficit was of long duration and that Mesmer's therapy really was effective in restoring vision. See D.W. Forrest: 'Von Senden, Mesmer, and the recovery of sight in the blind', *American Journal of Psychology* (1974) 87, pp.719–22.

24 F.A. Mesmer: *Mémoire . . .* , pp.72–3.

25 According to Friedrich Melchior von Grimm (Baron): *Correspondence littéraire, philosophique et critique adressée à un souverain d'Allemagne*, 5 vols. (Paris, 1813). A biography of Maria-Theresia Paradis is to be found in the *Allgemeine deutsche Biographie*, Vol. 25 (Leipzig, 1887). It contains no mention of Mesmer.

26 According to Buranelli, *op. cit.*, p.87, Mesmer complained on at least one occasion in writing from Paris of his wife's stupidity and extravagance, but nothing further is known of their relationship.

Chapter 2: Mesmer in Paris

1 F.A. Mesmer: *Précis historique des faits relatifs au magnétisme animal jusqu'en avril 1781* (London, 1781), in Robert Amadou (ed.): *Franz-Anton Mesmer: Le magnétisme animal* (Paris, 1971). There is no reason to doubt Mesmer's description of his activities in Paris from his arrival there until April 1781 which he published in his *Précis historique . . .* There is no independent account, even Burdin & Dubois refer to it and their treatment of Mesmer is anything but sympathetic. See C. Burdin & Fréd. Dubois: *Histoire académique du magnétisme animal* (Paris, 1841).

2 Leroy did, in fact, put Mesmer's letter to the Academy, whose members, notably Vicq d'Azir, forcibly argued that they should let the matter drop.

3 Antoine Mauduit published an account of his treatment in his *Mémoire sur*

les différentes manières d'administrer l'électricité et observations sur les effets qu'elles ont produits, which was published in 1784. He seems to have had many successes in spite of Mesmer's contention in 1781 that he had none to date.

4 Mesmer reported a successful cure of this patient in his *Précis historique . . .*, p.115, note 27.

5 F.A. Mesmer: *ibid.*, p.117.

6 F.A. Mesmer: *ibid.*, p.194

7 E.M. Thornton: *Hypnotism, Hysteria and Epilepsy: an Historical Synthesis* (London, 1976) p.24.

8 According to C. Burdin & Fréd. Dubois: *op. cit.*, p.7. A louis d'or was made up of 24 livres. It would be misleading to try to give an equivalent in modern currency: a skilled artisan at the time earned about 500 livres a year.

9 C. Deslon: *Observations sur le magnétisme animal* (Paris, 1780). According to Deslon, Mesmer had diagnosed a growth on the liver and had warned Deslon that the cure was unlikely to be complete. Deslon died seven years later while receiving magnetic treatment for an exacerbation of the complaint.

10 F.A. Mesmer: *op. cit.*, p.128.

11 Mesmer seems to have come to this conclusion from experiments such as those carried out with the asthmatic sufferer in his demonstration before the Academy of Sciences. The hallucinations mentioned in the text were occasioned by Mesmer's 'reversal of the magnetic poles' by means of alternate left and right hand passes beneath the subject's nostrils, whereupon the man reported the smell of sulphur. (One presumes that Mesmer must have made a previous statement to the audience about the phenomenon in the subject's hearing, and the subject then fulfilled Mesmer's expectations.)

   A humorous contemporary treatment of the notion of anatomical poles was provided by Jean-Jacques Paulet in his *Mesmer justifié* (Paris, 1784).

12 The *Journal de Médecine* and the *Gazette de Santé* were the two main sources of professional antagonism and carried critical reviews of both Mesmer's and Deslon's books.

13 Jacques de Horne: *Réponse d'un médecin de Paris à un médecin de province, sur le prétendu magnétisme animal de M. Mesmer* (Paris, 1780).

14 F.A. Mesmer: *op. cit.*, p.126.

15 Charles Deslon: *op. cit.*, p.124.

16 Mesmer's letter is reprinted in his *Précis historique* . . . , pp.187–90.

17 Jean Vinchon: *Mesmer et son secret* (Paris, 1937), p.68.

18 It is unclear why the book was first published in London. The manuscript was originally written in German; the stylistic improvement may thus be due to the use of his native language by the author and to idiomatic translation.

19 F.A. Mesmer: *op. cit.*, p.103.

20 Friedrich Melchior von Grimm (Baron): *Correspondence littéraire, philosophique et critique adressée à un souverain d'Allemagne* (Paris, 1813) Vol.II, pp.459–61.

21 *Ibid.*, p.462.

22 Nicholas Bergasse: *Lettre d'un médecin de la Faculté de Paris à un médecin du collège de Londres* (La Haye, 1781).

23 This cure is reported in M.S. (M.S. Mialle): *Exposé par ordre alphabétique des cures operées en France par le magnétisme animal, depuis Mesmer jusqu'à nos jours* (Paris, 1826), Vol.II, pp.81–2.

24 Nicholas Bergasse: *Considérations sur le magnétisme animal* (La Haye, 1784), p.30.

Chapter 3: Year of Crisis

1 A copy of this document is to be found in Etienne Charavay: *Le Général La Fayette, 1757–1834* (Paris, 1898) pp.104–5. Lafayette became an enthusiastic convert to Mesmerism, a fact that he made known in a letter of 14 May to George Washington. For correspondence between Lafayette and Washington, and Mesmer and Washington, see D.M. Walmsley: *Anton Mesmer* (London, 1967) pp.120–2.

2 Guillotin did not invent the guillotine; he advocated it as a humane method of execution appropriate for members of all social classes.

3 Antoine Laurent Lavoisier & Pierre Simon (Marquis de Laplace): *Memoir on Heat: Read to the Royal Academy of Sciences, 28 June 1783* (tr. Henry Guerlac, New York, 1982).

4 This account is based on that given by Louis Figuier in his *Histoire du merveilleux dans les temps modernes* (Paris, 1860) Vol.III, pp.179 ff.

5 Friedrich Melchior von Grimm (Baron): *Correspondence littéraire, philosophique et critique, adressée à un souverain d'Allemagne* (Paris, 1813) Vol.II, p.457.

6 Louis Figuier (*op. cit.*, p.189) makes the unlikely claim that the arrangements for Maria-Theresia's visit were made by Deslon in order to discredit Mesmer.

7 Louis Figuier: *ibid.*, p.186.

8 In F. Podmore: *Mesmerism and Christian Science* (London, 1909) p.55.

9 Louis Figuier: *op. cit.*, p.169.

10 According to Louis Figuier: *op. cit.*, p. 176.

11 Louis Bergasse: *Un défenseur des principes traditionelles: Nicholas Bergasse (1750–1832)* (Paris, 1910) p.29.

12 Extracts from the Baron de Corberon's journal are given in Robert Darnton: *Mesmerism and the End of the Enlightenment in France* (Cambridge, Mass., 1968) pp.180–2. An account of the content of Mesmer's lectures to the Society was provided in the form of aphorisms by Caullet de Veaumorel, the physician to the King's brother and an apostle of Deslon. See F.A. Mesmer [Caullet de Veaumorel]: *Aphorismes de M. Mesmer dictés à l'assemblée de ses élèves* (Paris, 1785).

   The 344 aphorisms give a reasonably comprehensive view of Mesmer's theories, expanded from the 1779 version, and provide details of practical procedures for magnetizing. We can note in this respect Mesmer's emphasis on observation of the patient's reactions, while maintaining a detached attitude without any emotional involvement, and the stress he laid on the necessity for the crisis without which there could be no lasting cure.

13 *Rapport des commissaires chargés par le Roi de l'examen du magnétisme animal* (Paris, 1784) 11 August. Quotations in the text are taken from the English translation by William Godwin: *Report of Dr Benjamin Franklin and the other Commissioners charged by the King of France with the Examination of Animal Magnetism* (London, 1785) reprinted in Maurice M. Tinterow: *Foundations of Hypnosis* (Springfield, Ill., 1970).

14 'Imagination' was one of Aristotle's faculties of the soul, which was extensively employed as an explanation of mental disorder and also enlisted to explain some cures. Towards the end of the nineteenth century it was largely replaced by the term 'suggestion'. See: Stanley W. Jackson: 'The imagination and psychological healing,' *Journal of the History of the*

Behavioral Sciences (1990) *26*, pp.345–58.

15 *Rapport des commissaires de la Société Royale de Médecine, nommés par le Roi, pour faire l'examen du magnétisme animal* (Paris, 1784) 16 August.

16 [A.L. de Jussieu]: *Rapport de l'un des commissaires de la Société Royale de Médecine, nommés par le Roi, pour faire l'examen du magnétisme animal* (Paris, 1784) 12 September.

17 *Rapport secret sur le magnétisme animal, rédigé par Bailly, au nom de la même commission* (same signatories as reference 13) 11 August. Quotations in the text are taken from the English translation in Alfred Binet & Charles Féré: *Animal Magnetism* (London, 1887) pp.18–25.

18 Robert Darnton: *op. cit.*, pp.86–7.

19 N. Bergasse: *Observations sur le magnétisme animal ou sur la théorie du monde et des êtres organisés, d'après les principes de M. Mesmer* (The Hague, 1784) p.29.

20 *Supplément aux deux rapports de MM. les commissaires chargés par le Roi de l'examen du magnétisme animal* (Paris, 1784). See F. Podmore, *op. cit.*, pp.9–23, for a full description of many of these cases. As Podmore points out, there are many mistakes in proper names, etc., a reflection of the haste with which the material was compiled.

21 *Ibid.*, p.30.

22 F. Thouret: *Extrait de la correspondance de la Société Royale de Médecine relativement au magnétisme animal* (Paris, 1785).

23 N. Bergasse: *op. cit.*

24 J.-B. Bonnefoy: *Analyse raisonnée des rapports des commissaires chargés par le Roi de l'examen du magnétisme animal* (Lyons, 1784).

25 J.M.A. Servan: *Doutes d'un provincial proposés à MM. les médecins commissionaires chargés par le Roi de l'examen du magnétisme animal* (Lyons, 1784).

26 Pierre Yves Barre & Jean Baptiste Radet: *Les docteurs modernes* (Paris, 1874).

27 Friedrich Melchior von Grimm: *op. cit.*, Vol.III, p.103.

28 Louis Figuier: *op. cit.*, p.193.

29 The opera ran for only five nights upon its first presentation in Vienna in January 1790, the year of the death of Mesmer's wife. He was not in Vienna

at the time, and during subsequent performances in Germany he was almost certainly in Switzerland.

30 A.J.F. Bertrand: *Du magnétisme animal en France* (Paris, 1826) p.49. Jacques Quen has described the materialistic bias of the medical profession in the late eighteenth century (*Journal of the History of the Behavioural Sciences*, 1975, *11*, pp.149–56) and Jan Goldstein has a full account of the development of the French medical profession in *Console and Classify* (New York, 1987). For a lively polemic on modern medical orthodoxy, see Brian Inglis: *Fringe Medicine* (London, 1964).

Chapter 4: The Aftermath

1 Louis Bergasse: *Un défenseur des principes traditionelles: Nicholas Bergasse (1750–1832)* (Paris, 1910) p.34.

2 Nicholas Bergasse: In Robert Darnton: *Mesmerism and the End of the Enlightenment in France* (Cambridge, Mass., 1968) p.114.

3 Robert Darnton's book contains an excellent account of Bergasse's development of the revolutionary theme.

4 Nicholas Bergasse: In Vincent Buranelli: *The Wizard from Vienna* (London, 1976) p.175.

5 A.M.J. de Chastenet (Marquis de Puységur): In Vincent Buranelli: *ibid.*, p.177.

6 F.A. Mesmer: *Lettre de l'auteur de la découverte du magnétisme animal à l'auteur des Réflexions préliminaires* (Paris, 1785).

7 Nicholas Bergasse: *Observations de M. Bergasse sur un écrit du Dr Mesmer, ayant pour titre: Lettre de l'inventeur du magnétisme animal à l'auteur des Reflexions préliminaires* (London, 1785).

8 According to D.M. Walmsley: *Anton Mesmer* (London, 1967) p.161.

9 F.A. Mesmer: *Mémoire de F.A. Mesmer, docteur en médecine, sur ses découvertes* (Paris, 1799), in Robert Amadou (ed.): Le magnétisme animal (Paris, 1971).

10 F.A. Mesmer: *ibid.*, p.309.

11 F A. Mesmer: *ibid.*, p.319.

12 D.M. Walsmley: *op. cit.*, p.170.

13 Karl Wolfart: In D.M. Walmsley: *ibid.*, p.171.

14 Karl Wolfart: *ibid.*, p.175 (Preface to 15).

15 Karl Christian Wolfart (ed.): *Mesmerismus. Oder System der Wechsel-wirkungen, Theorie und Anwendung des thierischen Magnetismus von Dr Friedrich Anton Mesmer* (Berlin, 1814). The poor quality of the translation was attested to by Rudolf Tischner in his biography: *Franz Anton Mesmer, Leben, Werk und Wirkungen* (Munich, 1928). Tischner was able to compare some of Mesmer's original manuscript with Wolfart's rendering.

16 W.H. Sheldon & S.S. Stevens: *The Varieties of Temperament* (New York, 1942).

17 C.D. Darlington: [Introduction to] F. Galton: *Hereditary Genius* (second edition, London, 1962) p.20. It is remarkable, considering the sexual morals of the time, that Mesmer's name was never linked with any of the many aristocratic ladies who frequented the baquet.

18 As in the virulent attack on animal magnetism mounted under the guise of an historical treatment by C. Burdin & Fréd. Dubois: *Histoire académique du magnétisme animal* (Paris, 1841).

19 As claimed by Stefan Zweig in his *Mental Healers* (London, 1933).

20 L. Chertok & R. de Saussure: *Naissance du psychoanalyste: de Mesmer à Freud* (Paris, 1973).

21 E.M. Thornton: *Hypnotism, Hysteria and Epilepsy: an Historical Synthesis* (London, 1976).

22 Eliot Slater & Martin Roth: *Clinical Psychiatry* (third edition, London, 1969) p.450.

23 Seizures might have a good effect on various disorders. See E.H. Reynolds: 'The pharmacological management of epilepsy associated with psychological disorders', *British Journal of Psychiatry* (1982) *141*, pp.549–57.

24 According to Puységur. See A.M.J. de Chastenet (Marquis de Puységur): *Les vérités cheminent, tôt ou tard elles arrivent* (Paris, 1815).

25 Karl Christian Wolfart: *op. cit.*, p.xiii. The interference came, as predicted, in 1856 when an encyclical letter from the Holy Roman Inquisition was sent to all bishops to prevent the abuse of magnetism in enabling somnambulists to predict the future and to call up the spirits of the dead. The text of the letter is to be found in Alfred Binet & Charles Féré: *Animal Magnetism* (London, 1887).

Chapter 5: Somnambulism

1 B.E. Poret (Marquis de Blosseville): *Les Puységur, leur oeuvres de littérateur, d'économie politique et de science* (Paris, 1873).

2 Antoine-Hyacinth's only publication concerned the island of Saint-Domingue: *Instructions nautiques sur les côtes et les débouquemens de Saint-Domingue* (Paris, 1821).

3 A.M.J. de Chastenet (Marquis de Puységur): *Mémoires pour servir à l'histoire et à l'établissement du magnétisme animal* (Paris, 1784).

4 *Ibid.*, p.28.

5 There is nothing in Mesmer's publications to indicate that he put any store on such control of the patient's mood. He was obviously well aware from his earliest experiments that it was possible to control perceptual and motor acts, and his Parisian experiences must have made him adept at controlling the crisis. A curious report by Charles Moulinie (in Louis Figuier: *Histoire du merveilleux dans les temps modernes*, Paris, 1860, Vol.III, p.168) mentions one of Mesmer's young servants who fell into a somnambulistic fugue lasting for several weeks, in which she followed her master wherever he went. Thus, Mesmer was also acquainted with the more bizarre manifestations of somnambulism.

6 A.M.J. de Chastenet (Marquis de Puységur): Letter of 17 May 1784 to Comte Maxime, *op. cit.*, p.32.

7 *Ibid.*, p.32.

8 This suggestion was made by Henri F. Ellenberger: *The Discovery of the Unconscious* (London, 1970) pp.189–191.

9 Prior to Puységur's publications, Mesmer had made no written reference to posthypnotic amnesia. However, Veaumorel quotes one of Mesmer's aphorisms, read to the Society of Harmony, which clearly implies that he was aware of it: '... those persons who are subject to the crises almost always lose all memory of their impressions on regaining the ordinary state.' Aphorism 261 in F.A. Mesmer [Caullet de Veaumorel]: *Aphorismes de M. Mesmer dictés à l'assemblée de ses élèves* (Paris, 1785). The actual date of the lecture is, however, unknown; Puységur's book appeared in December 1784, and it would therefore seem possible that Mesmer should be given priority, although the discovery was of little moment to him. De Jussieu was in fact the first to draw attention to the phenomenon in print. (A.L. de Jussieu: *Rapport de l'un des commissaires ...*, Paris, 1784).

10 A.M.J. de Chastenet (Marquis de Puységur): *op. cit.*, (second edition, Paris, 1809) p.104.

11 *Ibid.*, p.225.

12 A.M.J. de Chastenet (Marquis de Puységur): *op. cit.* (first edition, Paris, 1784) pp.65–86.

13 A good discussion of these cases is contained in A. Bertrand: *Traité du somnambulisme et des différentes modifications qu'il présente* (Paris, 1823).

14 A.M.J. de Chastenet (Marquis de Puységur): *Recherches, expériences et observations physiologiques sur l'homme dans l'état de somnambulisme naturel et dans le somnambulisme provoqué par l'acte magnétique* (Paris, 1811) p.54.

15 Puységur's, and indeed Mesmer's, use of a tree as a baquet was probably not unconnected with the importance of the tree in French folklore as a source of healing. Paul Sébillot in his voluminous work on French folklore mentions the way in which peasants of the seventeenth century attached themselves with ropes to certain trees in order to transfer their illness to the trees, a practice which he relates to earlier tree worship (*Le folk-lore de France*, Paris, 1906, Vol.II, pp.411–23).

16 J.M.P. Chastenet (Comte de Puységur): *Rapport de cures opérées à Bayonne par le magnétisme animal* (Bayonne, 1784). The Marquis' own first publication took a similar title and appeared anonymously as a pamphlet in the same year: *Détails des cures opérées à Buzancy* (Soissons, 1784).

17 M. Cloquet: Letter dated 13 June 1784, in Alphonse Teste: *Manuel pratique du magnétisme animal* (Paris, 1843), tr. D. Spillan (London, 1843) p.193.

18 A.L. de Jussieu: *op. cit.*

19 Victor Race and Henri Joly were subsequently replaced as family physicians by Agnes Burguet, whom Puységur had under treatment for the rupture of blood vessels in her breast. He devotes many pages to a consideration of her treatment and of her therapeutic abilities – which do not seem very remarkable, consisting largely of prescriptions for cough syrup for Puységur and his son. See Chapter 14 of his *Recherches...* (Paris, 1811). According to C. Burdin & Fréd. Dubois (*Histoire académique du magnétisme animal*, Paris, 1841, p.241), Mme Burguet, the wife of an iron founder, became notorious in Paris where she was known as 'La Maréchale'. She certainly seems to have led Puységur a pretty dance,

summoning him at short notice home from Paris or having herself taken
there for treatment on numerous occasions. Puységur later explained why
this was necessary: he believed her life was sustained over a period of
twelve years only through his will, although luckily she had the ability to
predict an imminent crisis so that he could hasten to her side! (*Bibliothèque
du magnétisme animal*, 1818, *4*, pp.11–39).

20 A.M.J. de Chastenet (Marquis de Puységur): *Mémoires . . .*, p.88.

21 *Ibid.*, p.211.

22 A.M.J. de Chastenet (Marquis de Puységur): *Du magnétisme animal,
considéré dans ses rapports avec diverses branches de la physique générale*
(Paris, 1807) p.149. The content of the lectures runs from pp.116–49.

23 *Ibid.*, p.163.

24 Henri F. Ellenberger: *op. cit.*, p.73.

25 The first piece had as co-author Nicholas Bergasse and was staged at Le
Théâtre National in 1790. Entitled *La Journée des Dupes*, it represented
an attack on those who might have profited from the recent upheavals,
and it is suitably scathing about the new 'freedoms' that bring restrictions
in their train.

26 J.H.D. Petetin: *Electricité animale prouvée par la découverte des
phénomènes physiques et moraux de la catalepsie hystérique* (Lyon,
1808).

27 A.M.J. de Chastenet (Marquis de Puységur): *Du magnétisme animal*,
pp.15–24. It is interesting that in spite of his views on the somnambulists'
passivity and lack of independence of the magnetizer, Puységur was
convinced early in his career that it would be impossible to make them
carry out actions against their own interests. Thus he reports asking one
young woman somnambulist if he could persuade her to undress; she
replied archly that she would take off her hat and shoes if he demanded
it, but no more. Another prospective subject, who was listening to the
conversation, assured Puységur that she would have to accede to his request
if he magnetized her. However, she proved to be as modest as her pre-
decessor, telling Puységur that she was no longer the same person when
magnetized as she was in the natural waking state. See his *Mémoires . . .*,
p.180 ff.

28 A vivid contemporary account of young Hébert's progress was provided
by a journalist, Hoffman, in the *Journal de l'Empire*, 8, 10, 13 November
1812. Hoffman's attitude was at this time one of provisional acceptance
of somnambulism, i.e., he accepted the reality of many cures and believed

in the sensory changes reported by somnambulists, but doubted the paranormal phenomena. By 1826, in another series of articles in the *Journal des Débats*, he had clearly shifted his position to one of complete distrust. A common increase in scepticism was one result of the magnetizers' stress on the marvellous abilities of their somnambulists.

M.S. Mialle, subsequently one of the founders of the Société du Magnétisme, was so impressed by Hoffman's earlier accounts of Hébert that he sought out Puységur for a cure of his personal illness, and, having achieved that, devoted two volumes to a long list of magnetic cures in which both Hébert and Victor figure. The volume was dedicated to Puységur. M.S. [M.S. Mialle]: *Exposé par ordre alphabétique des cures opérées en France par le magnétisme animal, depuis Mesmer jusqu'à nos jours, 1774–1826* (Paris, 1826).

29 A.M.J. de Chastenet (Marquis de Puységur): *Les fous, les insensés, les maniaques et les frénétiques ne seraient-ils que des somnambules désordonnés?* (Paris, 1812). Puységur showed Hébert to Gall, the inventor of phrenology, and to Pinel, the founder of French psychiatry. Both remained sceptical regarding animal magnetism.

30 Puységur seems to have believed that he had again cured Victor, to judge by his interim report of 21 April in the *Bibliothèque du magnétisme animal*, 1818, *4*, pp.135–42. However, Victor died shortly afterwards.

31 A.M.J. de Chastenet (Marquis de Puységur): *Les vérités cheminent, tôt ou tard elles arrivent* (Paris, 1815).

Chapter 6: Minor Magnetists

1 J.P.F. Deleuze: *Histoire critique du magnétisme animal* (second edition, Paris, 1819) Vol.I, pp.217–8.

2 J.P.F. Deleuze: *Instruction pratique sur le magnétisme animal* (Paris, 1835). Tr. Thomas C. Hartshorn (Providence, U.S.A., 1837) p.110.

3 Aubin Gauthier: *Histoire du somnambulisme* (Paris, 1842) p.290. Deleuze had translated Erasmus Darwin's *Loves of the Plants* in 1799 and had published his own *Eudoxe, or Conversations on the Study of the Sciences, Letters and Philosophy* in 1801.

4 J.P.F. Deleuze: *Histoire . . .* (first edition, Paris, 1813) Vol.I, p.12.

5 J.P.F. Deleuze: 'Définition du magnétisme', *Annales du magnétisme* (1816) *8*, p.120.

6 J.P.F. Deleuze: *Histoire* . . . (1813) Vol.I, p.52.

7 *Ibid.*, p.44.

8 *Ibid.*, p.72.

9 Deleuze mentions that if the legs are omitted from the magnetizer's passes the patient may complain of a loss of sensation in them. It is strange that so little use was made by the early magnetizers of these spontaneous anaesthesias, which had been noted by the 1784 Commissioners and attributed by them to the constrained posture of patients around the baquet.

10 Although Puységur himself stated that patients can be cured without entering somnambulism, he admitted that the failure to do so was not so satisfying for the magnetizer, who could then learn nothing of the patient's illness as it was impossible to question him (*Du magnétisme animal,* Paris, 1807, Chapter XII). In practice he concerned himself only with somnambulists, according to his son, who reported the fact in a conversation with Aubin Gauthier, *op. cit.*, p.289.

11 J.P.F. Deleuze: *Histoire* . . . (1813) Vol.I, p.84.

12 *Ibid.*, p.85. Tardy de Montravel, one of the most enthusiastic of early magnetizers, had published as early as 1785 an account of the appearance of the magnetic fluid as seen by somnambulists. They saw it streaming from the magnetizer, making liquids luminous, etc. (A.A. Tardy de Montravel: *Essai sur la théorie du somnambulisme magnétique,* London, 1785.)

13 *Ibid.*, p.123.

14 E.J. Dingwall (ed.): *Abnormal Hypnotic Phenomena* (London, 1967) Vol.I, p.15.

15 J.P.F. Deleuze: *Mémoire sur la faculté de prévision* (Paris, 1834).

16 E.J. Dingwall (ed.): *op. cit.*, p.20. Other magnetists, notably Aubin Gauthier, were also insistent on the incompatibility of experimental demonstration and cure. It was thought that, as somnambulists were directing their own treatment, putting them on public display could have the effect of disturbing their progress. On the contrast between therapists and experimenters, see Jacqueline Carroy-Thirard: 'Hypnose et expérimentation', *Bulletin de Psychologie*, *34*, No.348, pp.41–50.

17 G.P. Billot: *Recherches psychologiques sur la cause des phénomènes extraordinaires observés chez des modernes voyants* (Paris, 1839).

18 *Ibid.*, p.132.

19 For the details of Faria's life, see D.G. Dalgado: *Mémoire sur la vie de l'abbé de Faria* (Paris, 1906).

20 Probably the manuscript of Volume One of what was to be a four-volume work. The first and only volume appeared posthumously in 1819: J.C. de Faria (Abbé de Faria), *De la cause du sommeil lucide, ou, étude de la nature de l'homme*. Reissued with preface and introduction by D.G. Dalgado (Paris, 1906). All references are to the 1906 edition.

21 *Ibid.*, p.154.

22 M. Rabbé: *Biographies universelles des contemporains* (Paris, 1834) Vol.II, p.1833.

23 J.C. de Faria: *op. cit.*, p.34.

24 Faria's book was dedicated to Puységur, who did not deign to notice it, but his omission is understandable in view of Faria's opinion that neither the fluid nor the will were involved in bringing about the trance.

25 According to J.F. Noizet: *Mémoire sur le somnambulisme et le magnétisme animal* (Paris, 1854). Translated into modern idiom, the characteristics of susceptible subjects, according to Faria, are the ability to pass readily from one state of consciousness to another (i.e., to dissociate), to have a labile autonomic nervous system, and to be suggestible. The validity of the first and last of these indicators has been established in recent research. See Ernest R. Hilgard's *Hypnotic Susceptibility* (New York, 1965) for a general survey of this work.

26 The account appeared in the *Gazette de France*, 21 August 1813.

27 J.C. Faria: *op. cit.*, p.35.

28 *Ibid.*, p.33.

29 *Ibid.*, pp.167–8.

30 *Ibid.*, p.51.

31 D.G. Dalgado, *op. cit.*, has shown many resemblances between Faria's life events and episodes in Dumas's novel.

32 Sources used for the Hôtel Dieu experiments were: M.S. [M.S. Mialle]: *Exposé par ordre alphabétique des cures opérées en France par le magnétisme animal, depuis Mesmer jusqu'à nos jours* (1774–1826) (Paris, 1826), section entitled *Vomissement du sang*; Alphonse Teste: *Manuel pratique de magnétisme animal* (Paris, 1843) p.158 ff.; Du Potet de Sennevoy: *An Introduction to the Study of Animal Magnetism* (London,

1838) Chapter 2; Aubin Gauthier: *op. cit.*, pp.314–23.

33 J.F. Clarke: *Autobiographical Recollections of the Medical Profession* (London, 1874) p.161.

34 Alphonse Teste: *op. cit.*, p.158.

35 P. Foissac: *Rapports et discussions de l'Académie Royale de Médecine sur le magnétisme animal* (Paris, 1833) p.276. The account given by Mialle (*op. cit.*) is somewhat more graphic. He claims that Récamier pricked Mlle Samson, pinched her five times as hard as he could, dropped her on to her seat and finally on to the floor, without her waking up. He finally desisted after Husson pleaded with him to stop. Although she gave no sign of pain during these proceedings, she afterwards complained bitterly of the bruising caused by Récamier's violent treatment.

36 P. Foissac: *op. cit.*, p.280. Rebouam's observation was attested to by six observers.

37 According to Mialle, Catherine Samson returned to treatment in August 1822 at La Pitié hospital, where Geoffroy now was, and he resumed her magnetic treatment himself. Another woman by the same name, but aged 65, died soon afterwards, and it appears to have been a confusion in names that led Récamier to claim in a paper to the Académie de Médecine (24 January 1826) that no sooner had the magnetists published their account of Mlle Samson's cure than she had to return to hospital to die.

38 Jules Cloquet: 'Ablation d'un cancer de sein pendant le sommeil magnétique', *Arch. gén. Méd.*, (1829), *I*, pp.131–4.

39 Léon Chertok: *Sense and Nonsense in Psychotherapy: the Challenge of Hypnosis* (London, 1981) p.5.

40 Alexandre Bertrand: *Traité du somnambulisme* (Paris, 1823) p.176.

41 *Ibid.*, p.233.

42 *Ibid.*, p.231, footnote.

43 Alexandre Bertrand: *Du magnétisme animal en France* (Paris, 1826).

44 *Dictionnaire de médecine par MM. Adelon, etc.*, 21 vols. (Paris, 1821–8). Rostan's article, *'Magnétisme'*, appeared in 1825. He had lost his initial scepticism after witnessing experiments performed by the neurologist, Georget, at the Salpêtrière hospital. He thought that magnetism must have a direct effect on the nervous system and that it should accordingly prove particularly efficacious in the treatment of general nervous diseases. However, its use was not limited to such diseases; beneficial effects could be observed on other patients in whom its action could reduce pain.

Chapter 7: Vision without Eyes

1 Esquirol was the leader of the French School of psychiatry and chief physician to the 'Division of Mad Women' at the Salpêtrière, while Georget was well known for his textbook on the physiology of the nervous system: *De la physiologie du système nerveux, et spécialement du cerveau* (Paris, 1821).

2 According to Foissac, who quoted from Georget's will, in Appendix to J. Deleuze: *Practical Instruction in Animal Magnetism* (second edition, tr. Thomas C. Hartshorne, Providence, 1837) p.155.

3 P. Foissac: *Mémoire sur le magnétisme animal adressé à MM. les membres de l'Académie des Sciences et de l'Académie de Médecine* (Paris, 1825).

4 P. Foissac: *Rapports et discussions de l'Académie de Médecine sur le magnétisme animal* (Paris, 1833), tr. J.C. Colquhoun under the title: *Report of the Experiments on Animal Magnetism* (London, 1833) p.199.

5 *Ibid.*, pp.144, 153.

6 *Ibid.*, pp.154–6.

7 *Ibid.*, p.168.

8 *Ibid.*, pp.149–51.

9 C.P.G. Hamard reported Oudet's work; see *Bulletin de l'Académie royale de Médecine* (1836) *I*, pp.343 ff.

10 C. Burdin & Fréd. Dubois: *Histoire académique du magnétisme animal* (Paris, 1841).

11 The report appeared in the *Bulletin de l'Académie royale de Médecine* (1837) *I*, pp.957–74.

12 Quoted by F. Podmore: *Mesmerism and Christian Science* (London, 1909) p.114.

13 H.M. Husson: *Opinion prononcée par M. Husson à l'Académie de Médecine séance du 22 août 1837 sur le rapport de M. Dubois (d'Amiens) relatif au magnétisme animal* (Paris, 1837).

14 Berna gave vent to his opinion in a booklet published in the following year: D.J. Berna: *Magnétisme animal: examen et réfutation du rapport fait par M.E.F. Dubois (d'Amiens) à l'Académie royale de Médecine le 8 août 1837, sur le magnétisme animal* (Paris, 1838). It is a pity that no experiments were done with Berna having knowledge of the words presented to the

somnambulist in order to ascertain if his former successes had been due to some kind of communication between himself and his subject, whether by small muscular movements, whispering, or even telepathy.

15 J.J.A. Ricard (ed.): *Le Révélateur* (Bordeaux, 1837–8). This journal is chiefly noteworthy for its reports of magnetic cures of deaf-mutes, which Ricard collected together and re-published in his *Traité théorique et pratique du magnétisme animal* (Paris, 1841).

16 J. Pigeaire: 'Lettre sur quelques faits de magnétisme animal', *Bulletin de l'Académie de Médecine* (1837–8) *II*, pp.540 ff.

17 A discussion of the campaign is to be found in C. Burdin & Fréd. Dubois: *op. cit.*, p.593.

18 Best known for his *Manuel pratique de magnétisme animal* (Paris, 1840), *Le magnétisme animal expliqué* (Paris, 1845), and *Les confessions d'un magnétiseur* (Paris, 1848).

19 F.J. Double: 'Rapport au nom de la Commission du Magnétisme pour le prix Burdin', *Bulletin de l'Académie royale de Médecine* (1840) *VI*, pp.21–5.

20 Gerdy's account first appeared in the same volume of the *Bulletin* as Double's report (pp.719 ff). It was then published under the title, *Remarques sur la vision des somnambules* (Paris, 1841). For more recent critical remarks on eyeless-vision, reference should be made to Podmore: *op. cit.*, pp.101–2, 118–121. E.J. Dingwall in his *Abnormal Hypnotic Phenomena* (London, 1967) Vol.I, pp.93 ff, provides an excellent description of the Pigeaire experiments as well as a critique of many others.

   Contemporary work in China is difficult to evaluate without further details of the experimental precautions observed. See Jon C. Shum: 'Reading without the eye? – reports from China', *Bulletin of the British Psychological Society* (1981) *34*, pp.125–6. From time to time newspapers carry reports of similar phenomena, for example, *Evening Press*, 2 November 1981. It is unfortunate that the physical scientists who commonly record these events seem to be among the more credulous investigators; the experimental procedures might best be vetted by clinical psychologists and professional conjurors.

21 For example, in Balzac's *Ursule Mirouet* (1841) and Dumas's *Memoirs of a Physician, Joseph Balsamo* (1847).

22 Aubin Gauthier: *Histoire du somnambulisme* (Paris, 1842). Gauthier wrote many pamphlets. Some were serious, such as his *Compérage magnétique réprimé* (Paris, 1846), which dealt with the responsibilities of magnetizers

and their somnambulists. Some were amusing, and some dealt with other unorthodox subjects such as water-divining and anti-vivisection. He also edited a periodical, *Revue magnétique* (1844–5) in which he lost no opportunity to castigate all those who did not think as he did.

23 Alphonse Teste: *Manuel pratique de magnétisme animal* (Paris, 1840) tr. D. Spillan (London, 1843).

24 *Ibid.*, p.204.

25 Alphonse Teste: *Le magnétisme animal expliqué* (Paris, 1845) p.425.

26 Alphonse Teste: *Manuel pratique* ...(1843). Chapter 14 is devoted to the case.

27 N.N. Frappart: *Lettres sur le magnétisme et le somnambulisme, à l'occasion de Mademoiselle Pigeaire* (Paris, 1840).

28 J.D. Du Potet de Sennevoy: *L'Université de Montpellier et le magnétisme animal, ou une verité nouvelle en presence de vieilles erreurs* (Béziers, 1836).

29 Alexandre Erdan: *La France mystique* (Paris, 1855).

30 J.D. Du Potet de Sennevoy: *Magie dévoilée* (Paris, 1852) tr. A.H.E. Lee under the title: *Magnetism and Magic* (London, 1927) p.94.

31 Alexandre Erdan: *op. cit.*

32 J.D. Du Potet de Sennevoy: *An Introduction to the Study of Animal Magnetism* (London, 1838) Chapter 7.

33 Elizabeth Blackwell: *Pioneer Work for Women* (London, 1914) p.124.

Chapter 8: The Spread of Magnetism To Britain and the USA

1 *The Gentleman's Magazine* had published extracts from the Franklin Commission's report (1785, *II*, p.945).

2 According to John Martin: *Animal Magnetism Examined: in a Letter to a Country Gentleman* (London, 1790).

3 *Ibid.*, p.6.

4 *Ibid.*, p.9.

5 George Winter: *Animal Magnetism* (Bristol and London, 1801).

6 Hannah More to Horace Walpole, September 1788: In William Roberts (ed.): *Memoirs of the Life and Correspondence of Mrs Hannah More* (second edition, London, 1834), Vol.II, p.120.

7 George Winter: *op. cit.*, p.34.

8 Mary Pratt: *A List of a few cures performed by Mr and Mrs de Loutherberg of Hammersmith Terrace without medicine* (London, 1789).

9 Philippe Jacques de Loutherberg: *The Romantic and Picturesque Scenery of England and Wales* (London, 1805).

10 George Winter: *op. cit.*, p.17.

11 John Martin: *op. cit.*, p.31.

12 John Haygarth: *On the Imagination, as a Cause and as a Cure of the Disorders of the Body; exemplified by Fictitious Tractors, and Epidemial Convulsions* (Bath, 1800).

13 *Ibid.*, p.2.

14 *Ibid.*, p.2.

15 *Ibid.*, p.43.

16 *Ibid.*, pp.23–4.

17 According to Haygarth, the French translation appeared in the *Mercure de France*.

18 Thomas Medwin: *The Life of Percy Bysshe Shelley* (2 vols., London, 1847) p.49.

19 Thomas Medwin: *The Shelley Papers* (London, 1833) p.120.

20 According to an account subsequently published by John Elliotson in the *Zoist* (1843) *1*, p.66.

21 Richard Chenevix: 'On Mesmerism, improperly denominated animal magnetism', *London Medical and Physiological Journal* (1829) *61*, p.219; *62*, pp.199, 315. Elliotson's memoranda of what he had seen were published in abridged form in Chenevix's paper. The effect of Chenevix's abridgement was to omit any unfavourable results, a fact to which Elliotson drew attention in his *Human Physiology* (fifth edition, London, 1840) p.681, footnote.

22 John Elliotson, *op. cit.*, p.68. The article contains the comments of the other observers. Criticisms of Chenevix also appeared in the *London Medical and Surgical Journal* (1829) p.484.

It can be noted that Elliotson generally preferred the term 'mesmerism' to 'animal magnetism', and the former does seem to be the term most generally used by English writers of the time, especially those who were favourable to the practice.

23 Jefferson's activities are mentioned in Robert Darnton: *Mesmerism and the End of the Enlightenment* (Cambridge, Mass., 1968) pp.89–90.

24 Charles Poyen St Sauveur: *Progress of Animal Magnetism in New England* (Boston, 1837).

25 J.P.F. Deleuze: *Practical Instruction in Animal Magnetism*. Tr. T.C. Hartshorn (New York, 1846).

26 O. Brownson: *The Spirit-Rapper: An Autobiography* (Boston, 1854).

27 J.S. Grimes: *Etherology and the Phreno-Philosophy of Mesmerism and Magic Eloquence* (Boston, 1850). J.B. Dods: *Electrical Psychology*. Revised and edited by H.G. Darling (London & Glasgow, 1851). The term 'electrobiology' was popularized by H.G. Darling, who was a former Professor of Physiology. He had a good platform manner and gave numerous demonstrations, visiting Britain in 1851.

28 A.J. Davis: *The Principles of Nature, her Divine Revelations, and a Voice to Mankind* (New York, 1847).

29 According to Henry Spicer, a British investigator. Quoted in Alan Gauld: *The Founders of Psychic Research* (London, 1968) p.15.

Chapter 9: Elliotson and the Okey Sisters

1 A general history of the hospital, but with an unduly critical attack on Elliotson and mesmerism, will be found in W.R. Merrington: *University College Hospital and its Medical School: A History* (London, 1976). Elliotson's address at the opening of the medical session in October 1832 will be found reprinted in Fred Kaplan (ed.): *John Elliotson on Mesmerism* (New York, 1982).

2 *Medical Times* (1844–5), *XI*, quoted by J. Milne Bramwell: *Hypnotism: its History, Practice and Theory* (third edition, London, 1913) pp.4–5.

3 *Medical Times* (1844–5), *XI*, quoted by F. Podmore: *Mesmerism and Christian Science* (London, 1909) p.126.

4   John Elliotson: 'On the ignorance of the discoveries of Gall evinced by recent physiological writers', *Lancet* (June 1837) *2*, pp.469–71.

5   According to J.F. Clarke: *Autobiographical Recollections of the Medical Profession* (London, 1874) pp.160–1.

6   J. Milne Bramwell: *op. cit.*, p.5. Apparently on one occasion an attempt was made in a court of law to discredit Elliotson's testimony because he used a stethoscope. See 'Remarks on Dr. Fraser's inconsistency. Note by Dr. Elliotson', *Zoist* (1852) *10*, p.73.

7   To put Elliotson's salary in context, it was only a very successful London consultant who could earn more than £1,500 a year. At the very top of the profession, Sir Benjamin Brodie earned between £8,000 and £10,000 a year as a consultant surgeon, while Sir Astley Cooper was reputed to receive between £15,000 and £21,000. For details of these and other aspects of Victorian medical practice, see M. Jeanne Peterson: *The Medical Profession in Mid-Victorian London* (London, 1978).

8   J.D. Du Potet de Sennevoy: *Le Magnétisme opposé à la médecine. Mémoire pour servir à l'histoire du magnétisme en France et en Angleterre* (Paris, 1840) p.186.

9   According to the earliest account of their meeting: in the *Lancet* (September, 1837) *2*, p.872.

10 'Eyewitness', Letter to *Lancet* (4 October, 1837). This was one letter in the first skirmish of a controversy which later was to become so bitter. Between September and November of 1837 there were other letters from 'Eyewitness' on 25 September and 30 October, and replies to them by W. Wood, Elliotson's clinical clerk, on 17 October and 6 November.

11 John Elliotson: *Human Physiology* (fifth edition, London, 1840) pp.684–5.

12 Du Potet de Sennevoy: *op. cit.*

13 There is some doubt over the spelling of the name: Elliotson always spelled it 'Okey', while Wakley, the editor of the *Lancet*, used the more likely spelling 'O'Key'.

14 'Abstract of Clinical Lecture by Dr. Elliotson', *Lancet* (9 September 1837) p.866.

15 John Elliotson: *op. cit.*, p.685.

16 *Professor Elliotson's Female Case Register No.16 (January – March 1839)* (London: University College Hospital Archives).

17 *Ibid*.

18 *Lancet* (14 July 1838) pp.546–9. Elizabeth apparently mesmerized the water herself, and even the observers did not know which was which! The *Lancet* provides a vivid account of the way she bullied Charlotte to try to make her confess, but Charlotte never did so, perhaps because the trance was genuinely involuntary. Elizabeth was quite unaware in her waking state that she had denounced Charlotte.

19 Dickens was to become and to remain a faithful friend of Elliotson throughout the difficult years ahead. They often dined together and Elliotson acted as Dickens' family doctor. Dickens also became an enthusiastic amateur mesmerist; see F. Kaplan: *Dickens and Mesmerism: the Hidden Springs of Fiction* (Princeton, 1975). Dickens' admiration for Elliotson is apparent in a letter of 1841: 'If I were to tell you what I know of his skill, patience, and humanity, you would love and honour him as much as I do. If my own life or my wife's, or that of either of my children were in peril tomorrow, I would trust it to him implicitly' (Charles Dickens to John Owers, 24 August 1841: In Walter Dexter (ed.): *The Letters of Charles Dickens* (London, 1938) Vol.2, p.369).

Although there is no mention of Thackeray in the case register, he too was a friend of Elliotson, who had treated him. Thackeray dedicated his novel *Pendennis* to Elliotson, and incorporated him as the character Dr Goodenough.

20 First report, *Lancet* (26 May 1838) pp. 282–8; second report, *Lancet* (9 June 1838) pp. 377–83, (16 June 1838) pp. 400-403; third report, *Lancet* (23 June 1838) pp. 441–46; fourth report, *Lancet* (7 July 1838) pp. 516–19; fifth report, *Lancet* (14 July 1838) pp. 546–9; sixth report, *Lancet* (21 July 1838) pp.585–90; seventh report, *Lancet* (28 July 1838) pp.615–20.

21 *Lancet* (7 July 1838) p.517.

22 *Ibid*. (14 July 1838) p.546.

23 *Ibid*. (21 July 1838) p.585.

24 *Ibid*. (18 August 1838) p.728.

25 For a life of Wakley, see Charles Brook: *Battling Surgeon* (Glasgow, 1945). A less favourable view is expressed by E.C. Sherrington: 'Thomas Wakley and Reform, 1832 to 1862' (Oxford D.Phil. thesis, 1973). For an account of the controversy with Elliotson, see J.H. Harley Williams: *Doctors Differ* (London, 1946).

26 *Lancet* (1 September 1838) p.806.

27 *Ibid.* (1 September 1838) p.811.

28 *Ibid.* (8 September 1838) p.835. The *Lancet* refused all articles on animal magnetism after 27 October 1838.

29 *Ibid.* (15 September 1838) p.873.

30 *Ibid.* (15 September 1838) p.876

31 J.F. Clarke: *op. cit.*, p.163.

32 John Elliotson: *Numerous Cases of Surgical Operations without pain in the Mesmeric State* (London, 1843) p.27.

33 John Elliotson: *Human Physiology*, p. 1183, footnote.

34 Charles Brook: *op.cit.*, p.145.

35 According to J.F. Clarke: *op.cit.*, p.176. My account is based on that given by Clarke.

36 John Elliotson to Medical Committee: In *Minutes of University College Hospital Committee (9 June 1838)* (London: University College Hospital Archives).

37 *Ibid.* (4 July 1838).

38 *Ibid.* (13 July 1838). The Committee, however, permitted the exhibition of a Sicilian youth with a prodigious memory on 13 August 1838, for which tickets were sold at ten shillings each.

39 *London Medical Gazette* (1838–9) *1*, p.54.

40 *Lancet* (1 December 1838) p.380.

41 *Ibid.* (15 December 1838) p.450.

42 The *Lancet* devoted seven pages to an anonymous and scurrilous attack by 'Eyewitness' (1 September 1838, pp. 805–11), and then saw fit to reprint it in the issue of 7 August 1841, pp. 694–9. The material later appeared as a pamphlet luridly entitled, *A full Discovery of the Strange Practices of Dr E. on the Bodies of his Female Patients! At his house ... with all the secret experiments he makes upon them, etc* (London, 1842).

43 John Elliotson: *Human Physiology*, pp.67–8. Among those impressed by Elizabeth's precognitive abilities was the mother of Anthony Trollope. Elizabeth was visiting the house where Anthony was ill and reported that she saw 'Jacky' up to his knees, which meant that the patient would recover (Eileen Bigland: *The Indomitable Mrs Trollope*, London, 1953, p.195).

44 John Elliotson: *Zoist* (1850) *8*, p.374.

45 Charles Dickens to George Cruikshank, 28 December 1838: In Madeline House & Graham Storey (eds.): *The Pilgrim Edition of the Letters of Charles Dickens* (Oxford, 1965, 1970) Vol.I, p.480.

46 Harley Williams: *op.cit.*, p.71. The meeting was reported in the *Lancet* (12 January 1839) pp.590–6.

47 *London Medical Gazette* (1840–1) *2*, p.234, Extract.

48 John Elliotson: *Human Physiology*, p.1181.

49 *Ibid.*, p.1179.

50 *Ibid.*, p.1182, footnote. Elliotson later produced yet another reason for discounting Wakley's experiments. Elizabeth was so sensitive to the mesmeric influence that having several persons standing close to her would inevitably send her into a trance, and that was the situation when the lead was tried. This explanation was also offered by Elizabeth herself when asked, in a trance, to explain why she had reacted. Unfortunately it leaves unanswered the lack of response to some of the mesmerized objects (John Elliotson, 'Cures of epileptic and other fits with mesmerism', *Zoist*, 1843, *1*, pp.422–3).

51 *Lancet* (13 June 1846) p.662.

52 John Elliotson: *The Harveian Oration, delivered before the Royal College of Physicians, London, 27 June 1846* (London, 1846) p.66.

53 *Ibid.*, p.68. The very next Harveian oration given by Dr Francis Hawkins was notable for its attack on mesmerists: 'Among quacks, the impostors, called mesmerists, are in my opinion the especial favourites of those, both male and female, in whom the sexual passions burn strongly, either in secret or notoriously. Decency forbids me to be more explicit' (*Zoist* (1849) *6*, p.404).

Chapter 10: The Mesmeric Campaign

1 A report by one visitor had earlier appeared under the title 'Visit to Dr. Elliotson's' in *Chambers Edinburgh Journal* (26 October 1838) pp.337–8.

2 J. Johnson, quoted in *Zoist* (1844) *2*, p.279.

3 *Ibid.*

4 L.E.G.E.: *Zoist* (1844) *2*, pp.351–69.

5 L.E.G.E.: *Zoist* (1843) *1*, pp.101–10; (1844) *2*, pp.295–311.

6 C.H. Townshend: *Zoist* (1855) *13*, pp.419–40. Townshend was a personal friend of Dickens and of Elliotson, and had visited the prison at Tothill Fields in their company. He was an active mesmerist and had published *Facts in Mesmerism* (London, 1840), a book which Dickens considered the best ever written on mesmerism (Fred Kaplan: *Dickens and Mesmerism*, Princeton, 1975, p.69).

7 T.S. Prideaux: *Zoist* (1845) *3*, pp.399–416.

8 Herbert Spencer: *Zoist* (1843) *1*, pp.369–85; (1844) *2*, pp.316–25.

9 Richard F. Burton: *Zoist* (1852) *10*, p.177.

10 Harriett Martineau: *Zoist* (1850) *8*, pp.301–2.

11 See, for example, Ferenc András Völgyesi: *Hypnosis of Man and Animals*, tr. M.W. Hamilton (London, 1966).

12 John Wilson: *Trials of Animal Magnetism on the Brute Creation* (London, 1839) pp.42–3.

13 John Elliotson: *Zoist* (1846) *4*, p.118.

14 Carl von Reichenbach (Baron): *Researches on Magnetism and on certain allied subjects, including a supposed new imponderable*, translated and abridged by W. Gregory (London, 1850) Abstract in *Zoist* (1846) *4*, p.349.

15 *Ibid.*, p.122.

16 John Elliotson: *Zoist* (1846) *4*, p.123.

17 John Elliotson: *Zoist* (1848) *6*, p.225.

18 V. Burq: *Nervous Affection: Metallo-therapia, or Metal-cure: new properties of metals illustrated through mesmerism* (Paris, 1851). Review by Elliotson in *Zoist* (1852) *10*, p.132.

19 *Ibid.*, p.270.

20 *Lancet* (21 July 1838) pp.585–90. Even as late as 1840, Elliotson was adamant that he had witnessed nothing paranormal: 'Often I have seen Baron Du Potet speak at the epigastrium and finger ends of the ecstatic and comatose patients: often heard him address them in a language with which they were unacquainted: often ask them when they would have another fit; but nothing, which, till I witness such things, I must consider supernatural, has yet occurred ... Yet I will continue a little longer with docility to enquire and learn, for of Baron Dupotet's perfect good faith I

entertain no doubt, however credulous he may be' (*Human Physiology*, fifth edition, London, 1840, pp.687–8).

21 John Elliotson: *Zoist* (1844) *2*, p.478. The reports are on pp.291–4 and 477–529. Elliotson was obviously impervious to the criticisms of Alexis made by John Forbes, whose exposé of the séances appeared in his *British and Foreign Medical Review* and elsewhere. See his *Illustrations of Modern Mesmerism from Personal Investigation* (London, 1845). On the other hand, sensible and reasonably detailed accounts, supportive of a paranormal explanation also appeared; for example, Edwin Lee's *Report upon the Phenomena of Clairvoyance or Lucid Somnambulism* (London, 1843). E.J. Dingwall has an excellently balanced account of Alexis in Vol.I of his *Abnormal Hypnotic Phenomena* (London, 1967).

22 *Zoist* (1854) *12*, p.32; (1852) *11*, pp.390–402.

23 Spencer T. Hall: *The Phreno-Magnet and Mirror of Nature* (1843) *1*, p.34.

24 John Elliotson: *Zoist* (1843) *1*, p.99. Elliotson's rebuke was mild compared with that of a later writer, Horatio Prater, who in his *Lectures on true and false Hypnotism, or Mesmerism* (London, 1851) calls Spencer Hall 'a wily impostor', who on lecture tours misled his largely working-class audiences with unscientific demonstrations and socially divisive comments. Spencer Hall's own report of his therapeutic and lecturing career seems modest and probable (*Mesmeric Experiences*, London, 1845). A useful short account of Hall's life appeared in the *Glasgow Examiner* (5 October 1844) by 'Quaker'.

25 John Elliotson: *Zoist* (1844) *2*, p.393 ff.

26 L.E.G.E.: *Zoist* (1850) *8*, p.230.

27 John Elliotson: *Numerous Cases of Surgical Operations without pain in the Mesmeric State, with remarks upon the opposition of many members of the Royal Medical and Chirurgical Society and others to the reception of the inestimable blessings of mesmerism* (London, 1843) p.65.

28 W. Topham and W. Squire Ward: *Account of a Case of Successful Amputation of the Thigh during the Mesmeric State, without the knowledge of the patient* (London, 1842).

29 Marshall Hall: 'Lectures in Webb Street', *Lancet* (28 October 1837) p.42.

30 John Elliotson: *op.cit.*, p.56.

31 *Ibid.*, p.33.

32 *Ibid.*, p.59.

33 James Esdaile: 'Surgical operations without pain in the mesmeric state', *Zoist* (1845) *3*, pp.380–9.

34 'More painless surgical operations in the mesmeric state. Communicated by Dr Elliotson', *Zoist* (1846) *4*, pp.193–218.

35 James Esdaile to John Elliotson, 11 October 1846: *Zoist* (1847) *5*, p.51. The account of the operation will be found in J. Milne Bramwell: *Hypnotism: its History, Practice and Theory* (third edition, London, 1913).

36 'Report of the Committee Appointed by Government to observe and report upon Surgical operations by Dr J. Esdaile, upon patients under the influence of alleged mesmeric agency. Printed by order of the Deputy Governor of Bengal. Calcutta, 1846', *Zoist* (1847) *5*, pp.51–7 (p.52).

37 James Braid thought the reason for the increased heart rate in the patients who did not move was the rigid cataleptic state into which they had been mesmerized, a result he regularly obtained with his own patients. The movements observed in the other patients were, he thought, merely reflex responses (*Medical Times* (1847) *15*, p.381).

38 'Report of the Committee', *Zoist* (1847) *5*, p.57.

39 'Dr Esdaile's First Monthly Report of the Calcutta Mesmeric Hospital, and his Experiments with Ether used with the same view as Mesmerism in Surgical Operations. Communicated by Dr Elliotson', *Zoist* (1847) *5*, pp.178–92 (p.191).

40 James Esdaile: 'A Review of my Reviewers' (Calcutta, 1848), in *Zoist* (1848) *6*, pp.158–173.

41 *Ibid.*, p.173.

42 Reported by Esdaile in his *Natural and Mesmeric Clairvoyance* (London, 1852) Preface, p.vii.

43 *Ibid.*, p.viii.

44 James Esdaile: 'Reports of the Mesmeric Hospital Calcutta', *Zoist* (1849) *7*, p.27.

45 James Esdaile to John Elliotson, 16 December 1853: *Zoist* (1854) *12*, pp.74–80.

46 John Elliotson: 'Dr Esdaile's return to England', *Zoist* (1851) *9*, pp.313–6.

47 James Esdaile to John Elliotson, 16 December 1853: *Zoist* (1854) *12*, pp.74–80.

48 'The Protest and Petition of James Esdaile, M.D., Surgeon H.E.I.C.S., to the Members of the American Congress', *Zoist* (1853) *11*, pp.294–7.

49 *Zoist* (1850) *8*, p.372.

50 John Elliotson: 'Dr Esdaile's testimony to the reality of clairvoyance', *Zoist* (1849) *7*, pp.213–23.

51 W.R. Merrington: *University College Hospital and its Medical School: a History* (London, 1976) p.34.

52 However, I have been informed by Mr Gibson, former county surgeon of Kildare, Ireland, that he has found it easy to produce very rapid trance in the case of seriously injured road-traffic victims.

53 Marina Warner: *Queen Victoria's Sketchbook* (London, 1979) p.121.

54 *Zoist* (1848) *6*, p.423.

55 Quoted without comment in *Zoist* (1850) *8*, p.273.

56 Details of the business of the Mesmeric Infirmaries were given in each issue of the *Zoist* from 1850 until 1856. I have also consulted J.D. Coleman: *Die Geschichte des Mesmerismus in Grossbrittanien und Irland* (Ph.D. thesis, Mainz, 1980).

57 According to J.F. Clarke: *Autobiographical Recollections of the Medical Profession* (London, 1874) p.172.

58 Richard Whately to Mrs Arnold, 17 April 1846: In E.J. Whately: *Life and Correspondence of R. Whately* (London, 1866) Vol.II, p.90.

59 John Elliotson: *Zoist* (1855–6) *13*, p.441.

60 Charles Dickens to E.S. Dallas, 12 December 1862: In Walter Dexter (ed.): *The Letters of Charles Dickens* (London, 1938) Vol.3, p.326.

61 Charles Dickens to John Elliotson, 20 February 1863: *Ibid.*, Vol.3, p.343.

Chapter 11: Braid and Hypnotism

1 Spencer T. Hall: *Mesmeric Experiences* (London, 1845) p.1.

2 Professor Williamson's account is published as Appendix A, pp.465–7, in J. Milne Bramwell: *Hypnotism: its History, Practice and Theory* (third edition, London, 1913). Lafontaine's demonstrations were of a similar nature in Paris, according to Horatio Prater: *Lectures on true and false Hypnotism, or Mesmerism* (London, 1851). Lafontaine's own hugely

popular *L'Art de magnétiser* (fifth edition, Paris, 1886) gives a fanciful account of his platform success and of his alleged cures of deaf-mutes.

3 James Braid: *Neurypnology*. In A.E. White (ed.): *Braid on Hypnotism* (London, 1899) p.102.

4 For example, *The Veil Uplifted and Mesmerism traced to its Source* by 'A Christian' (London, 1852), where hypnotism, mesmerism and 'electropsychology' are all castigated as supernaturally evil because of the enhanced powers supposedly attainable in the trance state. Other common allegations refer to the weakening of will-power in mesmerized subjects, and the growing tendency for some to ascribe Christ's cures to mesmeric powers. Both criticisms will be found in an anonymous tract: *Mesmerism Considered* (Glasgow, 1852) (B.M.: *Tracts of Animal Magnetism*, 7410.c.37, 1–14).

5 James Braid: *Satanic Agency and Mesmerism reviewed*. Summarized in J. Milne Bramwell: *op.cit.*, pp.22–3.

6 James Braid: *Neurypnology*, p.94.

7 *Ibid.*, p.184.

8 *Ibid.*, p.199.

9 *Ibid.*, p.210.

10 James Braid: 'Observations on the phenomena of phrenomesmerism', *Medical Times* (1843) *IX*, p.74.

11 James Braid: 'On the power of the mind over the body: an experimental inquiry into the nature and cause of the phenomena attributed by Baron Reichenbach and others to a "new imponderable"', *Medical Times* (1846) *XIV*, pp.214, 252, 273. Published as a separate: *The Power of the Mind over the Body* (London and Edinburgh, 1846).

12 A.E. White: *op.cit.*, pp.35–6.

13 Braid tells us that he received heavy correspondence from eminent persons in support of his views: *Medical Times* (1847) *XV*, p.381.

14 *Zoist* (1854) *12*, p.32.

15 A.E. White: *op.cit.*, p.31.

16 *Ibid.*, p.17.

17 James Braid: In J.M. Bramwell: *op.cit.*, p.25.

18 Braid did submit one letter, requesting information about trance states in

India, which was published (*Lancet* (1845) *2*, p.325). In its obituary of Braid, the *Lancet*, true to form, placed its emphasis on Braid's pre-hypnotic activities, on his skilful surgery of club-foot and squint (*Lancet* (1860) *1*, p.335).

19 James Braid: 'Facts and observations as to the relative value of mesmeric and hypnotic coma, and ethereal narcotism, for the mitigation or entire prevention of pain during surgical operations', *Edinburgh Medical and Surgical Journal* (1847) *67*, pp.5–88. This paper was preferred to one offered earlier by Esdaile (see Chapter 10, note 45).

20 J.C. Colquhoun: *An History of Magic, Witchcraft, and Animal Magnetism* (London, 1851) Vol.I, p.xxxiii. Colquhoun was not well regarded by the more reputable mesmerists. For example, Elliotson's response to *Isis Revelata* concluded with these words: 'Mr Colquhoun would have rendered real service to mesmerism, if, instead of compiling so much rubbish, and displaying such ignorance and credulity, with a dogmatism and coarseness which have prevented me from being at all delicate with him, he had collected unquestionable facts only and gone to work experimentally, like a philosopher, and communicated his results to the public' (*Human Physiology*, fifth edition, London, 1840, p.693).

21 A modern advocate of a similar view is D.B. Cheek, whose investigations suggest that patients retain a memory of what was said in the operating theatre when they were under surgical anaesthesia. See D.B. Cheek: 'Unconscious perception of meaningful sounds during surgical anesthesia as revealed under hypnosis', *American Journal of Clinical Hypnosis* (1959) *1*, pp.101–13. Also B.W. Levinson: 'States of awareness during general anesthesia', in J. Lassner (ed.): *Hypnosis and Psychosomatic Medicine* (New York, 1967) pp.200–7.

22 The date is that of the third edition, but neither of the earlier editions is known.

23 James Braid: *Magic, Witchcraft, Animal Magnetism, Hypnotism and Electro-Biology: being a Digest of the latest Views of the Author on these Subjects* (London, 1852, third edition) pp.53–4.

24 *Ibid.*, pp.111–18.

25 *Ibid.*, p.49.

26 John Hughes Bennett: *The Mesmeric Mania of 1851* (Edinburgh, 1851). Another more violent critic of Darling and of mesmerism in general was Andrew Buchanan, Professor of Physiology at Glasgow University, whose pamphlet makes the point that susceptible subjects are predominantly

young women and all of them have weaknesses of the nervous system, of the intellect, or of moral principle! See his *On Darlingism, misnamed Electro-Biology* (Glasgow, 1851).

27 James Braid: *The Physiology of Fascination and the Critics Criticized* (Manchester, 1885).

28 James Braid: *Hypnotic Therapeutics, illustrated by cases, with an appendix on table-turning and spirit-rapping* (Edinburgh, 1853) p.33.

29 These details are contained in J.M. Bramwell, *op.cit.*, where the best bibliography of Braid's publications is to be found.

30 Hippolyte Bernheim: *De la suggestion et ses applications à la thérapeutique* (Paris, 1886) pp.220–3. Bernheim does, however, credit Braid with the discovery of waking suggestion in his experiments on the Reichenbach phenomena. See J. Braid: *The Power of the Mind over the Body* (London and Edinburgh, 1846) pp.22–3.

31 D.G. Dalgado: *Braidisme ou Fariadisme* (Paris, 1907).

32 James Braid: *Observations on Trance: or, Human Hybernation* (London and Edinburgh, 1850) p.43.

Chapter 12: Charcot at the Salpêtrière

1 Georges Didi-Huberman: *Invention de l'hystérie: Charcot et l'iconographie photographique de la Salpêtrière* (Paris, 1982) p.17.

2 According to Sigmund Freud's obituary notice of Charcot in James Strachey (ed.): *The Standard Edition of the Complete Psychological Works of Sigmund Freud* (London, 1966) Vol.III, p.11. No complete biography of Charcot has yet been written. Georges Guillain's standard work: *J.-M. Charcot (1825-1893). Sa vie. Son oeuvre* (Paris, 1955); tr. P. Bailey, (London, 1959) stresses Charcot's neurological discoveries made at the height of his fame. It needs to be supplemented by A.R.G. Owen's *Hysteria, Hypnosis and Healing: the Work of J-M. Charcot* (London, 1971), which concentrates on his work with the neuroses. These books have been my main sources of reference. Their somewhat laudatory tone is difficult to reconcile with the more critical comments of Axel Munthe: *The Story of San Michele* (London, 1936); Léon Daudet: *Souvenirs et polémiques* (Paris, 1992); and the brothers Goncourt: *Journal. Mémoires de la vie littéraire* (Paris, 1956). Henri Ellenberger provides a succinct and vivid account of Charcot in *The Discovery of the Unconscious* (London, 1970), and Ruth Harris places Charcot clearly in historical context in her introduction to

Ruth Harris (ed.): *J-M. Charcot: Clinical Lectures on Diseases of the Nervous System* (London, 1991).

3 Georges Guillain: *op.cit.*, p.51.

4 Axel Munthe: *op.cit.*, p.206. Munthe had reason to dislike Charcot, who had expelled him from the Salpêtrière when he had attempted to smuggle out a young hysterical patient.

5 Léon Daudet: *op.cit.*, pp.134–5.

6 Sigmund Freud: *op.cit.*, p.13.

7 Jean-Martin Charcot: *Lectures on Diseases of the Nervous System*. Translated by George Sigerson (London, 1889) Vol.III, p.13.

8 Pierre Janet: *The Major Symptoms of Hysteria* (New York, 1907) pp.272–7.

9 In his book with Paul Richer: *Les démoniaques dans l'art* (Paris, 1887), Charcot provides many examples of works of art depicting hysterical attacks.

10 In Ruth Harris: *op.cit.*, pp.95–7. The poor experimental method of this and other of Charcot's demonstrations led to later more controlled investigations, discussed in Chapter 14.

11 Désiré-Magloire Bourneville & Paul Régnard: *Iconographie photographique de la Salpêtrière vols.I–III* (Paris, 1876-80). The Salpêtrière had been the scene of earlier attempts to portray the insane. In 1822–3, Théodore Géricault, a friend of Georget, had painted ten realistic portraits of inmates.

12 *Ibid.*, Vol.II, p.128.

13 This device was suggested to Charcot by a patient ('Geneviève').

14 Jean-Martin Charcot & Pierre Marie, 'Hysteria', in D. Hack Tuke (ed.): *Dictionary of Psychological Medicine* (London, 1892) Vol.I, p.629.

15 Jean-Martin Charcot: *op.cit.*, Vol.III, p.289.

16 E. Azam: *Hypnotisme et double conscience* (Paris, 1893). Azam was always eager to claim his priority. He is best known for his work on double personality with a famous somnambulist, Félida.

17 Paul Broca: 'Sur l'anesthésie chirurgicale provoquée par l'hypnotisme', *Bull.soc.chir.Paris* (1859) *10*, pp.247–70. Among Broca's audience was the aged Professor Cloquet, to whom credit for the first surgical operation under magnetism is due. In her biography of Broca, Frances Schiller points out that Broca tried hypnotism with two patients but failed with one. The surgeon, Follin, tried to hypnotize three more patients, none of

whom became completely anaesthetized. See Frances Schiller: *Paul Broca* (London, 1979).

18 A.J.P. Philips [J-P. Durand de Gros]: *Cours théorique et pratique de braidisme ou hypnotisme nerveux* (Paris, 1860).

19 C. Lasegue: 'Des catalepsies partielles et passagères', *Arch. gén. méd.* (1865) *2*, pp.385–402.

20 Richet's studies are summarized in his book: *L'homme et l'intelligence* (Paris, 1884).

21 These curious transfer effects are probably best regarded as the simplest form of symptom substitution. According to Janet, they could occur in naive patients with no suggestions from the operator (Pierre Janet: *op.cit.*, pp.298–303).

22 Copper bracelets to relieve 'rheumatism' are still with us today; they, too, presumably depend on an autosuggestive effect for their occasional success.

23 Reported in A.R.G. Owen: *op.cit.*, p.185.

24 Pierre Janet: *Psychological Healing*, tr. E. and C. Paul (London, 1925) Vol.I, p.170.

25 Jean-Martin Charcot: 'Sur les divers états nerveux déterminés par l'hypnotisation chez les hystériques', *C.R.hebd.Acad.Sci.* (1882) *44*, pp.403–5. Charcot was elected to the Academy by 46 votes to 12.

26 The amusing story was told by Charcot's colleague, Charles Richer, of a patient, who, in the act of stealing some photographs from a drawer, was rendered cataleptic by the sound of a gong in an adjoining laboratory, and was thus caught *in flagrante delicto*.

27 A short account of these experiments is to be found in Theta H. Wolf's biography: *Alfred Binet* (Chicago, 1973) pp.46–7.

28 Jean-Martin Charcot: *Lectures on Diseases of the Nervous System* (London, 1889) Vol.III, p.305.

29 *Ibid.*, p.308. The fact that it was impossible to hypnotize these two hysterics does not seem to have shaken Charcot's faith in his theory, although it obviously entailed a modification in the use of hypnotic susceptibility as a diagnostic aid. Subsequently, the patient *Pin* apparently recovered sensation in his affected arm but continued to suffer from hysterical attacks. *Porcz* also recovered from his paralysis but relapsed after an argument with another patient.

30 Sigmund Freud: *op.cit.*, p.22.

31 Her later history is well documented. She transferred to the Hôtel Dieu and became a patient of Jules Janet, brother of the more famous Pierre, who succeeded in revealing under hypnosis a second and healthier personality. As *Blanche II*, she returned to work at the Salpêtrière but succumbed to cancer induced by the radiological work on which she was engaged. See A. Boudouin: 'Homage à Charcot: quelques souvenirs de la Salpêtrière', *Paris-Medical* (1925) *15*, p.519. Also Henri Ellenberger: *op.cit.*, pp.98–9. Jules Janet's paper on Blanche is summarized by Frederick W.H. Myers in his *Human Personality and its Survival of Bodily Death* (London, 1903) Vol.I, pp.447–8.

32 Frederick W.H. Myers: *op.cit.*

33 This count is based on the bibliography compiled by Max Dessoir: *Bibliographie des Modernen Hypnotismus* (Berlin, 1888).

Chapter 13: The Triumph of Suggestion

1 A.A. Liébault: *Du sommeil et des états analogues, considérés surtout au point de vue de l'action du moral sur le physique* (Paris, 1866). A more widely circulated rumour of the book's failure claimed that only one copy was sold in ten years.

2 According to Henri F. Ellenberger: *The Discovery of the Unconscious* (London, 1970) p.86.

3 J. Delboeuf: *Le magnétisme animal à propos d'une visite à l'école de Nancy* (Paris, 1889). Quoted by Frank A. Pattie: 'A brief history of hypnotism', in Jesse E. Gordon: *Handbook of Clinical and Experimental Hypnosis* (New York, 1967) p.34.

4 J. Milne Bramwell: *Hypnotism: its History, Practice and Theory* (third edition, London, 1921) p.31.

5 However, both Bramwell and Moll claim that Liébault accepted magnetic doctrine, at any rate for a time in his later life, after finding his therapeutic passes effective with infants, a fact he did not think completely explicable in terms of suggestion. See Albert Moll: *Hypnotism* (second edition, London, 1890) pp.358–9.

6 J. Delboeuf, quoted by E.M. Thornton: *Hypnotism, Hysteria and Epilepsy* (London, 1976) p.176.

7 Hippolyte Bernheim: *De la myocardite aiguë ramollissement inflamm-atoire, etc.* (Strasbourg, 1867); *Des fièvres typhiques en général, etc.*

(Strasbourg, 1868); *Leçons de clinique médicale* (Paris, 1877).

8 Bernheim was an ardent Alsatian nationalist. Pierre Janet was also very dismissive of Braid, and his book *Psychological Healing* (London, 1925) contains several examples of prejudice against non-Frenchmen. Janet's opposition to psychoanalysis probably arose from pique at being over-shadowed by the genius of Freud.

9 Hippolyte Bernheim: *De la suggestion dans l'état hypnotique et dans l'état de veille* (Paris, 1884) pp.1–2.

10 *Ibid.*, p.36.

11 Hippolyte Bernheim: *De la suggestion et ses applications à la thérapeutique* (Paris, 1886) p.93.

12 *Ibid.*, p.94.

13 *Ibid.*, p.95.

14 Freud was much struck by Bernheim's demonstration that it was possible to overcome posthypnotic amnesia by persistence. He adopted a similar technique with hysterical patients in order to recover repressed memories, but the attempt was shortlived and was soon replaced by the method of free association. It should be noted that Bramwell's assertion to the effect that Bernheim was merely re-hypnotizing his subjects to a signal cannot hold water or Bernheim would presumably have had to re-awaken them after their spoken recall. There is no mention of this occurrence. See J. Milne Bramwell: *op.cit.*, p.106.

More recently, Frank Pattie has concluded on the basis of Bramwell's criticism that Freud was illogical in using the persuasive technique with patients who had not been in a previous trance. However, if it were not a question of re-entering a trance state but of circumventing a defensive amnesia there would seem to be nothing illogical about Freud's extension of the method. See Frank A. Pattie: 'A brief history of hypnotism', in Jesse E. Gordon (ed.): *Handbook of Clinical and Experimental Hypnosis* (New York, 1967).

15 Hippolyte Bernheim: *op.cit.* (1886) p.164.

16 *Ibid.*, p.218.

17 J.L.R. Delboeuf: *Le magnétisme animal à propos d'une visite à l'école de Nancy* (Paris, 1889) p.10.

18 Alfred Binet: *Revue philosophique* (November 1886) p.562.

19 Hippolyte Bernheim: *La Revue de l'hypnotisme* (1887–8) *2*, pp.322–5.

20 J.L.R. Delboeuf: *op.cit.*, p.8.

21 J.L.R. Delboeuf: 'Influence de l'éducation et de l'imitation dans le somnambulisme provoqué', *Revue philosophique* (1886) *22*, p.143.

22 Alfred Binet & Charles Féré: *Le magnétisme animal* (Paris, 1887) pp.142–3.

23 Jean-Martin Charcot: 'Du vigilambulisme hystérique', Lecture of 2 December 1890, in Georges Guinon: *Clinique des maladies du système nerveux. M. le professeur Charcot* (Paris, 1892) Vol.2, p.171.

24 P. Richer & G. Gilles de la Tourette: 'Hypnotisme', in A. Dechambre & C. Lereboullet (eds.): *Dictionnaire encyclopédique des sciences médicales* (Paris, 1889) p.72.

25 J. Luys: *Hypnotisme expérimental. Les émotions dans l'état d'hypnotisme et l'action à distance des substances médicamenteuses ou toxiques* (Paris, 1890).

26 P. Marrin (1889) cited in Dominique Barrucand: *Histoire de l'hypnose en France* (Paris, 1967) p.143. A large part of Ernest Hart's book: *Hypnotism, Mesmerism and the New Witchcraft* (London, 1893) was devoted to an attack on Luys.

27 A. Pitres: *Leçons cliniques sur l'hystérie et l'hypnotisme* (Paris, 1891) p.327.

28 H.-E. Beaunis: *Le somnambulisme provoqué. Etudes physiologiques et psychologiques* (Paris, 1886).

29 Hippolyte Bernheim: *op.cit.* (1884) p.34.

30 J. Liégois: *De la suggestions et du somnambulisme dans ses rapports avec la jurisprudence et la médecine légale* (Paris, 1889), p.129.

31 G. Gilles de la Tourette: *L'hypnotisme et les états analogues au point de vue médico-légal* (Paris, 1887) p.203.

32 For a modern review of this whole topic, see: J.R. Lawrence & C. Perry: *Hypnosis, Will, and Memory: A Psycho-legal History* (New York, 1988).

33 J. Milne Bramwell: 'What is hypnotism?', *Proceedings of the Society for Psychical Research* (1896–7) p.236.

34 Luis Montoro, Helio Carpintero & Francisco Tortosa: 'Los origenes de los congresos internacionales de psicología', *Revista de Historia de la Psicologia* (1983) *4*, pp.43–57.
    Subsequent International Congresses of hypnotism were held infre-

quently, with the Second in 1900 and the Third in 1965. Since then regular meetings have occurred every three years.

35 William James: 'The Congress of Physiological Psychology at Paris', *Mind* (1889) *14*, pp.614–16.

36 Freud had visited Bernheim, to whom he had introduced a patient he had been unable to hypnotize, and had then accompanied Bernheim and Liébault to the Congress. Bernheim told Freud on this occasion that he himself was not so successful with private patients (Sigmund Freud: *An Autobiographical Study*, in James Strachey (ed.): *The Standard Edition of the Complete Psychological Works of Sigmund Freud*, London, 1961, Vol.XX, p.18).

37 Hippolyte Bernheim: *Hypnotisme, suggestion, psychothérapie* (Paris, 1891) p.24.

38 J.P. Durand de Gros [A.J.P. Philips]: *Cours théorique et pratique de braidisme* (Paris, 1860) p.158.

39 Hippolyte Bernheim: *op.cit.*, (1891) p.31. Bernheim did not originate the concept of ideodynamism, which seems to have first been put forward by James Mill and extended and popularized by W.B. Carpenter. See Kurt Danziger: 'Mid-Nineteenth-Century British Psycho-Physiology: A Neglected Chapter in the History of Psychology', in William R. Woodward & Mitchell G. Ash (eds.): *The Problematic Science: Psychology in Nineteenth-Century Thought* (New York, 1982) pp.119–46.

40 *Ibid.*, p.500.

41 Alfred Binet: *Les altérations de la personnalité* (Paris, 1892) p.68.

42 According to Theta Wolf: *Alfred Binet* (Chicago and London, 1973) p.64.

43 J. Milne Bramwell: *op.cit.*, p.433.

44 According to Charcot's secretary, Georges Guinon, in Georges Guillain: *J.-M. Charcot 1825-1893. His Life – His Work* (London, 1959) p.176.

45 G. Gilles de la Tourette: *Traité clinique et thérapeutique de l'hystérie d'après l'enseignement de la Salpêtrière* (3 vols., Paris, 1895).

46 J. Babinski: 'Définition de l'hystérie', in J. Babinski: *Oeuvres scientifiques* (Paris, 1934) pp.457–64.

47 Pierre Janet: *Psychological Healing* (London, 1925) Vol.I, pp.187–92. Janet refers to Teste, Despine and Du Potet.

48 John Elliotson: 'Cures of epileptic and other fits with mesmerism', *Zoist*

(1843) *I*, p.449.

49 Nicholas P. Spanos & Jack Gottlieb: 'Demonic possession, mesmerism
    and hysteria: a social psychological perspective on their historical interre-
    lations', *Journal of Abnormal Psychology* (1979) *88*, pp.527–46.

50 Jacqueline Carroy-Thirard has a most interesting discussion of the contem-
    porary attitude towards the female hysterical patient ('Figures de femmes
    hystériques dans la psychiatrie française au 19ième siècle', *Psychanalyse
    à l'Université*, 1979, *4*, pp.313–24). Also, for an extended treatment of
    the role of the experimental subject, see her *Hypnose, suggestion et
    psychologie: l'invention de sujets* (Paris, 1991).

51 André M. Weitzenhoffer: 'What did he (Bernheim) say? A postscript and an
    addendum', *International Journal of Experimental and Clinical Hypnosis*
    (1980) *33*, pp.24–31.

52 J. Milne Bramwell: *op.cit.*, p.31.

53 Barbara Tuchmann provides a vivid account of the period in *The Proud
    Tower* (London, 1966).

54 According to Barrucand (*op.cit.*, p.181), Bérillon's antipathy towards
    Bernheim was so great that he continued his attacks long after Bernheim's
    death, until as recently as 1944.

Chapter 14: The Twentieth Century

1 Pierre Janet: *Psychological Healing* (London, 1925) Vol.I, p.200.

2 Sigmund Freud: *An Autobiographical Study*, in James Strachey (ed.): *The
   Standard Edition of the Complete Psychological Works of Sigmund Freud*
   (London, 1961) Vol.XX, p.27.

3 Léon Chertok: 'The discovery of the transference', *International Journal
   of Psychoanalysis* (1968) *49*, pp.560–76.

4 Sigmund Freud: 'The dynamics of transference', in *Standard Edition*,
   Vol.XII, p.106. Cogent criticisms of the explanation of hypnosis in terms
   of suggestion have been offered from quite different standpoints than the
   psychoanalytic one. An early attempt was that of Milne Bramwell in his
   Hypnotism: its History, Practice and Theory (third edition, London, 1921)
   pp.308–39. More recently, H.J. Eysenck has made a notable effort to clarify
   the nature of suggestibility (see H.B. Gibson: *Hans Eysenck*, London, 1981,
   pp.48–60). For a further discussion of suggestibility and hypnosis, see
   Kenneth S. Bowers: *Hypnosis for the Seriously Curious* (Monterey, Calif.,

1976) Chapter 6.

5 Sigmund Freud: *Group Psychology and the Analysis of the Ego*, in *Standard Edition*, Vol.XVIII, p.127.

6 An excellent account of Janet's life and work will be found in Henri Ellenberger: *The Discovery of the Unconscious* (London, 1970).

7 Pierre Janet: *L'automatisme psychologique: essai de psychologie expérimentale sur les formes inférieures de l'activité humaine* (Paris, 1889).

8 M. Prince: *The Dissociation of a Personality* (New York & London, 1906).

9 Freud's only explanation of multiple personality is merely descriptive and is couched in terms of identification with several other persons, these identifications seizing hold of consciousness in turn. (Sigmund Freud: *The Ego and the Id*, in *Standard Edition*, Vol.XIX, pp.30–1.)

10 M. Boor: 'The multiple personality epidemic: additional cases and inferences regarding diagnosis, etiology, dynamics and treatment', *Journal of Nervous and Mental Disease* (1982) *170*, pp.302–4.

11 A critical modern account of these cases will be found in Ray Aldridge-Morris: *Multiple Personality: an Exercise in Deception* (Hove & London, 1989).

12 See, for example, Aubrey J. Yates: *Behavior Therapy* (New York, 1970).

13 E.L. Rossi (ed.): *The Collected Papers of Milton H. Erickson on Hypnosis* (New York, 1980), 4 vols.

14 A useful discussion of Erickson's techniques will be found in: André M. Weitzenhoffer: *The Practice of Hypnotism* (New York, 1989), 2 vols.

15 For example, the extraordinary findings reported in: L.F. Cooper & M.H. Erickson: *Time Distortion in Hypnosis* (Baltimore, 1954).

16 C.L. Hull: *Hypnosis and Suggestibility* (New York, 1933).

17 E.R. Hilgard: [Introduction to] C.L. Hull: *Hypnosis and Suggestibility* (New York, 1961).

18 J-M. Charcot: *Clinical Lectures on Diseases of the Nervous System*. Ed. Ruth Harris (London, 1991), pp.15–19.

19 Alfred Binet & Charles Féré: *Animal Magnetism* (London, 1887) p.134.

20 C.L. Hull: *op.cit.*, p.229.

21 *Ibid.*, p.391.

22 Hilgard was best-known for his overview with D.G. Marquis: *Conditioning and Learning* (New York, 1941) and for his standard reference book: *Theories of Learning* (New York, 1948).

23 J.W. Friedlander & T.R. Sarbin: 'The depth of hypnosis', *Journal of Abnormal and Social Psychology* (1938) *33*, pp.453–75.

24 A.M. Weitzenhoffer & E.R. Hilgard: *Stanford Hypnotic Susceptibility Scale, Forms A and B; Form C* (Palo Alto, 1959; 1962). Some years later Weitzenhoffer was critical of his own earlier work with Hilgard on the grounds that the scale did not measure the increase in suggestibility required by Hull's definition of hypnosis, but as Hilgard pointed out it would obviously be no easy matter to construct a scale embodying this requirement. See E.R. Hilgard: 'A neodissociation interpretation of hypnosis', in Stephen Jay Lynn & Judith W. Rhue (eds.): *Theories of Hypnosis* (New York, 1991), p.87.

25 E.R. Hilgard: *Hypnotic Susceptibility* (New York, 1965).

26 J.R. Hilgard: *Personality and Hypnosis: A Study of Imaginative Involvement* (Chicago, 1979).

27 E.R. Hilgard: *Divided Consciousness* (New York, 1977).

28 J.F. Kihlstrom: 'Conscious, subconscious, unconscious: a cognitive approach', in K.S. Bowers & D. Meichenbaum (eds.): *The Unconscious Reconsidered* (New York, 1984). Frederick J. Evans: 'Hypnotizability: individual differences in dissociation and the flexible control of psychological processes', in Stephen Jay Lynn & Judith W. Rhue (eds): *op.cit.*

29 R.W. White: 'A preface to a theory of hypnotism', *Journal of Abnormal and Social Psychology* (1941) *36*, pp.477–505. T.R. Sarbin: 'Contributions to role-taking theory: I Hypnotic behavior', *Psychological Review* (1950) *57*, pp.255–70.

30 T.X. Barber & D.S. Calverley: '"Hypnotic behavior" as a function of task motivation', *Journal of Psychology* (1962) *54*, pp.363–89.

31 K.S. Bowers: 'The effects of demands for honesty upon reports of visual and auditory hallucinations', *International Journal of Clinical and Experimental Hypnosis* (1967) *15*, pp.31–6. The similarity of the situation of the task-motivated subjects to those in Milgram's well-publicised studies of forced compliance are striking. See Stanley Milgram: *Obedience to Authority* (London, 1974).

32 M.T. Orne: 'The simulation of hypnosis: why, how, and what it means', *International Journal of Clinical and Experimental Hypnosis* (1971) *19*,

pp.183–210.

33 P.W. Sheehan & K. McConkey: *Hypnosis and Experience: The Exploration of Phenomena and Process* (Hillsdale, NJ., 1982).

34 A summary of his theoretical position will be found in N.P. Spanos: 'A social psychological approach to hypnotic behavior', in G. Weary & H.L. Mirels (eds.): *Integrations of Clinical and Social Psychology* (Oxford, 1982) pp.231–71.

35 Nicholas P. Spanos: 'History and historiography of hypnosis', in Steven Jay Lynn & Judith W. Rhue (eds.): *op.cit.*

36 N.P. Spanos: 'Experimental research on hypnotic analgesia', in N.P. Spanos & J.F. Chaves (eds.): *Hypnosis: The Cognitive-Behavioral Perspective* (Buffalo, N.Y., 1989).

37 Kenneth S. Bowers & Thomas M. Davidson: 'A neodissociative critique of Spanos's social-psychological model of hypnosis', in Steven J. Lynn & Judith W. Rhue (eds.): *op.cit.*

38 *Ibid.*

39 D.R. Gorassini & N.P. Spanos: 'A social-cognitive skills approach to the successful modification of hypnotic susceptibility', *Journal of Personality and Social Psychology* (1986) *50*, pp.1004–12.

40 The importance of gaining rapport should not be overlooked. See J.D. Gfeller, S.J. Lyon, & W.E. Pribble: 'Enhancing hypnotic susceptibility: Interpersonal and rapport factors', *Journal of Personality and Social Psychology* (1987) *52*, pp.586–95.

41 N.P. Spanos: 'Hypnotic behavior: Special process accounts are still not required', *Behavioral and Brain Sciences* (1986) *9*, pp.776–81.

42 The point is similar to the objections made to Hull's research by Erickson. It was elaborated upon by Ronald E. Shor: 'The fundamental problem in hypnosis research as viewed from historic perspective', in Erika Fromm & Ronald E. Shor (eds.): *Hypnosis: Research Developments and Perspectives* (New York, 1973).

43 G.F. Wagstaff: *Hypnosis, Compliance and Belief* (Brighton, 1981).

44 A good perspective on current theories will be found in Stephen Jay Lynn & Judith W. Rhue (eds.): *op.cit.* A full assessment constitutes the epilogue of Alan Gauld's *A History of Hypnotism* (Cambridge University Press, 1992), a book to be generally recommended for its extensive coverage of the European literature.

45 For an account of modern therapeutic practice, see H.B. Gibson & M. Heap: *Hypnosis in Therapy* (Hove and London, 1991). A general survey will be found in David T. Rowley's *Hypnosis and Hypnotherapy* (London and Sydney, 1986).

46 D.V. Sheehan & O.S. Surman: 'Follow-up study of hypnotherapy for smoking', in David T. Rowley, *op.cit.*

47 A.A. Mason: 'A case of congenital ichthyosiform erythrodermia of Brocq treated by hypnosis', *British Medical Journal* (23 August 1952) pp.422–3. Eight subsequent cases were failures, but it should be borne in mind that Mason was not an experienced hypnotist and these patients may not have been capable of the deep trance which could have been crucial.

48 T.H. McGloshan, F.J. Orne, & M.T. Orne: 'The nature of hypnotic analgesia and placebo response to experimental pain', *Psychosomatic Medicine* (1969) *31*, pp. 227–46. For an extensive discussion of the use of hypnosis as an analgesic, see E.R. Hilgard & J.R. Hilgard: *Hypnosis in the Relief of Pain* (Los Altos, Calif., 1983).

49 W.S. Kroger: *Clinical and Experimental Hypnosis in Medicine, Dentistry, and Psychology* (Philadelphia, 1977).

50 David Oakley, Phyllis Alden, & Marcia Degun Mather: 'The use of hypnosis in therapy with adults', *The Psychologist* (1996) *9*, pp.502–5.

51 Peter Gay: *Freud: A Life for our Time* (London, 1988) pp.90–6.

52 Chris R. Brewin: 'Scientific status of recovered memories', *British Journal of Psychiatry* (1996) *169*, pp.131–4. Richard A. Gardner: 'Belated realization of child sex abuse by an adult', *Issues in Child Abuse Accusations* (1992) *4*, pp.177–95.

53 John F. Kihlstrom: 'The recovery of memory in laboratory and clinic', *Paper presented to the 1993 joint convention of the Rocky Mountain Psychological Association and the Western Psychological Association.*

54 Jean-Roch Lawrence & Campbell Perry: *Hypnosis, Will, and Memory* (New York, 1988).

55 L.G. Echterling & D.A. Emmerling: 'Impact of stage hypnosis', *American Journal of Clinical Hypnosis* (1987) *29*, pp.149–54.

56 Michael Heap: 'The nature of hypnosis', *The Psychologist* (1996) *9*, pp.498–501.

57 W.P. Morgan: 'Hypnosis and sports medicine' in G.D. Burrows &

L. Dennerstein (eds.): *Handbook of Hypnosis and Psychosomatic Medicine* (Amsterdam, 1980).

58 Alan Richardson: 'Mental practice: a review and discussion', *Research Quarterly* (1967) *38*, pp. 95–107, 263–73.

59 D.E. Gibbons: *Applied Hypnosis and Hyperempiria* (New York, 1979).

60 C. Baudoin: *Suggestion and Auto-Suggestion*, tr. E. & C. Paul (London, 1920).

61 The best introduction to autogenic training is Wolfgang Linden: *Autogenic Training* (London, 1990). H. Benson & M.Z. Klipper in *The Relaxation Response* (London, 1976) were responsible for the view that the benefits sprang from the muscular relaxation required by many of these therapeutic systems.

62 See David O'Connell: *Jetlag: How To Beat It* (London, 1997).

Index

Figures in **bold** type indicate that the subject is treated inclusively

Abernethy, John, 153
Academy of Sciences (Berlin), 9, 98
Academy of Sciences (Munich), 11–12
acupuncture, 175–6
ailments *see* treatment
amnesia *see* memory
amputation, 180, 181, 182
anaesthesia
  chemical, 184–5, 186, 188
  mesmeric/hypnotic, 101, 107, 179,
    180, 181–2, 186–7, 188, 205, 226,
    233, 234
analgesia
  mesmeric/hypnotic, 95, 101–2, 114,
    115, 138, 180–3, 185, 186, 187,
    188, 189, 193, 221, 234, 248, 262,
    265–6, 269
Andry, Charles, 19, 39
Angelesey, Marquis of, 144
animal heat, 51, 96
animal magnetism, 56, 101, 110, 212,
    223, 224, 228
  Bergasse on, 35, 42, 53, 57–8, 60
  Bertrand on, 98, 102–3, 106
  Braid on, 196–7, 198, 203–4, 208
  Burton on, 171
  Chenevix on, 130–2
  Colquhoun on, 205, 208
  criticisms of, 41, 50–4, 114, 116,
    119–20, 152, 157–8, 160, 162–3,
    180
  defences of, 54–5, 116, 122, 161, 167
  Deleuze on, 87–93
  Deslon on, 22, 27–9, 38, 53
  Du Potet on, 98, 122–4

Elliotson on, 132, 139–51, 160–1,
    167, 172, 174, 176–7, 191–2
Esdaile on, 187–8
Faria on, 96–8
Gébelin on, 40
Mainauduc on, 126
Mesmer on, 6, 1–11, 12, 16, 23–7,
    33–4, 37–8, 62–4, 66–9, 237
Puységur on, 70–1, 78–9, 81–2
Reichenbach on, 172–4
Royal Academy of Medicine
    Commission on (1831), 110–14
Royal Academy of Sciences
    Commission on (1784), 39, 44–53,
    64, 66
Shelley on, 129–30
spread of, 82, 125–35
stages in, 146–7, 250–1
Wakley on, 154–8, 162–3
with animals, 171–2
Annales du magnétisme animal, 82
arc-en-cercle, 218, 251
d'Artois, Comte, 22
attitudes passionelles, 218
Augustine (Charcot's patient) *see*
    Glaiz, Louise
autogenic training, 276
autohypnosis, 135, 176, 205, 276–7
l'automatisme psychologique (Janet),
    258
Azam, E., 221

Babinsky, J., 245, 246, 250
Bailly, J.S., 39, 61
Balzac, Honoré de, 120

baquets, 21, 25, 27, 38, 55, 58, 64, 66, 68, 96, 103
  cures at, 20–1, 54
  death at, 41, 56
  in Haiti, 70
  origin of, 20
  phenomena at, 67–8
  Royal Academy of Sciences Commission on (1784), 44–5, 46
  trees as, 21, 75, 89, 103
Baquet de Santé (Barre and Radet), 56
Bar, Alphonsine (Charcot's patient), 223, 227
Barber, T.X., 267, 268
Barth, Joseph, 13, 14
Beauchamp, Sally (Prince's patient), 258–9
Beaunis, Henri-Etienne, 243, 252
Bentley, Charlotte, 142
Bergasse, Nicholas, 35, 36, 42, 43, 53, 54, 57–61, 65
  Considérations sur le magnetisme animal, 57
Bérillon, Edgar, 253
Berna, J., 115–16
Bernard, Prudence, 207
Bernheim, Hippolyte, **229–53**, 255, 256, 265
  disagreements with Charcot, 228, 235–7, 240
  induction technique, 233
  on Braid, 211, 232, 233, 234
  on Faria, 211, 232
  on Liébault, 232, 238, 248, 252
  on Luys, 242
  on Pitres, 243
  on suggestion, 233–40, 246, 247–8, 252, 253
  personality, 232, 252
  treatment, 239, 252
  De la suggestion dans l'état hypnotique et dans l'état de veille, 232
  De la suggestion et ses applications à la thérapeutique, 236
  Hypnotisme, suggestion, phychothérapie, 247
Berny, Madame de, 20
Berthollet, Claude, 41, 42

Bertrand, Alexandre, **98–109**, 120, 231
  experiments, 99–100, 105
  on imagination, 103, 106, 107
  on intellect, 108
  on magnetic fluid, 103,106
  on the paranormal, 106, 107, 108
  on somnambulism, 103–4, 106–8
  on telepathy, 105–6
  on treatment, 106
  Du magnétsime animal en France, 106
  Traité du somnambulisme, 103
Bibliothéque de médecine, 102
Bibliothèque du magnétisme animal, 82
Bicêtre, 110, 213
Billot, J.P., 92
Binet, Alfred, 231, 239, 242, 246
  defence of Salpêtrière, 241, 242
  experiments, 239–41, 262
  on suggestion, 249
  use of magnets, 225–6, 237, 243
  Le magnétisme animal (with Féré), 241
  Les altérations de la personnalité, 249
Blackwell, Elizabeth, 124
Blackwood's Magazine, 179
Blumenbach, J.F., 137
Borie, G. de, 39
Bonnefoy, J.B., 54
Bosch, Anna von (wife of Mesmer), 2, 16
Bourdois de la Motte, M.M.J., 113
Bourneville, Désiré-Magloire, 219–20, 222, 227
Braid, James, 186–7, **193–208**, 233, 234, 261, 269
  appearance, 211–12
  Charcot, influence on, 221, 222, 223
  Elliotson, relationship with, 177, 204
  induction technique, 177, 194–5, 197–8, 203, 208, 211
  Liébault, influence on, 229, 231
  on electrobiology, 208–9
  on hypnotism, 196–8, 206–8, 210
  on mesmerism, 195, 196, 198, 203, 204, 208, 211–12
  on the paranormal, 207–8
  on phrenohypnotism, 199–202
  on Reichenbach, 202–3

Braid, James – *cont.*
  on role of operator, 177
  on suggestion, 197–8, 202, 207, 209, 211, 212, 234
  personality, 194, 211–12
  Hypnotic Therapeutics, 209, 211
  Magic, Witchcraft, Animal Magnetism, Hypnotism and Electro-biology, 206
  Neurypnology, 196
  Observations on Trance: or, Human Hybernation, 205
  On the Distinctive Conditions of Natural and Nervous Sleep, 210
  Physiology of Fascination, 210
  The Power of the Mind over the Body, 202
Bramwell, Milne, 231, 232, 245, 249, 253, 256
Briquet, Pierre, 217
Brissot, Jacques-Pierre, 42, 60, 61
British and Foreign Medical Review, 179
British Association, 195
Brodie, Sir Benjamin, 132, 160
Broca, Paul, 221
Brouillet, A., 219, 228
Brownson, Orestes, 133
Burdin, C., 117, 119
  Histoire académique du magnétisme animal (with Dubois), 120
Burq, Victor, 175, 176, 222–3
Burton, Sir Richard, 171

Cagliostro, Count Alessandro, 60
Caille, C.A., 39
Calcutta Medical Journal, 186
Calcutta Mesmeric Hospital, 185, 189
Canterbury, Archbishop of, 126–7
Canton, John, 5
Carleton Skills Training programme, 270
catalepsy, 144, 196, 202, 203, 207, 223, 224, 233, 248, 262; *see also* paralysis; hysteria, symptoms of
Charcot, J.-M., 213–28, 232, 243, 245, 246, 249–53, 257, 261, 262, 269
  appearance, 215

as neurologist, 216–17
criticisms of, 215, 235–7, 240
diagnostic method, 213–15
induction technique, 223, 224–5
on Bernheim, 242
on hypnotism, 223–8
on hysteria, 217–21
on therapy, 215, 226–7
personality, 215, 250, 251, 252
Chastellux, F.-J., marquis de, 60
Chaulnes, duchesse de, 30, 31, 33
Chenevix, Richard, 130–2, 139, 180
childbirth, 27, 181,188
chloroform, 186
clairvoyance, 63, 80, 81,94, 95, 115–16, 134, 177, 188, 196, 205, 208
Clarke, J.F., 154, 158
Cloquet, Jules, 102, 180, 181, 223
Cloquet, M., 75–6
clownism, 217
Cobbett, William, 153
Colquhoun, J.C., 205, 207, 208
  An History of Magic, Witchcraft and Animal Magnetism, 205
  Isis Revelata, 205
Comédie Italienne, 55
Congresses, International
  of Experimental Psychology (1892), 249, 252
  of Experimental and Therapeutic Hypnotism (1889), 246–7
  of Physiological Psychology (1889), 245–6
Considérations sur le magnétisme animal (Bergasse), 57
Cooper, Sir Astley, 160
Cooper, Samuel, 160
Corberon, Baron de, 43
Copland (physician), 181
Così fan tutte (Mozart), 56
Coué, Emil, 276
The Count of Monte Cristo (Dumas), 98
credivity (*credivité*), 247, 253
crime, 170, 243–5, 246
crisis, mesmeric, 41, 55, 110
  de Jussieu on, 77
  Deslon on, 22, 28

Mesmer on, 10, 26–7, 69
Puységur on, 70–1, 72, 75–6, 77, 83
Royal Academy of Sciences
   Commission on (1784), 45, 49–53,
   107, 243
Thornton on, 67
Cruikshank, George, 143
Cue (mesmerist), 126

Dalgado, D.G., 211
Darcet, J., 39
Darling, H.G., 209
Darlington, C.D., 66
Dauder, Léon, 215
Davis, Andrew Jackson, 134
   The Principles of Nature, 134
Deimann (physician), 9
de Jussieu, A.L., 39, 51, 77
*De la suggestion dans l'état hypnotique
   et dans l'état de veille* (Bernheim),
   232
*De la suggestion et ses applications à la
   thérapeutique* (Bernheim), 236
Delboeuf, J., 232, 240–1, 245
Deleuze, J.P.F., 82, **84–93**, 96, 97, 105,
   108, 120, 122, 133
   induction technique, 87–8
   theory, 88–90
   treatment, 88
   *Histoire crtique du magnétisme
     animal*, 85, 93
delirium, 4, 71, 81, 140, 141, 147, 164,
   218
dentistry, 273
Deslon, Charles, 22, 33, 38, 39, 40, 42,
   55, 66, 67, 125, 126, 243
   Faculty of Medicine, controversy
     with, 28–9, 56
   illness of, 22, 56
   on imagination, 50
   Mesmer, relations with, 34–5, 36
   Royal Commission, relations with,
     28, 44, 46, 47–8, 49–50, 52, 53–4
   *Observations sur le magnétisme
     animal*, 27
Despine, Prosper, 251
Dickens, Charles, 143, 153, 165, 191–2
Didier, Alexis, 176, 177, 179

Dingwall, E.J., 90–1
dissociation, 257, 260, 264, 266, 267,
   269
Docteurs modernes, Les (Barre and
   Radet), 55–6
Dods, J.B., 133–4
Dreyfus affair, 253
Dubois, R., 115, 116, 117, 120
   *Histoire académique du magnétisme
     animal* (with Burdin), 120
Ducie, Earl of, 189
Du magnétisme animal en France
   (Bertrand), 106
Du somneil et des états analogues
   (Liébault), 229
Dumas, Alexandre, 98, 120, 247
   The Count of Monte Cristo, 98
Dumontpallier, V.V.A., 246
Duport, Adrien, 60, 61
Du Potet de Sennevoy, J.D., Baron,
   110, 117, 125, 131, 138–40, 154,
   251, 271
   appearance, 98–9
   demonstrations, 122–4, 133, 138
   experiments, 99–101
   personality, 123
   treatment, 101, 139, 140
   Journal du magnétisme, 122
   Magie dévoilée, 123
Durand de Gros, J.-P. [pseud. Philips,
   A.J.P.], 221–2, 232, 247

*Edinburgh Medical and Surgical
   Journal*, 205
Eeden, F. van, 246, 249
electrobiology, 134, 208–9, 221
electrotherapy, 1, 2, 13, 19, 227
Elliotson, John, 132, **136–92**, 197, 203,
   223, 227, 249, 250
   appearance, 136, 138
   controversy with hospital, 149,
     159–61, 164–5
   controversy with Wakley, 154–9,
     162–3, 165–7, 193
   finances, 138, 191
   illness of, 191
   induction technique, 140–1, 144,
     145, 146–7, 150

Elliotson, John – *cont.*
  on Braid, 177, 204
  on Burq, 175
  on the paranormal, 176–7
  on Reichenbach, 174, 203
  personality, 136–7, 163, 178, 192
  treatment, 137, 141–2, 146, 160, 164,
    179
  use of metals, 151, 154–6, 166, 175–6
  use of water, 150, 156–7
  Human Physiology, 137, 165
  Numerous Cases of Surgical
    Operations without Pain in the
    Mesmeric State, 181
epilepsy, 9, 19, 54, 67–8, 110, 112, 132,
    138, 142, 146, 175, 190, 198,
    216–18, 226
epileptoid stage, 217
épopte, 94, 95, 96
d'Eprémesnil, J.-J. Duval, 56, 60, 61
Erickson, Milton, 260–1
Esdaile, James, **181–8**, 189, 190
  belief in magnetic fluid, 188
  induction technique, 181, 183, 187
  on chemical anaesthesia, 184–5, 186,
    187, 188
Esquirol, J.E.D., 110
ether, 184, 186
exorcism, 11, 12, 269

Faculty of Medicine (Paris), 19, 22,
    28–9, 30, 39, 56
Faculty of Medicine (Vienna), 11, 16,
    17, 19
Faraday, Michael, 131–2
Faria, J.C. de, abbé, **93–8**, 105, 130
  appearance, 94
  background, 93
  influence on others, 103, 130
  induction technique, 93, 94–5
  theory, 94, 96–7
fascination, 209, 210
fatigue, 47, 48, 113, 114, 119, 131, 175,
    222, 241, 258, 262
Féré, Charles, 225, 231, 237, 240–1,
    242, 243, 249, 262
  Le magnétisme animal (with Binet),
    241

Fleury (painter), 213
fluid, magnetic, 19, 102, 106, 176, 192,
    193, 208
  criticisms of, 45–6, 96, 103, 133, 177,
    198
  propagation of, 21, 42, 82
  storage of, 20
  theory of, 24–6, 40, 57–8, 67, 84,
    87, 88–90, 134, 139, 172, 176,
    199
fluid, universal, 2, 5, 6, 17, 23, 25, 28,
    42, 44, 67, 78, 79
Foissac, P., 110, 111, 113, 114
Forbes, John, 179
Forel, Auguste, 254
formes frustes, 215, 218, 227
Fox family, 134
Franklin, Benjamin, 3, 39, 46, 47, 49
Franklin Commission *see* Royal
    Academy of Sciences (Paris)
Frappart, N.N., 121–2
French Revolution, 61, 79, 82
Freud, Sigmund, 216, 227, 246, 255–6,
    257, 260
Friedlander, J.W., 265
fugue, 257, 258

Galen, 134
Gall, Franz, 225
Gassner, Johann, 11–12
Gauthier, Aubin, 85, 120
Gébelin, Court de, 40–1, 58
  Monde primitif, 40
Geoffroy (physician), 101
Georget, E.J., 108, 110
Gerdy, P.N., 119–20
Gilles de la Tourette, G., 241, 245, 246,
    247, 250
Glaiz, Louise (Charcot's patient), 220,
    223, 225, 227
glass harmonica, 3, 10, 21
Gleason, Cynthia, 133
globus hystericus, 217
Glück, C.W., 3
Gregory, William 209
Grimes, J.S., 133–4, 208
Grimm, Melchior, Baron von, 34–5,
    40, 55

Guillain, Georges, 221
Guillotin, J.I., 39, 61

Haiti, 70, 133
Hall, Marshall, 102, 144
Hall, Spencer T., 177–8, 193, 200
hallucinations, 18, 68, 230, 233, 234, 259, 263, 265, 266
 retroactive, 237–8
 see also hysteria, symptoms of
Hancock, Harriet, 142
Hartshorn, Thomas, 133
Harveian Oration (1846), 166–7
Haussay, Chevalier du, 20
Haydn, F.J., 3
Haygarth, John, 128–9
Hébert, Alexandre, 81
Hell, Father Maximilian, 5–6, 9, 28
Henry, Prince of Prussia, 43
Herring (physician), 154
Hervier, Father Charles, 50
hidden observer, 266, 269
Hilgard, Ernest, 262, 265–7, 269, 270
Hilgard, Josephine, 265
Hippocrates, 9
Histoire académique du magnétisme animal (Burdin and Dubois), 120
Histoire critique du magnétisme animal (Deleuze), 85, 93
An History of Magic, Witchcraft and Animal Magnetism (Colquhoun), 205
Holland, G.C., 132
Hollaway, John, 126
Horne, Jacques de, 27
Hortense (Teste's subject), 118–19
Hospice de la Charité, 110
Hôtel de Coigny, 36, 37, 60
Hôtel Dieu, 98, 101, 106, 110, 122, 131, 175, 246, 247
Hull, Clark, 261–5
 on Binet, 262
 on hypersuggestibility, 264–5
 Hypnosis and Suggestibility, 262
Human Physiology (Elliotson), 137, 165

Husson, H.M., 98, 99, 100, 101, 111, 114, 116, 117
hypermnesia *see* memory
hypersuggestibility, 261, 264–5, 266
Hypnosis and Suggestibility (Hull), 262
Hypnotic Therapeutics (Braid), 209, 211
hypnotiques, grandes, 239
hypnotism/hypnosis
 Bernheim on 232–9, 247–8
 Braid on, 196–8, 206–8, 212
 Charcot on, 223–8
 depth of, 230, 235, 248, 265
 Elliotson on, 204
 Erickson on, 260–1
 Freud on, 255–6
 Hilgard on, 265–7
 Hull on, 261–4
 Janet on, 257–8
 Liébault on, 229–32
 major hypnotism, 223–5, 237, 240, 242
 minor hypnotism, 227, 240
 role theory of, 267, 268–9
 Spanos on, 268–71
 stages (states) of, 224–5, 236, 237, 240, 242, 246, 250–1
 state theory of, 264, 267
hypnotisme, grand see hypnotism, major
hypnotisme, petit see hypnotism, minor
Hypnotic Therapeutics (Braid), 170, 172
Hypnotisme, suggestion, psychothérapie (Bernheim), 247
hypnotization *see* trance induction
hysteria, 54, 68, 94, 106, 110, 132, 217, 230, 234, 235, 236, 242, 245, 249, 250, 251, 257, 264
 in men, 220–1, 226
 major, 217–18, 220
 minor, 218
 symptoms of, 4, 9, 11, 67, 80, 121, 139, 146, 175, 187, 197, 217–19, 222, 226–7, 239
hystérie, grande see hysteria, major
hystérie, petite see hysteria, minor

ideodynamism, 234, 247–8
imagination, 18, 41, 129, 157, 171, 193
  Bernheim on, 239
  Bertrand on, 103, 106, 107, 109
  Braid on, 209
  Charcot on, 221
  Deslon on, 50, 53
  Elliotson on, 161, 192
  Faria on, 97
  Royal Academy of Medicine
    Commission on (1826), 114
  Royal Academy of Sciences
    Commission on (1826), 49–52, 67
imitation, 41, 50, 67, 171, 200
Ingenhousz, Jan, 7–8, 14, 28
Institutions of Physiology
  (Blumenbach), 137
intellect, improvement of, 71–2, 103,
  107, 108
Isis Revelata (Colquhoun), 205
Itard, J.M.G., 111

Jackson, J. Hughlings, 67
James, William, 246
James-Lange theory, 199
Janet, Pierre, 246, 247, 249, 254, 256
  on stages of hypnosis, 250–1
  theory of, 257–8, 260, 266
  treatment, 257
  L'automatisme psychologique, 258
jar-phoonka, 183
Jefferson, Thomas, 133
jet lag, 277
Johnson, James, 153, 169–70, 180
Joly, Henri, 73, 77–8
Joseph II, Emperor, 12
Journal de Paris, 55
Journal du magnétisme, 122
Julie (Teste's subject), 121

Kornmann, Guillaume, 35, 59, 60

Lafayette, M.J., marquis de, 37–8, 60,
  61, 66, 132–3
Lafontaine, Charles, 193–4, 195, 197
Laënnec, R.T.H., 111, 137
Lamballe, princesse de, 30
Lancet, 139, 144, 149, 152, 153, 154,
  156, 157, 159, 161, 166, 167, 168,
  181, 189, 205
Lansdowne, Lord, 132
Larochefoucauld, duc de, 101
Larrey, Hippolyte, 102
Lasègue, C., 222
Lavoisier, A.L., 39, 61
Lawrence, Jean-Roch, 275
Leeson, John, 152
Le magnétisme animal (Binet and
  Féré), 241
Lenoir, Jean-Pierre, 52
Léonie (Janet's subject), 258
Leroy, Charles, 17–18, 39
Les altérations de la personnalité
  (Binet), 249
Liébault, Auguste, 211, 229–32, 235,
  238, 246, 247, 248, 252
  on sleep, 229–30
  on suggestion, 230
  treatment, 230, 231–2
  Du sommeil et des états analogues, 229
Liégois, Jules, 243–4, 246
Lind, Jenny, 211
Liston, Robert, 159–60, 166, 180, 184,
  188
London Medical and Physical Journal,
  153
London Medical Gazette, 161, 165,
  166
Louis XVI, King of France, 22, 29, 40,
  51, 56, 61
Lourdes, 239, 247
Loutherberg, Philippe de, 126–7
Luys, J., 242
Lys (Charcot's patient), 220

McNeile, Rev. James, 195
Madeleine (Puységur's subject), 80–1
Magendie, F., 111, 137
magic, 98, 123
*Magic, Witchcraft, Animal Magnetism,
  Hypnotism and Electro-biology*
  (Braid), 206
magnats, 92
Magnetismomania (Vernet), 95
magnets, 5–6, 8–10, 24, 67, 173–4,
  202–3, 222–3, 225, 237

magnetism *see* animal magnetism; mineral magnetism
Mainauduc, John Boniot de, 125–6, 127
Majault (physician), 39
Malmaison, comtesse de la, 20
Manuel pratique de magnétisme animal (Teste), 121
Maria-Theresia, Empress of Austria, 1, 12, 13, 14
Marie Antoinette, Queen of France, 30, 31–3, 60, 61, 62
Marrin, Paul, 242
Martin, John, 127–8
Martineau, Harriet, 171, 177
Mason, A.A., 272–3
Mauduit, Antoine, 19, 39
Maurepas, J.F.P., comte de, 30, 31
Mazarin, Cardinal, 213
Mead, Richard, 2, 24
Medical Chirurgical Review, 153, 169
medical profession, 142, 153, 212, 251
acceptance and use of hypnotism by, 198, 228
opposition to animal magnetism by, 27, 54, 102, 106, 120, 168, 185–6, 204
opposition to hypnotism by, 204–5, 254
opposition to new ideas by, 167, 204
Medical Times, 136, 179, 202, 205
mediums, 104, 135
Medwin, Thomas, 129
Mémoire de F.A. Mesmer, docteur en médecine, sur ses découvertes (Mesmer), 62
Mémoire sur la découverte du magnétisme animal (Mesmer), 7, 23
memory, 103, 148, 230, 257
enhanced (hypermnesia), 95, 262, 263
loss of (amnesia), 68, 76, 95, 107, 236, 238, 257, 258, 265, 269, 274
menstruation, 132
Mercure de France, 42
Mesmer, Franz Anton, 1–69, 70–1, 77, 85, 86, 89, 90, 120, 122, 130, 237, 277

appearance, 17, 65–6
education, 1
finances, 21, 30, 35, 59–60, 62, 125
in old age, 64–5
induction technique, 5, 6, 7, 10, 19, 23, 38–9
letter to Marie Antoinette, 31–3
marriage, 2, 16
medical thesis, 1–2
personality, 17, 62, 65–7, 83
theory, 2, 23–7, 33–4, 66–7, 82, 84
treatment, 2, 4–7, 10–16, 18–21, 26–7, 31, 35, 68–9, 82
Mémoire de F.A. Mesmer, docteur en médecine, sur ses découvertes, 62
Mémoire sur la découverte du magnétisme animal, 7, 23
Mesmerismus, 65
Précis historique des faits relatifs au magnétisme animal jusqu'en avril 1781, 33
Mesmeric Infirmaries, 189–90, 191
The Mesmeric Mania of 1851 (Bennett), 209
mesmerism *see* animal magnetism
Mesmerismus (Mesmer), 65
mesmerization *see* trance induction
Mesnard, Brittania, 142
metals, 6, 151, 152, 154–6, 166, 173–6
Mills, George, 143–6, 149, 150, 151–2, 154
mineral magnetism, 44, 237
Mitouard, M., 80
Monde primitif (Court de Gébelin), 40
monoideism, 206, 210
Moore, Thomas, 146
More, Hannah, 126
moxa, 51, 101
Mozart, Leopold, 3, 4
Mozart, Wolfgang, 3, 16, 56
multiple personality, 257–60, 269
Munthe, Axel, 215
Myers, Frederick, 228, 246

Nancy, School of, 228, 232, 239, 241, 243, 245, 246, 247, 250, 252, 253, 255
neodissociation, 266–7, 271

Neurypnology (Braid), 196, 198, 201, 206, 221

New Nancy School, 276

Newton, Sir Isaac, 2, 24

Noizet, F.J., 98, 231

Norwich, Bishop of, 146

Numerous Cases of Surgical Operations without Pain in the Mesmeric State (Elliotson), 181

Observations of Trance: or, Human Hybernation (Braid), 205

Observations sur le magnétisme animal (Deslon), 27

odyllic force, 174

Oesterlin, Francisca, 4–8, 68, 71, 83

Okey, Elizabeth, 140–59, 163–4, 166, 169, 170, 172, 174, 176, 177, 178, 179, 189, 250–1

On the Distinctive Conditions of Natural and Nervous Sleep (Braid), 210

Orne, Martin, 268

Ossine (Mesmer's patient), 12

Ost (physician), 15

Oudet, M.J., 115

Paget, Sir Charles, 144

pain, 5, 8, 13, 22, 23, 44, 46, 47, 48, 51, 58, 65, 100, 105, 130, 140, 141, 167, 183, 217, 220, 239, 255, 258, 273; *see also* analgesia

Paradis, Maria Theresia von, 12–16, 25, 40

paralysis, mesmeric-hypnotic, 95, 132, 194, 209, 226, 228; *see also* catalepsy

paranormal, 63, 69, 74, 81, 83, 90, 97, 107, 109, 111–19, 120, 176, 179, 196–7, 205, 209, 234; *see also* spiritualism

Paris, School of *see* Salpêtrière, School of

Parker, John, 126

Parker, J.B., 190

Parlement of Paris, 53, 56

passes, magnetic, 96, 103
   Braid on, 196

Chenevix, used by, 131

Deleuze, used by, 87

Deslon, used by, 46, 48

Du Potet, used by, 138

Elliotson, used by, 140, 144–5, 146, 147, 148

Hervier, used by, 40

Janet, used by, 258

jar-phoonka, used in, 183

Lafontaine, used by, 194

Mesmer, used by, 19, 67

Wilson, used by, 171–2

Paul, Saint Vincent de, 213

Perkins, E., 128

Perrier (mesmerist), 250

Perry, Campbell, 275

Petetin, J.H.D., 79–80, 108, 188

Petit (Du Potet's subject), 112–13

Petronille (Georget's patient), 110

Philips, A.J.P. *see* Durand de Gros, J.-P.

phrenohypnotism, 199–202

Phrenological Society of London, 137

phrenology, 137, 169–71, 177–8, 199–202, 211

The Phreno-Magnet and Mirror of Nature, 177

Physiology of Fascination (Braid), 210

The Power of the Mind over the Body (Braid), 202

Pigeaire, J., 117–18

Pigeaire, Léonide, 117–18, 119, 120, 122

Pin (Charcot's patient), 220, 226

Pinel, P., 213

Pitres, A., 242–3

Pius VI, Pope, 12

placebo, 247, 273

Plantin, Madame (Cloquet's patient), 114

Poissonier, P.I., 39

poltergeist, 134

Porcz (Charcot's patient), 220, 226

posthypnotic suggestion *see* suggestion, posthypnotic

Potier (actor), 95

Poyen St. Sauveur, Charles, 133

Pratt, Mary, 126–7

Précis historique des faits relatifs au magnétisme animal jusqu'en avril 1781 (Mesmer), 33
Prescott (mesmerist), 126
Preyer, Wilhelm, 210
Prideaux, T. S., 170
Prince, Morton, 258–9, 266
The Principles of Nature (Davis), 134
Prout, William, 132
psychical research *see* paranormal
psychoanalysis, 34, 256
Psycho-Physiology: embracing Hypnotism, Monoideism and Mesmerism (Braid), 210
Puyfontaine, marquis de, 251
Puységur, A.-H.-A. de Chastenet, comte de, 70, 78, 133
Puységur, A.-M.-J. de Chastenet, marquis de, 38, 43, 51, 59–60, 66, 69, **70–83**, 84, 86–90
    mentioned, 96, 108, 120, 122, 126, 134, 224, 252
    induction technique, 172, 176, 177–8
    personality, 74, 83
    treatment, 71–3, 81–2
    theory, 78–9
Puységur, J.-M.-P. de Chastenet, comte de, 43, 75

Quain, Richard, 160
Quarterly Review, 179

Race, Victor, 71–3, 77, 78, 81–2, 108
rapport, 80, 84, 92, 104, 212, 230, 248, 264
Rebouam (mesmerist), 101, 110
Récamier, C.A., 99, 101–2, 122
Régnard, Paul, 219–20
regression, 149
Reichenbach, K.L., Baron von, 172–4, 176, 202–3
relaxation, 217, 260, 264, 273
Renterghem, A.W. van, 231, 246
Revue de l'hypnotisme, 253, 254
Revue de psychothérapie et de psychologie appliquée, 254
Ribes (physician), 112
Ricard, J.J.A., 117

Richardson (physician), 154
Richer, Paul, 222, 227, 242, 251
Richet, Charles, 222, 245
Riddle, E.E., 263
Robespierre, Maximilien, 61
Rohan, Cardinal de, 60
Rosière (actor), 55
Rostan, Louis, 108–9
Rousseau, Jean-Jacques, 58
Roux, F., 115
Royal Academy of Medicine (Paris), 102, 115, 117, 175
    1826 Commission of, 109, 110–14
    1831 Commission of, 114
    1837 Commission of, 115–16
    1838 Commission of, 117–19, 122
Royal Academy of Sciences (Paris), 17, 18, 41, 221, 223
    1784 Commission of, 39, 44–50, 55, 57, 67, 89, 125, 155
    secret report of Commission, 51–3, 68
Royal Medical and Chirurgical Society, 180, 181
Royal Society (London), 150
Royal Society of Medicine (Paris), 18, 19, 29, 54
    1784 Commission of, 39, 50–1

Saint-Domingue *see* Haiti
St. Thomas's Hospital, 131
Sallin (physician), 39
Salpêtrière hospital, 108, 110, 212, 213, 215, 222, 224, 225
    Binet's experiments at, 225, 231, 249
    Burq at, 175, 222
    Charcot's improvements to, 215
    Freud's visit to, 227
    iconography of, 219–20
    Janet at, 257
Salpêtrière, School of, 228, 236, 237, 239–41, 244–7, 249, 251, 252
salutations, 218
Samson, Catherine, 99–101, 122
Sand, George, 118
Sandby, Rev. G., 189
Sarbin, T.R., 265, 267
Sauvage, Céline, 111

scientific method, 11, 34, 97, 101, 109, 114, 124, 128, 188, 271
Servan, J.M.A., 54
Shelley, Percy Bysshe, 129–30
Simon, Th., 249
sleep, hypnotic/mesmeric *see* trance
sleep, lucid, 93, 95
sleep, natural, 75, 219
    relationship with hypnotic state, 63, 101, 132, 197, 207, 210, 229–30, 231, 239, 248, 252, 262, 264
    relationship with hypnotizability, 94, 206
sleep-walking, 130
Société du Magnétisme, 82
Society for Psychical Research, 212
Society of (Universal) Harmony, 87, 132
    Bayonne branch, 75
    Lyons branch, 43
    Paris branch, 35–6, 37–8, 41, 42–3, 53, 54, 57, 59, 60, 70, 75, 82, 126
    Strasbourg branch, 78, 79, 87
somnambulism, 77,81
    Bertrand on, 103, 106–8
    Charcot on, 223, 224
    Deleuze on, 89–90, 91
    Faria on, 94, 96
    Liébault on, 230
    Mesmer on, 63, 68
    Puységur's discovery of, 72, 82, 86, 89
    Royal Academy of Medicine Commission on (1826), 109, 114, 116
somnambulists
    accuracy of, 74, 91
    as mediums, 135
    as 'physicians', 76–7, 134
    numbers of, 89, 111, 114, 230, 239
    paranormal abilities of, 80–1, 83, 88, 92, 104–6, 107–9, 111–14, 115–21, 123–4
    personalities of, 91, 94, 107, 238
    predictions of, 73–4, 90
    treatment of, 102, 193, 194, 252
sommeil lucide see sleep, lucid
Spanos, Nicholas, 268–70

Spencer, Herbert, 171
spiritualism, 91–2, 134–5
stage hypnotism, 275–6
Stalnaker, J.M., 263
Stanford Hypnotic Susceptibility Scale (Hilgard and Weitzenhoffer), 265, 267
Stanhope, Earl of, 189
Stebbing, Rev., 148
Stevenson, Robert Louis, 258
    The Strange Case of Dr Jekyll and Mr Hyde, 258
stigmata, 219
Stockholm Society of Magnetists, 92
Stoerk, Anton, 2, 6–7, 9, 13, 14, 15, 16
Stone, G.W., 209
The Strange Case of Dr Jekyll and Mr Hyde, 258
suggestibility, 238, 240, 246, 247, 248, 249, 252, 262, 264–5, 266
suggestion, 147, 260
    Bernheim on, 211, 230, 233–40, 246, 247–8, 252, 253
    Binet on, 241, 249
    Braid on, 197–8, 202, 207, 209, 211, 212, 222
    Charcot on, 223, 226–7, 242
    Durand de Gros on, 222
    effects on body, 74, 101, 243
    Freud on, 255–6
    Hull on, 264
    in behaviour therapy, 260
    in Charcot's practice, 252
    in crime, 244–5
    indirect, 261
    in Puységur's practice, 71
    in waking state, 234, 235, 264, 267
    Janet on, 254, 257
    Liébault on, 230, 231
    posthypnotic, 95, 121, 226, 230, 234, 265
    Royal Society of Medicine Commission on (1784), 51
    Spanos on, 269, 270
Sunderland, La Roy, 133
Swedenborg, Emanuel, 134
Swieten, Gerard van, 1, 2

Tavistock, Frances, 142
telepathy, 63, 72, 81, 105, 106, 107, 108, 109, 123–4
Teste, Alphonse, 118–19, 120–2, 250
  Manuel practique de magnétisme animal, 121
theosophy, 91
therapy *see* treatment
Thompson (physician), 185
Thomson, Anthony Todd, 160
Thornton, E.M., 67–8
thought transference *see* telepathy
Thouret, M.A., 54
time estimation, 74, 107, 108–9, 112, 121
Topham, W., 180–1
Townshend, Rev. C.H., 170, 192
tractors, 128–9
Traité du somnambulisme (Bertrand), 103
trance, 121, 124, 132, 138, 142, 163, 232, 238–9, 248, 250, 263, 264
  anaesthesia in, 138
  analgesia in, 101–2, 188, 189
  behaviour of Okey sisters in, 140–1, 144–51, 154–7, 163–4, 172, 176
  depth of, 230, 235, 265
  genuine or feigned, 77–87, 114,115, 120, 156–9
  hibernation as, 205–6
  history of, 120, 251, 268–9
  in epilepsy, 67
  paranormal aspects of, 62, 77, 80–1, 99–100, 105–6, 119, 135
  sensory changes in, 131, 196
  Shelley composes in, 130
  varieties of, 103, 146–7, 260
trance induction
  by electrobiology, 133, 209
  by ether, 184, 186
  by eye fixation, 171, 177, 194, 196, 197, 198, 209, 211, 224, 229, 243
  by *jar-phoonka*, 183
  by metals, 151, 152, 154–6, 166, 174
  by pressure, 224, 242
Transactions du magnétisme animal, 120
transcendental meditation, 276

transference, 85, 192, 256
treatment, mesmeric/hypnotic, 45–52, 111, 127, 189–90, 249, 255
treatment of particular ailments
  anxiety, 272
  apoplexy, 75
  appetite, loss of, 239
  asthma, 47, 105, 272
  battle stress, 260
  blindness, 12–16, 23, 28, 54, 127
  burns, 190
  cancer, 54, 127
  child abuse, 274
  chorea, 142, 190
  convulsions, 11, 40, 47
  deafness, 73, 133, 197
  demonic possession, 269
  depression, 9, 274
  dropsy, 18
  epilepsy, 9, 19, 54, 110, 142, 146, 190, 198
  eye condition, 21, 35, 47, 51
  fever, 99
  gastro-intestinal conditions, 239
  habits, 272
  headache, 73, 81, 140, 198
  hypochondria, 54
  hysteria, 4, 9, 12, 54, 106, 110, 121, 132, 141, 146, 187, 197, 239, 273
  hystero-epilepsy, 140
  ichthyosis, 272–3
  incontinence, 239
  inflammation of the lungs, 71
  insomnia, 239, 258
  kidney disease, 40
  lactatory disorder, 210
  lameness, 127
  liver obstruction, 48
  lockjaw, 146
  lower back pain, 272
  menstrual disturbances, 239
  military fever, 28
  multiple personality, 257–60, 269
  muscular spasm, 13, 198
  muscular strain, 51
  neuralgia, 232, 239
  neurasthenia, 258
  obsessive-compulsive states, 274

treatment of particular ailments – *cont.*
  obstruction of bowels, 23, 48, 54
  palpitations, 198
  palsy, 127
  paralysis, 9, 20, 54, 190, 198
  paroxysms, 129
  pericarditis, 190
  phobias, 274
  psychosis, 247, 274
  rheumatism, 54, 198, 239, 272
  rupture, 127
  St Vitus' dance, 47
  schizophrenia, 274
  scrofula, 47
  sensory deficit, 198
  skin disorders, 272
  sleep-walking, 239
  stomach pains, 21, 22, 35, 99
  stress, 272
  swelling, 47
  toothache, 71, 190
  torticollis, 197
  tumor, 47, 182, 187
  ulcers, 23
  vomiting, 21, 99
  writer's cramp, 239
  tremor, 213, 214, 216, 217, 221,
    262–3
trees, magnetization of, 21, 49, 75, 89,
  103

unconscious, the, 97
University College (London), 164, 249
University College Hospital (London),
  136, 138, 139, 159, 160, 162, 164,
  166–7, 169, 176, 181,184
Unzer, Johann, 7, 9

Vauzesmes, Roussel de, 28–9
Vernet, Jules
  Magnetismomania, 95
Vicq-d'Azyr, Félix, 19, 20
Victoria, Queen, 188
Villagrand, Paul, 113
Vinchon, Jean, 32
vision
  disturbances of, 198, 219
  fixation of, 194, 196, 197, 198

prevention of, 81, 202
without eyes, 107, 108–9, 112–13,
  115–20, 177, 207
see also treatment of particular
  ailments: blindness
Vogt, Oskar, 254
Voisin, Auguste, 247
voodooism, 70

Wagstaff, Graham, 271
Wakley, Thomas, 153–9, 161–3, 165–6,
  178, 181, 193
Walpole, Horace, 126
Ward, W. Squire, 180–1
water (magnetized), 6, 10, 20, 42, 121,
  142–3, 150, 152, 156–7, 188, 232
Webb, Alan, 187
Weitzenhoffer, André, 265
Whately, Richard, Archbishop of
  Dublin, 189–90
White, R.W., 267
Whymper, Surgeon-Major, 131
will and will-power, 38, 51, 87, 96, 115,
  131, 132, 133, 195, 209, 210, 259,
  274–5
Willermoz, Jean-Baptiste, 43
William IV, King, 153
Williams, G.W., 263, 264
Williamson (academic), 194
Wilson (ophthalmist), 194
Wilson, John, 171–2
Winter, George, 126, 127
witch hunt, 219
Witt (Charcot's patient) *see* Wittman,
  Blanche
Wittman, Blanche, 227–8, 240–1,
  244–5
Wolfart, Karl, 64, 69, 82
Wood, William, 140, 143, 146, 147,
  148, 155, 165, 169

Yedal (mesmerist), 126

Zeitschrift für Hypnotismus, 254
Zen buddhism, 34
Zoist, 169–70, 174, 176–9, 181, 187,
  188, 189, 190, 203
Zwelferine (Mesmer's patient), 12